Third Edition ─────────────────

CONTEMPORARY SOCIOLOGICAL THEORY
Continuing the Classical Tradition

─────────────────

RUTH A. WALLACE
George Washington University

ALISON WOLF
University of London

PRENTICE HALL
Englewood Cliffs, New Jersey 07632

Library of Congress Cataloging-in-Publication Data

Wallace, Ruth A.
    Contemporary sociological theory : continuing the classical
tradition / Ruth A. Wallace, Alison Wolf. — 3rd ed.
        p.   cm. — (Prentice Hall series in sociology)
    Includes bibliographical references (p.   ).
    ISBN 0-13-172586-6
    1. Sociology.   I. Wolf, Alison.   II. Title.   III. Series.
HM51.W15   1991
301—dc20   90-35412
                                                       CIP

To Our Families and Students

Editorial/production supervision and
    interior design: E. A. Pauw and Karen Buck
Cover design: Marianne Frasco
Manufacturing buyer: Ed O'Dougherty

Prentice Hall Series in Sociology
Neil J. Smelser, Editor

 ©1991, 1986, 1980 by Prentice-Hall, Inc.
A Paramount Communications Company
Englewood Cliffs, New Jersey   07632

Printed in the United States of America
10   9   8   7

ISBN 0-13-172586-6

Prentice-Hall International (UK) Limited, *London*
Prentice-Hall of Australia Pty. Limited, *Sydney*
Prentice-Hall Canada Inc., *Toronto*
Prentice-Hall Hispanoamericana, S.A., *Mexico*
Prentice-Hall of India Private Limited, *New Delhi*
Prentice-Hall of Japan, Inc., *Tokyo*
Simon & Schuster Asia Pte. Ltd., *Singapore*
Editora Prentice-Hall do Brasil, Ltda., *Rio de Janeiro*

CONTENTS

PREFACE

This book discusses and analyzes sociological theory as it is practiced today. Its major focus is on those writers whose work has most influenced social theory and the way sociologists currently approach and analyze their subject matter.

Contemporary sociology, at almost every point, builds on and incorporates the classics, and especially the work of Marx, Durkheim, Weber, Simmel, and Mead. We believe that the best way to study and understand theory is to follow the ways in which the work of classical writers has been incorporated into that of later sociologists, and to see how theoretical insights are actually used by people to explain social developments. We have therefore described the contributions of classical theorists directly when discussing the historical roots of each perspective. Throughout the text we also point out the many ways in which contemporary theorists and researchers alike make active use of classical ideas.

In the following pages we describe the central ideas and arguments of these thinkers and the ways in which they provide a number of quite distinct perspectives on society and social behavior. Although we also present some assessment and criticism of their theories, our purpose is to provide readers with a clear summary of modern sociological theory's arguments, not to engage in a detailed critique of each approach or to espouse a particular perspective. To give readers as clear an idea as possible of the authors' own style and presentation, we have included a number of direct quotations in the text. We have also tried particularly to show how sociological theories inform social scientists' empirical research and to demonstrate the close links between sociological theory and the ways in which we all, sociologists and nonsociologists alike, deal with and try to understand our world. To this end we have included throughout the book empirical examples of how a given perspective is used in both sociological research and more general explanation.

While we have made every effort to avoid unnecessary jargon and to express ideas as simply and as clearly as possible, much of the subject matter is, inevitably, quite complex. We have tried, therefore, to follow Albert Einstein's dictum, "Everything should be made as simple as possible, but not one bit simpler." At the same time it is not a precondition for the reader to be a student of sociology already. We conceive of our audience as comprising anyone interested in the contributions social science can make to understanding our social world.

We have been very aware during our work of the old but still raging debate about whether any writers, but especially social scientists, can deal objectively with their subject matter. In one sense, namely our choice of what writers and what aspects of their work to present, our own values and preferences must obtrude. Within that framework, however, we have tried unashamedly to maintain the traditional scientific values of unbiased description, objectivity, and, indeed, reason; for while they may never be fully realizable, it seems to us of the utmost importance that scholars—and the world—not abandon them as standards. We have also paid particular attention to whether or not a given perspective is successful in dealing with and answering a range of concrete questions and problems.

Plan of the Text

This revised text discusses five major perspectives of modern sociological theory: functionalism, conflict theory, theories of rational choice, symbolic interactionism, and phenomenology. It also provides an overview of recent theoretical developments. In addition to generally updating the text, and, in particular, the empirical and everyday examples, this new edition has a number of major changes: (1) a new section on neofunctionalism (including Niklas Luhmann's work), (2) an expanded section on Jürgen Habermas, (3) a new section on recent theories of rational choice, (4) a new section on a social theory of emotion, (5) a discussion of the structuration theory of Anthony Giddens, and (6) inclusion of feminist contributions and feminist critiques within each of the major perspectives. Other changes include (1) expanded treatment of the contributions of Simmel, Durkheim, Thomas, and Goffman; (2) clarification of key concepts; (3) more extensive coverage of European contemporary theorists, including Bourdieu and Boudon; and (4) a discussion in Chapter I of the structure of sociological theories, including subject matter, assumptions, methodology, and objectives.

Chapter I discusses the structure of sociological theories and their practical importance as a way of analyzing and understanding how human societies work. It also introduces important questions about the role of women in contemporary society and the workings of the formal educational system. Each major theoretical perspective can provide important but partial answers to these questions, and they correspondingly provide a theme woven throughout the book.

The following five chapters then follow a common pattern. In each case, we set out the basic assumptions and key concepts of the theory concerned and the questions it raises and attempts to answer. We identify the intellectual roots of the approach and discuss the insights which the contemporary theorists derived from previous scholars. We then describe in detail the work of the perspective's major theorists, with particular emphasis on their most recent or current arguments. Throughout each section we stress the reciprocal relationship between theory on the one hand and sociological research and general social observation on the other. We show how contemporary theorists themselves use their approaches to analyze concrete phenomena, including but not confined to the educational system and the role of women, and how the research of their colleagues draws on and embodies different theoretical perspectives. We also illustrate how the outlook of contemporary theorists is reflected in the way nonsociologists look at and discuss the world. Chapter VII discusses a number of theoretical developments of considerable interest and relevance to contemporary sociology: namely, sociobiology and alternative approaches to analyzing social structure. Finally, Chapter VIII synthesizes the major perspectives' contributions to answering the questions posed in Chapter I, and briefly discusses historical trends in social theory.

This book has been a joint effort throughout, with no senior or junior authorship. Ruth Wallace took primary responsibility for the chapters on functionalism, symbolic interactionism, and phenomenology, and Alison Wolf for the chapters on conflict theory, theories of rational choice, and alternative perspectives.

In writing this book, we have learned a great deal and have both come to appreciate more fully the insights and achievements of the theorists we describe. We would like to acknowledge our intellectual debt to them and also to the many students whose questions and comments have contributed to our work.

Herbert Blumer, Anthony Heath, Patricia Lengermann, J. Clyde Mitchell, Robert Moran, Whitney Pope, Neil Smelser, and Martin Wolf all made major contributions to our thinking through their suggestions and questions on this or earlier editions. Our editors, Edward Stanford, Susan Taylor, Bill Webber, and Nancy Roberts, as well as a number of Prentice Hall reviewers—including Meredith B. McGuire (Trinity University), Janet Mancini Billson (Rhode Island College), Richard Robbins (University of Massachusetts–Boston), Marvin Scott (Hunter College)—gave us useful suggestions.

We would also like to acknowledge the help of Janet Saltzman Chafetz, Ralf Dahrendorf, Christine Dolan, Vance Grant, Wade Hook, Iain McLean, Carlyle Maw, Kathryn Orlans, Vernon Reynolds, David Sciulli, R. Stephen Warner, and Jacqueline Wiseman.

We thank Joy Alexander for encouraging us to write on theory and Edmund Wolf for his help in translating. Without the time so generously given by Winnie Potter, Rebecca Wolf, and James Coriden, this book would still be in manuscript. Jonathan, Benjamin, and Rachel Wolf maintained our sense of proportion and helped by being themselves.

R.A.W.
A.W.

I

THE UNDERSTANDING
OF SOCIETY

The Structure of Sociological Theory

Theory and Understanding: The Examples of Formal
Education and the Role of Women in Contemporary Society

Reading modern sociological theory has not been something to which people have generally looked forward with delight. Often they see it as just so many groups of rarefied abstractions related only to each other, like a set of crossword puzzles, free-floating above the "real world" of schools, factories, and suburbs, elections, weddings, strikes, muggings, and tennis matches. This is a mistake. Far from being able to separate theory from real life, our whole way of looking at the world depends on our theoretical perspective. To read sociological theory is to understand a great deal more about what we and our world are like and how unordinary and ambiguous the most taken-for-granted and everyday aspects of our life may be.

When sociologists "do sociology," they do not come to their subject matter cold, their minds a blank. Whether their topic is the way people deal with death, or the whole evolution and probable future of modern society, they focus on particular aspects of what is going on.[1] They approach their subject with certain assumptions, they emphasize particular research methods, and they have particular types of questions they want answered. This means that their research is based on the ways of looking at things which "sociological theories" advance. What the theories do is to lay these out in an explicit and systematic way.

Very much the same is true of the world outside sociology. In some famous remarks, John Maynard Keynes, whose own ideas dominated government economic management from the Second World War until the present, argued that ideas "both when they are right and when they are wrong, are more powerful than is commonly understood. Indeed, the world is ruled by little else. Practical men, who believe themselves to be quite exempt from any intellectual influences, are usually the slaves of some defunct economist. Madmen in authority, who hear voices in the air, are distilling their frenzy from some academic scribbler of a few years back."[2] The different ways of looking at our society that contemporary sociological theories advance are reflected in the arguments and observations of society's members as a whole.

The effect that "sociological theory" may have on people's behavior and on the course of history is demonstrated most dramatically by the work of Karl Marx. But a journalist trying to explain Watergate and the resignation of Richard Nixon, a marriage counselor grappling with rising divorce rates, and new students on campus trying to understand what is going on, also draw on notions about how people behave and how social institutions work which embody certain "theoretical" assumptions. Furthermore, our very ability to talk about "the President's unconstitutional behavior" or about "granting someone a degree" depends on a whole range of facts

[1]For the use of theoretical perspectives to discuss these particular topics, see Chapter III (Collins), Chapter V(Part II: Blumer), and Chapters II (Parsons) and III (Habermas).

[2]John Maynard Keynes, *The General Theory of Employment, Interest and Money* (London: Macmillan and Co., Ltd., 1936), p. 383.

about ourselves and our listeners. Sociological theories do not comprise a world of formal, empty boxes, irrelevant to the world of work and family, power, freedom, discrimination, and oppression. Far from it. They have everything to do with that world—how we see it, understand it, and explain it, as well as how we act in it and thus what it becomes.

THE STRUCTURE OF SOCIOLOGICAL THEORY

Sociological theorists are distinctive because they express their assumptions or hypotheses very systematically and discuss in a very comprehensive way how far their theories explain social life. Even more important, they provide new insights into behavior and the workings of societies. These, in turn, are disseminated, and in years to come they may affect the ideas of many who have never read the original work.

The systematic way in which sociological theory sets out its ideas is a quality it shares with the "theory" of any other discipline: psychology, physics, genetics, and the rest. Shared, too, is a second important quality: it relates innumerable events, with many apparent differences, to general principles that bring out their similarities. Student protests, strikes, and food riots may all be treated as examples of conflict within hierarchical organizations, and the important qualities they have in common may be thus defined.[3] Similarly, counselors' interviews with high school students and trials for murder may both be examined in the light of what they show about the shared ideas of a society's members and the creative and unpredictable dynamics of human interaction.[4]

However, although sociological theory shares the essential systematizing qualities of all theory, in other ways it often differs from what is usually meant by the term. The classical definition of a theory[5] is essentially a *deductive* one. It starts with definitions of some general concepts (and, often, a few clearly stated assumptions); lays out rules about how to classify the things we observe in terms of these different categories; and then puts forward a number of general propositions about the concepts. Once observers have classified their subject matter, a generalized "theory" allows them to deduce logically a number of quite specific statements about its nature and behavior. The laws of Mendelian genetics are a good example, for their general statements about the pairing of genes and distribution of characteristics among offspring can be used to deduce statements about an enormous range of species. Since such theories are also very powerful instru-

[3]See Chapter III.
[4]See Chapters V and VI.
[5]One of the best such discussions can be found in Ernest Nagel, *The Structure of Science* (New York: Harcourt, Brace and World, 1961), especially pp. 90–105.

ments in predicting and hence manipulating our environment, they are essential to almost every aspect of modern life, from stockbreeding to manufacturing skateboards.[6]

Much sociological theory is of this very clearly defined type; but much is not. Robert Merton, whose own functionalist theory we discuss later, has emphasized that "much of what is described in textbooks as sociological theory consists of general orientations towards substantive materials."[7] For example, if a "theory" puts forward a number of very general propositions about human motivation, it may imply that some sorts of behavior are more likely than others and thereby provide the observer with a handle on a situation. However, it will supply very little in the way of concrete propositions.

Such general propositions are not, in themselves, inconsistent with the idea of a deductive social science. Some theorists whose work is of this kind are very interested in making predictive or testable statements about social organization and the development of society.[8] Others, however, are not concerned with such deductive "scientific" theory at all. Indeed, they may deny that such an approach is valid when one is dealing with the behavior of human beings.[9] Instead of being about regularities in the content of human behavior or the nature of social organization, their general statements describe how people's social interaction proceeds.[10]

Because of these differences, sociological theory may look like a group of perspectives with very little in common except their general and formalizing approach and their concern with understanding human behavior. However, even those theories which are furthest removed from the deductive model involve a set of concepts, which are often described as the most elementary "building blocks" of any theory. Basically, a concept can be described as a word or symbol that represents a phenomenon (a label we use to name and

---

[6]The actual process of scientific research and discovery is far more complex than this description of theoretical structure implies. Good (and very different) discussions of what is involved in scientific theory construction are to be found in Karl Popper, *The Logic of Scientific Discovery* (London: Hutchinson, 1959); Thomas Kuhn, *The Structure of Scientific Revolutions* (Chicago: University of Chicago Press, 1970); Stephen Toulmin, "From Form to Function: Philosophy and History of Science in the 1950's and Now," *Daedalus*, 106, no. 3 (Summer 1977); Nagel, *The Structure of Science*.

[7]Robert K. Merton, *Social Theory and Social Structure*, Enlarged Edition (New York: The Free Press, 1968), p. 141.

[8]See, for example, the work of Dahrendorf on the importance of conflict, or much of Parson's theory (Chapters III and II).

[9]See, for example, the work of Garfinkel (Chapter VI) and Blumer (Chapter V).

[10]For good discussions of the debate about whether social science is essentially different from natural science and whether it requires different and unique types of theory and argument, see Peter Winch, *The Idea of a Social Science and Its Relation to Philosophy* (London: Routledge and Kegan Paul, 1958); George Caspar Homans, *The Nature of Social Science* (New York: Harcourt, Brace and World, 1967); Randall Collins, *Conflict Sociology: Toward An Explanatory Science,* Chapter I (New York: Academic Press, 1975); Anthony Giddens, *The Constitution of Society* (Cambridge, England: Polity Press, 1984).

classify our perceptions and experiences) or an abstract idea generalized from particular instances. Durkheim's concept, anomie, and Marx's concept, alienation, are classic examples of sociological concepts.

The key concepts of a theory also enable us to "see" parts of social reality that may have escaped us otherwise. Concepts are an essential first step in understanding and analyzing social phenomena. Throughout this book we will define the central concepts of each theory to enable the reader to see the various aspects of social reality revealed by each perspective and thus to have a better understanding of society.

Among the major dimensions along which sociological theories differ, we have already identified their acceptance or rejection of the deductive model drawn from natural science.[11] This is a crucial aspect of their *methodology*. Theories also differ in three other significant aspects. These are their *subject matter*, the *assumptions* underlying their approach, and the *types of questions* they believe social theory can and should answer. The following section provides an overview of the current main alternatives as exemplified by the theories discussed in this text.

Subject Matter

In their subject matter, theoretical perspectives divide rather clearly between those perspectives that are concerned with the large-scale characteristics of social structure and roles, or *macrosociology*, and those concerned with person-to-person encounters and the details of human interaction and communication, or *microsociology*.

Functionalism and conflict theory are the two approaches concerned with the overall characteristics of social structure and the general nature of social institutions. They emphasize the relations between (and implications of) general categories of social position, such as Marx's "classes" or the "affectively neutral" relationships which Parsons saw as predominant in industrial societies. It is in the context of functionalism and conflict theory that discussions of social evolution, the most wide-ranging of all sociological subjects, are found.

This does not mean that macrosociological theories necessarily consider the perceptions and decisions of individual people to be irrelevant to their arguments. We would agree with Smelser that "hypotheses that link positions in the social structure with behavior always rest on at least implicit psychological assertions,"[12] and particularly on general ideas about human nature. But these theorists pay most attention not to individual psychology, but rather to organizations and institutions within society and to the socially

---

[11]For a full discussion of the particular senses in which these terms are used, see the section on methodology.

[12]Neil J. Smelser, ed., *Sociology: An Introduction,* 2nd ed. (New York: John Wiley, 1973), p. 13.

prescribed roles that individuals play in them. They spend relatively little time analyzing the dynamics of individual action.

The perspectives of symbolic interactionism and phenomenology could hardly be more different, for they examine human interaction in the minutest detail. They discuss how, for example, the behavior of a supermarket clerk, faced with an obstreperous customer and trying to "make sense" of the situation, depends on individual experiences and individual perceptions, as well as on social prescriptions; or how, sentence by sentence, a teacher and child understand (or fail to understand) each other. The concepts used by these microsociological approaches do not categorize aspects of social structure but instead consist of the vocabulary required to discuss the particular actions of people.

The rational choice theories discussed in Chapter IV are less easily categorized. Although they concentrate on individuals' decisions and choices, these theories—Blau's in particular—attempt to link them to such structural qualities as a society's legitimacy. Nonetheless, compared to functionalists or conflict theorists, sociologists using a rational choice perspective are predominantly concerned with microsociological issues.

Assumptions

Sociological theorists' most important underlying assumptions concern human nature, and throughout the text we have attempted to underline and contrast the different views of human beings. Theorists differ, in particular, in whether they view human behavior as *essentially determined* and so in principle predictable, or whether they emphasize human *creativity*. The clearest contrast is between, on the one hand, functionalism and exchange theory, and on the other, symbolic interactionism and phenomenology.[13]

The most explicit philosophical statement of the first view will be found in George Homans' work. Homans' arguments emphasize the role played by individuals' choices and decisions, but his whole approach is based on the belief that human behavior has causes and thus in principle is fully explicable. It may be *practically* impossible to find the underlying origins of different tastes and to predict any given decision, but they are nonetheless determined, Homans would argue, by a combination of particular prior circumstances and by universal principles or laws.

The same view is apparent in functionalism. Durkheim, Parsons, and Merton treat behavior as ultimately predictable, a function of certain underlying forces and needs and of the particular set of internalized norms and values characteristic of a society. Again, it is not that functionalists' explanations ignore individual decisions—indeed, Parsons' action theory is built

---

[13]Rational choice theorists outside exchange theory use a rather less deterministic model in which individuals' given values and objectives nonetheless are treated as firm predictors of behavior.

around individual motives. The point is, however, that functionalists see the behavior as ultimately determined and so in principle fully explicable— exactly the "scientific" attitude that Merton remembers exciting him and leading him into social science.[14]

Conflict theory is less wholeheartedly deterministic, but its underlying orientation is the same. The "analytical" theorists, Dahrendorf, Coser, and Collins, show this most clearly. Their search for general explanatory propositions implies that, by and large at least, behavior is determined and predictable. However, in general, the same is true for the more critical and utopian writers. Marx's whole theory of evolution is ultimately determinist.

What conflict theorists do emphasize is the point of view of *purposive individuals and groups* acting to secure their ends. The same is true of rational choice theorists. By contrast, functionalists are more interested in identifying and describing the general values and norms of a society or group, and in analyzing the role these play in events, they treat behavior as considerably more *passive*.

However, it is the microsociological perspectives of symbolic interactionism and phenomenology that most emphasize human action, and their assumptions about human nature are fundamentally different. All the social sciences (and also, we would add, the biological sciences) differ from natural sciences, such as geology or physics, in that they deal with purposive behavior. In humans this involves a very wide range of symbols and meanings—things that are intrinsically unobservable.[15]

Symbolic interactionists and phenomenologicts believe that this view of the individual as active and creative also makes it impossible to predict behavior and develop sociological "laws" of a scientific type. Thus, although symbolic interactionists do not deny the existence of important regularities in behavior, they emphasize instead the *creative* way in which people interpret meaning during the course of an interaction. They distinguish between the "me" that incorporates learned attitudes and meanings and the innovative and unpredictable "I."[16] Phenomenology is also concerned with the continual nature of interpretation, but rather than contrasting the "I" with the "me," phenomenologists point to the pervasive nature of inferences and assumptions. Our whole social world and experience of society and social interaction are, they argue, things that we build up as we go

---

[14]See Chapter II.

[15]Behaviorist psychology is an attempt to dispense with any discussion of unobservables and to describe and predict behavior without going into what happens inside the "black box" of the human or animal mind. We feel that this is unlikely to be successful even with rats, and it is noticeable that Homans, one of the theorists who refers to the approach, nonetheless makes meanings and values a central part of his own explanations.

[16]It should be pointed out that predicting an individual's behavior and predicting average or group behavior are not the same; the impossibility of doing the first does not in itself imply that the second is also impossible. To predict group behavior, we need only know how most people will react most of the time.

along, not things that are objectively "real." Consequently, one should not develop concrete propositions that impose a misleading character of fixed meaning and structure on this process.

In addition to the crucial difference over whether or not human behavior is determined, perspectives also differ on whether they assume that human beings are motivated essentially by *interests* or by *values*. The difference is clearest in the case of functionalism and conflict theory, but it is also relevant to other perspectives.

Functionalists assume, more or less explicitly, that people's motives and behavior are largely a function of the social values they internalize. In other words, people's basic purposes are formed by their birth into a particular society; they do not exist independently. Functionalism also recognizes underlying "needs" or "functional imperatives" that are common to all human beings and that all societies must and do meet; but these tend to be sketched in very cursorily. It is socially instilled values that are emphasized. Conflict theorists, by contrast, emphasize "interests," which they often treat as self-evident but which include being free from subjugation, being in a position of power, and possessing more rather than less wealth and status. These theorists see interests as primary, common to all societies, and the main force behind human behavior in every case. Indeed, when conflict theorists discuss values specific to a given society, it is usually to describe their role in deceiving people about their true interests.

Other perspectives also imply that either "values" or "interests" are primary. Symbolic interactionism sees "values" as incorporated into the "me"; "interests" hardly appear in work done within this perspective. Phenomenology also emphasizes values rather than interests in its argument that people "trust" others to behave in certain situation-specific ways, and it sees such underlying trust as the basis of human behavior. Exchange theory, on the other hand, talks specifically about the importance of social values and tastes, which define people's preferences; but in practice it tends to base its arguments on objectives that are seen as universal—and therefore easily assumed—such as social acceptance or status. To that degree, it moves closer to conflict theory's idea of universal "interests."

Methodology

The third important respect in which the perspectives of modern theory differ is in their methods of argument and research, in particular whether they advocate deductive or inductive reasoning. With a *deductive* (or natural science) approach, one begins with explanatory hypotheses about a research problem and uses logical reasoning to deduce its empirical implications. In this approach the "recipe" for theory building requires that the basic concepts be spelled out before they are used in the formulation of hypotheses. For example, Durkheim's basic concepts (egoism, altruism, anomie, and fatalism) were used as key independent variables in his analysis of suicide rates.[17] The hypotheses are then tested on data in the real world.[18]

Scientists using the *inductive* approach begin instead by observing, by immersing themselves in the data. They feel that to start analysis with a clearly defined hypothesis is too rigid and may lead analysts to ignore important aspects of their subject. It is far better, they suggest, to get to know a subject and situation well and gradually build up, or induce, descriptions and/or explanations of what is really going on. In an inductive approach, the key concepts emerge in the final analysis of the research process. For example, Goffman's extensive observations in a mental hospital led him to create the concept "total institution."[19] Induction implies an inference from the particular to the general. In both deduction and induction, however, the theorist is concerned with clearly defined concepts that can be used to help understand what is going on.

Functionalism, conflict theory (with the exception of the Frankfurt School), and rational choice theory are essentially deductive. They logically derive, or "deduce," arguments and hypotheses from prior, more general propositions. For example, the functionalist Robert Merton argues that deviance results from a lack of congruence between values and opportunities;[20] the conflict theorist Ralf Dahrendorf explains industrial conflict by relating it to the more general principles of conflict of organization;[21] and Randall Collins devotes considerable effort to the defense and advocacy of deductive "scientific" social analysis. Marxist theory can also be placed most easily on the deductive side of the divide. It relates social evolution to material changes, and the superstructure of politics and ideas to the substructure of economic life. However, its mode of argument is also consciously different in its emphasis on dialectical reasoning and identifying how social events emerge from contradictions within the existing order (rather than on tracing out a step-by-step progression).[22] Finally, rational choice, and especially exchange theory as presented by Homans, is also clearly and self-consciously deductive in form.[23] Homans sets out his basic propositions and then deduces others from them, showing how, for exam-

[17]See Chapter II for a discussion of Durkheim's approach.

[18]The argument is that, strictly speaking, you cannot prove that a hypothesis is *true*, because there might always be some other explanation for your data which hasn't occurred to you. However, data which are clearly inconsistent with your hypothesis can show that it is *false*. See Karl Popper, *The Logic of Scientific Discovery* (London: Hutchinson, 1959).

[19]See Chapter V for a discussion of Goffman's approach.

[20]See Chapter II.

[21]See Chapter III.

[22]See Chapter III. Marx's economics is especially close to mainstream deductive argument.

[23]Peter M. Blau's *Inequality and Heterogeneity: A Primitive Theory of Social Structure* (New York: The Free Press, 1977), although not a part of exchange theory, is quite as formally deductive in its approach.

ple, conformity to group norms may follow from individuals' valuation of social approval.[24]

Symbolic interactionism and phenomenology provide very clear contrasts, for their proponents observe and experience a situation first and then infer or "induce" from it what is going on. Symbolic interactionists feel that deductive reasoning implies falsely that action and interpretation are simplistically determined by prior events. Sociologists should instead concentrate on understanding—through the use, above all, of participant observation—how people in a particular situation see things and then build up from there. Phenomenologists are even more antagonistic toward deductive social science. This position is connected with the perspective's general assumptions. Phenomenologists believe that deductive theories, by proposing general "positivist" law, falsely imply the existence of a single objective "reality" about which one can advance testable generalizations. Instead, phenomenology argues, what any human being describes is his or her own view of reality, based on tacit assumptions. Ethnomethodologists, in particular, appear to be confident in their own ability to describe how people order their experiences. However, their view leads them to see sociology's task as not to derive general causal laws but to observe the ordering of experience directly and to use the "documentary method of interpretation" to identify regular patterns of meaning.

The deductive model is also rejected, for different reasons, by a third group, the "critical" theorists. They attack what they call "traditional," or "positivist," theory for suggesting that its deductive arguments can be assessed objectively and for aiming at pure knowledge. However, their work is not inductive in the fashion of symbolic interactionism or phenomenology. Its proponents have no faith in "participant observation," and they have attacked phenomenology for relying on intuition.[25] Their "critical theory" assumes that fact and value are inseparable, and they propose their own antipositivist approach. In particular, they relate social phenomena to their notion of historical possibilities different from and superior to the current reality, and they believe in the possibility of "reason" as a standard against which to measure alternatives.[26]

Sociological theorists also differ in whether they advocate a heavy reliance on *quantitative data*. This aspect of their methodology tends to be related to whether they adopt a deductive model, since the scientific idea of hypothesis testing is associated with using quantitative data. However, the link is by no means universal. A deductive exchange theorist like Homans is very quantitative in his approach; most conflict theorists, like Collins, are

---

[24]See Chapter IV.
[25]Martin Jay, *The Dialectical Imagination* (Boston: Little, Brown, 1973), p. 82.
[26]Max Horkheimer, *Critical Theory* (New York: Herder and Herder, 1972).

moderately so, within the limits set by historical information. However, a functionalist like Parsons makes fairly little use of quantitative data.

Among inductive theorists in sociology there is a general dislike on principle of quantitative techniques. Symbolic interactionists believe that quantitative techniques distance the observer from the area of life being studied and ignore important aspects of meaning not built into the measurement instrument. Phenomenologists distrust them because they imply that social phenomena can be measured objectively—although some, such as Cicourel, believe that they be can be useful if the analyst is aware of their limits. However, there is no necessary connection between induction and a distrust of quantitative methods. An analyst who believes in inducing propositions from experience may also believe in subsequently using quantitative methods for verification.

Objectives

The final respect in which the major perspectives of contemporary theory differ from each other is in their ultimate objectives—in particular, whether they aim largely at describing things or at explaining, or even predicting, them. Ultimately, all sciences and social sciences are concerned with increasing our comprehension of things, with providing accounts that make us feel that we now *understand* what is going on to a greater degree than we did before. But such accounts may be ranged along a spectrum, from what are more or less detailed redescriptions of what is happening (often employing unfamiliar terms and ways of looking at things but hardly concerned with identifying causal chains) to explanations that reinterpret things by relating them back to different and more general concepts. At their most precise and fully developed, such explanations may not only increase one's understanding but allow one to make quite specific predictions. This is what makes scientific deductive explanation such a powerful technological tool. Explanation and prediction are not identical, however. Important explanations that refer back to general principles may not permit much in the way of prediction—the theory of evolution is a case in point. Conversely, the ability to predict can rest simply on tight statistical correlations and not on much "understanding" at all.

One of our favorite examples of what this distinction means is the story of Dr. John Snow. During a nineteenth-century cholera epidemic, he suggested to the authorities that they could stop the spread of the disease if they simply removed the handles from all the water pumps! Snow was not a madman. He had noticed that the poorhouse inhabitants, who had their own well, were free from the disease, unlike people drinking water from the main pumps. But although Snow was quite correct about the correlation between catching cholera and drinking the water that carried it, he understood fairly little about the way cholera operates. This distinction between prediction and explanation has, in turn, encouraged many philosophers of science to emphasize explanation, not prediction, as the heart of deductive science.[27]

Among the major perspectives of sociological theory, we find, not surprisingly, that objectives are closely associated with methodology and with whether the perspective accepts a scientific model for social science. Thus, symbolic interactionism and phenomenology place relatively the greatest emphasis on descriptive analysis. Phenomenology's concern with describing events follows naturally from its rejection of the idea of general and objective laws about reality. Users and advocates of the symbolic interactionist perspective also tend to feel that general explanatory arguments are likely to ignore and miss so much of people's experiences that they are seriously flawed and inadequate. However, by taking into account numerous factors and occurrences that can be missed in everyday, casual observation, such descriptions greatly increase our understanding.

Functionalism, conflict theory, and exchange theory aim at explaining phenomena in terms of more general principles. Of the three, functionalism is closest to the descriptive end of the spectrum. Talcott Parson's work, for example, largely consists of redescribing society as a system and providing new classifications, but it does not explain how its parts develop, although other parts of functionalist theory are more fully explanatory.

Conflict theorists are more concerned with explanation than are functionalists. They also derive propositions that are generally predictive, though usually not to the extent of predicting particular historical events. Their work involves some redescription—as when they talk of "ideology" or "alienation"—but their main concern is to provide a detailed explanation of how events and institutions are created by the actions and interests of different groups with different resources and by changes in technology, economic organization, ritual, and ideas. In using such explanatory propositions as a basis for prediction, Marx is by far the most ambitious, although other theorists, such as Habermas, have attempted to predict the future development of existing society.

Finally, of all the perspectives discussed in this text, rational choice, and especially exchange theory, is the least concerned with description and the most concerned with explanation and prediction. This is not to imply that its proponents are interested only in correlations of the pump-handle type, for they discuss in great detail what goes on inside people's minds in an attempt to understand the origins of actions and behavior. However, this objective further reinforces the tendency of exchange theorists and other rational choice theorists to concentrate on a limited range of subjects involving individual and small-group behavior. On a wider scale, they would agree that the complexity of social affairs makes precise prediction impossi-

[27]Toulmin, "From Form to Function," pp. 152–53.

ble[28] and that by taking as its subject the whole sprawling complex of "human society," sociology has chosen an area it cannot fully explain, let alone predict.

The fact that sociological theory does not form a cumulative body of work comparable to physics or even neoclassical economics does not mean that we have an impasse with one approach merely contradicting another. The test of a theory is ultimately whether it helps us to understand, and each of the theories discussed here sheds light on a different aspect of human society. In Popper's words, they are all "nets cast to catch what we call 'the world'—to rationalize, to explain and to master it";[29] and it is for this reason that each deserves recognition as part of contemporary sociological theory.

THEORY AND UNDERSTANDING: THE EXAMPLES OF FORMAL EDUCATION AND THE ROLE OF WOMEN IN CONTEMPORARY SOCIETY

Formal education and gender are two aspects of life in modern industrial society with which we all have direct experience and which affect our lives in countless ways. This makes them both excellent areas in which to see how well sociological theory illuminates our everyday world. In the chapters that follow, we have consistently selected examples of sociological research and nonsociological writing which bear on education and gender. Each theoretical perspective can illuminate some but not all aspects of a social phenomenon; by returning frequently to the same themes, we hope that the reader will be able to understand more easily the strengths and weaknesses of each perspective.

In modern societies, an increasing proportion of people's lives and a large part of national income are given to formal education. In America, for example, about one adult in four now studies or works in an educational institution. About 75 percent of students complete high school, compared to 6 percent in 1900; more than one in five graduate from college, compared to 1 in 50 at the turn of the century.[30] Moreover, the length of people's education and their success in passing courses, getting good grades, and entering prestigious colleges have a considerable impact on their later opportunities and careers.

In the case of both education and gender, two questions in particular relate very clearly to our experiences. Our questions for education are:

[28]Homans, in fact, would argue that at this level the distinction between history and sociology becomes meaningless.

[29]Popper, *The Logic of Scientific Discovery*, p. 59.

[30]U.S. National Center for Education Statistics, *Digest of Education Statistics* (Washington, D.C.: U.S. Government Printing Office, 1988).

First, why is the amount of time we spend in formal schooling so long, and the educational system of industrialized countries so big compared to the past? And second, within our own schools and classes, why do some students do well and continue through high school, college, and graduate school, while others drop out as soon as they possibly can, after years of guerilla war with the authorities?

Our questions for gender both relate to the roles of women in contemporary society. First, why, among full-time workers, do female college graduates in the United States make annual average salaries that are *lower than those earned by male high school graduates?*[31] Second, why do boys and men, at home, school, and work, tend to be aggressive and to dominate the situation, while girls and women tend to be caring and to take on less important "supportive" roles?

We suggest that our readers keep these general themes and research questions in mind as they progress through the text. Each theoretical perspective can be seen as effectively providing a piece of the puzzle. In Chapter VIII, we assemble and synthesize what each offers. We hope that, in bringing their contributions together, it will be apparent how, together, these very different approaches can provide coherent explanations of apparently bewildering social phenomena.

[31]In 1985 the average annual earnings of full-time female workers in the United States who were college graduates was $21,362; whereas the average earnings of male full-time workers who were high school graduates was $22,852. See United States Census Bureau, *Current Population Reports,* Series P-60, No. 156 (Washington, D.C.: U.S. Printing Office, 1985), Table 36.

II ———————————

FUNCTIONALISM

———————————

INTRODUCTION

Because it held the dominant position among contemporary sociological theories for a number of years, we begin with functionalism. Typically, a major portion of the required modern theory readings for students of sociology in the United States has been devoted to works by Talcott Parsons and Robert Merton. Some sociologists have even taken the position that sociological analysis and functional analysis are one and the same. Such was the thrust of Kingsley Davis's presidential address to the American Sociological Association in 1959, which was titled "The Myth of Functional Analysis as a Special Method in Sociology and Anthropology."[1]

Davis argued that sociology involves (1) examining the role (or function) that an institution or type of behavior plays in society and the way it is related to other social features and (2) explaining it in essentially "social" terms.[2] This, Davis felt, is also the nature of functional analysis. The debate continues, however, for there are many sociologists who disagree with Davis's arguments about the nature of sociology and are opposed to any effort to label the discipline as functionalist. Indeed, as we shall see in the ensuing chapters, other perspectives tend to define themselves in terms of and in contrast to functionalism.

This perspective is often labeled "structural-functionalism" because of its focus on the functional requisites, or "needs," of a social system that must be met if the system is to survive and on the corresponding structures that meet these "needs." According to this view, social systems have a tendency to perform certain tasks that are necessary for their survival, and sociological analysis, therefore, involves a search for the social structures that perform these tasks or meet the "needs" of the social system. Over the years, the approach's two major theorists, Talcott Parsons and Robert K. Merton, have often been referred to as structural-functionalists. We call this perspective *functionalism* for two reasons. First, it clarifies the link to the functionalism of its forerunners, especially Durkheim, Radcliffe-Brown, and Malinowski. Second, both of our major theorists prefer the term *functionalism*. Merton's use of the term *functional analysis* has been consistent over the years. Parsons abandoned the term "structural-functionalism" when he revised the concepts of function, structure, and process. In his revision, function is the master concept for systems analysis; and structure and process are parallel concepts, designating

---

[1]Kingsley Davis, "The Myth of Functional Analysis as a Special Method in Sociology and Anthropology." *American Sociological Review*, 24 (1959), 757–72.

[2]It is interesting to compare Davis's arguments with the exchange theory of George Homans, who argues that satisfactory "sociological" explanation must ultimately be psychological. See George Homans on "psychological reductionism," Chapter IV.

which functional elements remain static (structural) or which are dynamic and changing (processual).[3]

Functionalism Defined

In answer to the question "What is functionalism?" we turn first to *A Modern Dictionary of Sociology*, which defines functionalism as:

> The analysis of social and cultural phenomena in terms of the functions they perform in a sociocultural system. In functionalism, society is conceived of as a system of interrelated parts in which no part can be understood in isolation from the whole. A change in any part is seen as leading to a certain degree of imbalance, which in turn results in changes in other parts of the system and to some extent to a reorganization of the system as a whole. The development of functionalism was based on the model of the organic system found in the biological sciences.[4]

Because it is concerned with the overall characteristics of social structure and the general nature of social institutions, functionalism has a macrosociological focus. What functionalists mean by the "interrelation of the parts of a social system" can be understood by looking at an airport. Its "parts" include the roles of airline ticket and reservation personnel, maintenance crews, pilots and flight attendants, passengers, air traffic controllers, restaurant workers, and luggage carriers, to mention a few. All these parts are interrelated, and you need only think of a disturbance in any one of the parts to realize their interdependence. Many changes could lead to disequilibrium of the airport as a social system, including the closing of runways due to inclement weather, a malfunctioning of the radar control system, and the Christmas or Thanksgiving "crunch" of passengers. Any of these disturbances can result in a "certain degree of imbalance," often to the point of a temporary breakdown in the system.

In analyzing social systems along these lines, functionalists emphasize three elements:

1. the general interrelatedness, or interdependence, of the system's parts;
2. the existence of a "normal" state of affairs, or state of equilibrium, comparable to the normal or healthy state of an organism; and

---

[3]See Talcott Parsons, "The Present Status of Structural-Functional Theory in Sociology," in Lewis A. Coser, ed., *The Idea of Social Structure: Papers in Honor of Robert K. Merton* (New York: Harcourt Brace Jovanovich, 1975), p. 67, where he states: "The hyphenated label 'structural-functionalism' has seemed to me to be decreasingly appropriate."

[4]George A. Theodorson and Achilles S. Theodorson, eds., *A Modern Dictionary of Sociology* (New York: Thomas Y. Crowell Co., 1969), p. 167.

3. the way that all the parts of the system reorganize to bring things back to normal.

One of functionalism's most important propositions is that there will always be some such reorganization and tendency to restore equilibrium. In the case of the airport, it is easy to define "normal" conditions and see how the system organizes to restore them: personnel will work harder, overtime will be set up, additional staff will be hired. In other cases, as we shall see, restoring equilibrium may be more difficult.

In analyzing how social systems maintain and restore equilibrium, functionalists tend to use shared values or generally accepted standards of desirability as a central concept.[5] Value consensus means that individuals will be morally committed to their society. The emphasis on values is the second most important feature of functionalism, alongside the stress on a system's interdependence and tendency to restore equilibrium. As such, it is in direct contrast to the other major macrosociological perspective, conflict theory. Whereas functionalism emphasizes the unity of society and what its members share, conflict theorists stress the divisions within a society and the struggles that arise out of people's pursuits of their different material interests.[6]

INTELLECTUAL ROOTS: THE INFLUENCE OF EMILE DURKHEIM

The most important intellectual ancestors of modern functionalism are the sociologists Comte, Spencer, Pareto, and Durkheim and, at a later date, the anthropologists Radcliffe-Brown and Malinowski. Comte, Spencer, and Pareto emphasized the interdependence of parts of the social system; Durkheim emphasized integration, or solidarity, which inspired both Radcliffe-Brown's and Malinowski's analyses of the function of social institutions.

Auguste Comte (1789–1857), who is commonly identified as the founder of sociology, derived his interest in "statics" (order) and "dynamics" (progress) in society from his general investigation of the foundations of social stability. Comte stated functionalism's basic assumption of the social system's interdependence when he said, "The statical study of sociology consists in the investigation of the laws of action and reaction of the different parts of the social system."[7] The functional concept of equilibrium also emerged when Comte declared that a lack of harmony be-

[5]See p. 24 for a functionalist definition of values.
[6]See Chapter III.
[7]Auguste Comte, *The Positive Philosophy*, trans. Harriet Martineau (London: Bell, 1896), Vol. II.

tween the whole and parts of the social system was "pathological." The concept of equilibrium was borrowed from biology's treatment of homeostasis. For instance, if you fall and scrape your knee, you know that eventually a scab will form as other parts of your body come to the rescue; soon it will be healed and your body's system will be in equilibrium again. Comte's work was replete with such comparisons between social and biological organisms.

Herbert Spencer (1820–1903) should also be mentioned as a forerunner of functionalism because of his concept of differentiation. By differentiation Spencer meant the mutual dependence of unlike parts of the system, which is brought about inevitably by an increase in societies' size. Modern functionalists similarly identify differentiation as an important aspect of a social system's interrelatedness and integration. Spencer's evolutionary theory generally resembled the theory that Durkheim later presented in *The Division of Labor in Society*—a theory that greatly influenced modern functionalists. However, there were two important differences. First, Durkheim did not insist on the inherent necessity of social differentiation, as did Spencer. Second, Durkheim's insistence that social facts were the proper subject matter for sociology directly contradicted Spencer's reductionist position that the cause of social progress was psychological; that is, that the determining factor was the individual's need for greater happiness. In these respects, functionalism follows Durkheim. Nonetheless, Parsons used Spencer's notion of social differentiation in his theory of social change.

Vilfredo Pareto (1848–1923) patterned his system of sociology on a physiochemical system characterized by interdependence of parts and adjustive changes, rather than on the biological organism. To Pareto, the "molecules" of the social system were individuals with interests, drives, and sentiments. He was the first sociologist to provide a precise description of a social system in terms of the interrelations and mutual dependencies among parts. In his discussion of how systems adapt and change while maintaining equilibrium, Parsons later borrowed Pareto's idea of a dynamic or "moving" equilibrium that produces harmony for the system.

Emile Durkheim

Emile Durkheim (1858–1917) is certainly the most important sociological forerunner of modern functionalism. Comte's influence on Durkheim and, in turn, Durkheim's impact on Radcliffe-Brown and Malinowski were of crucial importance to its development. Parsons said that Durkheim was one of his most important intellectual role models. He mentions him specifically "in terms of substantive influence in the shaping of problems and of many elements of empirical and conceptual structure which has been central to my thinking."[8] Similarly, Robert Merton states that Durkheim was, besides those under whom he studied directly, one of the two from whom he learned most.[9]

However, Durkheim's theoretical influence extends beyond functionalism. Erving Goffman and Peter Berger have also incorporated some of Durkheim's ideas into their own symbolic interactionist and phenomenological perspectives. Randall Collins, a conflict theorist, incorporates Durkheim's ideas on ritual into his work.[10]

Emile Durkheim was born at Epinal in Lorraine, France. His father, grandfather, and great-grandfather had been rabbis, but though he studied for a time at a rabbinical school, Durkheim decided not to follow in their steps.[11] Family finances and his father's illness made Durkheim's early days as a college student difficult, but he finished his degree at the Ecole Normale Superieure, and because of his many publications in philosophy and social science, he was invited to teach at the University of Bordeaux in 1887. In 1902 he moved to the University of Paris, where he taught until his death.

Durkheim viewed teaching as almost a sacred duty, for many of the students in his courses were the future secondary teachers of France. In addition to teaching and research, Durkheim found time to establish, with a small number of colleagues, the first French Sociology journal, *Année sociologique*. He was also fiercely patriotic, and during World War I helped to organize a committee for the publication of studies and documents on the war to explain the French position to other countries. Durkheim's only son, André, was killed while fighting for the French cause in 1916. That blow, combined with overwork, led to a stroke and Durkheim's subsequent death in 1917, at the age of 59.

Some of Durkheim's most important functionalist ideas are a result of his lifelong interest in the concept of integration, the incorporation of individuals into the social order. Integration (or social solidarity) is important for the maintenance of social equilibrium. *The Rules of Sociological Method* and his works on religion and education are most often cited as his most important contributions to functionalism, but even in his first great work, *The Division of Labor in Society*, he was examining the function of the division of labor.

Durkheim viewed social evolution as a movement from the mechanical solidarity of tribal societies to the organic solidarity characteristic of industrial societies. He argued that primitive societies were characterized by a strong collective conscience, which he defined as "the totality of beliefs and

---

[8]Talcott Parsons, "On Building Social System Theory: A Personal History," *Daedalus* (Fall 1970), 873.

[9]See Coser, *The Idea of Social Structure*, p. 96.

[10]See Chapters III, V, and VI.

[11]See Steven Lukes' *Emile Durkheim: His Life and Work* (New York: Harper and Row, 1972) for a comprehensive treatment.

sentiments common to average citizens of the same society." As the division of labor increased, so too did individualism. There was a corresponding decrease in collective conscience and a shift to organic solidarity, character-ized by the interdependence of roles[12] and a lack of self-sufficiency that held people together.

Durkheim set out to create a proper subject matter for sociology, the realm of social facts. He defined a social fact as that "which is general over the whole of a given society whilst having an existence of its own, indepen-dent of its individual manifestations." His examples of social facts are laws, morals, beliefs, customs, and fashions. Durkheim later elaborated on the meaning of social facts and used the term institution, meaning the "beliefs and modes of behavior instituted by the collectivity." He defined sociology as "the science of institutions, their genesis and their functioning."[13] Durk-heim thus made it clear that he viewed macrostructural (large-scale or society-wide) phenomena as sociology's proper subject matter.

In *The Rules of Sociological Method,* where he discusses social facts, Durkheim sees functions as "general needs of the social organism."[14] He then proceeds to make his case for explanation of social facts by social rather than nonsocial causes. He applied his method in his well-known study *Suicide,* where he focused on suicide rates, a social fact, rather than on individual suicides.

Durkheim's discussion of punishment provides an excellent example of the strengths and weaknesses of both his and much later functionalist analysis. Punishment is, he argues, a social reaction to crime. It serves not simply the obvious functions of retribution for the criminal and general deterrence of crime; it also fulfills the generally unrecognized but critical function of maintaining the intensity of collective sentiments, or what modern functionalists call shared values (in this case, the objection to criminal activity). Punishment, Durkheim argues, "has the useful function of maintaining these sentiments at the same level of intensity, for they could not fail to weaken it if the offenses committed against them re-mained unpunished."[15]

However, Durkheim's explanation of what causes societies to adopt punishment is less satisfactory. He points out, quite correctly, that the func-tion something performs does not explain its existence in the first place, and he states, "We will, therefore, discover more easily the function if the cause is already known." However, he then goes on to engage in exactly that circular-ity of reasoning he attempted to avoid in distinguishing cause from function;

[12]Emile Durkheim, *The Division of Labor in Society* (Glencoe, Ill.: The Free Press, 1964), p. 49.

[13]Emile Durkheim, *The Rules of Sociological Method,* edited and with an introduction by Steven Lukes (New York: The Free Press, 1982), pp. 45 and 59.

[14]Ibid., p. 123.

[15]Ibid., p. 124.

he argues that punishment exists *because* of the function it performs in maintaining collective sentiments, which then in turn "cause" punishment.

In other words, at first Durkheim says that punishment is a consequence, or dependent variable:

But when he discusses the consequences of punishment for the society, he says:

Thus, in Durkheim's argument, the cause is, after all, the function, as we can see in the illustration. One could ask the chicken or the egg question of Durkheim. We shall find that this problem of circularity and "explaining" things by the functions they perform recurs throughout functional analysis.

Durkheim's most famous concept, anomie, is central to his study *Suicide*.[16] Literally translated from the French, anomie means normlessness, a situation where rules or norms are absent. Besnard recently defined an anomic situation as one "characterized by indeterminate goals and unlimited aspirations, the disorientation or vertigo created by confrontation with an excessive widening of the horizons of the possible."[17] Durkheim described two types of anomie: acute anomie, which is the result of an abrupt change, like a business crisis or a divorce; and chronic anomie, a state of constant change, characteristic of modern industrial society. Durkheim focused on chronic anomie, for he was concerned about what was going on in his own country and in other industrialized countries.

Durkheim did not take a neutral position regarding suicide; he saw it as a social problem and was concerned about the increasing rates of suicide

[16]Emile Durkheim, *Suicide: A Study in Sociology,* translated by John A. Spaulding and George Simpson, edited and with an introduction by George Simpson (Glencoe, Ill.: The Free Press, 1951).

[17]Philippe Besnard, "The True Nature of Anomie," *Sociological Theory,* 6 (1988), 91–95.

in industrialized countries. He had also been touched personally by this phenomenon, for it was the suicide of his closest friend, Victor Hommay, which prompted him to embark on an empirical study of suicide.[18]

A description of the central argument of Durkheim's *Suicide* may clarify the deductive (or natural science) approach. Durkheim's study does not simply describe the suicide rates in Europe in the nineteenth century. Instead he begins with the basic assumption that too much or too little regulation or integration (cohesion) is unhealthy for a society, and from this he derives specific hypotheses about suicide. To demonstrate Durkheim's approach and clarify what "middle-range" theory is about, Robert Merton restated Durkheim this way:

1. Social cohesion provides psychic support to group members subjected to acute stresses and anxieties.
2. Suicide rates are functions of unrelieved anxieties and stresses to which persons are subjected.
3. Catholics have greater social cohesion than Protestants.
4. Therefore, lower suicide rates should be anticipated among Catholics than among Protestants.[19]

In typical functionalist fashion, Durkheim bases his theory on social cohesion or solidarity and on two specific societal "needs," regulation and integration. His major hypothesis is that societies characterized by too much or too little regulation or integration will have high suicide rates. Anomie, a state of normlessness, is the term Durkheim uses for lack of regulation, and he is deeply concerned about its effects. Anomie, he says, is a pathological state for society, one aspect of which is a rise in suicide rates. As we shall see later, in his concern for the state of society Durkheim is very like Marx. Whereas Durkheim saw modern society as afflicted with anomie, Marx described it as marked by alienation. The concept of anomie holds an important place in modern functionalism, as does alienation in conflict theory. However, whereas Durkheim emphasizes people's need for firmly established and common social norms, Marx sees alienation as the pernicious result of a social order that tightly controls its citizens, and he argues that mankind needs far greater freedom from regulation.[20]

Again unlike Marx, Durkheim attempted to make his theory of sui-

---

[18]See Ruth A. Wallace and Shirley F. Hartley, "Religious Elements in Friendship: Durkheimian Theory in an Empirical Context," in Jeffrey C. Alexander, ed., *Durkheimian Sociology: Cultural Studies* (New York: Cambridge University Press, 1988), pp. 93–106.

[19]See Robert K. Merton, *Social Theory and Social Structure*, rev. and enl. ed. (New York: The Free Press, 1957), p. 151.

[20]See Chapter III for Marx's definition and discussion of alienation.

cide empirically verifiable by further defining and operationalizing his concepts. For instance, he considered a situation clearly anomic when a crisis or a sudden social change causes discontinuity between people's actual experiences and their normative expectations. Events of this type, which Durkheim suggested will create anomie and on which empirical data can be collected, include the sudden death of a spouse and economic depressions. Anomie, Durkheim hypothesized, will in turn lead to high suicide rates. Using the deductive approach, Durkheim not only made his hypotheses testable; he actually tested some of his hypotheses with data that had been collected by government officials. He found, for example, that widows and widowers did indeed have higher suicide rates than married people and that suicide rates were higher during a depression than they were during periods of economic stability.[21]

Durkheim's most important contribution to functionalism is *The Elementary Forms of the Religious Life*.[22] Here he shows how in the most primitive tribes religion was a strong integrative force through its instillation of common values and identification. We have already referred to the central role values play in functionalist explanation; functionalism again closely follows Durkheim's approach, referring to values as "widely shared conceptions of the good"[23] or "beliefs that legitimize the existence and importance of specific social structures and the kinds of behavior that transpire in social structure."[24] Smelser presents the example of belief in free enterprise as a societal value that "endorses the existence of business firms organized around the institution of private property and engaged in the pursuit of private profit."[25] Another of the hallmarks of functional analysis, the persistent search for integrative forces, is an aspect of the general stress on interdependence and equilibrium, which we mentioned above. Durkheim, who again shared modern functionalism's concerns, is interested in religion largely because he considers religion to be especially effective in developing common values—and so a very good source of integration. Durkheim's search for an equally strong integrative force in modern society led him to

---

[21]See Durkheim, *Suicide*.

[22]Emile Durkheim, *The Elementary Forms of Religious Life* (New York: Collier Books, 1961).

[23]Marie Augusta Neal, *Values and Interests in Social Change* (Englewood Cliffs, N.J.: Prentice-Hall, Inc., 1965), p. 9.

[24]See Neil J. Smelser, *The Sociology of Economic Life* (Englewood Cliffs, N.J.: Prentice-Hall, Inc., 1963), p. 27.

[25]Ibid. See also Robin M. Williams, Jr., "Change and Stability in Values and Value Systems," in Bernard Barber and Alex Inkeles, eds., *Stability and Social Change* (Boston: Little, Brown, 1971), pp. 123–59. Williams describes values as generalized criteria for desirability of conduct and norms as specific obligatory demands, expectations, and rules that are legitimated by values.

see the public school system as the functional alternative to religion for the transmission of values in modern society.[26]

Two anthropologists who adopted Durkheim's functional analysis in their work were Bronislaw Malinowski (1884–1942) and Arthur Radcliffe-Brown (1881–1955). Both were interested in Durkheim's work, and it was Malinowski who first used the term "*functional*" for this type of analysis.[27] One of the links between their work and modern functionalism in sociology was forged when Talcott Parsons studied under Malinowski at the London School of Economics.

Malinowski's and Radcliffe-Brown's levels of analysis differed, however. Malinowski was concerned with psychological needs and functions, which he believed all societies developed ways of fulfilling; Radcliffe-Brown was concerned with sociological ones—the functions of institutions in the social system. For instance, on the question of the function of magical rites, Malinowski believed that the individual's needs are the causal factor. He argued that magic was used more in open-sea fishing than in inland fishing because of the individual's feelings of danger and insecurity on the open sea. Magic both developed and functioned to reduce these feelings. Radcliffe-Brown, on the other hand, treated magic in terms of its social functions. He believed that societies define what is dangerous and threatening, and individuals are taught by society to have appropriate responses to these situations. Thus, according to Radcliffe-Brown, magical rites exist to maintain an orderly society; their function is social, not individual. When Parsons developed his functionalist framework, he borrowed more heavily from Radcliffe-Brown, who emphasized social needs and social explanation, than from Malinowski. However, Parsons did incorporate Malinowski's theories when he introduced the personality system, along with the cultural and social systems, in his systems of action.

Although modern functionalism has roots in the work of Comte, Spencer, and Pareto and is also indebted to Malinowski and Radcliffe-Brown, it owes its greatest debt to Durkheim. We now turn to Durkheim's most important heirs, Talcott Parsons and Robert Merton.

---

[26]During the First World War, in which his own son was killed, Durkheim hailed the success of the public school system:

> All peoples . . . render homage to the virtues she (France) has shown, the heroism of her troops, to the grave and calm endurance with which the country has borne the frightful calamities of a war unparalleled in history. What does this mean if not that our educational methods have produced the best effects that could be expected of them; that our public school has made men of the children confided to it.

Emile Durkheim, "The School of Tomorrow," in Ferdinand Buisson and Frederic E. Farrington, eds., *French Educational Ideals of Today* (New York: World Books, 1919), pp. 185–92.

[27]See Chapter IV for Malinowski's contribution to exchange theory.

PART ONE
Talcott Parsons: Grand Theory

BACKGROUND

Talcott Parsons (1902–1979) was the son of a Congregational minister who later served as president of Marietta College in Ohio. Parsons did his under-graduate work at Amherst, where he majored in biology. As he describes it in his intellectual autobiography, he was "converted" to the social sciences in his junior year, but owing to faculty turnover he was unable then to pursue his interests in detail.[28] It is important to keep in mind this early interest in biology, however, because the direction he took in sociology was clearly rooted in biological studies and their concern with the interdependence of an organism's parts.

A year at the London School of Economics, where Parsons studied under Malinowski, was followed by an exchange fellowship to Heidelberg, where he encountered Max Weber's work for the first time and where he wrote a doctoral dissertation on "The Concept of Capitalism in Recent German Literature," treating, among others, Marx and Weber. Parsons played an important part in introducing Weber to America when he trans-lated *The Protestant Ethic and the Spirit of Capitalism* (1930) and when he later analyzed Weber's theoretical perspective in what is now Volume II of *The Structure of Social Action* (1937).

Following a year of teaching at Amherst, Parsons went to Harvard as an instructor in 1927[29] and taught there until he was retired as Emeritus Professor in 1973. After that he continued to teach as a visiting professor at such universities as Pennsylvania, Rutgers, and California at Berkeley. He also continued to publish, to present papers at professional meetings, and to give guest lectures. Shortly before his death in May 1979, he was continu-ing work on such topics as sociobiology (the study of the biological bases of human behavior), interdisciplinary studies, and the cultural system level (the level of analysis that focuses on the question of meaning, or symbolic systems) in his general theory of action.[30] The indicators of his stature in the profession include his numerous publications, his presidency of the

[28]We have relied on Parsons' autobiographical statement and on Benton Johnson's monograph throughout this section. See Parsons, "On Building Social System Theory," pp. 826–81, and Benton Johnson, *Functionalism in Modern Sociology: Understanding Talcott Parsons* (Morristown, N.J.: General Learning Press, 1975).

[29]From 1927 to 1930 he was in the economics department. Harvard's sociology depart-ment was established in 1930.

[30]From personal interview with Parsons on February 16, 1977.

American Sociological Association in 1942 and the Eastern Sociological Society in 1949, his participation at international meetings, and his reputation throughout the world of sociology. His critics, both positive and negative, are numerous; and his work serves as a major reference point in modern sociological theory.[31]

The major portion of this chapter will be devoted to a discussion of Parsons' contributions to functionalism: his systems of action, his action schema, the pattern variables, the system problems, and his theory of evolutionary change.

PARSONS' SYSTEM LEVELS

We have already seen that the concept of a system is at the core of any discussion of Parsonian theory. As Parsons puts it, "The concept of system in the action field as in others, has been central to my thinking from a very early stage."[32] His general theory of action, in which he gives his overall picture of how societies are structured and fit together, includes four systems: the cultural system, the social system, the personality system, and the behavioral organism as a system.

How does Parsons define his four system levels? First of all is the "cultural system," in which the basic unit of analysis is "meaning," or "symbolic system." Some examples of symbolic systems are religious beliefs, languages, and national values. As we would expect, at this level Parsons focuses on shared values. When, for instance, societal values are internalized by a society's members (when they make society's values their own), "socialization" takes place; and socialization is a very powerful integrative force in maintaining social control and holding a society together.

The preeminence of the cultural system in Parsons' thinking is illustrated in his statement:

> It is quite clear that the high elaboration of human action systems is not possible without relatively stable symbolic systems where meaning is not contingent on highly particularized situations. . . . It is such a shared symbolic system which functions in interaction which will here be called a cultural tradition.[33]

---

[31]Two festschrifts have already been published. See Alex Inkeles and Bernard Barber, eds., *Stability and Social Change* (Boston: Little Brown, 1971), and Jan J. Loubser, Rainer C. Baum, Andrew Effrat, and Victor Lidz, eds., *Explorations on General Theory in Social Science: Essays in Honor of Talcott Parsons* (New York: The Free Press, 1976). For a complete bibliography through 1977, see Talcott Parsons, *Action Theory and the Human Condition* (New York: Free Press, 1978).

[32]Parsons, "On Building Social System Theory," p. 849. See Walter Buckley's critique of the way functionalists like Parsons use "system" in his *Sociology and Modern Systems Theory* (Englewood Cliffs, N.J.: Prentice-Hall, Inc., 1967).

[33]Talcott Parsons, *The Social System* (New York: The Free Press, 1951), p. 11.

Heads of state often draw on the functionalist perspective in their speeches. The following excerpts from President John F. Kennedy's inaugural address on January 20, 1961, exemplify a leader's appeal to shared values on both national and international levels:

> Let every nation know . . . that we shall pay any price, bear any burden, meet any hardship, support any friend, oppose any foe to assure the survival and the success of liberty.
>   . . . In your hands, my fellow citizens, more than mine, will rest the final success or failure of our course. Since this country was founded, each generation of Americans has been summoned to give testimony to its national loyalty.
>   . . . And so, my fellow Americans: ask not what your country can do for you—ask what you can do for your country.
>   My fellow citizens of the world: ask not what America will do for you, but what together we can do for the freedom of man.[34]

The social system is the next level in Parsons' scheme, and it is the one on which he has elaborated the most. Here the basic unit is "role interaction." Parsons devoted an entire book to this topic, and in it he defined the social system:

> A social system consists in a plurality of individual actors interacting with each other in a situation which has at least a physical or environmental aspect, actors who are motivated in terms of a tendency to the "optimization of gratification" and whose relation to their situations, including each other, is defined and mediated in terms of a system of culturally structured and shared symbols.[35]

In Parsons' definition of a social system, *plurality* can mean two or more, and *actors* can be people or collectivities. Thus, a social system can be made up of anything from two people interacting in a restaurant to the relationships within NATO or the Warsaw Pact, where the actors are member nations. The relationship of the social system to the cultural system is apparent in Parsons' reference to "culturally structured and shared symbols," which define the way actors interact. In addition, Parsons shows how the other two systems penetrate the social system as well. He refers to "individual actors" whose motive is self-gratification because of the nature of their personality system, and he brings in a "physical or environmental aspect," which sets boundaries around this situation where interation takes place and is itself a function of the behavioral organisms involved.

According to Parsons, the basic unit of the personality system is the

[34]*Public Papers of the Presidents of the United States: John F. Kennedy* (Washington, D.C.: United States Government Printing Office, 1962), pp. 1–3. Thanks to Anne Kanour for drawing our attention to this source.

[35]Parsons, *The Social System*, p. 5.

individual actor, the human person. His focus at this level is on individual needs, motives, and attitudes, such as the "motivation toward gratification," which he emphasizes in the definition we have quoted. As we shall see, "motivation toward gratification" corresponds to both conflict theory's and exchange theory's explicit assumptions that people are "self-interested" or "profit maximizers."[36]

In the fourth system, the behavioral organism, the basic unit is the human being in its biological sense—that is, the physical aspect of the human person, including the organic and physical environment in which the human being lives. In referring to this system, Parsons explicitly mentions the organism's central nervous system and motor activity.[37] One of Parsons' later interests was in sociobiology, which is the study of the biological basis of social behavior.[38]

Parsons' view of socialization will illustrate how all these systems are interrelated. At birth we are simply behavioral organisms; only as we develop as individuals do we gain any personal identity. How, then, do people become socialized? As we mentioned earlier, Parsons says that people internalize the values of a society; that is, they make the social values of the cultural system their own by learning from other actors in the social system what is expected of them. In other words, they learn "role expectations" and so become full participants in society. Thus, the values come from the cultural system; the corresponding normative or role expectations are learned in the social system; the individual identity comes from the personality system; and the biological equipment comes from the behavioral organism.

Let us take a concrete social system and see how socialization "works" within it. Consider a juvenile gang. If one of the values of that gang is the ability to steal cars, then juveniles who wish to become full members of that gang not only will have to make that value their own (cultural system), but they must also know how much of such behavior is expected of them. In social system terms, they must conform to normative expectations. Also, their own identity must be involved in their membership: membership in the gang must answer certain needs or drives in their own personalities. The behavioral organism is also involved, since potential gang members must possess a certain dexterity and physical skills to steal cars successfully and live up to the expectations of the gang.

This example should help illustrate the interpenetration of all four systems. Parsons does not consider his four system levels to be mutually exclusive; rather, they exhibit the interdependence that functionalism consistently stresses. In the following section, we discuss Parsons' action

---

[36]See Chapters III and IV.

[37]Talcott Parsons, *The System of Modern Sociology* (Englewood Cliffs, N.J.: Prentice-Hall, Inc., 1971), p. 5.

[38]See Chapter VII for a discussion of sociobiology.

schema, which is a framework for describing actual behavior within the context of the four systems and which is central in his general theory of action.

PARSONS' THEORY OF ACTION

Parsons' action theory starts with an "actor," who could be either a single person or a collectivity. In Figure 2-1, the actor (1) is Ann Doe. Parsons sees the actor as motivated to spend energy in reaching a desirable goal or end, as defined by the cultural system (2), which for Ann Doe is a B.A. degree. The action takes place in a situation (3), which includes *means* (facilities, tools, or resources) and *conditions* (obstacles that may arise in the pursuit of the goal. Ann Doe, for instance, has the intellectual ability and the money for tuition, but she is employed full-time. Taking courses that are scheduled after work hours, getting time off during work hours, or changing to a job that will allow her the needed time is essential in her situation. The means and conditions involved could, then, make a situation precarious. Finally, and this is extremely important in Parsons' action theory, all the above elements are regulated by the normative standards of the social system (4); in Ann Doe's case, she must pass all courses required for her degree. Actors cannot ignore the rules of the game; the rules define their ends and how they behave, and normative expectations must be fulfilled by any actor who is motivated to pursue a goal. Because the norms have been internalized by the actor, she or he is motivated to act appropriately. Now we can see both why it could be said that norms are at the heart of Parsons' theory of action and why Parsons considers the "cultural system" that legitimates them to be primary.

FIGURE 2-1   Parsons' Theory of Action

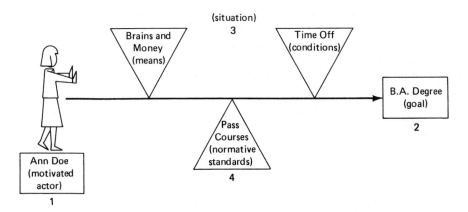

In Chapter I we drew a distinction between theories in the scientific sense, from which one can logically deduce concrete propositions and hypotheses, and "general orientations" to analysis. We can see that Parsons' all-encompassing general theory of action belongs more to the latter than to the former category. It provides concepts that are appropriate for describing a wide range of behavior and for emphasizing the interdependence of society's components rather than direct statements about what people will do in different situations or the structure of actual societies. However, Parsons also provides some more specific arguments about how different societies work when he elaborates on the normative expectations and cultural goals that dominate his action schema. The next section discusses this aspects of Parsons' thought.

THE PATTERN VARIABLES

As we saw in the preceding section, Parsons was initially preoccupied with the formulation of the action schema. In it, he portrayed purposive actors who were oriented to goals but had to fulfill certain conditions—themselves defined by normative expectations—before they could be gratified. Parsons felt that his next intellectual task was to develop clearer specifications of what different contingencies and expectations actors were likely to face. He wanted to show that their situation is not entirely unstructured and uncertain. Therefore, he formulated the pattern variables, which categorize expectations and the structure of relationships. They make the abstract action schema more explicit.

This portion of Parsons' work is based on Ferdinand Toennies' (1855–1936) *gemeinschaft-gesellschaft* typology. (A typology is an analysis based on types.) Toennies was interested in contrasting primitive communities (*gemeinschaft*) with modern industrial (*gesellschaft*) societies. Community (*gemeinschaft*) is characterized by a predominance of close personal bonds or kinship relations; society (*gesellschaft*) is characterized by a predominance of more impersonal or business-type relationships. Durkheim, following Toen-

TABLE 2-1   Parsons' Pattern Variables

EXPRESSIVE (GEMEINSCHAFT)	INSTRUMENTAL (GESELLSCHAFT)
Ascription	Achievement
Diffuseness	Specificity
Affectivity	Neutrality
Particularism	Universalism
Collectivity	Self

nies, analyzed the types of solidarity in primitive and modern societies. He labeled the former "mechanical solidarity" (where the collective conscience was strong) and the latter "organic solidarity" (where the collective conscience was weak owing to the rise of individualism).[39] Like Toennies and Durkheim, Parsons considers the difference between the two to be fundamental. He labels relationships in traditional societies, which are predominantly personal and stable, "expressive," and relationships in modern society, which are predominantly impersonal or businesslike, "instrumental."

Even in modern society both types of relationships exist and are needed. Parsons uses this "need" to analyze sex role differentiation in the family. He argues that the instrumental leadership role must be accorded to the husband-father, on whom the reputation and income of the family depend.[40] Likewise he states that because of the occupational responsibilities of the father, the mother must take on the expressive leadership role in the socialization of the children. Feminists have argued that Parsons' statement regarding the positive functions of this instrumental/expressive division of labor in the family was an attempt to justify the status quo. They have criticized Parsons' theory of gender socialization as oppressive for both genders, but particularly for women.

Parsons went beyond a simple twofold typology of expressive/instrumental. His pattern variables are a fivefold elaboration of the traditional-modern typology. Parsons' own definition of a pattern variable is "a dichotomy, one side of which must be chosen by an actor before the meaning of a situation is determinate for him, and thus before he can act with respect to that situation."[41] In other words, each pattern variable represents a problem or a dilemma that must be solved by the actor before action can take place.

Table 2-1 summarizes the pattern variable scheme. In each case the choices that actors typically and appropriately make differ according to the type of society. The appropriate choices for traditional societies are on the left-hand side (expressive), and the appropriate choices for modern societies are on the right-hand side (instrumental).

The first choice actors must make is between ascription and achievement, or, as they are sometimes labeled, "quality" and "performance." The dilemma here is whether to orient oneself toward others on the basis of what they are (that is, on the basis of ascribed qualities, such as sex, age, race, ethnicity) or on the basis of what they can do or have done (that is, on the basis of performance). For example, in modern societies such as ours, employers are expected to orient themselves toward potential employees

---

[39]See our earlier discussion of these two types of solidarity, pp. 20–21.

[40]Talcott Parsons, *Essays in Sociological Theory* (New York: The Free Press, 1954), pp. 422–23.

[41]Talcott Parsons, *Toward a General Theory of Action*, edited with Edward A. Shils (Cambridge: Harvard University Press, 1951), p. 77.

on the basis of the work that they have done in the past and that they could be expected to do in the future, not according to their color, age, sex, or family connections. Thus, employers should choose the performance, or achievement, side of the pattern variable dichotomy, rather than the ascriptive, or quality, side. When, for instance, a young member of a famous family is hired for a job over others with better performance qualifications, an outcry from the public is to be expected. There remain situations, however, in which the choice is expected to be at least partly ascriptive. For example, one must be a certain age to qualify for acceptance into the armed service. If it could be proved that a person lied about age, negative sanctions from authorities in the armed service would be in order. It is important to keep in mind that what we are discussing here is the *appropriate* choice between ascriptive and achievement options. Parsons places normative expectations at the core of the decision; the either-or choice is not an arbitrary one. Thus, in Ann Doe's case, which we used in discussing Parsons' action schema, normative standards dictate that she pass her courses; if she fails, she does not achieve the goal of a B.A. degree no matter what her ascriptive qualities.

The second pattern variable is diffuseness or specificity. Here the issue is the range of demands in the relationship. If the number and types of demands or responsibilities are wide-ranging, it is a diffuse relationship; if the scope is narrow or very limited, the relationship is functionally specific. For instance, you can expect a lot from a very close friend—from spending hours being a good listener for you, to volunteering services, such as house- or plant-sitting, to lending you a variety of things, including money. This is what Parsons means when he talks of a diffuse relationship. On the other hand, if the relationship in question is between dentist and patient, the dentist's interest in the patient is restricted to the care of the teeth, and the patient is expected to be on time for the appointment, to sit still, to open and close his or her mouth as directed, and to pay for the dentist's services. This is a functionally specific relationship. Moreover, the type of relationship it is predefines its limits. If either doctor or patient makes demands that are not connected with the care of the teeth, such as asking personal questions about family, business, or sex life, a negative sanction can be expected; the patient will be angry and may even stop seeing the dentist altogether. In short, there aren't many things you can't ask your close friend to do for you; that relationship is based on nonexclusion. A specific relationship like the one between dentist and patient is one in which all irrelevant behavior should be excluded and in which what is relevant is very specifically defined. Parsons' argument is that in modern societies, the appropriate choice generally involves specifically defined behavior, whereas in a traditional society, most relationships are diffuse.

The third pattern variable is affectivity or affective neutrality. Here the issue is simply whether or not the actor can expect emotional gratification in the relationship. An engaged couple can certainly expect to relate to each other with affectivity; on the other hand, a high school teacher and student are expected to opt for neutrality. Parsons' view of the school system in the United States, incidentally, is that when children enter the system at approximately age six they are used to the affective relationships of family life. At school, they learn that they can "get away" with some measures of affectivity, such as clutching the teachers's hand, but only in the first one or two years of schooling. In his article "The School Class as a Social System," Parsons describes how education becomes more of a "bloodless existence" as students progress through the grades and argues that this is important for children's survival in a society in which affective neutrality and instrumental, rather than expressive, expectations are predominant in the occupation structure.[42]

The fourth pattern variable is particularism or universalism. Here the choice is between reacting on the basis of a general norm or reacting on the basis of someone's particular relationship to you or one's membership in a particular group. Because a teacher in our society is expected to treat all students equally—that is, according to universalistic criteria—it would be difficult for parents or relatives to have their own students or relatives as students in their own classrooms. A good librarian is in the same predicament; librarians are expected not to cancel charges incurred by a relative or close friend on overdue books. An example of particularism is the "old boy" system, which worked effectively for some time in many occupations in the United States when hiring was done on a particularistic basis. Although this used to be socially acceptable, and in many countries still is, it is no longer the orientation that United States employers are expected to take.[43] In general, questions of "discrimination" involve choices being made on the basis of particularistic criteria rather than the universalistic criteria that modern societies believe in and prescribe.

A fifth pattern variable, the collectivity-self orientation, involves the dilemma of whether private interests can be gratified or some collective obligation or duty must be fulfilled. Self-interest is highly institutionalized in the business world, for example, where the profit motive is pursued legitimately. By contrast, civil servants are expected to carry out their duties in the best interests of the public, so appropriate role behavior is oriented to the interests of the collectivity rather than to self-interests. Although Par-

---

[42]Talcott Parsons, "The School Class as a Social System: Some of Its Functions in American Society," in A. H. Halsey, Jean Floud, and C. Arnold Anderson, eds., *Education, Economy, and Society* (New York: The Free Press, 1961), pp. 434–55. Expressive choices are appropriate in the private sphere of the family, however.

[43]Changes in normative expectations resulting from changes in laws or guidelines do not ensure conformity, as we have learned from the civil rights movement in the United States. Witness, for instance, the backlog of cases to be inspected by the Equal Employment Opportunity Commission.

sons originally included collectivity-self, it tended to disappear from his own formulations of the pattern variables after 1953.[44]

Look back for a moment at the first pattern variable described, ascription or achievement. You can see that there is some resemblance between the first and fourth set of pattern variables. Universalism is very similar to achievement, or performance, and particularism is similar to ascription, or quality. As with his system levels, Parsons does not view the pattern variables as mutually exclusive. Rather, a given society or situation is generally characterized by pattern variables that are related to each other. In particular, the pattern variables falling in the "expressive" category are likely to occur together, as are those falling in the "instrumental" category.

Now that we have described all the pattern variables, we can better understand how they can be used to characterize a role relationship. The role relationship of teacher toward student is achievement oriented, functionally specific, affectively neutral, and universalistic. All these choices happen to be on the instrumental side, and this is in line with Parsons' argument that the instrumental variables predominate in an industrial society, particularly in the professions.

Because Parsons thinks the instrumental side of the pattern variables is characteristic of modern or industrial societies, he clearly implies a need for institutions with socializing functions. In his discussion of the school class, Parsons points out some of these implications for the school, which is a "focal socializing agency" for the child from the first grade through entry into the labor force.[45] As Parsons puts it, "It is essential that the teacher is not a mother to her pupils, but must insist on universalistic norms and the differential reward of achievement."[46] Whereas it was appropriate for the children to concentrate on the expressive side of pattern variables in the expressive, or *gemeinschaft*, atmosphere of the home, it is in the school that they learn that they are expected to tread a predominantly instrumental path in our society. The school thus provides the type of workers needed in an industrial society.

Although Talcott Parsons admitted to being an "incurable theorist" (on the dedication page of *The Social System*), he has also been concerned with the empirical application of the pattern variables. He assumes that the pattern variables can be combined in a number of different ways to de-

---

[44]See Talcott Parsons, "Pattern Variables Revisited," *American Sociological Review*, 25 (1960), 467–88. Parsons says his view now is that the collectivity-self orientation was "an unduly restricted formulation of an element in the organization of action components at the level next above that designated by the primary pattern variables" (480). In other words, he sees it on a more abstract level than the other four.

[45]Much of this argument is reminiscent of Durkheim's ideas on education. See Emile Durkheim, *Moral Education*, ed. Everett Wilson (New York: The Free Press, 1973).

[46]Parsons, "The School Class as a Social System," p. 444.

scribe various role relationships, and he points to the need for empirical research to show the types and numbers of these combinations.[47]

The results of one of his rare ventures into empirical research are reported in *The Social System* in a chapter entitled "Social Structure and Dynamic Process: The Case of Modern Medical Practice."[48] In this chapter Parsons utilizes the pattern variable scheme as he describes the doctor-patient role relationship. In gathering data for his study of medical practice, Parsons engaged in both participant observation and interviews with physicians at Tufts Medical Center and Massachusetts General Hospital.[49] As might be expected, he depicts the doctor's role as predominantly instrumental. Because of the high levels of technical competence required, the doctor's position is seen as an achieved status; one is not "born" a doctor (though being the child of a doctor may help).[50] Parsons points out that the complexity and subtlety of the knowledge and skill required, and the consequent length and intensity of training, demand performance or achievement criteria as well as a universalistic orientation. For instance, a doctor must concentrate on making the patient well, and in this respect all patients must be treated the same.

Likewise, affective neutrality is necessary because the physician is expected to treat problems in "objective scientifically justifiable terms."[51] For this reason surgeons do not ordinarily operate on family members. Finally, since a doctor is a specialist in matters of health and disease, specificity of function is involved. Patients do not, for instance, ordinarily consult their doctors about their income taxes; even though physicians may be helpful in this matter, that is not their area of expertise.

What distinguishes the medical profession from many other professions, in Parsons' eyes, is the collectivity orientation. Although we would point out that there is clearly a great profit to be gained from the practice of medicine, Parsons discusses the "ideology" of the profession, which emphasizes the obligation of the physician to put the "welfare of the patient" above his or her personal interests. He believes that the medical profession draws a line between itself and business and commercial operations, and he compares medicine with the clergy in this respect; in both cases, the profit motive is *supposed to be* "drastically excluded."[52]

---

[47]See Benton Johnson, *Functionalism in Modern Sociology: Understanding Talcott Parsons*, p. 28.

[48]See Parsons, *The Social System*, pp. 428–79.

[49]Parsons, "On Building Social System Theory," p. 835. This may come as a surprise to those who thought that Parsons had never engaged in empirical research.

[50]One could argue that there is an ascribed element inherent in the doctor's role, as the expense of medical school education makes it easier for those born of wealthy parents to aspire to the medical profession in the United States.

[51]Parsons, *The Social System*, p. 435.

[52]Ibid.

Parsons points out that the particular patterning of the doctor's role is related to cultural tradition and that the specialization of technical competence is a characteristic of that role in contemporary America. In tribal societies the role of medicine man could be an ascribed status, passed on from parents to children. As a medicine man, his behavior to others and theirs to him were defined by and varied according to particularistic variables. In addition, because the medicine man might often be consulted on many matters unrelated to health and sickness, diffuseness of function, rather than specificity, would be the norm. We might also expect to see more affectivity exhibited, because of close tribal ties. Thus, the patterning of the "appropriate choices" would be different in tribal societies. The contrast between the roles of medicine man and physician illustrates the general shift from an expressive orientation in *gemeinschaft* societies to an instrumental orientation in industrial, or *gesellschaft*, societies. As we explained earlier, this shift is at the heart of the pattern variable scheme.

If we assume, in the Parsonian framework, that individual actors are socialized and thus are motivated to meet the demands of societal expectations, then we can expect actors to make appropriate choices about the pattern variables, and we can predict their behavior on the basis of information about values and normative expectations. However, there are situations in which the choice is not simply a matter of one or the other. For instance, teacher-parents who have their own children as students in the classroom will find the parent role conflicting with the teacher role in many instances. The choice in this case is not always either a universalistic or a particularistic one; the blood relationship "muddies the waters" considerably, for the decision involves both universalism and particularism. Thus, the pattern variable scheme is not as neat as it appears at first glance, either as a way of clarifying and describing role relationships or as a way of predicting people's appropriate choices. On their own, the pattern variables do not tell the sociologist how people will behave when faced with role conflicts, a problem to which, as we shall see later in the chapter, Robert Merton has devoted considerable attention. In addition, it is questionable whether socialization is as effective, or people's behavior as simply and clearly a function of normative expectations, as Parsons's approach implies. In other words, people's "appropriate" choice may very frequently not be their actual one. The occurrence of nonprescribed, or what Parsons would call "deviant," behavior will occupy us again in the context of our next topic: Parsons's work on "systems problems" and equilibrium.

THE FUNCTIONAL SYSTEM PROBLEMS—AGIL

Shortly after Parsons worked out the pattern variable scheme, he embarked on his next intellectual mission. He wanted to reduce the lack of certainty in his action schema about what goals actors would pursue, and he wanted to specify further the pattern variables. The ideas he developed—which have been referred to variously as the "system problems," the "functional imperatives," the "AGIL Model" (based on the first letters of the four functions he devised), or the "four-function paradigm"—were his attempt to incorporate into his theory propositions about the nature of goals.

Interestingly enough, this work evolved from Parsons' collaboration with Robert F. Bales in experiments on leadership in small groups. Bales observed changes in the quality of activity as the small groups attempted to solve their task problems. In a typical meeting the groups would begin by requesting and providing information which would solve the problem of a *common orientation* to the task. The groups would then attempt to solve the problem of *evaluation* and make decisions about the task at hand. Next they would attempt to ensure a degree of consensus through *social control.* The cycle, if successful, would conclude with activity expressing *solidarity* and *tension reduction,* like joking and laughing, to repair any damage done to social integration and to bring the groups back to a state of equilibrium.[53]

A careful reading of *Working Papers* will reveal that Bales's small groups were made up entirely of Harvard undergraduates, whom Bales recruited through the Harvard employment service. In the early 1950s those groups would have been made up almost entirely of white, upper-middle or upper-class, Protestant males. The group's homogeneity raises questions about generalization.[54]

According to Bales' general theory, the same people cannot undertake task ("instrumental") behavior and social ("expressive") behavior, but both behaviors are necessary to a viable small group. However, Meeker and O'Neill show that subsequent research provides little support for the idea that task and social roles are incompatible. They conclude that the dimension of task versus social orientation is no longer justified as an explanation of sex differences in behavior in task groups.[55]

Parsons decided that Bales' categories for analyzing small group interaction and the activities all small groups engage in could, if reconceptualized, be expanded beyond small groups to include *all* systems of action. This led Parsons to the four-function paradigm. In it, Parsons identifies the major problems action systems must solve if they are to develop and survive—the problems existing systems cope with successfully.

---

[53]See Talcott Parsons, *Working Papers in the Theory of Action,* with Robert F. Bales and Edward A. Shils (New York: The Free Press, 1953), pp. 140–43.

[54]For a feminist critique of the evolution of the functional system problems, see Ruth A. Wallace, "Introduction," pp. 1–19, in Ruth A. Wallace, ed., *Feminism and Sociological Theory* (Newbury Park, Calif.: Sage, 1989).

[55]See Barbara F. Meeker and Patricia A. Weitzel-O'Neill, "Sex Roles and Interpersonal Behavior in Task-Oriented Groups," in Joseph Berger and Morris Zelditch, Jr., eds., *Status, Rewards, and Influence* (San Francisco: Jossey-Bass, 1985), pp. 379–405.

Parsons' work in this area addresses in intricate detail the determinants of and requirements for his basic interest—equilibrium. Equilibrium, which basically means a state of balance of a system, was developed as a theoretical concept in sociology by modern functionalists. The following definition of "social equilibrium" illustrates the relationship between equilibrium and functionalism:

> [Social equilibrium is] the concept that social life has a tendencey to be and to remain a functionally integrated phenomenon, so that any change in one part of the social system will bring about adjustive changes in other parts. The initial change creates an imbalance, but a functional adjustment of the parts occurs to recreate an integrated, adjusted and relatively stable system.[56]

As we noted at the beginning of this chapter, functionalism's model of society as interdependent and self-equilibrating is similar to the biological model of an organism. Parsons traces his own early interest in equilibrium to W. B. Cannon's idea of homeostatic stabilization of physiological processes, as well as to his exposure to biology at Amherst.[57] In the case of society, he argues that certain institutions or structures maintain equilibrium by fulfilling "needs" and solving recurring problems—much as a biological organism does in its physical environment. These structures, in turn, function because certain mechanisms ensure that they operate appropriately on a day-to-day basis. In his discussion of system problems, Parsons sets out his views on what any action system "needs" to achieve equilibrium. His discussions of socialization, the internalization of societal values, and social control concern the way in which society maintains equilibrium over time.

Parsons argues that all action systems face four major problems (or have four major "needs"): adaptation; goal attainment; integration; and pattern maintenance, or, as he later renamed it, "latent pattern maintenance-tension management." In the context of the social system, Parsons usually pictures society or the social system as a large square, which he divides into four equal parts. These parts are the four functional system problems, which are represented by the letters AGIL.[58] (See Figure 2-2).

What does Parsons mean by the letters AGIL in his famous "square"? By *A,* adaptation, he means the problem of securing sufficient resources from the environment and distributing them throughout the system. Social

---

[56]George A. Theodorson and Achilles G. Theodorson, eds., *A Modern Dictionary of Sociology,* p. 133.

[57]Parsons, "On Building Social System Theory," p. 849.

[58]For Parsons, a society and a social system are not synonymous. "A society," he says, "is a type of social system . . . which attains the highest level of self-sufficiency as a system in relation to its environments" (*Societies; Evolutionary and Comparative Perspectives* [Englewood Cliffs, N.J.: Prentice-Hall, Inc., 1966], p. 9). As we have seen, a social system may range from an international organization to a nuclear family.

institutions are interrelated systems of social norms and roles that satisfy social needs or functions and help to solve social system problems. Examples of social institutions are the economy, the political order, the law, religion, education, and the family. If it is to survive, a social system needs certain structures or institutions that will perform the function of adaptation to the environment. Taking the United States as a social system, a Parsonian analysis would point to the economy as the social institution that meets this need, or solves the problem of securing sufficient resources; it would identify production or the wealth that results as the central question.

The *G* stands for goal attainment, the system's need to mobilize its resources and energies to attain system goals and to establish priorities among them. This system problem is essentially the concern of political institutions. Basically the function of decision-making bodies, goal attainment's central question is the nature of power as a means of implementing social decisions.

Integration, the *I* in the box, is at the heart of the four-function paradigm, because the solution to this problem has been a priority for functionalists, especially since Durkheim. By integration, Parsons means the need to coordinate, adjust, and regulate relationships among various actors or units within the system to keep the system functioning. In the social system of the United States, legal institutions and courts meet the need for social control; the central question is the implementation of norms, or influence.

The fourth system need, the *L* in Parsons' box (latent pattern maintenance-tension management), is twofold: first, the need to make certain that actors are sufficiently motivated to play their parts in the

FIGURE 2-2   Parsons' Four-Function Paradigm Applied to the United States as a Social System. (Adapted from Figure 3, p. 53 in Talcott Parsons and Neil J. Smelser, *Economy and Society* [Glencoe, Ill.: The Free Press, 1956], p. 53. Reprinted with permission of Routledge and Kegan Paul.)

A adaptation	G goal attainment
Economic	Political
Educational, Religious, Family	Legal
L latent pattern maintenance – tension management	I integration

system or maintain the value "pattern"; and second, the need to provide mechanisms for internal tension management. This problem is one of keeping the value system intact and guaranteeing the conformity of the members of the system by transmitting societal values. In the United States the relevant social institutions are family, religion, and education, and the central question is moral commitment to shared values.

One of Parsons' later involvements in empirical research was related directly to the AGIL schema. With Gerald Platt, Parsons engaged in a study of higher education by means of a sample survey of members of American colleges and university faculties.[59] In *The American University*, the theoretical framework for the study, the structure of higher education is described as "specializing in implementing the cultural patterns of cognitive rationality"[60]; the rational or "scientific" approach to generating knowledge and searching for truth and the whole range of teaching and learning within this framework. Parsons' and Platt's data on faculty teaching goals show that cognitive rationality is the paramount shared value within the American system of higher education.[61] Thus, the American system of higher education transmits and maintains values central to modern American society; it has a pattern maintenance function and so is placed in the L box.

In Figure 2-2 we presented the four-function paradigm in terms of social structures and pictured the United States in Parsonian fashion. However, things are not necessarily so neat. In simpler societies there is more of a tendency to collapse functions. The Parsonian breakdown for the United States does not fit, for example, the pygmy tribes of the African forests who engage in little division of labor (typical of a *gemeinschaft* society) and, as members of the tribe, all participate in hunting, hut building, socialization of the young, and social control in general. Again, in a centrally planned totalitarian state, such as communist China, the party may be the institution responsible for both economic production and the direction of resources and setting of priorities, so that G and A are collapsed into one. Conversely, in a market economy the institutions concerned with G spill over into A: "priorities" are set by market forces affecting supply and demand and not by central political decision making.

This points to a general problem with Parsons' four functions. Because they are analytic categories, the four functions are not necessarily

[59]Talcott Parsons and Gerald M. Platt, *The American University* (Cambridge: Harvard University Press, 1973). Although no major monograph with analysis of the data from this study has appeared, a number of articles have been published. See, for example, Gerald M. Platt, Talcott Parsons, and Rita Kirshstein, "Faculty Teaching Goals, 1968–1973," *Social Problems*, 24 (1976), 298–307; Gerald Platt, Talcott Parsons, and Rita Kirshstein, "Undergraduate Teaching Environments; Normative Orientations to Teaching Among Faculty in the Higher Educational System," *Sociological Inquiry*, 48 (1978), 3–21; and Gerald M. Platt, "The American University: Collaboration with Parsons," *Sociological Inquiry*, 51 (1981), 155–65.

[60]Parsons and Platt, *The American University*, p. 394.

[61]See Platt, Parsons, and Kirshstein, "Undergraduate Teaching Environments."

clearly separable. Institutions do not necessarily fit neatly into one "box," and the scheme in itself cannot be used to predict what institutions a society will develop or what functions a given institution will fulfill. Rather, the paradigm serves as a way of classifying institutions after the event.

The complexity of applying the four-function paradigm becomes even more apparent when one realizes that Parsons believes the same problems face every system; this means not just the larger social system but each of its subsystems as well. We can look at the family as a social structure that fulfills the larger social system's need for latent pattern maintenance-tension management, as in Figure 2-2; but we can also look at the family itself as a social system with the same four problems to be solved. Thus, we can picture the L box in our diagram of the United States as itself a social system divided into four boxes of its own. Parsons' viewpoint regarding the family was consistently a traditional one, so it is not surprising to find him assuming that it is the father who solves the problem of adaptation by being the breadwinner. The father also makes the major decisions, thus fulfilling the goal attainment function, and he plays a dominant role in coordinating and adjusting family relationships to keep the system integrated. The mother's chief functions are to transmit family values to the children and to create and maintain an atmosphere where tensions can be released ($PM-L$). Once again, however, things may be far less neat and predictable than Parsons implies, especially in a period when the traditional family is less and less the statistical norm. Husband and wife may contribute equally to "adaptation"; or the wife may be the major breadwinner; or the state may play a crucial role through welfare, unemployment benefits, or social security payments. The other three functions may be shared as well. Parsons' scheme identifies universal functions but cannot in itself predict how they will be met.

AGIL and Equilibrium

The crucial point to remember about the four system needs is that Parsons considers them to be the prerequisites for social equilibrium. Their continuing operation on a day-to-day basis is in turn ensured, according to Parsons' theory, by two mechanisms: socialization and social control. If socialization "works," all members of a society will be committed to shared values, make the "appropriate" choices among the pattern variables, and generally do what is expected of them in terms of adaptation, integration, and so forth. For example, people will marry and socialize their children (L), and within the family, fathers will, as they "should," be the breadwinners (A). Moreover, such successful socialization produces what Parsons refers to as "complementarity of expectations." This means that both parties involved in an interaction situation share and accept the same cultural values and normative expectations, so that each actor knows what the other expects, and their responses complement each other. Actors are motivated to meet the demands of societal expectations, and do interact appropriately: the happy result is equilibrium.

Parsons' work tends to imply that this situation of complementary expectations and behavior and of equilibrium is the one that obtains the bulk of the time. However, he does also deal with situations of "disequilibrium," in which the balance of society is disturbed and in which, he argues, forces come to play that restore equilibrium. Thus, from day to day, there will occur cases of deviance, and norms regarding role interaction will be transgressed, as in the case of a motorist who drives through a red light. In Parsonian terms, it is then that social control comes into play, and negative sanctions are used to make recalcitrant actors conform. A police officer will probably give a ticket to the deviant motorist. In Parsons' view every society has general social control mechanisms, like the police and courts, that operate to deal with deviance, bring behavior back into line with expectations, and restore equilibrium again.

As we have seen, "role interaction" is the basic component of a social system in Parsons' theory. However, Stacey and Thorne, in arguing against the term *sex and/or gender role,* or an emphasis on the process of sex and/or gender role socialization, state that the notion of role

> focuses attention more on individuals than on social structure, and implies that "the female role" and "the male role" are complementary (i.e., separate or different but equal). The terms are depoliticizing; they strip experience from its historical and political context and neglect questions of power and conflict. It is significant that sociologists do not speak of "class roles" or "race roles."[62]

In Parsons' view, by ensuring "appropriate" role interaction, the two mechanisms of socialization and social control generally promote and maintain equilibrium in the social system. However, disequilibrium may arise because of changes or strains in the social system that affect the way the four "system needs" are met. Parsons is vague about the origins of strain. In introducing the concept, he says only, "Let us assume that, *from whatever source* (emphasis ours), a disturbance is introduced into the system . . .";[63] thus the source of disequilibrium may be anything from an earthquake to a severe economic depression to a revolution. Whatever the source of the strain, Parsons believes society adjusts in response to disturbances in order to restore equilibrium.

At the beginning of this chapter we used the example of an airport to show what functionalists mean by systems adjusting to restore equilibrium.

[62]Judith Stacey and Barrie Thorne, "The Missing Feminist Revolution in Sociology," *Social Problems,* 32, no. 4 (April 1985), 307.

[63]Parsons, *The Social System,* p. 252.

We can also show what this would mean in Parsonian terms by using the two social systems we have just been discussing: the family and the United States. For a family of the traditional sort, the father's unexpected death would be a source of strain, and the family as a system would be in disequilibrium. If the father had been the sole breadwinner, the family would not be solving the problem of adaptation effectively until either the mother obtained a full-time job or the older children went to work full- or part-time. A family council meeting might divide the mother's and father's household tasks among the other members of the family to free the mother for outside work. Temporary adjustments in the form of money loaned by family and friends and some budget cuts could also aid in the reequilibrating process. In any case, the father's death would cause repercussions throughout the family as a system, and the system would be in disequilibrium until some adjustments were made.

What happens when there is disequilibrium in a larger social system, such as the United States? Many Americans experienced such disequilibrium directly at the time of the assassination of John F. Kennedy. In Parsonian terms, the G box, or the goal-attainment function, was badly disturbed, for until Lyndon Johnson took the oath of office, the most important decision-making position in the government was vacant. If we look back, we can see how rapidly the necessary actors were assembled for the oath-taking ceremony: Parsons would see this as an example of a system reacting quickly to an acute disequilibrium.

Parsons' model provides a way of looking at society that focuses our attention on the interdependence of different institutions, on the way human societies everywhere grapple with similar problems in spite of their surface differences, and on the continuities in social life and how they are secured. However, as many critics have pointed out, it leaves a great deal unexplained. In discussing the origins of modern functionalism, we pointed out that Durkheim's "explanation" of something according to the function it performed was a recurring problem. This circularity is certainly apparent in Parsons' work. He fails to specify the mechanisms by which systems develop ways to meet their needs or deal with functional exigencies, and he does not specify the method by which systems respond to disequilibrium. Rather, Parsons' model assumes that the existence of various needs somehow ensures that they will be met. Again, the sources of deviance and disequilibrium are never dealt with in concrete detail, and Parsons' theory of deviance has been criticized because it "stands most in need of greater specification, of the conditions under which one type of deviance tends to excite one type of social control: and of the conditions under which social control tends to be effective or ineffective. Such specification would give his paradigm greater theoretical adequacy and bring it closer to direct testability.[64]

[64]Neil J. Smelser and R. Stephen Warner, *Sociological Theory: Historical and Formal* (Morristown, N.J.: General Learning Press, 1976), p. 204.

Parsons' concern with the interdependence of society's parts and his theory of social equilibrium have had enormous influence on contemporary sociology. From the start, however, he has also met with intense criticism; as we mentioned earlier, many sociologists have defined their work and their concerns in opposition to Parsons.[65] We have already touched on some of the problems with Parsons' theory: the fact that his classificatory schemes and list of essential functions, or needs, do not allow one to predict in advance the actual structure and institutions a society will develop; the way in which he fails to deal adequately with role conflict; and his failure to specify the mechanisms by which equilibrium will necessarily be restored. However, what has caused the most impassioned criticism is the fact that Parsons is not neutral about the survival and development of social systems. Instead, his formulation of functionalism implies that equilibrium is intrinsically desirable.

Above all else, Parsons' system is a system in equilibrium because each actor is morally committed to perform culturally and socially expected functions. As Parsons puts it, "Many complex processes are necessary to maintain the functioning of any societal system; if its members never did anything, a society would very soon cease to exist."[66] Indeed, if cultural values are fully inculcated and if all actors and all units do what is expected of them, the system can hardly fail to be in equilibrium. Suppose, however, that people do not do what is expected. Parsons treats "deviance" in a way that implies disapproval, saying very little about its origins or justification but instead discussing it as a source of disequilibrium to which negative sanctions are appropriately applied. But is it? Parsons' critics, especially those who apply a conflict perspective to social analysis, argue that his approach implies approval of the status quo, at the expense of discounting the conflicts of interest, inequalities, or outright oppression that a social system may incorporate. As one such analyst argued,

> To maintain and transmit a value system, human beings are punished, bullied, sent to jail, thrown into concentration camps, cajoled, bribed, made into heroes, encouraged to read newspapers, stood up against a wall and shot, and sometimes even taught sociology. To speak of cultural inertia is to overlook the concrete interests and privileges that are served by indoctrination, education and the entire complicated process of transmitting culture from one generation to the next.[67]

By contrast, another conflict theorist stated, "No one of his contemporaries developed a theory of society of comparable complexity. . . . Any

---

[65]See Chapters III, IV, and V.

[66]Parsons, *Societies: Evolutionary and Comparative Perspectives*, p. 21.

[67]Barrington Moore, Jr., *Social Origins of Dictatorship and Democracy: Lord and Peasant in the Making of the Modern World* (Boston: Beacon Press, 1966), p. 486.

theoretical work in sociology today that failed to take account of Talcott Parsons could not be taken seriously."[68]

SOCIAL CHANGE

Early Work

A frequent criticism of Parsons' work, arising out of his emphasis on equilibrium, is that he failed to develop a theory of social change. It is easy to see how such a charge arises, for a system in equilibrium would seem to imply inertia, or lack of change. However, Parsons has in fact addressed social change, both through a chapter in *The Social System* entitled "The Processes of Change in Social Systems," and in particular through his more recent model of evolutionary social change, which we discuss in the next section.

In his early work on social change, Parsons states clearly that he is dealing with changes *within* social systems and not changes *of* social systems.[69] He begins his chapter on social change with the explicit assumption that the system is a boundary-maintaining one—that is, a system that within its boundaries maintains its distinctiveness from its environment rather than merging with its surroundings to produce completely new configurations. He points out that socialization and social control operate to keep people in line and maintain continuity. Correspondingly, Parsons' ideas about social change center on slow and adjustive changes that have already been introduced into the system and on the ways the system reequilibrates to produce a state of affairs that is not identical to the one before, but rather a "moving equilibrium."[70]

The chapter of *The Social System* dealing with social change does show that Parsons' theory has a dynamic aspect and is not, as critics have charged, purely static. Indeed, in defense of Parsons, Johnson has recently argued that these criticisms are distortions of Parsons' work, because Parsons has always viewed social order as a problem to be explained, not something to take for granted; Parsons uses equilibrium as a theoretical construct, not a description of empirical reality. Johnson maintains that Parsons' chapter on social change has been misrepresented, and he argues:

> In other words, in the real world there is no such thing as equilibrated interaction; there are only degrees of approximation to it. Special processes are

---

[68]Jürgen Habermas, "Talcott Parsons: Problems of Theory Construction," *Sociological Inquiry*, 51 (1981), 173–74. See also Chapter III, pp. 122–24.

[69]Parsons, *The Social System*, p. 486.

[70]For an example of a functionalist whose approach does not include a stress on stable equilibrium, see William F. Ogburn, *Social Change* (New York: B. W. Huebsch, 1922).

required to produce and maintain whatever approximations actually exist. In fact, analyzing their processes is what the chapter in question is all about.[71]

Moreover, Parsons goes on to say that no change is possible unless the vested interests that are bent on maintaining the system as such are overcome.[72] This particular statement is one with which conflict theorists would certainly agree, and it modifies the impression given by so much else of Parsons' work that the status quo is by definition desirable. However, as we noted earlier, Parsons conceives of change as a very gradual process. This is the basis for Dahrendorf's argument, which we shall meet in the following chapter, that functionalism is inadequate for dealing with social change.[73]

In general, throughout *The Social System,* Parsons associates change with "deviance" and "strain," which must be controlled in the cause of equilibrium; he uses terms with negative overtones, such as *imbalance, coping mechanisms, strain,* and *disturbance,* when discussing conflict or change.[74] Parsons views the individual actor as a person who does *not* welcome strain and conflict, who is disturbed by them, just as the social system is, and who strives to restore equilibrium. On the personality system level, he states, "the individual actor deals with elements of strain and conflict" by means of "mechanisms of adjustment," such as withdrawal from interaction situations that cause strain or conflict.[75] In the next chapter, we shall have occasion to criticize some conflict theorists for ignoring the fact that people value security; Parsons, by contrast, tends to overemphasize it.

Parsons admits that his theory of change is "fragmentary and incomplete" and concludes his chapter by saying, "We do not in the present state of knowledge possess a general theory of the process of change in societies as a whole," and he admits that what he has outlined is a "partial explanation in terms of certain elements."[76] A lack of completeness and specificity is undeniable. Parsons hypothesizes, for instance, that strain in the interactive system can lead to anxiety, fantasy, hostility, or defense mechanisms, but he fails to specify under what conditions strain will precipitate one or the other outcome.[77]

Parsons' Evolutionary Model

Parsons' ideas on social change were not fully developed until the early 1960s, when he wrote *Societies: Evolutionary and Comparative Perspec-*

[71]Johnson, *Functionalism in Modern Sociology,* p. 35.
[72]Parsons, *The Social System,* p. 492.
[73]See Chapter III.
[74]See, for instance, Parsons, *The Social System,* p. 491.
[75]Ibid., p. 203.
[76]Ibid., p. 534.
[77]Ibid., p. 485.

tives. Looking at change from an evolutionary perspective was not a new direction for him; in fact, Robert Nisbet has argued that the concerns of the early sociologists can best be understood as an attempt to comprehend the almost total transformation of society taking place around them.[78] The "two revolutions"—the dramatic upheaval of the French Revolution and the gradual but even more far-reaching Industrial Revolution—signaled the disappearance of both the old aristocratic political order and the agrarian society in which the vast bulk of the population tilled the soil, as their fathers and grandfathers had before them. Intellectuals living in such an era could hardly fail to think in terms of the development and evolution of society from one form to an entirely new one.

Consequently, we can trace the "intellectual roots" of Parsons' evolutionary thinking to, among others, Auguste Comte, the creator of "sociology," who believed that man progressed through three states of thought and corresponding types of society: theological, metaphysical, and the dawning "positivist" model.[79] Herbert Spencer subsequently applied the concepts of Darwin's evolutionary theory directly to society, arguing that societies, too, progress from simpler to more complex forms[80] as they grow in size; we will see how Parsons includes this process of differentiation in his model. Durkheim wrote that because of population density, "mechanical" solidarity (societies held together because individual differences were minimized, and people had common beliefs and occupations—similar to Toennies' *gemeinschaft* society) was replaced by the "organic" solidarity of more advanced societies (held together by the interdependence of a highly complex division of labor—similar to *gesellschaft* society).[81] Most important of all for the future, Marx developed a theory of history in which society was seen as evolving inevitably, through conflict, toward the communist utopia.[82]

Parsons' evolutionary model, then, marks a revival of interest in the evolutionary development of human society.[83] Basically, Parsons' ideas on evolution are an outgrowth of his pattern variable typology and his four-function paradigm.

In his evolutionary model, Parsons is developing and extending Durk-

[78]Robert A. Nisbet, *The Sociological Tradition* (New York: Basic Books, 1966).

[79]Comte, *The Positive Philosophy.*

[80]Herbert Spencer, *The Principles of Sociology* (New York: Appleton, 1896).

[81]Durkheim, *The Division of Labor in Society.*

[82]See Chapter III.

[83]A group of cultural anthropologists has also revived the biological analogies of Spencer. Among the most important are Marshal Sahlins, Elman Service, and David Kaplan, who argue that one can classify the degree of society's evolution in terms of its overall potential for appropriating nature's energy—something to which, in their view, culture is crucial. See Marshall D. Sahlins and Elman R. Service, eds., *Evolution and Culture* (Ann Arbor, Mich.: University of Michigan Press, 1960). For an alternative theory of economic evolution and its implications for social development, see John Hicks, *A Theory of Economic History* (Oxford: Oxford University Press, 1969).

heim's ideas again. Like Durkheim, Parsons sees the primitive or prehistorical stage, when kinship relations and a religious orientation in the world were prominent, as the first stage of societal evolution. In addition, he posits an intermediate stage characterized by a written language and therefore the availability of documents and history. The modern, or third, stage is characterized by formal relationships and procedures and—most important—the institutionalization of law and full adult literacy.[84]

Echoing Durkheim and using Spencer's concept of differentiation, Parsons argues that continually increasing differentiation (that is, the division of a unit or system into two or more units or systems "which differ in both structural and functional significance for the wider system,"[85]) is the key to evolution of social systems. In other words, in the change from primitive societies to modern societies, the change from a situation in which roles are fused to a situation in which roles have been allocated to different role incumbents is what creates and signifies the shift to a different evolutionary level. This shift is crucial, above all, because it permits greater control of the environment. Parsons points out, for example, that economic production is more efficient in specialized factories than in self-sufficient households.[86]

In elaborating on and extending this basic model of evolution, Parsons identifies a number of evolutionary "universals," which he defines as "any organizational development sufficiently important to further evolution that, rather than emerging only once, it is likely to be 'hit upon' by various systems operating under different conditions."[87]

First of all, he argues, language, kinship organization, religion, and rudimentary technology are prerequisites if communities are to "break out of" the primitive stage at all and become what we think of as full societies. Then follow, in order, the six major evolutionary universals: social stratification, cultural legitimation, bureaucratic organization, money economy and markets, generalized universalistic norms, and democratic associations. This evolutionary sequence starts from and is made possible by greater differentiation, and as societies develop and acquire these structures they become still further differentiated (as well as changing in other ways).

Parsons' evolutionary model incorporates both structures and processes.[88] The structures (patterned and stable relationships) are social stratification, cultural legitimation, bureaucratic organization, money and markets, generalized universalistic norms, and democratic associations; in fact,

---

[84]Parsons, *Societies: Evolutionary and Comparative Perspectives*, pp. 26 and 27. See also Talcott Parsons' *The System of Modern Societies* (Englewood Cliffs, N.J.: Prentice-Hall, Inc., 1971).

[85]Parsons, *Societies; Evolutionary and Comparative Perspectives*, p. 22.

[86]Ibid.

[87]Parsons, "Evolutionary Universals in Society," *American Sociological Review*, 29 (1964), 339–57.

[88]See pp. 16–17.

the structures are the six evolutionary universals. The processes (evolutionary changes taking place in the system) are differentiation, adaptive upgrading, inclusion, and value generalization.

Parsons proposes that social stratification is the first structure likely to evolve from an increase in differentiation.[89] Thus, he adds the notions of ranking and of occupations carrying "higher" and "lower" prestige to role differentiation as such. Earlier in his career, Parsons presented a theory of stratification in which he said that certain jobs have high prestige and are the best paid because of the amount of talent and skill they require; the money, time, and energy spent in training people for them; and the need to attract the most capable individuals to them.[90] Thus, Parsons believes that modern schools serve a crucial function for society, not only in teaching values but also in acting as stratifying agents that identify children's skills and so determine their future occupations. Parsons' basic argument here is that a stratification system is both desirable and necessary in a complex industrial society; it fills occupations effectively and keeps the entire social system functioning smoothly. Consequently, social stratification is an "evolutionary universal," because without it a highly differentiated society cannot be maintained.

This functionalist analysis of social stratification is one of the most debated parts of Parsons' theory. Conflict theorists, in particular, disagree with Parsons' analysis.[91] Some regard a stratification system as the antithesis of the classless society they believe in and consider possible. They think that functional theory, by emphasizing the necessity of stratification, takes an essentially conservative stance. Others agree with functionalists that stratification is inevitable, though they do not use the term *necessary*, with its connotation of social "needs." However, they disagree with the functionalist explanation of how and why stratification is inevitable. They see stratification as an aspect of the unequal distribution of power in society, with those who have more power, for whatever reason, using it to secure greater prestige and wealth. Finally, a number of sociologists see the functionalist view as one-sided rather than completely wrong. It tends to imply a perfect "meritocracy" and to ignore the fact that the talent of people born into lower status groups, such as the poor, women, or minority groups, often goes undiscovered.[92]

As we have mentioned, Parsons sees differentiation as the key to the

---

[89]See Talcott Parsons, ed., *Sociological Theory and Modern Society* (New York: The Free Press, 1967).

[90]Talcott Parsons, "An Analytic Approach to the Theory of Stratification," *American Journal of Sociology*, 45 (1940), 843.

[91]See Chapter III.

[92]See Mark Abrahamson, *Functionalism* (Englewood Cliffs, N.J.: Prentice-Hall, Inc., 1978), pp. 57–74, for a full treatment of the functional theory of stratification. He discusses the arguments of Davis and Moore, Tumin, and others.

evolution of social systems. Without differentiation of role allocation and, he would argue, the accompanying social stratification, specialization and technological development would be impossible. The second evolutionary process, adaptive upgrading, involves the idea of control or dominance of the environment,[93] and this, too, is advanced by the development of each of the "universals." Parsons relies on Weber's notion of rationalization to conceptualize the main trend of social change. In Weber's view, modern society has rationalized and made calculable and predictable what in primitive society had seemed to be governed by chance. According to Weber, an increase in rationalization is accompanied by increasing bureaucratization. He attempted to document this within various social institutions.[94]

Parsons feels that the process of evolutionary change involves the enhancement of societies' adaptive capacities—their ability to attain a wide variety of goals despite environmental difficulties. Societies involved in this process would, for example, tend to reward inventors of scientific or technological innovations with both money and fame; indeed, there have been Americans who have made fortunes from outstanding inventions.

We can illustrate how some of the structures, or evolutionary universals, fit into the processes of evolutionary change by considering a bureaucracy. Parsons states that bureaucratic organization, which involves further differentiation, gives societies an adaptive advantage because the specialization it entails means better utilization of talent and a more flexible response to environmental exigencies. In addition, money economies and markets enhance a society's adaptive capacity because they provide increased economic flexibility. Finally, a society has an adaptive advantage when it has cultural legitimation—when the cultural definition of "we-ness" is expanded well beyond the kinship group to the larger society and is institutionalized. A country has cultural legitimation when the notion of "nation" not only emerges but is accepted by its citizens. This enhances the nation's capacity to carry on collective action. Since cultural legitimation is a precondition for both bureaucratic organization and money economies and markets, it is also necessary for a society's adaptive upgrading.

In addition to differentiation and adaptive upgrading, Parsons adds two more processes to his model of evolutionary change. One is a sort of desegregation process, which he calls "inclusion."[95] For adaptive upgrading to take place in the United States, for example, people can no longer be excluded from certain jobs because of race, sex, age, religion, or national origin. Society must recognize that groups that have been excluded are capable of contributing to the functioning of the system. In other words,

[93]Here there is a similarity between Parsons and the conflict theorist Habermas on evolutionary change. See Chapter III.

[94]See Lewis A. Coser, *Masters of Sociological Thought* (New York: Harcourt Brace Jovanovich, 1977), pp. 233–44, for a discussion of Weber's notion of rationalization.

[95]Parsons, *Societies: Evolutionary and Comparative Perspectives*, p. 22.

the more skills that are developed without regard to ascriptive characteristics, the more specialized members there will be in society, and the more productive the social system will be.

To inclusion Parsons adds "value generalization." The new type of social system emerging in this evolutionary process must have a value pattern that is "couched at a higher level of generality in order to legitimize the wider variety of goals and functions of its sub-units."[96] In other words, higher levels of differentiation, adaptive upgrading, and inclusion cannot coexist with a parochial value system that is shared by only a portion of the members of the social system. Robert Bellah's idea of the civil religion in America is an example of value generalization. Whatever its label, this religion is neither Protestant, Catholic, nor Jewish; it can encompass an extremely wide variety of believers and nonbelievers because it is basically a religion of patriotism.[97] A civil religion that espouses the values of life, liberty, and the pursuit of happiness legitimizes a much wider variety of goals and functions than does any one of the three major religions in America. It also provides a more general value pattern that is necessary for a society with a wide variety of members.

The direction of the evolutionary processes is from differentiation to adaptive upgrading to inclusion to value generalization. Figure 2-3 shows an example of how each of these processes has occurred in American society. A change from medicine man to nurse, pharmacist, or surgeon is an illustration of differentiation in medicine; a progression from epidemics to control of disease illustrates adaptive upgrading in the health field; a change in medical school enrollments (and in higher education in general) from discriminating in favor of white Anglo-Saxon male Protestants to opening professions to minorities and females illustrates inclusion; and finally, in the religious area, a shift from a predominantly Protestant value system to American civil religion is an example of value generalization.

Miriam Johnson uses Parsons' four evolutionary processes to explain the rise of the feminist movement in the United States.[98] She cites Parsons' argument that modernization brings about a clearer differentiation between personality and society which is related to the increasing autonomy of individuals.[99] She then argues that "the perception of gender inequality itself depended in part on a process of differentiation by which people's identities and sense of self-worth became separable from the roles they played and the activities they pursued." The process of *differentiation*, ac-

---

[96]Ibid., p. 23.

[97]Robert N. Bellah, "Civil Religion in America," *Daedalus*, 96 (1967), 1–21.

[98]Miriam Johnson, "Feminism and the Theories of Talcott Parsons," in Wallace, ed., *Feminism and Sociological Theory*, pp. 101–118.

[99]Parsons, *Societies: Evolutionary and Comparative Perspectives*, p. 24.

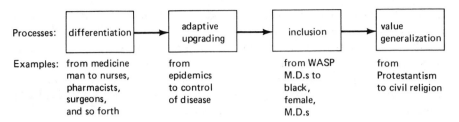

FIGURE 2-3 Parsons' Evolutionary Model Applied to Processes in the United States

cording to Johnson, "made possible the understandings that have characterized western feminism."[100]

With regard to the process of *inclusion,* she argues that reactivated efforts to pressure states into ratifying the Equal Rights Amendment epitomized the push for inclusion. Feminists hoped that the passing of this amendment would enhance equal acess to jobs, equal pay, and equal opportunity for women. Johnson is quick to add that inclusion has not been a smooth process; women's wages are still far below those of men; and, regardless of whether they work outside the home or not, women continue to take major responsibility for child care.

Johnson further argues that the inclusion of educated women into the occupational world outside the home on an equal basis with men has led to *adaptive upgrading* because it released more trained capacity into the system. Finally, she makes the point that much of feminist writing could be described as an effort to bring about a redefinition of dominant (male) societal values; in Parsonian terms, it has been an effort to achieve *value generalization.*

The limited success of the women's movement illustrates a weakness in Parsons' model of social change: strain, tension, and resistance to the inclusion process should be inserted. This, then, raises a question about resistance to differentiation, adaptive upgrading, and value generalization as well. In fact, we would argue that Parsons' evolutionary theory would be strengthened if strain, tension, and resistance to change were inserted into each of the four change processes.[101]

Parsons rejects the older evolutionary view that all societies follow an inevitable and uniform course of development, but he does assume that human history reveals an evolutionary trend toward an increase in adaptive

---

[100]Johnson, "Feminism and the Theories of Talcott Parsons."

[101]In addition, Frank Lechner, a neofunctionalist, in "Modernity and Its Discontents," in Jeffrey C. Alexander, ed., *Neofunctionalism* (Beverly Hills, Calif.: Sage, 1985), pp. 157–76, argues that we should turn Parsons on his head and use his social change theory as a basis for conceptualizing four functional sources of *dis*order. For instance, Lechner argues that inclusion can create resistance. It means breaking up what were once closely knit groups, bound together by collective sentiment. Such a process will cause pain, tension, and opposition. Women and other groups occupying a marginal position in society will be quick to recognize that this interpretation helps to explain the unevenness of their "inclusion."

capacity.[102] He is not claiming that societies all progress gradually and evenly through these evolutionary processes. Rather, he is identifying a number of crucial characteristics, which he sees as central to the way societies develop and which cannot be grafted onto any existing society in an arbitrary fashion.[103] Parsons would argue that if we want to understand the differences between modern society and the Aztecs, we should find out which of these central institutions they possess and then see how they differ. We should consider each society's degree of adaptive upgrading, inclusion, and the rest. Similarly, Parsons would be dubious about efforts to introduce democracy or a modern legal system into a tribal, kin-based society.[104]

Parsons is cautiously optimistic about possibilities for social change. In his theory, evolution and progress emerge as synonymous, democracy as a logical and stable social development. Though he does not conceal his admiration for American democracy, Parsons synthesizes his American pragmatism with the pathos of European theory. For example, Parsons and Jürgen Habermas, who is a critical conflict theorist, consider many of the same features to be central to social evolution—though the overtones are quite different.[105]

Parsons' theory of social change, which emphasizes gradual, smooth adjustments if the institutions of liberal democracy are to be retained, is not a departure from his functionalist perspective; it is an elaboration of it. Parsons does not think an evolving social order is dysfunctional; it leads to change *within*, but not to change *of*, the system. Parsons never attempted to explain either sudden or total societal change. A communist coup would be difficult to explain in the Parsonian framework.[106]

Throughout his work Parsons was certainly indebted to Emile Durkheim. Societal progression, as Durkheim saw it, was from the undifferentiated structures of primitive societies (characterized by mechanical solidarity) to structural differentiation in modern societies (characterized by organic solidarity). In summarizing Parsons' thinking on change, we can see that his vital interest in the problem of order is much like Durkheim's preoccupation with integration. Both Durkheim and Parsons prefer a gradual, careful adjustment of the system, and this stance leads them to evolutionary models.[107]

[102]See Johnson, *Functionalism in Modern Sociology*, p. 41.

[103]Parsons, "Evolutionary Universals in Society," pp. 339–57.

[104]For a study which tested Parsons' evolutionary theory, see G. L. Buck and A. L. Jacobson, "Social Evolution and Structural-Functional Analysis: An Empirical View," *American Sociological Review*, 33 (1968), 343–55.

[105]See Chapter III.

[106]See Chapter III. See also Kenneth Bock's critique in his article, "Evolution, Function, and Change," *American Sociological Review*, 28 (1963), 229–37.

[107]See Robert N. Bellah, "Durkheim and History," *American Sociological Review*, 24 (1959), 447–61, for a description of Durkheim as evolutionist and functionalist.

PART TWO
Robert K. Merton: Middle-Range Theory

BACKGROUND

Robert King Merton was born in 1910 of Jewish immigrant parents in a South Philadelphia slum, where his father was a carpenter and truck driver. He grew up with a passion for learning and won a scholarship at Temple University. There he received his B.A. and became interested in sociology while taking an introductory sociology course taught by George E. Simpson. Recalling this experience, Merton has said, "It wasn't so much the substance of what Simpson said that did it. It was more the joy of discovering that it was possible to examine human behavior objectively and without using loaded moral preconceptions."[108]

With the help of a fellowship, Merton received a doctorate from Harvard University, where he was one of Parsons' earliest and most important graduate students. Looking back over his career at Harvard, Parsons stated that of the significant relations he had with graduate students, "the most important single one was with Robert Merton." He adds, "For a considerable time, Merton and I came to be known as the leaders of a structural-functional school among American sociologists."[109]

While at Harvard, Merton was also influenced by Pitirim Sorokin, who was not sympathetic to Parsons' work.[110] Sorokin shared Parsons' propensity for large-scale theorizing, but he balanced this with an equally strong interest in empirical research and statistical studies. It was Paul K. Lazarsfeld who influenced Merton to become active in empirical research,[111] and Merton was closely associated with him at the Bureau of Applied Social Research at Columbia University until Lazarsfeld's death in 1976.[112] Parsons saw himself as an "incurable theorist," but Merton has been actively engaged in empirical research since 1941, when he joined the faculty at Columbia, where he is still at work. He currently holds the title of

---

[108]Much of the background material here is based on the excellent biographical sketch by Morton M. Hunt, "How Does It Come To Be So?" Profile of Robert K. Merton, *The New Yorker*, 36 (January 28, 1961), 39–63.

[109]Parsons, *On Building Social System Theory*, pp. 833 and 849.

[110]Ibid., p. 832.

[111]See the dialogue between Lewis A. Coser and Robert Nisbet entitled "Merton and the Contemporary Mind," in Lewis A. Coser, ed., *The Idea of Social Structure: Papers in Honor of Robert K. Merton* (New York: Harcourt Brace Jovanovich, 1975), pp. 3–10. This work also contains an excellent bibliography (see pp. 497–552).

[112]See Lazarsfeld's chapter, "Working with Merton," ibid., pp. 35–66.

University Professor Emeritus, a rank for a handful of Columbia faculty who are professors-at-large.

Merton's two classic essays on the relationship between sociological theory and empirical research appear as chapters in his best-known book, *Social Theory and Social Structure*. Unlike Parsons, Merton does not stop with abstract theory and typology; he formulates empirical hypotheses and very often tests them in the "real world" by gathering data himself and analyzing the results.[113]

In 1957 the American Sociological Society elected Robert K. Merton its president. Not all of Merton's contributions to sociology are functionalist.[114] Some of his most important contributions to functionalism are his work on middle-range theory, his clarification and refocusing of functional analysis, his theory of deviance, and his work on role-sets.

THEORIES OF THE MIDDLE RANGE

One of the most important ways in which Merton diverged from Parsonian functionalism was in his decision to abandon the quest for an all-encompassing theory. He chose, rather, to take the path of what he calls "middle-range theories." As Merton himself explains:

> At the summit of human thought, some sociologists are seeking a single unified theory—a generalized body of explanations as to what cements society together, how institutions fit into a social framework, how discrepant values arise and work their changes upon a society, and so on. My friend and occasional colleague, Talcott Parsons, is doing just that, and, I think, making useful progress. But for most of our energies to be channeled that way would be decidedly premature. Einstein could not have followed hard on the heels of Kepler, and perhaps we haven't even had our Kepler yet. Just as it would stifle sociology to spend all its time today on practical problems before developing theory sufficiently, so it would to spend all its time on abstract, all-encompassing theories. Our major task today is to develop *special* theories, applicable to limited ranges of data—theories, for example, of deviant behavior, or the flow of power from generation to generation, or the unseen ways in which personal influence is exercised.[115]

[113]See, for example, his work on propaganda, which he describes in Chapter XVI of *Social Theory and Social Structure*, "Studies in Radio and Film Propaganda," pp. 563–82. See also his study (with George P. Reader, Patricia L. Kendall, and others) of the changing attitudes of medical students, *The Student-Physician: Introductory Studies in the Sociology of Medical Education* (Cambridge: Harvard University Press, 1957).

[114]The sociology of science, in particular, has been a central interest of Merton's. We recommend the festschrift edited by Lewis A. Coser, *The Idea of Social Structure: Papers in Honor of Robert K. Merton* (1975).

[115]Merton in Hunt, "How Does It Come To Be So?" p. 44.

Theories of the middle range, then, transcend sheer description of social phenomena. They are theories with limited sets of assumptions, from which specific hypotheses can be derived and tested empirically. In Merton's view, middle-range views would gradually consolidate into more general theory. What he sets out to do is to "fill in the blanks" between raw empiricism (what is referred to by some sociologists as the "fishing expeditions" of researchers who cross-tabulate data with abandon and with no guiding theoretical framework) and grand or all-inclusive theory of the type Parsons was working on in his general theory of action.[116]

In his plea for theories of the middle range, Merton is standing on the shoulders of such great sociologists as Durkheim and Weber. Two classical examples of middle-range theories are Durkheim's *Suicide*, which we discussed earlier, and Weber's *The Protestant Ethic and the Spirit of Capitalism*, an analysis of the importance of a religious belief system (Calvinist asceticism) in the rise of capitalism in the West.[117] What Merton is advocating is not a new approach, then, but a proliferation of works like these classics. His own work on such phenomena as medical students' attitudes and patterns of influence are good examples of middle-range theories. Durkheim's study of suicide rates provides an example of the kind of middle-range theory Merton was advocating. It also furnished a concept, anomie, that Merton found very fruitful in developing his own theory of deviance, though he defined anomie somewhat differently.

CLARIFYING FUNCTIONAL ANALYSIS

Merton has devoted considerable attention to what he calls the "codification of functional analysis in sociology."[118] This work displays some important differences from Parsons' functionalism. For one thing, Merton's functional paradigm is not open to criticisms of inherent conservatism and teleology ("explaining" things by their function). At the same time, however, Merton offers fewer specific propositions about the structure of societies than Parsons does. His notion of functionalism is closer to the general orientation that Kingsley Davis identified with sociology as a whole than it is to Parsons' own theories.

As we have seen, functionalists in general conceive of society as a system of "interrelated parts." This is equally true of Merton, who argues that the "central orientation of functionalism" is expressed in the practice of interpreting data by establishing their consequences for larger structures

[116]See C. Wright Mills' critique of both Parsons' grand theory and of abstracted empiricism in *The Sociological Imagination* (New York: Oxford University Press, 1959), pp. 25–75.

[117]See Chapters III and IV.

[118]Merton, *Social Theory and Social Structure*, p. 73.

in which they are implicated.[119] Merton is also deeply interested in social integration, or equilibrium. Like Durkheim and Parsons, he analyzes society with reference to whether the "cultural" and "social" structures are well or badly integrated;[120] is interested in the contributions of customs and institutions to the persistence of societies;[121] and defines functions as those contributions or consequences that "make for the adaptation or adjustment of a given system."[122] Finally, Merton thinks that shared values are central in explaining how societies and institutions work, thus sharing the other major distinguishing concern of all functionalist analysis.

However, through his paradigm Merton clarifies and refocuses some major aspects of functionalist theory. The most important are his emphasis on dysfunctions, his distinction between manifest and latent functions, his concept of functional alternatives, and his insistence on the importance of uncovering and understanding the mechanisms by which functions are fulfilled.

Dysfunctions

Talcott Parsons' work tends to imply that all existing institutions are inherently good or "functional" for society; this tendency has been one of the major points of attack on functionalism and the one that arouses the most emotion among its critics. Merton explicitly dissociates himself from such a position. Instead, he emphasizes the existence of "dysfunctions" and encourages sociologists to be active in identifying them.

Merton's concept of dysfunctions involves two complementary but distinct ideas. The first is that something may have consequences that are generally dysfunctional; in his words, an item may have "consequences which lessen the adaptation or adjustment of the system."[123] The second is that these consequences may vary according to whom one is talking about; the sociologist must ask the crucial question, "Functional and dysfunctional for whom?"

An excellent example of what Merton means by generally dysfunctional consequences can be found in his own discussion of bureaucracy. On the whole, bureaucracy appears as a functional institution for industrial society in that bureaucratic specialization means better utilization of talent and more effective response to the exigencies of the environment. However, Merton's understanding of dysfunctions makes him aware of what may happen when adherence to bureaucratic rules becomes an end in itself—a situation he calls "ritualism" in his theory of deviance. He illus-

[119]Ibid., pp. 100–101.
[120]Ibid., p. 217.
[121]Ibid., p. 87.
[122]Ibid., p. 105.
[123]Ibid.

trates this aspect of bureaucracy with a pathetic incident involving Bernt Balchen, Admiral Byrd's pilot in the flight over the South Pole:

> According to a ruling of the Department of Labor Bernt Balchen . . . cannot receive his citizenship papers. Balchen, a native of Norway, declared his intention in 1927. It is held that he has failed to meet the conditions of five years' continuous residence in the United States. The Byrd Antarctic voyage took him out of the country, although he was on a ship carrying the American flag, was an invaluable member of the American expedition, and in a region to which there is an American claim because of exploration and occupation of it by Americans, this region being Little America. The Bureau of Naturalization explains that it cannot proceed on the assumption that Little America is American soil. This would be *trespass on international questions* where it has no sanction. So far as the bureau is concerned, Balchen was out of the country and *technically* has not complied with the law of naturalization.[124]

Although adherence to the rules is ordinarily a moral and social "good" and therefore "functional" for society, in this case it was dysfunctional—not only for Balchen but also for "society," because the rigidity resulted in the loss of a superb person as a citizen. Merton's knowledge of general dysfunction thus makes him aware of the "dark underside" of bureaucracy in a way not generally associated with functionalism. He is close to Weber, who saw bureaucracy as an efficient, "rational" way of dealing with problems, necessary to a modern state and to the end of feudalism and yet prospectively tyrannical because of its inflexible ritualism, its insistence on rules for everything. Merton is even close to the neo-Marxist conflict theorist, Habermas, who sees rationalistic bureaucracy as an impressive technical development that threatens human freedom.[125]

Merton's second point—that an institution need not be generally functional or generally dysfunctional but may instead be functional for some people and groups and dysfunctional for others—is an even clearer shift away from a functionalism that implies approval of the status quo. In some ways it approaches conflict theory. Merton talks in terms of whether institutions and practices are "functional" or "dysfunctional" for people, whereas conflict theorists generally refer to people's "interests" and the degree to which these are served. However, they share a concern with the differing benefits that various groups obtain from the social order and with the way these benefits explain the origin, persistence, or decline of social institutions.

We can see what Merton means by dysfunctions and why it is important for sociologists to bear them in mind by looking at such supposedly indispensable institutions as marriage and family living. People commonly think of these institutions as crucial to the "health of society." Yet marriage

[124]Ibid., p. 254.
[125]See Chapter III.

and family life may not be functional for some types of individuals at all. They may be happier with such functional alternatives as joining "collectives," renting in singles' apartment complexes, living together as unmarried couples, or living in religious communities. Only by recognizing the dysfunctional aspects of marriage and family living can we explain the development and persistence of these alternatives. Again, as functionalists from Durkheim on have tended to emphasize, an institutionalized and established religion may help to integrate a society by creating common values and identification with the group. However, Merton points out, such a religion is hardly functional for dissidents who are victims of an Inquisition, and religious conflicts and wars are dysfunctional for large segments of the societies involved.[126]

In *Social Theory and Social Structure*, Merton asks, "What are the consequences, functional and dysfunctional, of positive orientation to the values of a group other than one's own?"[127] His interest in this phenomenon, labeled *anticipatory socialization*, is exemplified in a recent study by a former student of Merton's, Helen Ebaugh. Ebaugh explores the process of role exit—"disengagement from a role that is central to one's self-identity and the reestablishment of an identity in a new role that takes into account one's ex-role." Her study concerns a variety of social groups, including ex-convicts, ex-nuns, ex-alcoholics, divorced men and women, mothers without custody, ex-prostitutes, ex-air traffic controllers, and transsexuals.

Anticipatory socialization is functional for both the aspiring individual and for the group he or she eventually enters. This is true when the seeking and weighing of role alternatives is taking place and, especially, as individuals come closer to a final decision to exit a role.

Prior identification with a group serves as a kind of bridge to membership in the group. Ebaugh found, for instance, that transsexuals identified with members of the opposite sex by cross-dressing and taking on the mannerisms of the opposite sex long before they underwent sex-change surgery. As she puts it, "In addition to shifts in orientation, attitudes and values, individuals at this point in the process also began rehearsing the roles they were anticipating."[128]

Gans' analysis of poverty demonstrates how a Mertonian functionalist approach can produce analyses that would generally be associated with "radical" conflict theory rather than "conservative" functionalism. Gans points out that when one distinguishes between different groups in a society, one can see that the existence of poverty serves a number of positive functions for different groups. For example, he claims, poverty ensures the existence of a group willing to serve in a peacetime army, provides the

---

[126]Merton, *Social Theory and Social Structure*, pp. 96–99.

[127]Ibid., p. 319.

[128]Helen Rose Fuchs Ebaugh, *Becoming an Ex: The Process of Role Exit* (Chicago: University of Chicago Press, 1988), p. 111.

upper classes with an outlet for charity and the gratification it brings, creates jobs for people in professions and occupations that "serve" the poor, and makes it possible for wealthier people to get dirty jobs and personal services performed at a slight cost. These functions, he suggests, help explain why poverty exists in technologically advanced societies: those who benefit from it wish to preserve it.[129]

Gans' analysis could also shed some light on a social problem of the 1980's—homelessness. We could point to the increase in homelessness in the United States as a dysfunction of the deinstitutionalization of mentally ill patients. By asking Merton's question "Who benefits?" we can uncover the travesty of leaving mentally ill people on the streets in the name of civil liberties, and we can inquire where the funds which were "recovered" from a dismantling of the mental health systems will be allocated. Without attention to latent functions, we miss the significance of an analysis by President Reagan, who said in a television interview that many of the nation's homeless people "make it their own choice" not to seek shelter and who also claimed that a "large percentage" of the homeless are "retarded" people who have voluntarily left institutions in which they were placed.[130]

Merton's concept of dysfunctions is also central to his argument that functionlism is *not* intrinsically conservative. It appears to be only when functionalists imply that everything is generally functional in its consequences[131]—something his concept of general dysfunctions denies—and when analysts treat "society" and its members as one and the same thing[132]— a view he sets out to demolish by asking, "Functional for whom?"

At the same time, Merton does retain a distinctively functional perspective. Unlike most conflict theorists, Merton believes that institutions and values can be functional (or dysfunctional) for society as a whole, not just for particular groups. He suggests that researchers should start with the hypothesis that persisting cultural forms may have a "net balance of functional consequences"[133] for society as a unit as well as for subgroups. Merton's emphasis on dysfunctions, to use a good functionalist word, balances Parsons' concern with social functions.

Manifest and Latent Functions

Merton's distinction between "manifest" and "latent" functions further clarifies functional analysis. Manifest functions are those consequences people observe or expect; latent functions are those consequences that are

---

[129]See Herbert Gans, "The Positive Functions of Poverty," *American Journal of Sociology*, 78 (1972), 275–89.

[130]Lou Cannon, "Reagan Cites 'Choice' by Homeless," *Washington Post* (December 23, 1988), p. A8.

[131]This is what Merton labels the "Postulate of Universal Functionalism."

[132]This Merton calls the "Postulate of the Functional Unity of Society." Ibid., pp. 79, 84.

[133]Ibid., p. 86.

neither recognized nor intended. Parsons tends to emphasize the manifest functions of social behavior; Merton pays particular attention to the latent functions of things and the increased understanding of society functionalist analysis can bring by uncovering them.

The notion of latent functions is not a totally new one. Durkheim's discussion of social cohesion as a consequence of punishment, which we outlined at the beginning of this chapter, was an analysis of the latent function of punishment (the manifest function being retribution). Similarly, the functional analysis of religion as a social integrator, to which we have referred, is concerned with religion's latent function. What Merton does is to emphasize both the distinction between manifest and latent and the way analysis of latent functions "precludes the substitutions of naive moral judgments for sociological analysis."[134] This distinction forces sociologists to go beyond the reasons individuals give for their actions or for the existence of customs and institutions; it makes them look for other social consequences that allow these practices' survival and illuminate the way a society works. As an example of the fruitfulness of such analysis, Merton cites Veblen's analysis of conspicuous consumption, whose latent function is to enhance one's status in the eyes of the world.[135]

Merton's own analysis of political machines shows how the distinction between manifest and latent functions can help explain the way institutions work and why they survive and thrive. The manifest function of political machines, especially in the context of ward politics, seems to be personal advancement through corruption, since it involves vote buying and similar law breaking. However, because they were so firmly rooted in the local neighborhood, ward politics and political machines were highly functional for such disadvantaged groups as new immigrants. They served to humanize welfare assistance by providing information about how hospitals worked, by marshaling legal aid, and by furnishing jobs; thus, they kept families together and broke down some of the isolation of immigrant groups. Merton started with the hypothesis that in spite of obvious surface dysfunctions, to survive and be influential the machine must serve important functions for some social groups. By asking "Who benefits?" and uncovering the machine's latent functions, he created a classic piece of sociological analysis.

Functional Alternatives

Functionalism's claim of providing specific propositions about how societies work, rather than simply general suggestions about how to set

---

[134]Ibid., pp. 124–25.

[135]It is worth noting that Veblen is generally considered essentially a "conflict theorist" (see Chapter III), and conflict theorists are, on the whole, very interested in the unadmitted and unseen consequences of people's actions and their relationship to people's interests. Merton's use of Veblen to illustrate the notion of latent functions again underlines his point that there is nothing intrinsically conservative about analyzing society in terms of things' functions, dysfunctions, and general interrelatedness.

about analyzing and explaining things, rests in large part on its argument that in order to persist, a society must have certain characteristics; and correspondingly, all societies will exhibit these characteristics. As we have seen, this argument is central to the work of Parsons, who lists such characteristics in his AGIL schema, and it is also apparent in the work of Malinowski, Radcliffe-Brown, and Durkheim. In much of Merton's work, functionalism serves more as a way of orienting oneself to one's material than as a set of propositions about the structure of societies. But Merton does share this central view, and he puts forward the concept of functional prerequisites, or *"preconditions functionally necessary* for a society."[136] At the same time, however, he emphasizes that there is no reason to suppose that particular, given institutions are the only ones able to fulfill these functions; therefore, a given social structure is in no way sacrosanct. On the contrary, there may be a wide range of what he terms "functional alternatives," or substitutes, able to perform the same task.

Merton's concept of functional alternatives also clarifies functionalist analysis because it explicitly rejects the idea that existing institutions are necessary and, by implication, good. Therefore, it encourages sociologists using a functionalist approach to question the indispensability of an existing social structure. For example, most functional theorists believe that religion maintains and inculcates certain norms and values central to the group[137] and thus combats the anomie that leads both to social disintegration and personal unhappiness. However, this function may be served by structures other than organized religion, and movements that might be interpreted as functional alternatives to religion seem to be cropping up almost daily in certain parts of America, particularly in California, the birthplace of many occult and therapeutic groups.[138]

Other functional alternatives can be found among the different types of higher education and vocational training existing in modern industrial societies. All of these perform the function of "sorting" people out for the adult world of work and classifying them as qualified for different types of occupations. But the different ways they do so may be more or less functional for different people. As Burton Clark points out, American society places great emphasis on encouraging people to achieve and on ensuring "equal opportunity" to do so, and it practices something close to an open-door admission to college. However, in practice, not everyone can become a nuclear physicist, veterinarian, or corporate executive. Colleges impose fairly strict criteria on performance, and many students would, if they entered a four-year college, inevitably encounter standards of performance they could not meet. Using terminology derived directly from Merton's work on deviance, Clark says there is "dissociation between culturally instilled goals and

[136]Merton, *Social Theory and Social Structure,* p. 87.
[137]A view shared, as Merton points out, by Marxists. Ibid., pp. 98–99.
[138]See Durkheim on the public school as a functional alternative, p. 24.

institutionally provided means of realization; discrepancy between ends and means is seen as a basic social source of individual frustration."[139]

For students who would fail in a four-year college, the two-year or junior college provides a functional alternative. It performs the same function of sorting students for the labor market, and it makes it clear to less academically oriented students that certain careers are not possible for them. And it does so at much less personal cost to such students, for whom the straight academic failure of the conventional college might be personally dysfunctional. Clark describes the "cooling-out" function of these colleges, which permit transfer to four-year colleges but also redirect students through testing programs and extensive counseling that serve to reorient students who need to redefine their goals. Although a four-year college is both personally functional for those who succeed scholastically and an appropriate way to train people for some careers, Clark shows how the two-year college can be a functional alternative for others because it provides alternative achievements that alleviate the personal stress caused by failure. It may also be socially functional because it may help prevent discontentment and deviance and may direct people successfully into other occupations.

In the wake of the contemporary women's movement, many functional alternatives to traditional marriages have emerged. The increasing use of day care facilities and, on a much smaller scale, househusbands are examples of functional alternatives to the mother staying at home. Other examples of functional alternatives to traditional marriages are commuting relationships, equal parenting, and greater husband participation in household work.[140]

Merton's notion of functional alternatives is thus important because it alerts sociologists to the similar functions very different institutions may perform, and it further reduces the tendency of functionalism to imply approval of the status quo. However, Merton makes very little progress in specifying what the "functional prerequisites" are that can be served in a variety of ways. Merton apparently does not consider Parsons' schema to be the definitive statement on the subject, but neither does he provide any concrete alternative list of his own. He recognizes the idea of functional requirements as an essential part of any functional analysis,[141] and refers frequently in his analysis to the degree to which a society is well or poorly adjusted.[142] But he never defines what the functional requirements for

---

[139]Burton Clark, "The 'Cooling-Out' Function in Higher Education," *American Journal of Sociology*, 65 (1960), 560. As Parsons might put it, the discrepancy creates strain or potential disequilibrium.

[140]See William Beer, *Househusbands* (South Hadley, Mass.: Bergin and Garvey, 1982), and Joseph H. Pleck, *Working Wives, Working Husbands* (Beverly Hills, Calif.: Sage, 1985).

[141]Merton, *Social Theory and Social Structure*, pp. 87 and 106.

[142]Ibid., e.g., p. 217. Merton's concept of integration seems to owe most to Durkheim and to include the necessity for cultural norms and actual institutions and opportunities to be in line with one another. See the discussion of his theory of deviance, which follows.

such integration are. Instead he refers to them as "one of the cloudiest and empirically most debatable concepts in functional theory."[143]

As might be expected from his remarks on middle-range theory, in general, Merton's achievement is to provide an excellent clarification of the requirements of functionalist theory and to show how a general functionalist orientation can be used fruitfully in empirical analysis, rather than to provide further general propositions about social structure and equilibrium. Merton's own summary of the logic of functional analysis in biology, which has so heavily influenced functionalism, makes very clear how many gaps remain. As Merton points out,

> First of all, certain functional requirements of the organisms are established, requirements which must be satisfied if the organism is to survive, or to operate with some degree of effectiveness. Second, there is a concrete and detailed description of the arrangements (structures and processes) through which these requirements are typically met in "normal" cases. Third, if some of the typical mechanisms for meeting these requirements are destroyed, or are found to be functioning inadequately, the observer is sensitized to the need for detecting compensating mechanisms (if any) which fulfill the necessary function. Fourth, and implicit in all that precedes, there is a detailed account of the structure *for which* the functional requirements hold, as well as a detailed account of the arrangement *through which* the function is fulfilled.[144]

A full functionalist theory of society would require comparable steps; but though Merton clarifies these requirements admirably, he does not himself fill them.

MERTON'S THEORY OF DEVIANCE

Though Merton's contributions to sociology are legion, his theory of deviance, which has been reprinted several times in different languages, is one of his best known. In developing his theory of deviance, Merton utilizes explanatory factors that are typical of functional analysis—namely, cultural goals and institutionalized norms. He uses anomie as a major independent variable; as we saw above, anomie is a term also used by Durkheim to explain suicide, which is a form of deviance. Let us recall that Durkheim's general definition of anomie was a lack of regulation, or normlessness. Merton's definition differs somewhat; for him, anomie is a discontinuity between cultural goals and the legitimate means available for reaching them. He applies his analysis to the United States, where the goal of monetary success is heavily emphasized but there is no corresponding emphasis

[143]Ibid., p. 107.
[144]Ibid., p. 103.

on the "legitimate avenues to march toward this goal."[145] The resulting anomie is, Merton argues, dysfunctional for American society in general and especially dysfunctional for those groups within the country who lack the means to the goal of monetary success. Thus, it is a source of strain for the system, in the Parsonian sense, and it leads to a considerable amount of deviance.[146]

In depicting his model graphically Merton chose to use a plus sign (+) to indicate acceptance of the goal of monetary success and/or the means to the goal, and he used a minus sign (−) to indicate the rejection (or unavailability) of the goal or means to it. He thus arrives at five modes of adaptation, or types of deviance. Our schematic presentation (Figure 2-4) differs from Merton's original one in that we have presented it with the relationship between the goal and means (his independent variable, anomie) first, followed by the modes of adaptation, or deviance typology (his dependent variable).

We can dispose of the mode of conformity very easily, for a person who attains monetary success by working hard and getting an education is the prototype of the successful American. Next, we can see that innovation (for example, racketeering) and ritualism (the type we mentioned earlier in discussing the Balchen case) are the only pure cases of anomie as Merton defined it, because in both of these there is discontinuity between the goals and means. Retreatism (for example, drug addiction) is a rejection of both monetary success and the means to it, and rebellion is a combination of a rejection of societal goals and means and a substitution of other goals and means.

Merton's prediction for the United States, where monetary success is highly valued and the legitimate means to it are unavailable for many, is that our society should have a lot of deviance and that it should most likely occur among the lower classes, who experience the structural blockages most keenly. In general his model is not clear, however, about when the various types will emerge or in what degree.

Although Merton did not test his hypotheses on deviance himself, they were stated empirically enough to guide other researchers,[147] and it has been said that the publication of this essay on deviance in 1938 in the *American Sociological Review* established Merton "once and for all as a major figure in sociology."[148]

[145]See Merton's chapter, "Social Structure and Anomie," in *Social Theory and Social Structure*, pp. 185–248.

[146]Parsons, in fact, borrowed from Merton's model in his own classification of deviant orientations. See Parsons, *The Social System*, p. 257.

[147]Light, for instance, recently stated that Merton's anomie theory is "still the orthodox sociological explanation of why ethnic and racial minorities have always been disproportionately involved in illegal enterprise in America." Ivan Light, "The Ethnic Vice Industry, 1880–1944," *American Sociological Review* (1977), 465.

[148]Hunt, "How Does It Come To Be So?" p. 52.

| | X $\longrightarrow$ Y | |
| (Anomie) | | (Deviance) |
Cultural Goals	Institutionalized Means	Modes of Adaptation
+	+	Conformity
+	−	Innovation
−	+	Ritualism
−	−	Retreatism
±	±	Rebellion

FIGURE 2-4 Goals, Means, and Adaptations: Merton on Deviance

THE ROLE-SET

Merton first published his article "The Role-Set: Problems in Sociological Theory" in the *British Journal of Sociology* in 1957.[149] Merton begins his analysis by defining status and role as Ralph Linton did: status means a position in a social structure with its corresponding rights and duties, and role means the behavior that is oriented to others' patterned expectations. As Linton conceived it, each status has a single role associated with it, and each person in society occupies many statuses.

Merton elaborates on Linton's conception by introducing the notion that each status involves not one but an array of roles; he labels this a *role-set*. A role-set is "that complement of role relationships in which persons are involved by virtue of occupying a particular social status." Each person, in turn, occupies various statuses, each of which has its own role-set, and Merton calls this a status-set. (See Figure 2-5.)

In his article, however, Merton concentrates on role-sets rather than status-sets. His article is devoted to an analysis of the social arrangements that integrate the expectations of those who are in the role-set, thus avoiding role conflict. True to form, Merton focuses on the problem of social structure and asks which are the functional elements—that is, which mechanisms counteract the potential instability of role-sets—and, on the other hand, which are the dysfunctional elements—that is, under which circumstances do the mechanisms of social control fail to operate. Although it was not Merton's own, we find the example of the college student's role-set excellent for purposes of illustration. Its members include professors, other students, academic advisers, the dean, the registrar, and dorm counselors. There is considerable potential for role conflict in this role-set. However, Merton identifies four important mitigating factors, which reduce the impact of these conflicts. Among the members of the role-set, some are more and some less involved in their relationship with the student, and Merton

[149]Ibid., pp. 106–20.

FIGURE 2-5   Merton's Role-Set

believes that such a differential degree of involvement mitigates the effects of diverse role expectations. Under most circumstances, other students in the role-set, for example, would be more involved with the student than the dean is. Another mitigating factor Merton discusses is that those in the role-set may be competing with each other for power. In some circumstances, their involvement in the conflict (or the resulting stand-off) may give the role incumbent more autonomy. Merton's third mechanism to alleviate role conflict is the insulation of role activities from observance by role-set members. For instance, the confidentiality built into the student-counselor relationship insulates the professors and the dean from learning about certain behavior of the student from the dorm counselor. Finally, another mitigating factor is the degree to which conflicting demands by members of a role-set can be observed. If it is obvious that demands conflict, it is the task of the members of the role-set and not of the role incumbent to resolve the contradictions; for example, a dean who calls a meeting of the student body during a scheduled class period will have to work out this conflict with the professors involved.

Merton then discusses the mutual social support among status occupants, which helps to resolve conflicts of expectations among members of the role-set. A familiar example on campus, of course, is the formation of various student associations, which is a way of coping and also a way of giving social support to students. The latent function of social support could be seen in the Free Speech Movement at Berkeley in the early sixties, for example.[150]

Finally, Merton mentions withdrawal as a control mechanism. In this case a member of the role-set breaks off role relations with other members; as Merton points out, however, this is an infrequent and limited option. It is true, for example, that a particular dorm counselor can resign from her job over conflict with a dean; but someone else will replace her, and the role-set is "amputated" only in the interim.

This discussion of the role-set illustrates Merton's emphasis on the analysis of dysfunctional elements and functional alternatives. He immediately looks at the social structural demands that are incompatible or conflicting and asks what the functional alternatives are. True to the functional

---

[150]See Coser on the "nonrealistic" aspects of conflict and revolution in Chapter III.

perspective, Merton looks on the role-set as a system of interrelated parts and asks how order among these parts is made possible.

Role-set analysis can also uncover certain inequities existing in our society. For instance, if one were to list the members of the role-set related to the status of mother and compare it to that of the father, one might discover that one status is overburdened. For example, does the school nurse always phone the mother when the child is sick, even when both parents work? By virtue of being a mother, is she, and not the father, automatically involved in role-relationships with the school nurse? And if demands are unequal, what are the likely consequences? Questions such as these are raised by Merton's analysis, and they are the impetus for needed research.

In concluding this section on Merton, we can see that in general he alerts functionalists to question and to evaluate critically the "contributions" of various social institutions. He also raises questions of inequality when he asks who benefits from certain structures, thus leading to a more radical view than Parsons.

NEOFUNCTIONALISM

Neofunctionalism is a recent theoretical development emerging in the mid-1980s, both in the United States and in Germany. In 1984 the American Sociological Association devoted two sessions to a conference on neofunctionalism at its annual meeting, where most of the papers presented were reappraisals and reconsiderations of the empirical implications of Parsonian theory.[151]

These papers were subsequently edited by Jeffrey C. Alexander, the leading proponent of neofunctionalism in the United States. In the introduction to *Neofunctionalism,* he suggests three similarities between neofunctionalism and neo-Marxism. Both include a critique of some of the basic tenets of the original theory, the incorporation of elements from antagonistic theoretical traditions, and a variety of competing developments, rather than a single coherent form. Alexander then argues that neofunctionalism is a tendency rather than a developed theory, and he elaborates on the various tendencies of neofunctionalism: (1) to create a form of functionalism that is multidimensional and includes micro as well as macro levels of analysis; (2) to push functionalism to the left and reject Parsons' optimism about modernity; (3) to argue for an implicit democratic thrust in functionalist analysis; (4) to incorporate a conflict orientation; and (5) to emphasize contingency (uncertainty) and interactional creativity.

[151]See Alexander, *Neofunctionalism.* See also Alexander's four-volume work, *Theoretical Logic in Sociology* (Berkeley: University of California Press, 1982).

What remains at issue today among neofunctionalists, however, are the following kinds of interrelated problems: How many researchers best characterize the relationship between conflict or contingency and social order? To what extent must Parsons' emphasis upon the relationship between social action and social order be reformulated in order to inform empirical research?

Alexander refuses to predict whether a "school" of neofunctionalism will actually emerge. Nonetheless, he views the movement to reappropriate Parsons as gaining momentum, and he is of the opinion that a critically revived Parsonian tradition should continue. In locating current contributors to neofunctionalism, it is useful to divide them into three categories. First, there is an earlier generation of functionalists who continue to contribute to the distinctively Parsonian tradition, such as Neil Smelser, Robert Bellah, Bernard Barber, and Victor Lidz. Second, there is the group led by Alexander in the United States and Niklas Luhmann and Richard Munch in Germany who are labeled by others or self-labeled as neofunctionalists, such as Dean Gerstein, Mark Gould, Paul Colomy, Frank Lechner, and David Sciulli. Third, there is another group whose works seem consistent with the thrust of neofunctionalism, but who have not yet characterized themselves as neofunctionalists and who may not in all instances appreciate being so labeled by others, such as R. Stephen Warner, Donald Levine, Rainer Baum, Jeffrey Prager, and Ino Rossi. The American reconsideration of Parsons will stand or fall, however, on the quality and quantity of empirical research in the next decade in light of this new development.[152]

More recently, Alexander has proclaimed that the anti-Parsonian period is over, because the battle was won in 1980.[153] Why did the anti-Parsonians win? He replies that the "challengers" (e.g., conflict, exchange, interaction, ethnomethodology, and Marxist theory) picked on significant issues, pointed up weaknesses in Parsons' theory, and thus eclipsed functionalism. Alexander's view is that today we are in a new post-Parsonian phase of sociological theorizing—a synthesizing movement—which is attempting to make the link between macro- and microsociological theories. This is actually quite consistent with his position on neofunctionalism. As Alexander puts it, among the theorists of this new generation involved in the synthesizing movement, "some pay a great deal of attention to Parsons, others do not. Still, theirs is exactly the same course that long ago Parsons set for himself: to end the 'warring schools' by developing a synthetic theory which incorporates the partial theories of the day."[154]

German theorists, on the other hand, tend to read Parsons through

---

[152]See David Sciulli and Dean Gerstein, "Social Theory and Talcott Parsons in the 1980s," *Annual Review of Sociology* (Palo Alto, Calif.: Annual Review, Inc., 1985).

[153]Jeffrey C. Alexander, *Twenty Lectures: Sociological Theory Since World War II* (New York: Columbia University Press, 1987).

[154]Ibid., p. 376.

the eyes of Niklas Luhmann, who spent a year in the early 1960s at Harvard studying under Parsons. Luhmann views Parsons' theory as a milestone because it "has been the only attempt to begin with a number of equally important functions and then to give a theoretical deduction to them. . . . No one else has dared to try this or even thought it was possible."[155] However, what Parsons' theory is missing, according to Luhmann, are the concepts of self-reference and complexity. His own work is an attempt to formulate a universal or "grand" theory of social systems which incorporates these concepts.

Luhmann says that a social system exists "whenever the actions of several persons are meaningful interrelated and are thus . . . marked off from an environment."[156] A social system thus emerges whenever any interaction takes place among individuals. According to Luhmann, there are three types of social systems: interaction systems (face-to-face interaction of human beings), organization systems (where membership is linked to specific conditions), and societal systems (the all-embracing social system, entire societies).[157]

Self-reference, according to Luhmann, is a condition for the efficient functioning of systems. It means that the system is able to observe itself, can reflect on itself and what it is doing, and can make decisions as a result of this reflection. Self-referential systems have the ability to "delineate their self identities."[158] They can describe themselves by setting up boundaries regarding what they are and what they are not; in other words, the system has "structural autonomy."[159]

Self-referencing, in Luhmann's view, takes place in all subsystems, such as politics, science, economy, family, education, and law. He provides us with an example of the self-referencing of a system when he says that the scientific subsystem "reflects on itself in fundamental theorizing and in its decisions to continue or discontinue its historically given traditions."[160] "Self-referential systems are not only self-organizing or self-regulating systems. . . . They exist as a closed network of the production of elements which reproduces itself as a network by continuing to produce the elements which are needed to continue to produce the elements."[161]

To argue that a system is self-referencing is to confer on the system a

[155]See Niklas Luhmann, *The Differentiation of Society* (New York: Columbia University Press, 1982), p. 59.

[156]Ibid., p. 70.

[157]Ibid., pp. 71–75.

[158]Niklas Luhmann, "Tautology and Paradox in the Self-Descriptions of Modern Society," *Sociological Theory*, 6 (1988), 26–37.

[159]Luhmann, *The Differentiation of Society*, p. 258.

[160]Ibid., p. 265.

[161]Niklas Luhmann, "Society, Meaning, Religion—Based on Self-Reference," *Sociological Analysis*, 46 (1985), 6. As this quote demonstrates, a combination of unclear definitions and highly abstract concepts makes Luhmann's theory very difficult to grasp.

capability for decision making. How much is gained by such a reification? It is one thing to suggest, as Parsons does, that a system has "needs," but quite another to say that it can "reflect on itself" and "make decisions." It seems to us that an example such as the one given above confuses the issue even further. After all, the scientific subsystem that "reflects on itself" consists, in the last analysis, of groups of scientists who do the reflecting and make the decisions.

Luhmann's position, however, is that the human subject or concrete social groups should not be the central point of social thought. Societal systems, according to Luhmann, are too complicated to be treated in this way. They cannot be treated as composed of human beings, but rather as being composed of communication units. Individuals, then, are merely part of the environment of a societal system. Subjective meaning is ruled out, as evidenced in his statement that "there is no plausible way to base systems theory on a Weberian concept of meaningful action."[162]

In Luhmann's theory the chief task performed by social systems is to reduce complexity.[163] Luhmann is convinced that Parsons' theory of action offers "only meager resources for handling complexity"[164] and that "a theory of society will have to concern itself with ideas such as the reduction of the extreme complexity and contingency of the world."[165] In Luhmann's view, greater complexity brings more choices, more possibilities. This means that choosing among alternatives is more difficult; it takes more noes to reach a yes. Think, for example, of the difficult decisions arising from those technological innovations which have produced an enormous variety of software programs for computers. How does one choose a word-processing program, for instance, when newer and more sophisticated versions are being introduced almost daily?

Luhmann argues that the fundamental problem of such a paradoxical world can be "solved, or "transformed into minor problems," by religion or by several functional equivalents of religion in modern society, including art, love, sovereign power, and making money.[166] What these alternatives have in common is that they provide at least some actors with shared standards of action accepted on faith. They allow complex sets of interactions to proceed in a world that would otherwise be chaotic and incomprehensible.

Luhmann is basically not as optimistic about the future as was Parsons. In Luhmann's view, the modern world is too complex for shared norms or even value generalization, and he criticizes Parsons for overestimating not only the social consensus that is functionally necessary but also the consen-

---

[162]Luhmann, *The Differentiation of Society*, p. 232.

[163]Ibid., p. xxvi.

[164]Ibid., p. 92.

[165]Ibid., p. 192.

[166]Luhmann, "Society, Meaning, Religion—Based on Self-Reference," p. 9.

sus that exists in actuality. What unites us, according to Luhmann, is "common acceptance of schematized [or structural] contingency."[167]

However, in our view there is little attraction to the idea of the world being united by a situation of unpredictability. How can groups be socially integrated simply by experiencing the same uncertainties?

In a more recent work, Luhmann points to the negative aspects (dysfunctions) of modernity. He views society as confronted with the full consequences of its structural selections, such as the ecological problems resulting from its own "rationality."[168] Luhmann also points to the growing awareness of and anxiety about global risks nourished by modern ecological problems and the struggle to maintain the level of social welfare. In fact, Luhmann describes this as the "era of unmasked anxiety."[169]

Luhmann's work and the work of Richard Münch have spearheaded the revival of functionalist theorizing in Germany.[170] Like neo-Marxism, the development of neofunctionalism, both in Germany and in America, involves a critique and a reinterpretation of the original work, rather than an attempt to repeat the debates of the 1950s and 1960s.

CONCLUSION

In discussing the characteristics of functionalism and the contributions of the major theorists throughout this chapter, we have raised questions about certain features of the functionalist perspective. This was not done to discourage the reader from appreciating and making use of the insights of functionalism. Rather, it was an attempt to uncover the weaknesses as well as the strengths of this perspective, and this, as we mentioned earlier, is one of our goals in writing this text.

As a matter of fact, those who prefer another perspective could, nonetheless, profit by a more thorough knowledge and understanding of functionalism than is common among many contemporary sociologists. The perspective provides considerable insights into how societies work and why institutions and customs exist. If there is some wisdom in the saying, "You have to know the system to beat the system," then functionalism can help those who are dedicated to radical social change to understand how the system operates. Nor, to appreciate functionalism, need one take sides with Parsons when, for instance, he argues that his general theory of action

---

[167]Luhmann, *The Differentiation of Society*, p. xix.

[168]Luhmann, "Tautology and Paradox in the Self-Descriptions of Modern Society," p. 36.

[169]Ibid., p. 33.

[170]See Richard Münch, "Talcott Parsons and the Theory of Action I and II," *American Journal of Sociology*, 86 (1981), 709–39 and 87 (1982), 771–826. For an American interpretation see Jeffrey C. Alexander, "The Parsons Revival in German Sociology," *Sociological Theory 1984* (San Francisco: Jossey-Bass, 1984), pp. 394–412.

encompasses conflict theory and there are not two theories, but one. One may, instead, agree with Dahrendorf or Coser, who see consensus (or functionalist) theory and conflict theory as two different sides of the coin.[171]

Does the assumption that consensus lies at the basis of any social order make this theory ideologically conservative? In arguing that functionalism is independent of any ideological implications, Parsons says that functional analysis has "nothing to do with political conservatism or a defense of the status quo."[172] In the past, however, functionalism has often been used as a conservative approach to the analysis of society in that strain and conflict were seen as dysfunctional for the social system, and anomie as a pathological state to be avoided. Many of those who were attracted to functionalism tended, in practice, to be more or less satisfied with the present system, and they were not neutral about its survival. However, with the revitalization of functionalist theorizing in the 1980s and the critique and reinterpretation of Parsons by neofunctionalists, we expect to see some new developments and extensions of this perspective.

To summarize, then, functionalism tends to stress values over interests, so that although it shows the independent importance of ideas and the links between power and social consent, it neglects the coercive aspects of power and the significance of people's conflicting objectives. Similarly, it emphasizes social control over social change, so that it analyzes adjustive but ignores disruptive change and overemphasizes the importance of security and the "needs" of society at the expense of interests and objectives that cannot be met without social change. In general, it also stresses structure over process, although Parsons' work on evolutionary change takes into account processes as well as structures; and it stresses macro- over microsociological analysis.

Its macro-sociological emphasis means that one is taking an aerial view of society when one views society from the functionalist perspective. It is not a "better" picture than that taken from the ground; it is simply a picture taken from a different angle. If we consider, for instance, the locations of the numerous television cameras at a political convention, we realize that each camera captures a piece of the reality but that no one camera by itself catches all of the action. So it is, we argue, with theoretical perspectives in sociology. In functionalism, most of the pictures are taken from on high, looking down on the action, and most of the pictures are developed as "stills." Nonetheless, a part of the total reality is contained in those pictures. In the following chapters, we shall see how other perspectives differ by emphasizing interests and change, the dynamic processes of individual behavior, and the "close-up" view of social interactions.

[171]See Chapter III.
[172]In Coser, *The Idea of Social Structure*, p. 73.

III

CONFLICT THEORY

INTRODUCTION: THE TWO TRADITIONS

Conflict theory is the major alternative to functionalism as an approach to analyzing the general structure of societies; and it is increasingly popular and important in modern sociology. It is also a less unified perspective than the others discussed in this book, and the disagreements among its proponents are often more bitter than those they have with theorists who use other approaches. However, conflict theorists of all types share a number of important assumptions and preconceptions. Together these create a distinctive way of looking at the world.

Functionalists, as we have seen, look at societies and social institutions as systems in which all the parts depend on each other and work together to create equilibrium. They do not deny the existence of conflict; but they believe society develops ways to control it, and it is these that they analyze. Conflict theorists' perceptions of society could hardly be more different. Where functionalists see interdependence and unity in society, conflict theorists see an arena in which groups fight for power, and the "control" of conflict simply means that one group is able, temporarily, to suppress its rivals. Functionalists see civil law, for example, as a way of increasing social integration, whereas conflict theorists see civil law as a way of defining and upholding a particular order that benefits some groups at the expense of others.

We can see how very different a view of things this perspective creates if we go back to the example we used in introducing functionalism—a modern airport. A functionalist perspective points out the way the different parts of an airport work together to keep the system functioning. Conflict theory is interested in the rivalries among different workers and management and in the position each group is in to do well for itself. A conflict theorist might point out that the air controllers want more staff and additional expensive equipment; that the pilots are continually trying to restrict entry into the profession in order to keep salaries high; that the porters, maintenance staff, and cleaners all belong to militant unions; and that all these groups are at odds with the airlines and terminal management, who want to keep costs down and profits up. The focus is on the shifting balance of power among competing groups, not on the equilibrium of interdependence and cooperation.[1]

This general "conflict" orientation incorporates three central and connected assumptions. The first is that people have a number of basic "inter-

---

[1]The contrast between equilibrium and conflict analyses of society is very old. One of the major modern theorists we discuss later, Ralf Dahrendorf, builds one of his expositions of conflict theory around the figure of Thrasymachus, a famous Greek sophist who appears in the work of Plato as a "conflict theorist" attacking the "equilibrium theory" that Plato puts in the mouth of Socrates. Ralf Dahrendorf, "In Praise of Thrasymachus," in *Essays on the Theory of Society* (Stanford, Calif.: Stanford University Press, 1968).

ests," things they want and attempt to acquire and which are not defined by societies but rather common to them all. Conflict theorists are not always explicit about this view of mankind, but it is present in all their work.

Second, and central to the whole conflict perspective, is an emphasis on power as the core of social relationships. Conflict theorists always view power not only as scarce and unequally divided—and therefore a source of conflict—but also as essentially coercive. This analysis leads, in turn, to a concern with the distribution of those resources that give people more or less power. For example, any conflict theorist would consider what happened to the American Indians to have been inevitable. The white settlers had greater numbers, greater wealth, and more advanced weapons; therefore, they were bound, such a theorist would argue, to seize lands and mineral wealth and give little in return. What is surprising, from a conflict perspective, is not that the settlers' religion and political beliefs did not stop them, but that the Indians were not simply exterminated.

The third distinctive aspect of conflict theory is that values and ideas are seen as weapons used by different groups to advance their own ends rather than as means of defining a whole society's identity and goals. We shall find that conflict theorists have a great deal to say about ideas as an aspect of groups' interests, especially under the categories of "ideology" and "legitimacy." In the case of America's treatment of the Indians, for example, conflict theorists would tend to interpret the notion of America's "manifest destiny" and the idea of "civilizing" the tribes as clear examples of how people develop ideas that suit their own interests.

The Two Traditions

The basic elements of conflict theory which we have described are common to all its proponents, but conflict theory can also be divided into two quite dissimilar traditions. These differ, above all, in their view of social science and in whether they believe that conflict can ever be eradicated. This chapter will discuss each separately.

The first group of theorists believes the social scientist to have a moral obligation to engage in a critique of society. It refuses to separate—or to admit that one can really separate—analysis from judgment or fact from value. Theorists in this group also generally believe that in principle a society could exist in which there were no longer grounds for social conflict. Therefore, these theorists are frequently considered utopian writers. The second group, by contrast, considers conflict to be an inevitable and permanent aspect of social life; it also rejects the idea that social science's conclusions are necessarily value-laden. Instead, its proponents are interested in establishing a social science with the same canon of objectivity as informs the natural sciences.

Theorists in the first group, where we will discuss modern Marxism and neo-Marxism, Habermas and his Frankfurt School forerunners, and C. Wright Mills, are most influenced by the work of Karl Marx. In the second group, where we describe the work of Ralf Dahrendorf, Lewis Coser, and Randall Collins, Marx's influence is still apparent, but the most important continuities are with the writings of Max Weber. We therefore turn now to a discussion of the roots of modern conflict theory in the work of these two classical thinkers, as well as to the influence of such writers as Veblen, Schumpeter, Simmel, the European élite theorists, and the American sociologists of the Chicago School.

INTELLECTUAL ROOTS

Power, Position, and Legitimacy: Marx and Weber

The basic elements of conflict theory were set out by two of the greatest early sociologists, Karl Marx and Max Weber. Much of Weber's work incorporates a debate with Marx and Marxist analysis, but in both these authors we find the same two concerns: first, with the way social positions bestow more or less power on their incumbents; and second, with the role of ideas in creating or undermining the legitimacy of a social position.

Karl Marx (1818–1883)   Conflict theory in sociology is the creation of Karl Marx. Indeed, Marxism and conflict theory are sometimes discussed as though the two were synonymous. There can also be no better example than Marxism of the close connection between a theorist's ideas and the events of the "real world"; for it is in the name of Marx's ideas that revolutionaries around the world attack existing forms of society and that organized Communist parties have ruled a large part of mankind.

Karl Marx was born in 1818 in Trier, Germany. His parents were Jews who had converted to Protestantism to avoid discrimination and loss of civil rights, and in particular, to protect his father's law practice. Marx also began to study law. However, at the University of Berlin he became fascinated by the philosophy of Hegel, who interpreted the whole of history as the process by which "Spirit" (and consequently humanity) progressed toward complete self-knowledge and a "rational" and "free" society. Marx became a Young Hegelian, one of a group of young philosophers who questioned many parts of the master's teachings while remaining beholden to his approach. Indeed, in later years, Marx came to see his own writings as upending Hegel's, replacing Hegel's emphasis on mind as the crucial determinant of history with his own "materialist" philosophy, which demonstrated that material factors determined events. He also became an antireligious radical, and after completing his thesis he worked as a writer and publicist in Paris and Belgium. During this period he wrote *The Communist*

Manifesto, which sets out a program for a revolutionary government and outlines his theory of social structures and social change. When the revolution of 1848 broke out in Germany, he returned to edit a radical newspaper. After the revolution failed, he went into exile again and settled in London, his home for the rest of his life.

During much of this period, Marx and his family were extremely poor; help from his friend Friedrich Engels, a socialist textile manufacturer, was vital. Nonetheless, his theories became increasingly well known and influential, especially outside England. He was consulted more and more frequently by Russian and German radicals and revolutionaries, and since his death, Communist parties have developed all over the world. Their dogma consists of the analyses of Marx and of Lenin, who led the first successful Communist revolution.

Because Marx's work is still used by so many writers in their analyses of contemporary society, we discuss it in additional detail later in the chapter. Of course, the ideas of many other long-dead writers are essential to contemporary analyses, but Marx's work is rather different. Marxist sociologists form a school whose analyses take place *within* the framework Marx created. In this sense, therefore, Marxism is an entirely contemporary theory.

The basic elements of conflict theory are all apparent in Marx's work. He believed, first of all, that people have an essential nature and predefined interests. Indeed, Marxists generally argue that if people do not behave in accordance with these interests it can only mean that they have been deceived about what their "true interests" are by a social system that works in others' favor. Second, Marx analyzed both historical and contemporary society in terms of conflicts between different social groups with different interests. Finally, he emphasized the link between the nature of ideas or "ideologies" and the interests of those who develop them, and he insisted that the ideas of an age reflect the interests of the "ruling class."

Marx emphasized the primacy of technology and of patterns of property ownership in determining the nature of people's lives and the course of social conflict. Whereas Marxist and, to a lesser degree, other "critical" conflict theorists retain this emphasis, other analysts from Weber on have seen it as an important, but only partial, explanation. Marx's work is also distinguished by its claim to predict the future and its belief in the possibility of a perfect, conflict-free, communist society. Such beliefs are accepted partly or in full by the more "critical" or "utopian" theorists, while being rejected by the analytic conflict theorists who draw on Weber. The divide between the two approaches thus derives from the central differences between Marx and Weber themselves.

Max Weber (1864–1920)   Max Weber was born into a prominent bourgeois German family. His father was an important member of the National

Liberal Party, with a seat in the Reichstag (Parliament); his mother came from a wealthy but also intensely religious and cultured background. There was considerable tension in his parents' marriage. As a youth, Weber tended to identify with his father. However, during his post-student years, when he was still financially dependent and living at home, he came to resent the older man and his authoritarian behavior. These conflicts played an important part in the complete breakdown Weber suffered in his early thirties.

Before and after this period, Weber was enormously productive, both in his intellectual work and in political activities. He held chairs at the universities of Freiburg and Heidelberg and produced a range of works on topics which included economic policy, political development, the social psychology of industrial work, the sociology of religion, economic history, and the methodology of social science. At the same time, he played an important role in Christian-Social political circles, producing papers on current issues. During this period his home was a center of German intellectual life.

The last years of Weber's life were also those of the First World War, of German defeat, of revolution and virtual civil war at home, and of the establishment of a German Republic. During this period Weber was intensely involved in politics. After initially supporting the war, he later urged peace overtures and called for widespread changes in the German political structure. He was a founding member of the Deutsche Demokratische Partei and was involved in writing the new constitution. But he also called the abortive 1918 revolution a "bloody carnival," something the left wing never forgave and which doomed proposals to have him join the government or become a candidate for President of the Republic.

For all his lifelong concern with the relationship between politics and intellectual thought, Weber had none of the utopian prophet about him. Like Marx, Weber wanted to identify the origins and essential characteristics of "modern" society, but he did not see modernization as the road to perfection. On the contrary: modern rationality could be an "iron cage," creating a narrow "disenchanted" world of bureaucratic officialdom.

Weber's analyses are complex and difficult to categorize, and they have had none of Marx's impact on the world. Nonetheless, a very large proportion of non-Marxist intellectuals would nominate him as the greatest of sociologists, and his ideas are the single most important influence on "analytic" conflict theory.[2] He is also of great importance to some of the

---

[2]Weber also, like Marx, continues to arouse considerable passion. Raymond Aron describes a Heidelberg conference to celebrate the centenary of Weber's birth. Emotions ran very high, and Herbert Marcuse, one of the critical sociologists we discuss later, attacked with fury the long-dead Weber's hostility to and disbelief in socialist utopianism. Raymond Aron, *Main Currents in Sociological Thought* 2 (Harmondsworth, Middlesex: Penguin Books, 1970), pp. 252–56.

younger sociologists in the "critical" tradition, most especially Jürgen Habermas. As we discuss below, much of Habermas' work on modernity and rationalization needs to be read as an ongoing debate with Max Weber.

Like Marx, Weber saw people's activities as largely self-interested. However, he believed that a historian or sociologist must recognize, in addition to such universal interests as the acquisition of wealth, the importance of goals and values specific to a society. For example, he suggested that the Calvinists' desire to save their souls found expression in the unique goal of simply accumulating wealth. This was seen as evidence of God's favor, whereas actually enjoying its fruits would be sinful indulgence.[3]

Weber analyzed the way people maneuver in pursuit of advantage in terms of both particular values and circumstances and more general sociological categories. He formulated *ideal types* by abstracting from different historical contexts the *essential elements of a general concept*. Real-life examples need not correspond exactly to the stylized ideal type: for example, it may be impossible to find any examples of bureaucracy which correspond in every particular to Weber's model of it. However, an ideal type is very important in making historical and contemporary events intelligible. For example, Weber argues that an essential element of modern bureaucracies is that they are organized around written documents ("the files") and around fixed rules which define precisely what officials can and cannot do. American and Soviet bureaucracies may differ in certain ways because of general differences between the two countries. But insofar as both are examples of the ideal bureaucratic type, we can see that they will also be alike in crucial ways, including how they deal with the public.

Weber was very concerned with power and with the ways in which some people secure domination over others. He distinguishes between unlegitimated domination and legitimated domination, which has *authority*, and he claims that certain people have the *right* to be obeyed. He suggests that there are three main foundations for successful claims to authority—or three "ideal types."

Charismatic authority rests on a leader's personal qualities, so that "the governed submit because of their belief in the extraordinary quality of the specific *person*. . . . The legitimacy of charismatic rule thus rests upon the belief in magical powers, revelations and hero worship."[4] Thus, Jesus' disciples followed him because of what he was, not because of some position which he held.

Traditional authority is also personal, but it is enjoyed because it has been handed down from the past. A king or a tribal chief may not person-

---

[3]Weber distinguishes among different types of social action, not all of which are "rational" and calculating in the sense implied here. See Chapter V for a discussion of Weber's ideas on the connection between action and meaning.

[4]*From Max Weber: Essays in Sociology*, edited and with an introduction by H. H. Gerth and C. Wright Mills (London: Routledge & Kegan Paul Ltd., 1970), pp. 295–96.

ally be very capable or effective, but he enjoys authority legitimated by custom. Weber argues that in general "patriachalism is by far the most important type of domination the legitimacy of which rests upon tradition. Patriachalism means the authority of the father, the husband, the senior of the house; . . . the rule of the master and patron . . . of the lord over the domestic servants and household officials . . . of the patrimonial lord and sovereign prince. . . ."[5]

Finally, *rational-legal authority* is derived from formal rules. Thus, modern bureaucrats are obeyed because and insofar as statutes empower them to do certain things and because our societies accept statutory law as the ultimate source of authority. According to Weber, the anchoring of legitimacy in particular sorts of rules is central to modern society's ongoing "rationalization" of everything.

Weber did not disagree with Marx's view that economic interests often underlie people's behavior, even when not acknowledged. However, he believed Marx to be wrong in identifying economic characteristics as the *sole* crucial determinant of both social structure and people's chances in life. Someone's religion, education, or political faction may, he argued, be as important a source of power and success. Instead of relying on Marx's category of class, Weber distinguished among classes, status groups, and parties, all of which could be more or less important for people's lives and serve as foci of group organization and conflict.[6] By a *class,* he meant people who shared the same position in economic life, whether this involved property, as in Marx's definition, or marketable skills. A *party* he defined as an association that exists to "secure power within a corporate group for its leaders in order to attain ideal or material advantages for its active members."[7] Examples include political parties seeking power in the modern state but also the factions that fought for control of Rome or the Italian city-states. Finally, *"status groups,"* as Weber's term Stände is generally translated, are groups whose distinctiveness lies not in their shared economic position but either in their shared mode of life—often founded on a common education—or in the prestige attached to their birth and family, as in the case of a hereditary aristocracy.[8]

Weber's argument has had great influence on modern "analytic" theorists who, like him, believe that economic factors are not always the major determinants of people's lives and power. His influence is also apparent in these theorists' discussion of the relationship between ideas and power. It is important to emphasize that, unlike Marx, Weber believed ideas and values

---

[5]Ibid., p. 296.

[6]Weber, *The Theory of Social and Economic Organization,* trans. A. M. Henderson and Talcott Parsons (New York: The Free Press, 1964), pp. 407–12, 424–29.

[7]Ibid., p. 407.

[8]Ibid., pp. 407–12 and 424–29. The medieval division of society into "estates" according to someone's degree of birth would correspond to Weber's idea of *Stände.*

to have an important, independent effect on history (as in the case of Calvinism and Confucianism) and did not consider them to be *simply* reflections of underlying interests. At the same time, he was aware of the role they could play in strengthening the position of a social group or a given social order. He emphasized, in particular, the importance of "legitimacy," the belief that someone's position and the system incorporating it are right and proper. This concept recurs in and influences much of modern conflict analysis.

Power, Position, and Legitimacy: Twentieth-century Theorists

Although the major elements of conflict theory were set out by Marx and Weber, a number of other theorists developed comparable ideas that have also had a significant impact on modern analysts. The most important are the élite theorists (namely Pareto, Mosca, and Michels), Thorstein Veblen, and Joseph Schumpeter.

Élite Theory   The most prominent élite theorists are Weber's contemporary, Vilfredo Pareto (1848–1923); Pareto's great rival, Gaetano Mosca (1858–1941); and Weber's friend, Robert Michels (1876–1936). Although in no sense did they form a school, they shared a number of important ideas.[9]

Their central argument was that only a small number of people in any organization can hold authority and that their occupation of these positions automatically places them at odds with those subjected to it. Moreover, these theorists contended, the élites who are in control generally share a common culture, and they are organized—not necessarily formally, but in the sense that they act together to defend their position, as well as using it to their own individual advantage. In other words, élite theory presents explicitly the argument that people's self-interest and the intrinsically unequal nature of power make conflict both inevitable and permanent.

Michels' main concern was with the so-called "iron law of oligarchy," the proposition that small groups in authority come to run political parties essentially for their own ends. Mosca was primarily concerned with the conflict between holders of political power and those they dominate. Indeed, Mosca upended Marx, identifying political positions as the source of domination in all other spheres, including the economic. Pareto, on the other hand, recognized the existence of other nonpolitical élites; but he emphasized the "governing élites" who rule a society, and the existence of

---

[9]Vilfredo Pareto, *The Treatise on General Sociology* (New York: Dover, 1963); Robert Michels, *Political Parties: A Sociological Study of Oligarchical Tendencies of Modern Democracy*, trans. Eden and Cedar Paul (New York: The Free Press, 1949); Gaetano Mosca, *The Ruling Class* (New York: McGraw-Hill, 1960). In the case of Pareto, whose influence on Parsons we have noted, the theory of élites comprised only a small part of his work.

ruling and subject classes who face each other like alien nations. The modern analytic theorists, especially Dahrendorf, have been most influenced by the élite theorists' insistence on authority and the state as dominant sources of power. Their general image of society as divided horizontally into an élite and a mass is also apparent in C. Wright Mills' social critique.

Thorstein Veblen (1857–1929)   Veblen's major importance for modern conflict theory lies in the fact that he was one of the very few early American sociologists to analyze the roots of power and conflict in a broad historical context. Early American sociologists were essentially empiricist and pragmatic in style, and only of America could it be said that here "sociology is practiced without socialism."[10] Instead, they tended to be reformers, like the highly influential Lester Ward, who approached "social problems" with a faith in government policies and gradualist reforms.[11] Veblen, by contrast, analyzed society in terms of the conflicting interests of different social groups, and he also denounced passionately much of the existing order. Among modern theorists, C. Wright Mills both continued this tradition and drew directly on Veblen in his discussion of status struggles.

Veblen, like Marx, believed that modern society is characterized by the conflict between opposing "economic" groups. In his case they are the "industrial" class, who actually make goods, and the "pecuniary" class, who are involved in finance and sales and whom he characterized as parasites living off the innovation and productiveness of the rest of the population.[12] Veblen was also interested in the constants of human nature that underlie social behavior. He argued that people desire passionately the esteem of others and that esteem is essentially a competitive affair, since for everyone to enjoy high status is a contradiction in terms. A very large part of people's behavior, Veblen argued, especially styles of consumption and leisure, can be explained by the struggle for high standing in the eyes of one's neighbors.

Joseph Schumpeter (1883–1950)   Of the generation that followed Weber, it was the Austrian Joseph Schumpeter who most clearly developed Weber's interest in how a group's success is rooted in its social position and in the importance of legitimacy. He also developed Marx's ideas about *changes* in the distribution of power and with them the process of human history. Schumpeter argued that "classes"—a term he used loosely to describe more or less organized and distinctive social groups—achieve power because they

---

[10]A. Salomon, *The Tyranny of Progress* (New York: Noonday Press, 1955), p. 22. As so often, the United Kingdom stood midway between America and the rest of Europe: more openly ideological than America, less so than the European mainland.

[11]"Radicals" of the period, such as E. A. Ross, often found it very difficult to make a career on American campuses.

[12]Thorstein Veblen, *The Theory of the Leisure Class* (New York: Modern Library, 1934).

command skills that are either new and innovative or that (because of changing circumstances) are far more important than they were in the past.[13] Their position can then be used to obtain further wealth and privilege, dispose of older groups, and protect themselves from competition.

Ultimately, however, because they fail to continue providing valued services and because new innovatory groups rise up, powerful classes are replaced by others. The new classes attack the old successfully and deny the legitimacy of their position. Thus, late-twentieth-century America contains large numbers of people whose occupations simply did not exist a short time ago. The success of, for example, the "computer jockeys" and the industries of Silicon Valley has created major shifts in the economic—and political—power of various states. In the United Kingdom the work force in traditional industries employing manual workers has shrunk enormously. The Labour Party finds it harder to win a general election for this reason. It simply has fewer "reliable" manual workers' votes than in the past.

Two of Schumpeter's own most interesting examples are the rise of imperialist warrior groups and the decline of the capitalist bourgeoisie. He argues that the medieval feudal aristocracy developed from warrior groups. They attained power in a society where war was continual, where people consequently sought armed protection, and where fighting skill had to be acquired and maintained over a lifetime.[14] As this situation changed with the rise of the modern state, modern arms, and the conscript army, the aristocracy's position declined. At present, Schumpeter argues, the capitalist class, which ascended because of its economic achievements, is in decline in its turn. Technological innovation has become institutionalized, and independent entrepreneurs are less important. Meanwhile, a new class of intellectuals, with its own group attitudes and group interests has arisen, undermining the legitimacy of the old order and creating for itself a new power base in the increasingly important government bureaucracies.[15]

Schumpeter had no belief in a conflict-free utopia, and he tended to regret the passing of capitalist society rather than use his work as a vehicle for criticism and advocacy of change. However, just as he acknowledged his great debt to Marx, so his own work has influenced "critical" modern theorists, as well as those who, like him, believe in an objective, analytic sociology. In particular, the influence of his ideas about capitalism's loss of legitimacy is apparent in the work of Jürgen Habermas, the most important active theorist in the tradition of the Frankfurt School.

---

[13]Joseph Schumpeter, *Imperialism and Social Classes* (Cleveland: Meridian Books, 1955).

[14]Ibid. The history of ancient Egypt is similar, Schumpeter suggests. The repulsion of the invading Hyksos created a new warrior class that then, under the "New" Empire, wrested power from the independent landlords of the "Old" and "Middle" periods.

[15]Joseph Schumpeter, *Capitalism, Socialism and Democracy* (London: Unwin University Books, 1943), pp. 131–55, Schumpeter's central argument is that current social trends and conflicts will lead in the end to some form of socialism.

The Web of Conflict:
Simmel and the Chicago School

In addition to the central tradition of conflict analysis, which we have just described, there exists a rather different approach to the study of conflict. It emphasizes the abstract qualities of a social order, rather than the origins and progress of actual conflicts, and is exemplified by the writings of Georg Simmel and the Chicago School.

Georg Simmel (1858–1918)   Among the great early sociologists, Simmel was the most interested in identifying universal patterns in human behavior. Whereas Marx and Weber wanted to understand what made a particular society operate, Simmel concentrated on developing what is almost a mathematics of society: a collection of statements about human relationships and social behavior that apply irrespective of the historical setting. He has influenced a whole range of modern theorists who are similarly interested in interpersonal relationships, including some conflict theorists, symbolic interactionists, exchange theorists, structuralists, and network analysts.[16]

Simmel's sensitivity to how human relationships form and change was related to his own background and his feelings of insecurity and rootlessness. He was born in Berlin, the youngest child of a Jewish businessman who had converted to Christianity. His father died when Simmel was still a child, and the boy was never close to his mother. He studied history and philosophy at the University of Berlin, and stayed on there as a "Privatdozent," an unpaid lecturer dependent on student fees. His lectures were enormously popular, and he published widely. Among his friends were many of the foremost academics and writers of the time, including Weber. Yet although he applied constantly for senior positions in German universities, he was constantly turned down, partly because of anti-Semitism and partly because he refused, in his work, to stay within a single academic discipline. It was only in 1914, at the age of fifty-six, that he was appointed finally to a chair at the University of Strasbourg.

The most important part of Simmel's analysis for later conflict theory is his insistence that association and conflict between individuals and social groups not only can exist side by side, but indeed are intimately related. One cannot divide people neatly into self-contained groups, with common interests which are different from those of people in other, self-contained, antagonistic groups. Marx's image is of a society divided horizontally into antagonistic blocks; Simmel's is of a society integrated by numerous crosscutting conflicts, in which those who stand together in one respect are opposed in another.

[16]See pp. 150, 177, 237, 336.

Simmel's insistence that "social action always involves harmony *and* conflict, love *and* hatred"[17] did more than reinforce the tendency of "analytic" conflict theorists to consider conflict a permanent condition. It also altered them to the way varying degrees of social contact and interdependence affect the nature of conflict. For example, Lewis Coser's discussion of how conflict can actually stabilize a society is based directly on Simmel's writing.

Robert Park and the Chicago School   An emphasis on conflict as a general and abstract principle of social life has been more typical of American than of European sociology. Robert Park (1864–1944), whose only formal training was in Simmel's courses in Berlin, built up the "Chicago School of Sociology," which is renowned for research into the social life and culture of the city.[18] He also developed a system of general concepts that described what were, for him, the central characteristics of social life. They consisted of competition, conflict, accommodation, and assimilation into a common culture.[19] Park argued that competition, which is universal and continuous among individuals, determines individual careers. Conflict arises rather over status and over the way super-ordination—power—is allocated socially. Conflict may thus involve groups as well as individuals. Park and his colleagues were more interested in analyzing racial antagonisms and conflict among different ethnic groups than the class struggles stressed by Marx and other Europeans, whose own societies were much more racially and culturally homogeneous. Once again, the influence of this rather different tradition is especially apparent in the work of Lewis Coser, one of the most important of American conflict theorists.

Summary

The most important historical influences on modern conflict theory are the writings of Karl Marx and Max Weber, and modern theorists can be divided into two groups according to who is the dominant influence upon them. A number of other sociologists who share the same general conflict perspective have also influenced modern theory; and American sociology, in particular, has been influenced by a different tradition of "conflict analysis" deriving from Simmel.

---

[17]Lewis A. Coser, *Masters of Sociological Thought: Ideas in Historical and Social Context* (New York: Harcourt Brace Jovanovich, 1971), pp. 184–85.

[18]This demonstrates an emphasis on understanding people's definitions of their own situation similar to the approach developed by symbolic interactionism, which is discussed in Chapter V.

[19]Robert E. Park and Ernest W. Burgess, *Introduction to the Study of Society* (Chicago: The University of Chicago Press, 1921).

PART ONE
Conflict Theory and the Critique of Society

This section covers the conflict theory of Marx and modern Marxist sociologists, of Habermas and the Frankfurt School analysts, and of C. Wright Mills. All the writers in this group are distinguished by their view of social science, their image of society as divided hierarchically into exclusive groups, and their belief in the possibility of an ideal social order. In general, we refer to them as "critical" theorists because they all use social science to criticize society, in particular, the "ruling class," the "power élite," or what is often called the "establishment." However, "critical theory" is also used more narrowly to refer to the work of the Frankfurt School.

Critical conflict theorists believe that social analysts should not separate their work from their moral commitments, and they see their theories as a force for change and progress. They also believe that objectivity is more or less impossible. For them social science is inextricably bound up with the particular views of a writer, which are in turn a function of his or her society, and fact is consequently inextricable from value. In other words, they reject the usual scientific view that whatever writers' own values or motives in writing may be, their theories stand or fall by whether independent factual evidence supports them. At the same time, "critical" conflict theorists feel sure that their own values and standards are the right ones, and therefore constitute a justified basis for social critique.

The particular focus of their critique is the way wealth, status, and power are distributed in society. Theorists of this type generally see society as divided rather clearly between a small group of powerful and privileged people and an exploited or manipulated mass. They are also inclined to use a "unicausal" theory of social structure and to see people's circumstances as primarily determined by one set of institutions, most often property. At the same time, they do not believe that society need be highly segmented and unequal. They contrast the societies they analyze with a better order of things and often compare the "irrational" present, in which human development is stunted, with an ideal and "rational" state of affairs, in which human potential will be fulfilled. This vision of a society based on values which they presume to be absolutely valid, as well as their concept of "real" human nature, are the starting points for their criticisms of actual societies.

In all of this, Marx is the dominant influence. The argument that ideas are a product of social circumstances *and for that reason not objectively correct* is his. Moreover, although he believed that his own theory was not open to the charge of being an "ideology," Marx also regarded his work as a form of political and moral action—an expression of the ideas that would guide the proletariat to inevitable victory. Marxists use the term *praxis* to describe actions informed in this way by theoretical considerations and, more precisely, revolutionary consciousness. In addition, Marx presented a two-class model of society, divided between oppressors and oppressed on the basis of property, and looked forward to the communist utopia in which humanity would realize its essential nature.

For the most part, conflict theory of this type has developed in Europe, particularly western Europe. In countries under one-party Communist rule, Marxism or Marxism-Leninism has been treated as essentially a state religion and not open to critical analysis and development. Philosophers, sociologists, and political theorists, such as Leszek Kolakowski, who engaged in such analysis, frequently have been forced into exile.[20] On the other hand, in western Europe intellectuals have continued to be greatly influenced by Marx. Although the organized Communist parties have themselves produced some important Marxist theorists, such as Antonio Gramsci in Italy, they too insist on doctrinal orthodoxy; and the major source of modern critical conflict theory is Marxist intellectuals outside the party hierarchies.

In America there was a strong Marxist and Communist element in intellectual life during the 1930s and 1940s. Nevertheless, although a number of sociologists and economists (such as Norman Birnbaum and Paul Sweezy) continued to use Marxist categories, Marxist analysis had little direct impact on American sociology in the twenty years immediately after the Second World War. During this period, the only widely known and influential "critical" sociologist was C. Wright Mills, who was heavily influenced by Marx but not in any clear sense a Marxist. During the Vietnam period, however, many younger American sociologists were involved with the New Left and were heavily influenced by various radical writers, but quite specifically by Marx. Consequently, the "critical sociology" of the Frankfurt tradition and other Marxist and neo-Marxist writings are becoming increasingly known and influential in American sociology. Marxian journals have been founded specifically devoted to this approach.[21]

---

[20]Kolakowski, one of the most eminent of modern European political philosophers, was expelled from the Communist Party in 1966 and dismissed from his chair of philosophy at Warsaw University in 1968. He was accused of corrupting youth by his reexamination of Marxist tenets. He is now a Fellow of All Souls' College, Oxford.

[21]In 1982 the *American Journal of Sociology* acknowledged this by publishing a Supplement devoted entirely to Marxist analyses. Its editors are, as they note, part of that "cohort of sociologists that has been most influenced by Marxist perspectives"—that cohort, in other words, then in its mid-thirties and now in its forties, that was in college in the mid to late 1960s. Michael Burawoy and Theda Skocpol eds., *Marxist Inquiries: Studies of Labor, Class and States*, Supplement to Vol. 88 of the *American Journal of Sociology*. More generally, the journal *Theory and Society* provides a forum for Marxist analysis.

MARXIST AND NEO-MARXIST SOCIOLOGY

This section discusses in some detail Marx's own analyses, as well as those of later Marxist scholars. As we noted above, Marxism remains an entirely contemporary theory because so many sociologists work *within* it, and we therefore present it as an integrated perspective. We describe Marx's theory of the economic basis of social organization, the classes and class conflict that arise around economic interests, and the importance of ideology in both maintaining and undermining a social order. We also consider Marx's comprehensive theory of social evolution and his prophecy of the ideal classless and stateless society to come; and we look at how some modern theorists[22] incorporate political and cultural factors into Marixst class analysis.[23]

The Economic Basis of Society

The distinguishing mark of Marxist analysis is that it identifies economic factors as the fundamental determinant of social structure and change. Other spheres of social life and the ideas and values that people hold are seen as shaped by and dependent on the nature of economic production. In Schumpeter's analogy, they play the role of "transmission belts," through which the social forces and group interests created by economic arrangements emerge into social life.[24]

Marx distinguished between three aspects of social organization. They are, first, the "material forces of production," or the actual methods by which people produce their livings; second, the "relations of production" that arise out of them and that include property relations and rights; and third, the "legal and political" superstructures and the ideas, or "forms of social consciousness," that correspond to the first two. He argued that in production, "men enter into definite . . . relations of production [which] correspond to a definite stage of development of their material productive forces. The sum total of these relations of production constitutes the economic structure of society, the real foundation. . . . The mode of produc-

---

[22]A common distinction is between more or less orthodox "Marxist" and those "Marxian" scholars who depend largely on Marx's categories and perspectives but whose theories diverge substantially from his.

[23]The books that have most influenced our interpretation of Marx are Joseph Schumpeter, *Ten Great Economists: From Marx to Keynes* (London: George Allen & Unwin Ltd., 1952); John Plamenatz, *Man and Society* (London: Longmans, 1963); George Lichtheim, *Marxism* (London: Routledge and Kegan Paul, 1961); Robert C. Tucker, *Philosophy and Myth in Karl Marx* (Cambridge: Cambridge University Press, 1964); Shlomo Avineri, *The Social and Political Thought of Karl Marx* (Cambridge: Cambridge University Press, 1970); Leszek Kolakowski, *Main Currents of Marxism* (Oxford: Oxford University Press, 1981); and Anthony Giddens, *A Contemporary Critique of Historical Materialism*, Vol. I (London: Macmillan, 1981) and Vol. II (Cambridge: Polity Press, 1985)

[24]Schumpeter, *Ten Great Economists*, p. 12.

tion of material life conditions the social, political, and intellectual life-process in general."[25]

In other words, in Marx's view, the actual mode of production is the basic causal factor that ultimately determines how societies are organized. In this sense his is a "materialist" theory of history, whereby "in changing their mode of production . . . [men] change all their social relations. The hand-mill gives you society with the feudal lord; the steam-mill society with the industrial capitalist."[26] At the same time, however, both the mode and the relations of production—the technology *and* the form of economic organization—are the *substructure* that defines both the nature of a particular society and its *superstructure* of law, government, and ideas.

In practice, both Marx and later Marxist writers tend to pay more attention to the effects of economic organization than of the mode of production alone. Indeed, this is a far more plausible approach. There was little difference in technology between, for example, the Roman Empire and medieval Europe, yet their social structures were very different. These differences were, moreover, often clearly related to differences in economic organization, such as Rome's use of numerous slaves and feudalism's system of serfdom.[27]

However, if one admits that economic organization rather than technology is the primary determinant of social structure, one also undermines, to a considerable degree, Marx's claim that a single principle "unlocks" the workings of society. If different forms of economic organization can coexist with a given technology, then these forms must result, at least partly, from other, noneconomic factors—the ideas and legal principles that Marxism relegates to the "superstructure," for example, or the principles of military organization, which Marxists generally ignore. Thus, many historians would argue that the different forms of economic organization in Rome and feudal Europe (and the wide-ranging differences in their social structure) can themselves only be understood in terms of their different legal codes and systems and their different military organization. A society with a centralized standing army is obviously different from one in which fighting is the task of feudal lords who owe service to the king but who are "paid" with grants of land—of which they are virtually independent rulers. And in that case, Marx's "economic theory of history" becomes, as its critics would argue, an insight of genius into the role of economic factors but not an all-embracing explanation.

---

[25]Karl Marx, Preface to *A Contribution to the Critique of Political Economy*, in *Karl Marx and Frederick Engels, Selected Works*, Vol. I (London: Lawrence and Wishart, 1962), p. 362.

[26]Marx, *The Poverty of Philosophy* (Moscow: Foreign Language Publishing House, n.d.), p. 122.

[27]See Marc Bloch, *Feudal Society*, trans. L. A. Manyon (Chicago: University of Chicago Press, 1962), for a discussion of the major differences between serfdom and slavery.

Class and the Economic Base of Conflict

Marx argued that all forms of economic organization that had existed at the time he wrote inevitably generated conflict between social classes, which were defined by their common economic position. *The Communist Manifesto* opens with a now-famous declaration: "The history of all hitherto existing society is the history of class struggles."[28] This statement embodies three important but separate propositions. The first is that people whose economic position, or "class," is the same also tend to act together as a group. The second is that economic classes are the most important groups to be found in society; their history is the history of human society. The third is that these classes are mutually antagonistic, and the outcome of their conflicts defines how society develops. Marx's theory of class is thus not simply a theory of social structure; it is also a theory of change.

Property and Class   Although we have been describing the Marxist concept of class as "economic," Marx actually used a more specific and restrictive definition. A class is made up of people who are alike in their relationship to property: they have none, or they have the same type.[29] Ultimately, the sort of work people do is not what matters. Thus, manual workers, clerks, technicians, and engineers belong to the same class because they own and are paid for their labor. They belong to a different class from capitalists and landlords, who own the instruments of production; from serfs, who only partly own their own labor because they are bound to a given lord and cannot go to work for someone else; and from slaves, who own no property at all.

If you look around a university campus, you will find the only "factor of production" most people there own is their labor. In Marxist terms they therefore belong to the same class: the proletariat. This will certainly be true of most of the students and also of a good number of the faculty, who work for a salary and who, although they probably own their homes, do not own any "means of production." On the other hand, some faculty and some students probably own a fair number of shares of stock; some mature students may also be running businesses; and, especially if the campus is M.I.T., some of the faculty are likely to be founders and owners of high-technology industries, which are offshoots of their work. Because they own property of this type, all the people in the second group belong to another,

---

[28]Karl Marx and Friedrich Engels, *The Communist Manifesto* (Harmondsworth, Middlesex: Penguin Books, 1967), p. 79.

[29]Marx distinguishes between a class "in itself" and a self-conscious (or "class-conscious") class "for itself." See p. 94. For discussions of what creates class-consciousness or group mobilization see also Dahrendorf's work (pp. 144–45), and the work of rational choice theorists (pp. 223–33).

different class of "capitalists." Marx, we should note, does not differentiate between shareholders, who simply provide capital, and entrepreneurs.[30]

Marxist theory argues that different classes inevitably have incompatible interests, because under systems of property-ownership, if one class makes economic gains, it must be at the expense of another. According to Marx, each of the major economic systems that existed in the past strengthened one particular class, which could then *exploit* others. He wrote that "Freeman and slave, patrician and plebeian, lord and serf, guild-master and journeyman, in a word, oppressor and oppressed, stood in constant opposition to one another, carried on an uninterrupted, now hidden, now open fight,"[31] and that "An oppressed class is the vital condition for every society founded on the antagonism of classes."[32] In bourgeois society, capitalists are the oppresssors, and the proletariat the oppressed.

In explaining what Marx meant by this, we must reiterate that Marx's general theory is the work of an analytical economist. His theory of exploitation is based on an economic theory of value,[33] and it is important to note that in its essentials, his was the value theory of the "classical" economist Ricardo. Nowadays, the "labor theory of value" is seen as a distinguishing aspect of Marxism, because it is only Marxist economists who continue to hold it. However, in Marx's own time it was standard theory.

Marx states that the *value* of a commodity is equal to the quantity of labor that went directly into making it. In a market economy, workers selling their labor will get for it the price of the labor that went into "making" them—that is, the cost of rearing, feeding, clothing, and housing them. However, what each of them produces at work will very likely amount to considerably more than this, and this "surplus value" will go not to them but to the capitalist. In Marx's theory, any surplus value appropriated by someone other than the worker is by definition exploitation, because only labor produces value. All systems of property therefore involve a basic conflict of interest because one group expropriates the product of another's labor.[34]

[30]Marx tends to assume that people will belong clearly to one class or another. If this is not the case, then it is also a great deal less likely that a well-defined "class conflict" will develop.

[31]Marx and Engels, *The Communist Manifesto*, p. 79.

[32]Marx, *The Poverty of Philosophy*, p. 196.

[33]For good critical discussions of Marxist economics, see Joseph Schumpeter, *History of Economic Analysis* (London: George Allen and Unwin Ltd., 1954), and Paul Samuelson, *Collected Scientific Papers*, ed. J. Stiglitz (Cambridge, Mass.: M.I.T. Press, 1966 and 1972). A good modern Marxist economic analysis is Paul M. Sweezy, *The Theory of Capitalist Development* (New York: Modern Reader Paperbacks, 1968).

[34]Marx's analysis is rejected by modern neoclassical economics, which explicitly separates judgments of how prices "ought" to be determined from descriptions of how they actually are, and so avoids discussions of what the "real" or "just" price of, say, a diamond may be. Modern economics argues that price is related to the "marginal cost" of producing goods, not to the sum of the "cost" of labor and "surplus value." It also argues that providing capital

Modern Marxist and Marxian sociologists retain Marx's emphasis on property relationships. Norman Birnbaum, for example, uses Marxist categories to analyze the United States. He attacks the argument that property ownership is no longer a crucial determinant of power and opportunity and that a meritocratic education system decides people's success. Birnbaum argues that educational success and "access to some of the more privileged educational institutions" are a function of family background. The "technocratic élite" is thus far from being a new group with interests and objectives quite separate from those of "capitalists."[35] Rather, Birnbaum contends, it operates modern organizations in the interests of "property" and is backed by government, with which it has a symbiotic relationship.

Class Conflict   Marx argued that at any one time, it is class struggle that defines the essential character of a society. It is the product of, first, the irreconcilable differences in interest between classes and, second, the fact that a class's common interests will encourage its members to group together for common action. However, at any given time, the degree to which members of a class recognize their interests will depend on their level of *class consciousness*. The dominant ideas of any era may stand in the way of their recognizing their class identity, but so too may the circumstances of their lives. The French peasants of the nineteenth century, for example, did not "form a class" in the active sense, according to Marx, because "there is merely a local interconnection among these small-holding peasants, and the identity of their interests begets no community, no national bond, and no political organization among them."[36] It is the task of the Marxist to encourage people—specifically the members of the exploited proletariat—to recognize and act upon their interests and to encourage and accelerate change and revolution, as well as understand its roots. Thus, one of the foremost young American Marxist sociologists recently argued that "class interests in capitalist society are ... potential objectives." They are "hypotheses about the objectives of struggles which

---

for production involves genuine costs for which people must be recompensed. For example, if you put money in the stock market or a bank savings account, thus enabling companies to borrow, invest, and expand, you thereby deny yourself the enjoyment of the things you could have bought. Your recompense for this cost is the interest or dividends you receive. Modern neoclassical economists argue that people are paid for saving because providing capital (and so foregoing consumption) involves genuine costs.

[35]Norman Birnbaum, *The Crisis of Industrial Society* (New York: Oxford University Press, 1969), p. 13. See also the work of Harry Braverman, e.g., *Labor and Monopoly Capital: The Degradation of Work in the Twentieth Century* (New York: Monthly Review Press, 1974), and Michael Burawoy, *Manufacturing Consent: Changes in the Labor Process Under Monopoly Capitalism* (Chicago: University of Chicago Press 1979).

[36]Karl Marx "The Eighteenth Brumaire of Louis Bonaparte," in *Karl Marx and Frederick Engels, Selected Works*, Volume I (London: Lawrence and Wishart, 1962), p. 334.

would occur if the actors in the struggle had a scientifically correct under-standing of their situations."[37]

What Marx provides here is a powerful theory of how groups form in society. However, critics have queried the degree to which members of a property class do always have common interests or tend to act in unison. For example, innovations are favored by those who introduce them, and feared by all those involved with established firms, whether as owners, employees, or union officials. Government policy often benefits one part of an industry at another's expense, for example, by limiting imports of cheap foreign coal or oil and so increasing energy costs. In America, Northern businessmen wishing to relocate to small Southern towns are often opposed by local employers, who fear the impact of higher wages and benefits, and welcomed by prospective workers for the same reasons.

Again, Marxists tend to see any change in an industry's job structure which increases the numbers of different jobs, productivity bonuses, etc., as a conscious effort to undermine solidarity and conceal workers' "fundamental" interests (in organized struggle) behind their "immediate," individual interests.[38] It is certainly true that a more diverse job structure in which pay is linked to individual effort is likely to create a less unified, or uniformly militant work force, as seems to be happening, for just these reasons, with the British miners. Non-Marxist conflict theorists, however, would not tend to discriminate between real and immediate interests. They would rather be inclined to say that individuals' situations have changed and so, there-fore, has the action which they perceive to be in their best interests. In consequence, the sorts of groups likely to take joint action have also altered.

Class and Patriarchy   Marxist theory has always seen women as op-pressed by capitalist society and the "bourgeois family." Marx and Engels argue that "the bourgeois sees in his wife a mere instrument of produc-tion."[39] In *The Origin of the Family*, Engels argues that, with the move from a subsistence economy to one "with inherited property," the man took control in the home, and the woman was degraded and reduced to servitude.[40] Wives are, he argues, worse off than ordinary prostitutes, for they sell their bodies once and for all into slavery.

[37]Erik Olin Wright, *Class, Crisis and the State* (London: New Left Books, 1978), p. 89. Marxists differ in how far they emphasize individual action and purpose. The "structuralist" Louis Althusser argues that "if we take seriously what Marx tells us about the real dialectic of history, it is not "men" who make history . . . but the masses in the relations of class struggle." Louis Althusser, *Politics and History* (London: New Left Books, 1977), p. 168.

[38]Katherine Stone, "The Origins of Job Structures in the Steel Industry," *Review of Radical Political Economics*, 6, no. 2 (Summer 1974), 113–73.

[39]Marx and Engels, *The Communist Manifesto*, pp. 77–78

[40]Frederick Engels, *The Origin of the Family, Private Property and the State* (New York: Penguin Books, 1972), trans. Alick West, p. 87. This was written by Engels using notes left by Marx before his death.

Although Marx and Engels took it for granted that there had always been a division of labor between men and women, they treat the family as strictly part of the superstructure, determined by the relations of production. The bourgeois family is a product of property; therefore, it will vanish with the vanishing of capital, and with it will vanish women's oppression. Women will be brought back into "public industry," and love will be the basis of relations between the sexes.

Marxist feminists find this analysis inadequate. Women's oppression is not, they argue, simply equivalent to the oppression of the proletariat by the bourgeoisie, for "domestic slaves are not exploited in the same way as wage slaves. They would have to be paid a wage for this to be true."[41] Instead, women's position has to be understood in terms of male supremacy as well as—and in combination with—capitalism.

Zillah Eisenstein defines *patriarchy* as the "male hierarchical ordering of society" and argues that it is rooted in biology rather than economics or history.[42] Patriarchal culture exerts control through the "sexual division of labor. . . . It designates the fact that roles, purposes, activity, one's labor, are determined separately."[43] As such it predates—and outlives—capitalism, but the two are nonetheless mutually reinforcing. Thus, "patriarchy . . . provides the sexual hierarchical ordering of society for political control . . . while capitalism as an economic class system . . . feeds off the patriarchal ordering."[44]

Marxist feminists argue that women stabilize the patriarchal structure of the family through their domestic work and child care. Patriarchal ideology defines women as nonworkers; hence they are either not paid at all (for domestic work) or can be hired at a lower wage than men because of their defined sexual inferiority. "The sexual division of labor and society remains intact even with women in the paid economy. Ideology adjusts to this by defining women as working mothers. And the two jobs get done for less than the price of one."[45]

Capitalism has intensified the sexual division of labor by separating the home from the place of work. It creates two distinctive kinds of work—wage labor and domestic labor—which is why, according to Marxist feminists, Marx's original analysis is inadequate. "The housewife emerged, alongside the proletariat—the two characteristic laborers of developed capi-

---

[41]Zillah Eisenstein, "Developing a Theory of Capitalist Patriarchy and Socialist Feminism," in Zillah Eisenstein ed., *Capitalist Patriarchy and the Case for Socialist Feminism* (New York: Monthly Review Press, 1979), p. 23. See also Lise Vogel, *Marxism and the Oppression of Women: Toward a Unitary Theory* (New Brunswick, N.J.: Rutgers University Press, 1983).

[42]Eisenstein, *Capitalist Patriarchy*, p. 17.

[43]Ibid., p. 17.

[44]Ibid., p. 28.

[45]Ibid., p. 29.

talist society."[46] Hence, abolishing capitalism and the bourgeois ruling class is not, in itself, an adequate solution to women's oppression. At the same time, insofar as the "traditional" family profits the bourgeoisie as a class, socialism is a necessary precondition to realizing woman's potential.

Culture, Ideology, and Alienation

Marx emphasized that feelings and opinions about people in power are of major importance: especially whether their position is viewed as right or whether people feel exploited and oppressed. He thus identified one of the major topics of conflict theory.[47] Marx's own discussion of the role of ideas in establishing control follows from his argument that the legal, political, and cultural superstructure is ultimately a reflection of underlying economic relationships. He argued that people in a class society believe a large number of things that are not correct but are rather a form of "ideology" whose main purpose is to legitimize the position of those currently in control. Such ideology stands in the way of other people realizing what their "real" interests are, so that, Marxists argue, they suffer from *false consciousness*. To Marx, religion was an excellent example of this process, an "opium of the masses" that muted discontent by focusing attention on a supposedly better world to come.

It is this part of Marx's thought which inspired his and his followers' criticisms of "objective" social reporting and analysis as imbued with the authors' prejudices. However, Marx did not—unlike later theorists such as the symbolic interactionists—reject the possibility of quantitative research as such, since he was sure that his own viewpoint was scientifically correct. Thus, in order to obtain adequate information on working class conditions, he drew up a long questionnaire which was distributed through workers' societies and groups in France. Questions ranged from "Is your work done by hand or with the aid of machinery?" to "Do you know any instances in which the Government has intervened to protect the workers against the exactions of the employers and their illegal combinations?"[48]

This questionnaire, devised at the very end of Marx's working life, is concerned entirely with the "outward" conditions of work. However, Marx also believed that class society was evil because, besides fostering exploita-

---

[46]Eli Zaretsky, "Capitalism, The Family and Personal Life," *Socialist Revolution,* 14 (1973), 114. Cited by Eisenstein, op. cit.

[47]As his description of the French peasantry shows, Marx did not believe that only "ideology" affected people's class consciousness. His remarks here anticipate many of the factors discussed by "analytic" conflict theorists interested in the way change actually occurs. See pp.167–72.

[48]Results were never published. Apparently very few workers were able or willing to work through its 101 items. The questionnaire (the Enquete Ouvrière) is reprinted in *Karl Marx: Selected Writings in Sociology and Social Philosophy,* ed. T. B. Bottomore and Maximilien Rubel (Harmondsworth: Penguin Books, 1961), pp. 210–18.

tion and false consciousness, the whole nature of its economic life created *alienation*. Marx felt that man has an essential nature, which he believed to be realized through creative work. (This notion is, we may note, quite different from Durkheim's, who felt that mankind needed limits and fixed norms. Durkheim was also concerned at the consequences of modern industrial society for human development; but his concept of *anomie*, or normlessness, appeals greatly to functionalists.[49]) For Marx, the division of labor, the institution of private property, and the whole "cash nexus" of commercial relationships alienate man not only from what he produces and the act of producing it, but also from both himself and his fellows. He views them in terms of the narrow standards of the work place, rather than as full "species-beings."[50] Consequently the abolition of property, and its attendant class relationships, would also end this alienation.

This part of Marx's thought has been given increasing attention in recent decades, and its influence is apparent far beyond strictly "Marxist" writings. Criticisms of the soullessness of modern work, or the actions of people opting for a self-supporting and/or communal life, all belong to the same broad strand of thought as Marx's early writing on alienation. It should be emphasized, however, that Marx did not share the romantic view that the country was inherently superior to the town, and the Industrial Revolution a catastrophe. On the contrary—capitalism and the wealth it produced were the necessary preconditions for the communist utopia.

Although Marx regarded culture and ideology as simply a reflection of the underlying economic substructure, contemporary sociologists generally see the "superstructure" as important in its own right. Many neo-Marxists, especially in Europe, believe that cultural factors play an independent role in maintaining class inequalities—and potentially in creating revolutionary change.[51]

Culture and Reproduction   The most influential work in this area is that of Pierre Bourdieu (b. 1930). Director of the Centre for European Sociology in Paris and a professor at the École des Hautes Études, Bourdieu is very much a "man of the left" whose work is imbued with Marxist concepts. However, he also believes strongly in the independent role of cultural and educational factors.[52]

[49]See Chapter II.

[50]By "man" Marx, in all his work, means the human species in the collective sense. World history is about the self-realization of generic man, of which the individual is a microcosm. See Tucker, *Philosophy and Myth*, pp. 129–30.

[51]Cf., the work of Gramsci. American left-wingers of the 1960s also saw students as a revolutionary vanguard. See Samuel Bowles and Herbert Gintis, *Schooling in Capitalist America: Educational Reform and the Contradictions of Economic Life* (New York: Basic Books, 1976).

[52]See, especially, Pierre Bourdieu and Jean-Claude Passeron, *The Inheritors: French Students and Their Relation to Culture*, trans. R. Nice (Chicago: University of Chicago Press, 1979) (published in France as *Les Héritiers*, 1964).

Bourdieu argues that parents provide children with a sort of cultural "capital" which makes them either more or less advantaged in educational terms. Those from privileged homes have the attitudes and knowledge—especially cultural knowledge—which make the education system a comfortable, familiar sort of place in which they can succeed easily. The "formal equality" of competitive examinations encourages people to believe that they succeed—or fail—by their own individual merit. Hence, upper-middle-class students have no trouble in reconciling left-wing views with their own privileged position. In fact, though, their position is the result of students' social origins taking effect through "more secret channels."[53] The education system can "ensure the perpetuation of privilege by the mere operation of its own internal logic."[54]

Bourdieu's theory is one of class *reproduction*—of how one generation of an (economic) class ensures that it "reproduces" itself and passes on its privileges to the next generation. Renaud Sainsaulieu, for example, describes reproduction theory as illuminating the "latent ideological functioning of the educational apparatus which, despite its overtly democratic recruitment and the formalization of its rules, carries out in fact a social selection based on the cultural criteria of the dominant class."[55]

Bourdieu argues that what is necessary for educational success is a whole set of "cultured" behavior. It is this which carries you confidently through higher education, job interviews, boardrooms, and the like. The children of middle- and upper-class families have this behavior; their working-class peers do not. Consequently, the former are able to succeed within the educational system, and their families can reproduce their class position from generation to generation in a legitimate and apparently "fair" way.

In his more recent work, Bourdieu elaborates his analysis using the concept of *habitus*. Habitus can be defined as "a system of durably acquired schemes of perception, thought and action, engendered by objective conditions, but tending to persist even after an alteration of those conditions."[56] Bourdieu sees the habitus as the key to reproduction because it is what actually generates the regular, repeated practices which make up social

[53]Ibid., p. 68.

[54]Ibid., p. 27.

[55]Renaud Sainsaulieu, "On Reproduction," *Revue Francaise de Sociologie*, 13, no. 3 (1972), 339–412; reprinted in Charles C. Lemert, ed., *French Sociology: Rupture and Renewal Since 1968*, trans. P. Lemert (New York: Columbia University Press, 1981), p. 153.

[56]The definition is Richard Nice's given on p. 156 of the English edition of *The Inheritors* with reference to Bourdieu's updating "Epilogue." For Bourdieu's full explanation of the term, see P. Bourdieu, *Outline of a Theory of Practice*, trans. R. Nice (Cambridge: Cambridge University Press, 1977). There are overlaps here with the individual actors' orientations defined by Parsons' "pattern variables," as well as Mead's discussion of meaning, but there are also crucial differences in conception. A habitus generates coherent actions and behaviors which are specific to a particular group or class and rooted in the latter's particular economic conditions. It is not universal (like Parsons' pattern variables) nor specific for an individual.

life[57] and because it is linked to the class structure. So-called personal style, "the particular stamp marking all the products of the same habitus, whether practices or works, is never more than a *deviation* in relation to the *style* of a period or class."[58]

In *The Inheritors* Bourdieu and his coauthor argue that a major reason for the rapid growth in higher education is that

> those fractions of the dominant class and middle class who are richest in economic capital (i.e., industrial and commercial employees, craftsmen and tradesmen) have had to make greatly increased use of the educational system in order to ensure their social reproduction. When class fractions who previously made little use of the school system enter the race for academic qualifications, the effect is to force the groups whose reproduction was mainly or exclusively achieved through education to step up their investments so as to maintain the relative scarcity of their qualifications and, consequently, their position in the class structure. . . . [This] generates a general and continuous growth in the demand for education and an inflation of academic qualifications.[59]

In other words, changes in the economic substructure have repercussions for education *because* is the mechanism for reproducing class advantage. Moreover, education is such a potent and effective mechanism precisely because it does not simply involve learning technical skills or acquiring knowledge. There has to be the accompanying general "culture." According to reproduction theory, whenever there is a big increase in the numbers holding a qualification, the major losers are those who do not have the "social capital to extract the full yield" from it.[60]

As noted above, Bourdieu differs from Marx in emphasizing that institutions of the superstructure can have relative autonomy—and increasingly so. In the past, changes in the mode of production led to changes in the relations of production more quickly, he argues, but today "the education system *depends less directly on the demands of the production system than on the demands of reproducing the family group.*"[61] The producers would actually like more control over the education system than they possess. Currently, a qualification gives its holder relative freedom and autonomy; the producers would like the technical skills without this. The education system is an

---

[57]Cf., the work of Anthony Giddens, who also relates social structure to repeated interpersonal activities. See Chapter VII.

[58]Bourdieu, *Outline of a Theory of Practice*, p. 86.

[59]Bourdieu and Passeron, *The Inheritors*, pp. 77–78.

[60]Ibid., p. 90.

[61]Pierre Bourdieu and Luc Boltanski, "The Education System and the Economy: Titles and Jobs," trans. R. Nice, in C. Lemert, *Rupture and Renewal*, pp. 141–51. Bourdieu's analysis has strong parallels with Randall Collins' analyses of the "gatekeeping" role of education. See below pp. 161–63.

object of political struggle between the sellers and buyers of labor power. The latter want their education to be as generally applicable as possible, and they seek a high return on their educational capital. The former want to buy educated labor cheaply and have an interest in suppressing the autonomy of the education system.[62]

Bourdieu's emphasis on the role of cultural "capital" may seem exaggerated to readers outside France. However, the French education system is highly centralized and competitive. Almost all members of the élite went not only to university but also to one of the Grandes Écoles—small, selective, autonomous institutions specializing in, for example, engineering or preparation for a government career. For a period in the late 1980s both the French prime minister and the leader of the parliamentary opposition were graduates of the same class of the same selective institution. This is not something that would surprise anyone in France. The cultural processes which Bourdieu emphasizes thus are likely to be more important and more visible in France than in, for example, the United States, with its more open education system. They may nonetheless exist in the United States as well.

Even in France, however, there is empirical evidence that suggests that Bourdieu's argument may be overstated. His own data show that, even in the arts faculties, class reproduction is only partial: many students are, in fact, from relatively less privileged homes. In addition, analysis of French survey data by Robinson and Garnier[63] suggests that education has not, in fact, become more important in "reproducing" ownership of businesses. Fathers who are (large or small) owners of business do not "convert" their capital into educational capital as a way of securing their sons' position. Conversely, education *can*, very strongly, assist sons of nonsupervisory workers to move up to supervisory positions. The authors also note how different women's life paths are from men's and conclude that if women perpetuate their class position, it is not generally through education.[64] Overall, it would seem, Bourdieu overstates his case for class reproduction, while being quite correct about the independent influence that educational institutions can wield.

---

[62]A contrasting view is present by Bowles and Gintis in *Schooling in Capitalist America*. The authors adopt a more conventionally Marxist perspective, arguing that, as part of the superstructure, education reflects capitalist industry's requirements for hierarchically organized labor and for employees who obey rules and their "superiors."

[63]Robert V. Robinson and Maurice A. Garnier, "Class Reproduction Among Men and Women in France: Reproduction Theory on Its Own Ground," *American Journal of Sociology*, 91, no. 2 (1985), 250–80

[64]This may be a misleading conclusion. The survey looked at women's current occupation and related it to their family of origin. However, in France, as elsewhere, women's jobs are often of lower status than either their education or their husband's job would suggest. Conversely, women still acquire status through their husbands, and education may be crucial as a way of meeting a potential husband and/or becoming a "suitable" wife for a high-status male.

Evolution and the Classless Society

Marx's social theory is essentially a theory of change and evolution, which looks back over the whole of history, forward to the future, and claims to explain and understand both. A given economic system has within it, Marx argued, the seeds of change: its own logic and the way it works necessarily produce its successor.

Marxists describe this process in terms of a given order's "contradictions," which develop over time until the whole system becomes unworkable and there is a violent, revolutionary shift to another order altogether, the "negation" of the previous one. This view of development and change as a pattern of inner conflict is known as *dialectical*.[65] Like many other elements in his theory, including alienation, Marx's idea of the dialectic is a reworking of a Hegelian concept. However, Hegel was interested in the development of self-awareness and "Spirit." Marx's concern was the evolution of human society through economic stages.

Marx identified four major types of class society, each with its "primary classes"—Asiatic, ancient, feudal, and bourgeois. The Asiatic mode is based on state-controlled irrigation and a system of royal despotism and ownership of all land; but Marx treats only the last three in detail as part of Western history. In each case, change involves the appearance of new classes. The barbarian military chieftains who overran the Roman empire replaced ancient society with a society of feudal overlords and serfs; in turn they were replaced by the capitalist bourgeoisie, the adversaries of the proletariat. The next stage, however, would be different, Marx prophesied, for the contradictions inherent in capitalism would usher in an ideal communist society, in which property and classes were abolished and alienation replaced by self-realization. In dialectical terms, communist society would "emerge phoenix-like from the ashes of capitalist society."[66]

The End of Capitalism   Marx argued that over time many smaller capitalists, along with the other distinctive groups of previous eras—small shopkeepers, peasants, handicraftsmen—would be swallowed up into the

---

[65]It is often expressed in terms of a "thesis" and its opposite, or "antithesis," producing a new "synthesis," thus:

$$\text{thesis}$$
$$\downarrow$$
$$\text{(tension)} \longrightarrow \text{synthesis}$$
$$\uparrow$$
$$\text{antithesis}$$

See Avineri, *The Social and Political Thought of Karl Marx*, p. 171. We have described the dialectic in a way we consider faithful to Marx's own use. However, we should note that it is also used in a more complicated and philosophical sense by a number of writers influenced by the Marxist philosopher George Lukács to discuss the relationships between human consciousness and historical reality.

[66]Ibid., p. 182.

proletariat, their skills obsolete or their capital too small for them to compete. Only two ever more strongly differentiated classes would remain. At the same time, capitalists would produce more and more, on the backs of the exploited work force, without the market expanding correspondingly. Competition would then force the capitalists to cut prices and wages, and the rate of profit would decline toward zero. The outcome would be misery for the masses—but also revolt and the end of capitalism.

Thus, Marx argues, "along with the constantly diminishing number of the magnates of capital, who usurp and monopolize . . . grows the mass of misery, oppression, slavery, degradation, exploitation; but with this too grows the revolt of the working-class, a class always increasing in numbers, and disciplined, united, organized. . . . The knell of capitalist private property sounds. The expropriators are expropriated."[67]

Marx's forecasts clearly have not been borne out. There has been neither increasing misery in the West nor a steady decline in the rate of profit. Moreover, although production is more "concentrated," ownership is not, and shareholders are more and more often trade unions or pension funds. Marxist analysts, however, have been at pains to show that the survival of capitalism is temporary.[68]

Lenin's theory of imperialism is the most influential such argument. In his great work *Capital,* Marx remarks that capitalist countries use their colonies as providers of raw materials, captive markets for their products, and treasure-grounds to loot.[69] From these remarks, Lenin developed a Marxist theory of imperialism. He argued that advanced capitalism's need for ever-expanding markets and profitable investment opportunities would dicate a foreign policy of imperialism and of destructive wars among individual rivals for colonial possessions.[70] Imperialism would, temporarily, stave off the time when profits vanished and capitalism disappeared.

These ideas are pervasive in the arguments both of Third World politicians and intellectuals who argue that the West exploited and exploits their countries, and of Western critics of their own governments. A good example is the work of Régis Debray, a French Marxist who spent a period with the South American guerillas led by Che Guevara, Castro's friend and associate, and who hit world headlines when he was arrested and imprisoned. Debray argues that the regimes of South America are an arm of the

[67]Karl Marx, *Capital,* Vol. I, trans. Samuel Moore and Edward Aveling, ed. F. Engels (London: Lawrence and Wishart, 1961), Chapter XXXII (Historical Tendency of Capitalist Accumulation), pp. 762–63.

[68]Serge Mallet, *La Nouvelle Classe Ouvrière,* 4th ed. (Paris: Editions du Seuil, 1969), suggests that class consciousness will increase in automated enterprises, because workers will develop a calculated awareness of their joint interests.

[69]Marx, *Capital,* Vol. I, Chapter XXXIII (The Modern Theory of Colonisation).

[70]Vladimir I. Lenin, *Imperialism: The Highest Stage of Capitalism* (New York: International Publishers, 1939).

ruling class and that under them there is taking place the "polarization of exploited and exploiters." Meanwhile, North American imperialism "has increased its forces in the field" under the guise of assistance—missionaries, Peace Corps volunteers, technical projects, sociological research, and the like. "In a word, all these close-knit networks of control strengthen the national machinery of domination."[71]

Critics argue, however, that although governments often have acted in pursuit of the economic interests of home investors, the Marxist theory of imperialism is inadequate and frequently wrong. They charge that it fails to account for the frequently "imperialist" policies of noncapitalist countries; for the fact that imperialism was characteristic of the early days of capitalism, before falling profits should have threatened; and for the fact that capitalist countries often do not act according to economic interest. Britain, for example, staged a complete military withdrawal from the oil-producing Persian Gulf states on which her industry depended.

Closely related to these ideas about imperialism is *dependency theory*, which has developed a view of the world as divided into *core* and *periphery*.[72] Like Marx and Lenin, dependency theorists analyze events as part of a particular historic process: the global expansion of capitalism. The core is industrially advanced and develops as a result of its own internal dynamics. In the dependent countries of the periphery, by contrast, what happens depends on the demands and requirements of the core.

These ideas have been developed furthest by Immanuel Wallerstein in his work on the "Modern World-System." He argues that what exists under capitalism is, for the first time, a truly global system held together by economic, not political or military, ties.[73] The growth of the modern capitalist world economy was made possible by the geographical expansion of the core countries of Western Europe. The explorations and conquests of the sixteenth century were followed by economic domination.

According to Wallerstein, different parts of the world-system specialize, or have different "functions." Thus, the periphery supplies raw materials for the enterprises of the core.[74] This difference is mirrored in the way labor is controlled in different areas. "Free labor is the form of labor control used for skilled work in core countries whereas coerced labor is used

---

[71]Régis Debray, *Revolution in the Revolution?* trans. B. Ortiz (Harmondsworth, Middlesex: Penguin Books, 1968), pp. 26, 52. Debray is now an adviser to President Mitterand of France. See also Irving M. Zeitlin, *Capitalism and Imperialism: An Introduction to Neo-Marxian Concepts* (Chicago: Markham Publishing Co., 1972).

[72]See especially André Gunder Frank, *Dependent Accumulation and Underdevelopment* (London: Macmillan Press Ltd., 1978).

[73]In the past there were world *empires*, such as that of Rome, but they were held together militarily, not economically.

[74]Wallerstein also talks of the "semi periphery," halfway between exploiter and exploited.

for less skilled work in peripheral areas. The combination thereof is the essence of capitalism."[75]

Wallerstein also argues that core areas developed strong states, and peripheral areas weak ones. In the early development of capitalism, states were important in providing social stability through their growing bureaucracies and monopoly of force. However, the capitalist world-system is one of *economic* integration, and it is through economic mechanisms that the core controls the periphery.

However, critics query whether underdeveloped countries were or are exploited in the sense of being impoverished by capitalist production. They point out that nineteenth-century America was a major recipient of foreign investments, as are today's fastest-growing countries[76] and that some of the richest countries in the "core"—such as Australia—are predominantly exporters of raw materials. More generally, Wallerstein's work has been criticized for "economic determinism," or underemphasizing the importance of political organization and other noneconomic factors.

Among these critics, Theda Skocpol and Anthony Giddens are notable because they draw on Marxist theory themselves to provide analyses of historical developments worldwide. In her own work on social revolutions, Skocpol argues that the ability of *states* to cope with both internal problems and the international system is of central importance. Because Wallerstein sees differences between states as simply reflections of economic conditions, he cannot explain satisfactorily either the origins of capitalism or the very different histories of different nations which supposedly share a core position.[77]

Giddens praises Wallerstein for emphasizing that in capitalism we have a truly global phenomenon, integrated economically; but he also urges recognition of "specifically political and military factors."[78] We can

[75]Immanuel Wallerstein, *The Modern World-System I: Capitalist Agriculture and the Origins of the European World-Economy in the Sixteenth Century* (New York: Academic Press, 1974), p. 127. See also his *The Modern World-System II: Mercantilism and the Consolidation of the European World-Economy 1600–1750* (New York: Academic Press, 1980), and *The Modern World-System III: The Second Era of Great Expansion of the Capitalist Economy, 1730–1840,* (New York: Academic Press, 1988).

[76]For a more detailed presentation of the arguments, see Zeitlin, *Capitalism and Imperialism;* Irving Louis Horowitz, *Three Worlds of Development,* 2nd ed. (New York: Oxford University Press, 1972); P. T. Bauer, *Dissent on Development* (London: Weidenfeld and Nicolson, 1971) and *Equality, the Third World and Economic Delusion* (London: Weidenfeld and Nicolson, 1981); and Robert W. Tucker, *The Inequality of Nations* (New York: Basic Books, 1977). Of course, it does not follow that because Marx's specific predictions were inaccurate, he was also wrong about the inevitable disappearance of capitalism. Many analysts, including Joseph Schumpeter, have agreed that it will disappear—but not because of the falling rate of profit.

[77]Theda Skocpol, "Wallerstein's World Capitalist System: A Theoretical and Historical Critique," *American Journal of Sociology,* 82, no. 5 (1977), 1075–90 and *States and Social Revolutions* (Cambridge: Cambridge University Press, 1979).

[78]Anthony Giddens, *The Nation-State and Violence: Vol. II of a Contemporary Critique of Historical Materialism* (Cambridge, England: Polity Press, 1985), p. 168. Giddens also criticizes Wallerstein for functionalism, as when "the existence of semi-peripheral regions is explained by reference to the "needs" of the world system." Ibid., p. 167. Giddens' own theory is discussed in Chapter VII.

talk of a world capitalist economy, he argues, provided we remember that it is only one aspect of the world-system and that the "globally encompassing nation-state system" is equally important. Unlike traditional states, the modern nation-state is a "power-container" which has swept other forms of state organization before it. This is partly because industrialism, from the beginning, was harnessed to provide new weaponry and partly because of the vast expansion of such states' administrative power.[79] They, as much as capitalism, define the nature of our modern world.

Capitalism in America   American Marxists are, not surprisingly, especially interested in the survival of capitalism; class-based groupings are less evident in the United States than in any other Western industrial country, and the advent of socialism does not seem very likely in the near future. In this context, Erĭk Olin Wright's work is of special interest. It attempts to show, empirically, that analyzing American society in terms of classes (in Marx's sense) is indeed the most fruitful approach to take. In his *Class Structure and Income Determination*, Wright used detailed survey data to examine how well Marxist categories "explain" (that is, can be used to predict) income, compared to such common occupational categories as "upper white collar," "lower white collar," "lower blue collar," "farmers," or "service workers."[80]

Wright defines classes in terms of their members' control over money and physical capital and over others' labor. This produces the classic Marxist categories of the "bourgeoisie," who control capital and direct labor, and the "proletariat," who do neither. However, when Wright applies these categories to the modern work force, only about 1 to 2 percent of workers can be classified as "bourgeoisie," and almost half are seen as falling into "contradictory" class locations—that is, not quite one thing or another. The latter are:

1. managers and supervisors (30–35 percent of the workforce)
2. semiautonomous employees
3. small employers (with "minimal" control over labor)

With so few bourgeoisie, by his definition, in existence, the survey data did not actually provide Wright with enough cases for analysis.[81] In

[79]Ibid., pp. 170–72, 255–311 passim.

[80]Erik Olin Wright, *Class Structure and Income Determination* (New York: Academic Press, 1979). Data were collected by the Institute for Social Research at the University of Michigan. Wright drew most heavily on the *Panel Study of Income Dynamics* (nearly 6,000 households), the 1969 *Survey of Working Conditions* (1,500 adults), and the 1973 *Quality of Employment Survey* (basically a replication of the *Survey of Working Conditions*).

[81]The "bourgeoisie" control labor as well as investments and the physical means of production; the "petty bourgeoisie" control only the latter.

FIGURE 3-1   Erik Olin Wright's Analysis of American Class Structure. (Illustration by Luca Perrone; reproduced from Erik Olin Wright, *Class Structure and Income Determination* [New York: Academic Press, 1979], p. xxv.)

practice, therefore, he looked at five "classes"—small employers, managers, supervisors, workers, and petty bourgeoisie (self-employed with no employees). On that basis he found that class *did* affect income:

> People occupying different class positions but with the same level of education and occupational status, the same age and seniority on the job, the same general social background, and working the same number of hours per year, will still differ substantially in their expected incomes. And people in different class positions can expect to receive different amounts of additional income per increment in education credentials, even if they do not differ in a variety of other characteristics.[82]

Figure 3-1 summarizes, for Wright, what these findings imply about the workings of American society.[83]

However, class position actually accounts for only 20 percent of the

[82]Wright, *Class Structure,* p. 162.
[83]The drawing was contributed to *Class Structure* by Luca Perrone (p. xxv).

variation in people's incomes—no worse, but also no better, than the standard (though more complicated) census-based occupational codes. Moreover, as pointed out above, since Wright simply assumes that the bourgeoisie is important, it does not appear in his data at all; and he puts many people into "contradictory" categories that are not Marxist classes at all. Altogether, critics of Marxist analysis are no more convinced than before that "class" is the primary factor in the analysis of society. Wright, they would argue, merely shows what we already know—that your position in the labor market affects your income![84]

Erik Olin Wright also believes that there is a constant tendency, under capitalism, to "deskill" jobs—that is, reduce them to routine, which makes it easier to supervise and control workers. "Thus, capitalists look for innovations which tend to reduce skill levels and reduce the autonomy of workers on the job."[85] The combination of overeducated workers and deskilled jobs is seen as a potentially potent route to class consciousness. It will make workers who traditionally have seen themselves as "middle-class" realize that their interests lie with the organization of the whole "working class."

A recent article by Olin Wright and Singlemann uses census data to argue that the Marxist view is more accurate than the opposite and very common argument that the labor force has become less "proletarianized," more skilled, and autonomous.[86] Their case is that *within* given industrial sectors there was a clear increase in the proportion of "working-class" jobs, i.e., jobs in which workers have little freedom to decide how to do them. At the same time, the sectors which expanded most in terms of *overall numbers* of jobs were those with relatively more "semi-autonomous" jobs and relatively fewer "proletarian" ones. For the economy as a whole, these two shifts tended to cancel each other out. Nonetheless, the authors argue, "within given economic sectors, there was a systematic tendency for those positions with relatively little control over their labor processes to expand during the 1960s and for those positions with high levels of autonomy to decline."[87] Moreover, they predict that "the rest of the century is likely to be characterized by a continuing and perhaps intensifying process of proletarianization."[88]

---

[84] An analysis that emphasizes the importance of education in maintaining and legitimating capitalist society is offered in Bowles and Gintis, *Schooling in Capitalist America*.

[85] Wright, *Class, Crisis and the State*, p. 65.

[86] Erik Olin Wright and Joachim Singelmann, "Proletarianization in the Changing American Class Structure," in Burawoy and Skocpol, eds., *Marxist Inquiries*, pp. 176–209. The authors used survey data in which respondents answered questions about the nature of their jobs as a means of classifying census job categories as managerial, semi-autonomous, or proletarian.

[87] Ibid., p. 198

[88] Ibid., p. 202. Wright also argues that people's class origins are crucial in creating class consciousness and awareness of class interests. Erik Olin Wright and Kwang-Yeon Shin, "Temporality and Class Analysis: A Comparative Study of the Effects of Class Trajectory and Class Structure on Class Consciousness in Sweden and the United States," *Sociological Theory*, 6, no. 1 (1988), 58–84; Erik Olin Wright, *Classes* (London: Verso, 1985).

This analysis provides an interesting alternative to the general view that industrial countries' populations are increasingly middle-class. However, even if Wright and Singelmann turn out to be correct in their predictions, it is not obvious that increased "class consciousness" is the probable result. It depends very much on what people's expectations really are and how quickly they adjust them, as well as on how far the population at large shares Marx's view of creative work as central to self-fulfillment. Surveys by Val Burris[89] and Steven Vallas[90] produced no evidence that people who were "overeducated" for their jobs or worked in highly automated sectors move to left-wing positions, become generally alienated from politics, or acquire strong class consciousness. The only discernible effects were a slight decrease in job satisfaction among the most highly overeducated and some feeling that, as automation increases, so does the machines' control over the worker.

Class, Society, and the State

Marx's belief in classless society rested on his argument that property is the essential determinant of class interest. This implies that if everyone has exactly the same relationship to property, there can be no class divisions. If no one owns land or capital and there are no rents and profits or returns to capital to be paid, labor will get all of its "surplus value," and exploitation will end. In other words, abolishing property will end social conflict. Orthodox Communists share this view, and other Marxists and socialists believe that the abolition of private property will remove many of the systematic conflicts they perceive in social life. Non-Marxists, of course, disagree, as do many Marxian analysts who share Marx's belief in the primary importance of economic factors. They question whether the abolition of property necessarily abolishes systematic differences of interest among social groups. Their reason for doing so is the existence of the state and state power.[91]

State Power   Marx described the state as an instrument of class rule, and he saw political domination as a reflection and expression of conflict between classes. He therefore argued that, with the establishment of a classless society, the state too would be abolished, and instead of a coercive structure, there would remain only routine and uncontroversial administra-

[89]Val Burris, "The Social and Political Consequences of Overeducation," *American Sociological Review*, 48 (August 1983), 454–67.

[90]Steven Vallas, "White-Collar Proletarians? The Structure of Clerical Work and Levels of Class Consciousness," *Sociological Quarterly*, 28, no. 4 (1987), 523–40. We are indebted to Christine Dolan for this reference.

[91]The autonomous role of the state is also the main factor cited by theorists such as Skocpol and Giddens in their critiques of Marxist evolutionary and world-system theory. See above pp. 104–6.

tive tasks.[92] It is not at all obvious, however, that this is likely, as we can see from Marx's own description of the state apparatus.

When Marx discussed the role of the state, with its legal authority, bureaucracies, law enforcement agents, and armed forces, he actually advanced two propositions—although he nowhere recognized them as different. The first was that the state made class exploitation possible by providing stability under which one group was able to remain dominant.[93] The other was that the state was actually an instrument of class rule (in the sense of being an arm of the exploiting class), and its purpose was to advance the exploiting class's interests.[94] These views imply very different interpretations of the role of government officials. The first, unlike the second, implies that officials may be seen as a separate group with independent interests and not merely as part of the ruling class. In that case, it is a good deal less plausible to suppose that a coercive state apparatus, the distinction between state and society, and the potential for conflict over state control will disappear.

Marx envisaged communist society as one in which scarcity had vanished—as a result of the achievements of bourgeois capitalism, which in this respect he greatly admired. He also talked as though the abolition of property would also cause all important differences between people to disappear. Consequently, there would be a single social will; economic production would proceed on the basis of universal consent; and a separate, coercive state apparatus would no longer be required. His critics argue that a society without scarcity is nowhere apparent and that even if it were obtainable there is no reason to suppose that people would always agree, for example, on where factories should be sited or whether and for how long school should be compulsory. Moreover, if scarcity did remain and production was no longer the responsibility of private individuals, state power would be far more, not less, important. There would be fierce conflicts over who controlled the powers of the state.[95] The result, critics contend, would be more like Marx's "Asiatic mode" than his communist vision.

An essentially Marxist analysis of the self-interested use of power in socialist societies is offered by Milovan Djilas in *The New Class*.[96] Djilas, who was a friend of Tito's and vice-president of Yugoslavia, was expelled from

---

[92]This stage would be preceded, however, by a period of great state activity, the "dictatorship of the proletariat," in which communism would be implemented.

[93]A good example is Marx's account of "The Civil War in France," in Marx and Engels, *Selected Works*, Vol. I (see especially pp. 516–18).

[94]See, for example, Marx and Engels, *The Communist Manifesto*.

[95]A society without private property could be organized around "workers' control" of businesses instead of central government planning. However, there would then be conflicts of interest between successful enterprises, who wished to retain their earnings and expand, and unsuccessful ones, who would favor restraint on competition and income redistribution.

[96]Milovan Djilas, *The New Class: An Analysis of the Communist System* (New York: Frederich A. Praeger, Inc., 1957).

the Yugoslav Communist Party in 1954 and has served long prison sentences for his views. In *The New Class,* Djilas argues (following Marx) that classes are essentially based on the property they control. Abolishing private property, however, has not meant the abolition of classes. Instead, he contends, in communist countries it has created a new class, the political bureaucracy, which controls all property (since all property is the state's) and uses it to appropriate to itself power and privilege at the expense of the rest of the population:

> As in other owning classes, the proof that [the political bureaucracy] is a special class lies in its ownership and its special relations to other classes. In the same way, the class to which a member belongs is indicated by the material and other privileges which ownership brings to him.
>
> As defined by Roman law, property constitutes the use, enjoyment, and disposition of material goods. The Communist political bureaucracy uses, enjoys, and disposes of nationalized property. . . . In practice, the ownership privilege of the new class manifests itself as an exclusive right, as a party monopoly, for the political bureaucracy to distribute the national income, to set wages, direct economic development, and dispose of nationalized and other property. This is the way it appears to the ordinary man who considers the Communist functionary as being very rich and as a man who does not have to work.[97]

A Marxian analysis which develops Djilas' assessment further is that of Ivan Szelenyi, a Hungarian sociologist who was forced to emigrate when he would not renounce his views. He argues that, with the development of state-socialist economies in the post-Stalin era, a new dominating class developed.[98] This was rather broader than the political bureaucracy described by Djilas. It was the intelligentsia as a whole which grasped class power. In Eastern Europe, Szelenyi points out, people moved constantly between important "bureaucratic" and "intellectual" positions. Thus:

> The present director of one of the comedy theaters in Budapest is a former high-ranking officer of the political police. His former boss in the Hungarian equivalent of the KGB is today the manager of a big salami factory. Today one may be an officer in the political police, but tomorrow one might be the only person licensed to produce political jokes, or one might supervise salami production or sociological research, as a manager or an academic. The line between intellectuals and bureaucrats is a very shaky one in terms of personal career patterns. . . . [It] is practically impossible to distinguish between the

---

[97]Ibid., pp. 44–45.

[98]Ivan Szelenyi, "The Intelligentsia in the Class Structure of State-Socialist Societies," in Burawoy and Skocpol, *Marxist Inquiries,* pp. 287–326. See also George Konrad and Ivan Szelenyi, *The Intellectuals on the Road to Class Power* (New York: Harcourt Brace Jovanovich, 1979), which the authors wrote in secret, burying the manuscript in the garden of a peasant cottage to forestall police raids.

technobureaucracy and the intelligentsia. Their living standards are practically identical. It is the level of power which stratifies them.[99]

Szelenyi argues that state-socialism shows that Marx was wrong to believe that property ownership was the major determinant of power. He believes, at the same time, that a "historical materialist" perspective in the Marxian tradition remains valid. Marx, he argues,

> defined his classes on the basis of ownership relations because in a capitalist market economy it was the private ownership of the means of production which legitimated expropriation.[100]

In socialist countries, by contrast, it is not property ownership and the market which define income and the distribution of "the surplus"—defined by Marxists as the difference between what labor produces and what is needed to keep it alive. Instead, the state expropriates and allocates the surplus. "Contemporary state socialism might be characterized by the antagonism between redistributors and direct producers."[101] These "redistributors" use Marxist ideals to legitimate their seizure of power as creators of a "scientifically" planned economy.

Szelenyi (and, by implication, Djilas) are contrasting socialist countries with Western ones, where they see classes with different relationships to private property as still the major groupings. By contrast, conflict theorists in the Weberian tradition would tend to see their analyses as strengthening the case for discussing power and conflict in terms of several different categories—class being one, political power another. Thus, Djilas' major point can be applied generally to argue that government employees should be viewed as a distinctive group with their own interests and power base[102] and that there are conflicts of interest between those who do and do not benefit from increased government spending and activity.[103]

[99]Ibid., pp. 297–98 passim.

[100]Ibid., p. 300.

[101]Ibid., p. 301. In recent work, Szelenyi discusses the "countervailing power" of workers in bureaucratically organized work places and, particularly the relative independence which, in Hungary, derived from part-time family farming and private, after-hours work. Ivan Szelenyi, in collaboration with Robert Manchin, Pál Juhasz, Balint Magyar, and Bill Martin, *Socialist Entrepreneurs: Embourgoisement in Rural Hungary*, (Cambridge, England: Polity Press, 1988).

[102]See Alain Touraine, *The Self-Production of Society* (Chicago: University of Chicago Press, 1977), for a Marxian analysis that ascribes an independent role to state organizations.

[103]One can use this approach to explain why, for example, businessmen and doctors generally vote Republican or Conservative, whereas equally "middle-class" teachers and social workers tend to vote Democrat or Labour.

Marxist Analysis: An Assessment

Marx's most important contributions to social analysis in general derive from two sources: his emphasis on the way that people in the same economic position tend to group together for common action and his explanation of why and how societies differ in terms of the characteristics of the groups that are generated by their economic life. As Kolokowski has noted, "No reasonable person would deny that the doctrine of historical materialism has been a valuable addition to our intellectual equipment. . . . [I]f it has become a commonplace, this is largely thanks to Marx's originality."[104]

However, this insistence on the primacy of economics means that Marxist analysts have a tendency to use a "Catch-22" approach. They assume in advance that economic and business interests lie behind things, proceed to find them, and then offer their explanation as "proof" of the original proposition. But the fact that on any particular occasion, one can generally find businessmen and others seeking to advance their economic interests means neither that this is the "real" explanation of what is going on nor that those involved are necessarily acting in the interests of their class as a whole.

The American South offers a good example of both the strengths and the weaknesses of Marxist analysis. Because of its focus on property relationships, Marxism identifies the pre–Civil War slave-owning South as a distinctive social order based on the ownership of human beings. A great part of the written history of the South and the Civil War has tended to interpret the South as essentially agrarian and therefore threatened by industrialization—or as itself merely a variant of capitalism, based on the plantations. As Eugene Genovese, the leading Marxist historian of the South, argues, neither approach explains the antagonism between North and South or the Civil War. An agrarian hinterland can grow prosperous as a market for manufactured goods and a supplier of food, and competition between farmer and industrialist is hardly a common cause of war. Or if the South was basically capitalist, why could the two sides not reach an accommodation?[105]

However, once we see slavery as the essence of Southern society and not just one of its many characteristics, however morally repugnant, it is apparent that the South was fighting to preserve a distinctive world. Much about the politics of the South also becomes comprehensible when we see it as a defense of this slavery-based social structure against not only the blacks

---

[104]Kolakowski, *Main Currents of Marxism*, Vol. III, p. 524. He also argues that, as an explanatory system, Marxism is dead. Ibid., p. 528.

[105]Eugene D. Genovese, *The Political Economy of Slavery: Studies in the Economy and Society of the Slave South* (New York: Pantheon Books, 1965), and *The World the Slaveholders Made: Two Essays in Interpretation* (New York: Pantheon Books, 1969).

who suffered under it but also other potential social groups whose interests it did not serve. Thomas Sowell, for example, points out that forced labor is always extremely inefficient economically.[106] A Southern slave's labor was potentially worth much more to him than to his owner, since he would work far harder and more productively for himself than when forced and driven for someone else. Even without adding in the price he would pay just to be free, "Selling a slave to the highest bidder would mean selling him to himself"[107]—a practice that was very common among slave-owning profit-maximizing Romans. However, although this might profit individual slave owners and the slaves themselves, it would certainly have undermined a society whose defining core was plantation slavery and whose ethic was fundamentally anticapitalist. Thus, very severe legal restrictions developed on the freeing of slaves.

However, Marxist theory does not explain adequately why the white population of the South supported this order so whole-heartedly, even through the terrible rigors of the Civil War.[108] Most whites were not slaveowners, and the poorly functioning Southern economy did not serve their economic interests any more than it did those of nascent industrialists facing a meager home market. Their support, we would argue, can be explained fully by the fact that the racial character of Southern society gave every white an automatic claim to superior *status*, so that "the notion that all men were created equal contradicted the facts of daily experience for most Southerners."[109]

Class interests are an even less adequate explanation of the system of racial segregation that succeeded slavery, under which the old classes of slaves and slaveowners no longer existed. The system of segregation was clearly against the interests of industrialists, for it denied skills to a large section of their potential work force. Under segregation, white and black "proletarians" conspicuously failed to group together to further shared class interests. The system did, however, offer benefits to whites as a whole—and benefits that were real, not a matter of "false consciousness." Their race alone gave them substantial advantages in power and opportunities—better education, for example, and less chance of being treated unjustly by the courts and police. Moreover, when change did come, it could also hardly be explained in terms of class conflict. Rather, it was the outcome of a civil rights movements, in which blacks of all classes and the power of the federal government were the essential agents of change.

[106]Thomas Sowell, *Race and Economics* (New York: David McKay Company, 1975).

[107]Ibid., p. 16.

[108]Now, we would add, do we believe that economic interests alone explain the behavior of the North. Moral indignation was one, though not the only, important factor at work.

[109]Barrington Moore, Jr., *Social Origins of Dictatorship and Democracy. Lord and Peasant in the Making of the Modern World* (Boston: Beacon Press, 1966), p. 121. We should emphasize that Moore's account of the South is not identical to our own. For an explanation of the Civil War from a rational choice perspective, see pp. 208–9.

CRITICAL THEORY:
THE FRANKFURT SCHOOL AND JÜRGEN HABERMAS

Although all the theorists discussed in this section provide a critique of contemporary society, the term *critical theory* is also associated specifically with the theorists of the Frankfurt School. The work of the older Frankfurt theorists only became well known among English-speaking sociologists in the 1960s. However, Jürgen Habermas, the most important active theorist of the Frankfurt School, is becoming increasingly influential in both Europe and the United States.

The analyses of the Frankfurt theorists owe a great deal to Marx, and, like him, they emphasize the importance of conflicts of interest based on property relationships. However, they are by no means orthodox Marxists. They owe a major debt to Hegel, and they draw more on Marx's early and more "Hegelian" work, such as his writings on alienation, than on his later, more economic analyses.[110] In addition, they are very interested in uniting psychoanalysis and Marxism, an effort toward which orthodox Marxism (or Marxism-Leninism) is highly unsympathetic. These different influences are apparent in the aspects of their "critical theory" described later: their view of social science, their critique of mass culture and its place in the "administered society," and Habermas' recasting of Marx's evolutionary theory, and emerging theory of "communicative action."

The Frankfurt School is so called because of its association with a single institution, the Institute of Social Research at the University of Frankfurt in Germany. The Institute was founded in 1923 with funds from one of its members, Felix Weil, and his wealthy father; its most important members were Max Horkheimer (1895–1973), Theodor Adorno (1903–1969), Herbert Marcuse (1898–1979), and Erich Fromm (1900–1980). All of them came from comfortable, middle-class Jewish homes, and all had fled Germany for America by the mid-1930s because their political views made the continuation of the Institute impossible. Marcuse remained in the United States and worked for the American State Department until the Korean War, when he returned to academic life. He taught at Columbia, Harvard, Brandeis, and the University of California, San Diego. Fromm, who broke with the Institute soon after his arrival in America, practiced psychoanalysis in New York and became a founder and trustee of the William Alanson White Institute of Psychiatry, Psychoanalysis, and Psychology. In 1949 he moved to Mexico because of his wife's health. There he started the Department of Psychoanalysis at the National Autonomous University of Mexico and founded and directed the Mexican Psychoanalytic Institute,

---

[110]Jay, for example, suggests that "on one level . . . the Frankfurt School was returning to the concerns of the Left Hegelians of the 1840's." See Martin Jay, *The Dialectical Imagination* (Boston: Little, Brown, 1973), p. 42.

while still commuting regularly to the United States and academic appointments in New York and Michigan.

Adorno and Horkheimer were persuaded by the city and the University of Frankfurt to return to Germany, where the Institute of Social Research was reestablished in 1949.[111] During the postwar period, they became estranged from Marcuse. Horkheimer's attitudes toward liberal capitalism changed; he came to regard it as a form of society, to be protected against the encroachment of "totalitarian administration."[112] Marcuse regarded this position as a betrayal of the group's beliefs.[113]

Jürgen Habermas shares many concerns with the older Frankfurt theorists and, like them, draws very much on a German philosophical tradition. Habermas was born in 1929 in Gummersbach, near Dusseldorf, where his father was a pastor and head of the local Bureau of Industry and Trade. He studied philosophy at Göttingen and in 1956 became Assistant to Adorno in Frankfurt. In 1961, at an unusually young age for a German academic, he became professor of philosophy and sociology at Heidelberg, and in 1964 he was awarded the chair at Frankfurt and made co-director of the Philosophical Seminar. He left Frankfurt in 1971 to become director of Munich's Max Planck Institute for the Study of Life in Technical and Scientific Society. He has since returned to Frankfurt.

Although the foremost members of the Frankfurt School were not themselves actively involved in politics, their work has been very influential among German student radicals. Furthermore, as we mentioned above, Marcuse was a writer of great importance to the American New Left. Consequently, the Frankfurt theorists are highly controversial; in fact, they were accused by the Minister President of one West German state of being directly responsible for the 1960s wave of urban terrorism in Germany. Nevertheless, there was considerable disagreement between the German student radicals and the Frankfurt School theorists. Habermas, who first became generally known at this period, emphasized repeatedly his solidarity with the movement as a whole, but he also denounced the views of some of its extremist leaders as "left-fascism," defended the importance of democratic institutions and the rule of law, and attacked the use of violence. Adorno had his classes broken up by students who considered him inadequately revolutionary. More recently, Habermas has been an active protagonist in

---

[111]Adorno was the most keen to leave, as he was probably the most unassimilated European of the group. A fellow refugee, Paul Lazarsfeld, described him on his arrival in America as "exactly as you would imagine a very absent-minded German professor, and he behaves so foreign that I feel like a member of the Mayflower Society." *The Intellectual Migration: Europe and America, 1930–1960*, ed. Donald Flemming and Bernard Bailyn (Cambridge, Mass.: Belknap Press at Harvard University, 1969), p. 301.

[112]Max Horkheimer, *Critical Theory*, trans. Matthew J. O'Connell et al. Preface to American edition (New York: Herder and Herder, 1972). These essays were written in the 1930s.

[113]Phil Slater, *The Origin and Significance of the Frankfurt School: A Marxist Perspective* (London: Routledge and Kegan Paul, 1977).

the "historians' dispute," an argument over the origins of Nazism and the Second World War which has riven West German intellectual and cultural life.

Critical Theory and the Nature of Social Science

At the core of the Frankfurt School's approach to social analysis are two propositions. The first is that people's ideas are a product of the society in which they live. Because our thought is socially formed, they argue, it is impossible for us to reach objective knowledge and conclusions, free of the influence of our particular era and its conceptual patterns. The second proposition is that intellectuals should not try to be objective and to separate fact from value judgment in their work. What they should adopt instead is a critical attitude to the society they are examining, an attitude that makes people aware of what they should do and has as its aim social change. Equally, intellectuals should maintain a critical attitude toward their work; they should examine and make explicit its relationship to the current state of society and socially created "knowledge."

It does not follow, however, that critical theorists consider one critical attitude to be as good as another. Unlike Marx, they admit that since they too are products of a particular society, their own work is subject to its influences and is not uniquely objective. Nevertheless, they also believe that there are such things as truth and knowledge and that their normative approach brings them closer to these than does mainstream, or "positivist," social science, with its attempts to separate value judgments from analysis.[114]

In their critique the Frankfurt analysts adopt the dialectical method of Marx and Hegel, emphasize the importance of a society's economic organization, and argue that "the class-related form of . . . work puts its mark on all human patterns of reaction."[115] Critical theory, Horkheimer argues, "does not . . . fall victim to the illusion that property and profit no longer play a key role, an illusion carefully fostered in the social sciences."[116] By contrast, "traditional" theory is itself part of the production process, and so it is "in the service of an existing reality."[117] The modern economy,

---

[114]See especially Max Horkheimer, *Critical Theory*, and Jürgen Habermas, *Theory and Practice*, trans. John Viertel (Boston: Beacon Press, 1972). Members of the Frankfurt School apply the term "positivist" to a wide range of work, most of which does not belong to the philosophical schools of "positivism" or "logical positivism" but does share an emphasis on the empirical testing of hypotheses and scientific objectivity. See also Stephen Turner and Regis Factor, *Max Weber and the Dispute over Reason and Value: A Study of Philosophy, Ethics and Politics* (Henley-on-Thames: Routledge and Kegan Paul, 1984); and Anthony Giddens. "Review Essay: Habermas's Social and Political Theory," *American Journal of Sociology*, 83, No. 1 (1977), 198–212.

[115]Horkheimer, *Critical Theory*, p. 245.

[116]Ibid., p. 236.

[117]Ibid., p. 217.

Horkheimer argues, "after an enormous extension of human control over nature, finally hinders further development and drives humanity into a new barbarism."[118] Critical theory incorporates this insight and is "the unfolding of a single existential judgment."[119]

The ideal standard by which critical theory judges the present is closer to the concept of *reason* as it is used by Hegel and other German philosophers than it is to Marx. Horkheimer, for example, argues that "the free development of individuals depends on the rational constitution of society" and that in a rational society there will cease to be a conflict between human potentialities and the organization of society around work.[120] However, what a "rational" society would be like remains almost totally unclear, and the Frankfurt analysts share none of Marx's confidence that it will one day be realized.

Defenders of traditional social science have always argued in reply that, whether or not writers can avoid incorporating their own values into their work, their theories stand or fall by the accuracy of their factual predictions. These—like a bridge built according to "twentieth-century science"—can be judged objectively. They also question whether critical theory has any reason to claim that it is less context-bound than other approaches. Jürgen Habermas has attempted to deal with this latter question and so "legitimate" critical theory, first through the concept of an "ideal-speech situation" and then through his elaborated discussion of communicative action. We discuss both of these topics below.

Culture, Personality, and the Administered Society   The Frankfurt analysts consider themselves "materialists" because of their emphasis on the importance of economic organization. During the 1930s, for example, they argued consistently that fascism was rooted in capitalism. For the most part, however, their studies are concerned with aspects of personality, culture, and thought, and not with social institutions. Horkheimer, Adorno, and their colleagues have always affirmed that thought and personality are rooted in the economic system, but unlike more orthodox Marxists they also argue that culture and ideology can play an independent role in society and that pure economic determinism is simplistic.

Much of the most important work in critical theory was carried out at a time when psychoanalysis was first becoming widely known and influential. The Frankfurt analysts were very interested in analyzing personality and behavior in terms of the interaction between the "socioeconomic substructure" and basic psychic drives. Their analyses are highly norma-

[118]Ibid., p. 227.
[119]Ibid., p. 227.
[120]Ibid., p. 216.

tive, emphasizing the way the economic system distorts or cripples the personality.

Erich Fromm shows the greatest interest in psychoanalysis. During the 1930s, when he was a central member of the group, Fromm was interested in the way a particular "libidinal" structure, formed and passed on in the family, could act as a social cement. At this period he argued that, for example, the "capitalist spirit" of rationality, possessiveness, and puritanism was linked to anal repression and orderliness.[121] Later, his analyses centered around the idea of "alienation," which he uses rather differently from Marx, to describe an individual's psychological experiences of the world.

Fromm argues that alienation is the "central issue . . . [in discussing] the effects of capitalism on personality."[122] Under capitalism, workers and managers alike are alienated because they are denied such "basic needs" as creativity and identity. Their work is entirely impersonal; their consumption is also alienated, for they acquire possessions whether or not they use or appreciate them. They are motivated by self-interest, not love, in their relationships with others, and they see themselves as "doctors" or "clerks," not people.[123] Moreover,

> The increasing emphasis on ego versus self, on having versus being, finds a glowing expression in the development of our language. It has become customary for people to say, "I have insomnia," instead of saying, "I cannot sleep"; or "I have a problem", instead of, "I feel sad, confused" or whatever it may be; or "I have a happy marriage" . . . instead of . . . "My wife and I love each other." . . . Modern man *has* everything: a car, a house, a job, "kids," a marriage, problems, troubles, satisfactions. . . . He *is* nothing. . . .
>   . . . There are no psychological shortcuts to the solution of [this] identity crisis except the fundamental transformation of alienated man into living man.[124]

The Frankfurt analysts indict modern society similarly in their massive study *The Authoritarian Personality*. This study, the most famous of the series on prejudice and anti-Semitism that Adorno, Horkheimer, and their colleagues conducted in America, clearly presented Adorno's views on the connections between personality and social structure.[125] *The Authoritarian Personality* concluded that the most prejudiced and anti-democratic individu-

---

[121]Erich Fromm, *The Crisis of Psychoanalysis* (New York: Fawcett World Library, 1975).

[122]Erich Fromm, *The Sane Society* (New York: Rinehart and Winston, 1956), p. 69.

[123]Ibid., p. 120–91.

[124]Erich Fromm, *The Revolution of Hope: Toward a Humanized Technology* (New York: Harper and Row, 1968), pp. 83–84 passim.

[125]Theodor Adorno et al., *The Authoritarian Personality* (New York: Harper, 1950). The study is rather atypical of critical theory in its use of detailed analysis of questionnaire items and the "scaling" of people's responses. Most critical theory involves assertions and arguments at a very general level, for which little detailed evidence is advanced.

als had distinctive personalities and came, on the whole, from homes where relationships between parent and child were characterized by dominance and submission and where family members were very intolerant of a lack of conformity. In other words, the factors that precipitate prejudice were clearly seen as psychological. At the same time, however, Adorno argued that the whole sample showed marked similarities in important degrees. The most prejudiced individuals simply demonstrated more clearly the overall and potentially fascistic cultural pattern produced by the social structure. The prejudiced person "must largely be considered the outcome of our civilization. The increasing disproportion of the various psychological 'agencies' within the total personality is undoubtedly being reinforced by such tendencies in our culture as division of labor, the increased importance of monopolies and institutions, and the dominance of the idea of exchange and of success and competition."[126]

The Critique of Mass Culture   Critical theory's discussion of culture displays the same deep pessimism as does its analysis of personality. Horkheimer argues that culture and ideology are not a simple reflection of the economic substructure, but a semiautonomous realm. They are crucial in maintaining and strengthening the existing order: "the obsolete social order is quickly patched up . . . [and] the antiquated cultural apparatus, in the form of the mental state of society's members as well as the network of concrete institutions, gains new force."[127] To the members of the Frankfurt School, popular culture is a means of manipulating the inhabitants of a totally "administered" society.

Thus, Adorno attacked jazz and popular music for its standardization, for distracting people and making them passive, and therefore for strengthening the current social order. Jazz, he argued, increases alienation.[128] He similarly despised astrology and the "attraction to the occult," which he called "a symptom of the retrogression of consciousness."[129] People turn to astrology, he argues, in an attempt to lure meaning out of a "frozen" world where humanity's "domination over nature, by turning into domination over man, surpasses all the horrors that man ever had to fear from nature."[130] Its practitioners exploit their clients, and by providing psychological reassurance they help sustain the current social structure.

---

[126]Ibid., p. 389.

[127]Horkheimer, *Studien über Autorität und Familie*, trans. Phil Slater, quoted in Slater, *Origin and Significance of the Frankfurt School*, p. 15.

[128]Theodor Adorno, "Uber Jazz," *Zeitschrift für Sozialforschung V*, 2 (1936). Adorno's major interest was music, and readers of Thomas Mann's great novel *Dr. Faustus* will be interested to know that Adorno was Mann's major source of information on music. See also Theodor Adorno, *Introduction to the Sociology of Music*, trans. E. B. Ashton (New York: Seabury Press, 1976), for some of Adorno's most interesting analyses.

[129]Theodor Adorno, "Theses Against Occultism," *Telos*, 19 (1974), 7.

[130]Ibid.

In his examination of the *Los Angeles Times* astrology column,[131] Adorno notes that the column's implication that work and pleasure are to be kept strictly apart befits a society in which people's functions as producers are rigidly divided from their consumption. He argues that:

> The columnist is very well aware of the drudgery of most subordinate functions in a hierarchical and bureaucratic setup . . . —[People] are encouraged to fulfill little and insignificant set tasks in a machinery. Thus, the admonition to work and not to allow oneself to be distracted by any instinctual interference has frequently the form that one should attend to one's *"chores."*
>
> > Dismal early A.M., forgotten by plunging into routine chores. (November 21, 1952, Leo)
> >
> > Keeping plugging at chores . . . (December 19, 1952, Sagittarius)
> >
> > Stick to attending chores . . . (December 27, 1952, Sagittarius)[132]

In *One-Dimensional Man* Herbert Marcuse paints a bleak picture of modern industrial societies in both the West and the Communist world.[133] Marcuse is more of a technological determinist than his former colleagues; he states that technical progress has made possible a "whole system of domination and coordination" that defeats all protests. Social control in the interests of the status quo, including conditioning by the mass media, is so powerful that even thought provides no source of criticism; it too is subordinated. Affluence assimilates into the existing order all those who once dissented, and in return for material goods people give up liberty. In doing so, they surrender to "false needs," which are "superimposed upon the individual by particular social interests in his repression."[134] Culture has been flattened in what Marcuse views as a totalitarian social order which has succeeded the previous liberal one and which has become "one-dimensional" because it has eliminated alternative ideas.

Marcuse's distaste for modern culture has struck a responsive chord, for very many of us have at some time been nauseated by yet more T.V. advertising or by the thought of life lived in "little boxes all the same." However, Marcuse has also aroused numerous critics. It is frequently pointed out, for example, that Marcuse's own work refutes his claim that all

---

[131]Theodor Adorno, "The Stars Down to Earth, The Los Angeles Times Astrology Column," *Telos*, 19 (1974), 13–90.

[132]Ibid., p. 47. The "fragmentation" of modern culture and the "atomisation" of experience are still seen by many radical social scientists as both central features of capitalist society and crucial to its continuation. See. e.g., David Held, "Crisis Tendencies, Legitimation and the State," in John B. Thompson and David Held, eds., *Habermas: Critical Debates* (London: The Macmillan Press Ltd., 1982), especially pp. 189–90.

[133]Herbert Marcuse, *One-Dimensional Man* (Boston: Beacon Press, 1964).

[134]Ibid., p. 70. Marcuse was also interested in psychoanalysis and argued that an integrated personality is impossible in modern civilization. See his *Eros and Civilization* (New York: Vintage Books, 1955).

criticism has been suppressed and that his writings generally advance little empirical evidence in support of his claims. Critics also disagree with his assertion that all industrial societies are essentially and similarly totalitarian, and they question his and other critical theorists' conviction that they, unlike the mass of people, know what people's "real needs" are.

Jürgen Habermas: Rationalization and Communicative Action

Jürgen Habermas shares with the original Frankfurt School theorists a belief in "reason" as a standard by which to judge—critically—our society and a concern with the links between culture, social structure, and personality. However, he provides a more comprehensive theory of social systems and evolution and develops further the Frankfurt School's ideas on how social analysis or critique should be conducted. He pays particular attention to the developments of the last century and the forces of change apparent in modern society.

Habermas has always paid great attention to the role of individuals' perceptions in maintaining or realizing social change. This emphasis is increasingly marked over time, notably in his massive *Theory of Communicative Action*,[135] in which the influence of phenomenology is very apparent. What is also increasingly obvious, however, is how far Habermas' work must be seen not simply as an elaboration of Marx but as an ongoing argument with Max Weber. He returns again and again to Weber's metaphor of bureaucratized society as an "Iron Cage,"[136] and one sympathetic commentator has described the *Theory of Communicative Action* as being "conceived as a second attempt to incorporate Max Weber into the spirit of Western Marxism."[137]

Like Weber (and like the older Frankfurt School analysts),[138] Habermas must also be understood in terms of a German tradition in which there is no strict separation of "sociology" from "philosophy." In this tradition, the concept of "reason" is far wider-ranging and imbued with values than our English use of the word implies.

---

[135]Jürgen Habermas, *The Theory of Communicative Action*, Vol. I: *Reason and the Rationalization of Society*, trans. Thomas McCarthy (London: Heinemann, 1985), and Vol. II: *Lifeworld and System: A Critique of Functionalist Reason*, trans. Thomas McCarthy (Cambridge, England: Polity Press, 1988).

[136]See above pp. 80–81.

[137]Michael Pusey, *Jürgen Habermas* (Chichester, West Sussex: Ellis Horwood, 1988) p. 105. We are indebted to Pusey's excellent review for pointing up the central role of Weber's diagnosis in Habermas' work. For commentaries on Habermas' work, see also Richard J. Bernstein ed., *Habermas and Modernity* (Cambridge, England: Polity Press 1985), and Thomas McCarthy, *The Critical Theory of Jürgen Habermas* (London: Hutchinson, 1978).

[138]See above pp. 115–17. The older Frankfurt analysts, however, did not engage so directly with Weber.

Evolution and Crisis   The major achievement of Habermas' earlier work, (especially *Legitimation Crisis* and *Communication and the Evolution of Society*) was to provide a recasting of Marx's theory of evolution.[139] Although his recent work modifies and expands the earlier model—for example, by changing some of the labels used—the basic categories have remained.

Habermas identifies a number of social formations, shown in Figure 3-2. "Primitive" societies are comparable to Marx's tribal ones; "traditional" societies would include both "ancient" and "feudal" ones; "liberal capitalist" describes the nineteenth-century capitalism Marx knew; and our own Western societies are examples of "organized" capitalism. Habermas classifies "state-socialist" societies as "post-capitalist" class societies "in view of their political-élitist disposition of the means of production."[140]

Habermas' mode of analysis is similar to Marx's in that he sees social evolution as a result of crises or "contradictions" inherent in a given system. These create "steering problems," which eventually make the system untenable. However, like other critical theorists, Habermas emphasizes the role played by people's ideas and consciousness. Underlying structural changes and contradictions manifest themselves in the breakdown of shared values or "normative structures," and the old social system disintegrates because such changes threaten people's feeling of social identity (and therefore social integration).[141]

In discussing such breakdown, Habermas focuses very much on the political organization of societies and on their legitimacy, meaning "*a political order's worthiness to be recognized.*"[142] In emphasizing legitimation, Habermas is like both Weber, who analyzed the comparable notion of authority,[143] and Parsons, who saw ideas or norms as central to system maintenance.[144] He argues that "problems of legitimacy are not a speciality of modern times. . . . In traditional societies, legitimation conflicts typically take the form of prophetic and messianic movements that turn against the official version of religious doctrine."[145] This is because it is here that the contradiction between the privileges of the dominant ruling class and the normative

---

[139]Jürgen Habermas, *Legitimation Crisis*, trans. Thomas McCarthy (Boston: Beacon Press, 1975), and Jürgen Habermas *Communication and the Evolution of Society*, trans. Thomas McCarthy (London: Heinemann, 1979). See also Jürgen Habermas, *Knowledge and Human Interests*, trans. Jeremy J. Shapiro (London: Heinemann, 1972).

[140]Habermas, *Legitimation Crisis*, p. 17

[141]Ibid., p. 3. Following Durkheim, Habermas describes this sitation as anomic.

[142]Jürgen Habermas, "Legitimation Problems in the Modern State," in *Communication and the Evolution of Society*, p. 178 (italics original).

[143]See above pp. 81–82.

[144]In Parsons' AGIL terms, we can see legitimation as involving systems of ideas which both support the political system's mobilization of resources for goal attainment (*G*) and also promote "latent pattern maintenance-tension management" (*L*)—the process of keeping a common value system intact. See above p. 40.

[145]Habermas, "Legitimation Problems in the Modern State," p. 181.

Social Formations

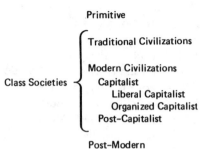

Primitive

Traditional Civilizations

Modern Civilizations
Class Societies   Capitalist
                          Liberal Capitalist
                          Organized Capitalist
                       Post-Capitalist

Post-Modern

FIGURE 3-2   Social Formations. (Adapted from Jürgen Habermas, *Legitimation Crisis* [Boston Beacon Press, 1975], p. 17.)

system of ideas which is supposed to legitimize them becomes apparent. Examples are the Hebrew prophets or the heretical movements of the Middle Ages. This does not, however, make legitimation crises in the state something separate from class conflicts. On the contrary, it is *through* the development of the state that societies moved away from production by and for families to a situation in which a dominating class appropriated wealth.

Habermas' focus on ideas as the mechanism of change makes his treatment very different from that of Marx, who treats the development of modern industry as a *deus ex machina* that catapulted humanity from feudal into capitalist society. Instead, it displays interesting parallels both with Schumpeter's approach, where the way capitalism destroys its own legitimacy was discussed as the central force behind its inevitable demise, and with that of some leading nonradical economic historians, who also focus on the role of the state and of "ideology" in determining how wealth is distributed.[146]

According to Habermas, the distinctive characteristic of liberal capitalism is the "depoliticization of the class relationship."[147] Before, control of the state by a small group was of central importance. Under liberal capitalism there is self-regulated market commerce, and the state's role is simply to maintain the general conditions of capitalistic production, especially civil law. Like Weber or Marcuse, Habermas notes the cumulative process of "rationalization" under capitalism and the corresponding disintegration of both traditional habits and the justification of practices by an appeal to tradition. Moreover, like Talcott Parsons (to whom he acknowledges an

---

[146]Unlike Habermas, they are also extremely interested in the effects of these on how much is *produced*. See E. L. Jones, *The European Miracle: Environments, Economies and Geo-politics in the History of Europe and Asia* (Cambridge: Cambridge University Press, 1981), and Douglass C. North, *Structure and Change in Economic History* (New York: W. W. Norton and Co. 1981).

[147]Habermas, *Legitimation Crisis,* p. 21.

intellectual debt),[148] he notes the general expansion of the secular domain and a shift from "tribal particularism to universalistic and at the same time individualistic orientations."[149]

However, in analyzing the probable development of modern society, Habermas believes that the trend from myth, through religion, to philosophy and ideology is of prime importance.[150] It means that "normative validity claims" (that is, arguments that something ought to be so) must be justified more and more explicitly. Instead of relying on appeals to tradition and authority, capitalism has based its claim to legitimacy on the notion that market exchange between equals is just. However, in a society where legitimacy rests on the workings of the market, economic fluctuations are direct threats to social integration. Such fluctuations may create very high unemployment or inflation, which wipes out people's savings, or may result in the virtual disappearance of a city's or state's traditional industries. In the process they make it clear to everyone involved that market ideology is incorrect. The market is not, in fact, a meeting place of equals, but a form of institutionalized power where some are better placed than others.[151]

In his discussion of contemporary "organized capitalism," Habermas is concerned above all with whether it has resolved this "fundamental contradiction." His answer is that it has not. There are serious "crisis tendencies" in modern Western societies, the most important of which undermine its legitimacy.

Habermas believes that the transition from liberal to organized capitalism involves two changes. The first is the rise of huge, oligopolistic firms and the disappearance of *competitive* capitalism. The second is the reemergence of the state, which increasingly replaces and intervenes in the market (thus signaling the end of *liberal* capitalism). In large part, the state's reemergence is a response to economic fluctuations and "steering problems." The state attempts to regulate the economic cycle and maintain growth and full employment; spends on education and research; provides the infrastructure of roads and utilities; and reduces the "social and material costs resulting from private production" through unemployment benefits, welfare, and the like.[152] The profit motive and the "continued private appropriation . . . of surplus value" remain crucial, however.[153]

The "recoupling" of the state and the economic system creates, Habermas argues, an increased need for legitimation, and in a rationalistic age the legitimation must be formal and explicit. Since the old bourgeois

[148]See Chapter II, p. 54.
[149]Habermas, *Legitimation Crisis*, p. 12.
[150]Ibid., p. 11.
[151]Ibid., pp. 25–26.
[152]Ibid., pp. 33–35.
[153]Ibid., p. 36.

ideology of fair exchange has broken down, the alternative is a system of "formal democracy."[154] *Genuine* participation in decision making would, he argues, make people aware of the contradictions in a society where production is the state's concern, but "surplus value" is individually appropriated. Such participation is not on offer.

This system is fragile, however. Habermas, following Marx, believes that the economic system itself is threatened by a falling rate of profit. Moreover, there is likely to be insufficient loyalty to the political system and a consequent "legitimation crisis." In its early days, capitalism had the remnants of tradition to maintain it. Now its own rationality has undermined traditions, and previously unquestioned norms and loyalties are publicly discussed and thereby weakened.

Related changes within the family further destroy the residues of tradition and the casts of mind that upheld the capitalist order.[155] While prebourgeois, authoritarian patterns of upbringing survived, people accepted rule by an élite rather than demanding participation;[156] but these patterns are vanishing, helped on their way by a self-conscious analysis of the ways we socialize children. Such an analysis further reduces the effectiveness of traditional child rearing because the latter's force depended on people not questioning it. Finally, the ideology of achievement is also disappearing. The welfare state makes hard work less important, and in a modern economy it is increasingly difficult to reward people for individual effort and hold them personally accountable.

Rationalization of the Lifeworld   Habermas elaborates his evolutionary theory by looking at it in terms of communication and the *lifeworld*—that is, in terms of how evolutionary change is actually experienced by individuals. Here, too, a direct line between Habermas and Weber is apparent. Weber argued that in social science we need subjective understanding of how other people see the world and of their "webs of meaning."[157] Habermas similarly argues for "intersubjective" projection into others' lifeworld—that is, for conceiving of what it would be like to be inside someone else's skin, experiencing the world as he or she does.

To an even greater extent, however, Habermas draws on the phenomenological tradition.[158] Edmund Husserl (1859–1938), the German philosopher who was the first to use the term "phenomenology," also employed the

---

[154]Ibid., p. 36.

[155]Ibid., pp. 48–49. These are discussed by Habermas in terms of the "social-cultural system" and "motivational crisis."

[156]Ibid., p. 76.

[157]For a discussion of Weber's concept of *verstehen* see Chapter V.

[158]This reached America primarily through the writing of Alfred Schutz. See Ch. VI, pp. 291–93.

concept of *Lebenswelt*, or *lifeworld*.[159] Husserl was referring here to the most fundamental levels of consciousness, levels of which we are not aware. These levels of consciousness structure all our perceptions and determine how we actually experience "reality." Adults in modern society, for example, take it for granted that time proceeds in one direction only and that once you have had your twentieth birthday, you can never be nineteen again. A three-year-old experiences reality rather differently and may declare that she wants to be two again after she has been twelve.

Seen this way, the process of "modernization" becomes coterminous with the rationalization of the lifeworld. Tribal societies are environments in which the "taken-for-granted" lifeworld is highly encompassing. People mix only with others who share the same lifeworld, so they are always able to communicate with each other and have no reason to become self-conscious about the structure of shared experience. One cannot conceive of meeting a phenomenologist amongst our hunting and gathering forebears or in a Viking settlement. Today, the "lifeworld" is increasing rationalized: instead of "knowing" that certain animals are unclean or that chiefs have a right to rule, we demand that things be justified in terms of very general principles—what Talcott Parsons calls "value generalization."

Habermas is concerned with the lifeworld as an aspect of his theory of *communicative action*. It is through the action of communicating, he argues, that "society" actually operates and evolves; this process is encompassed and structured by the actors' lifeworlds.[160] One of his own examples is that of an older worker at a German building site telling the newest recruit to go and get the mid-morning beer. The actual remark would probably be brief, almost offhand, but it has built into it all sorts of assumptions. It takes it for granted that a mid-morning "beer break" is a normal and acceptable custom and that there is a natural hierarchy based on age and/or length of service at the building site. A young English carpenter working in Germany might be extremely surprised at the order, since beer is not readily available at 11 A.M. in the United Kingdom. He would nonetheless probably share enough of the underlying "lifeworld knowledge" to understand, act accordingly, and, in so doing, become more integrated into German life.[161]

---

[159]See also the writings of Thomas Luckmann, who in *Life-World and Social Realities* (London: Heinemann, 1983) states that "the lifeworld forms the setting in which situational horizons shift, expand or contract. It forms a context that, itself boundless, draws boundaries. . . . Lifeworld analysis [is] an attempt to describe reconstructively, from the internal perspective of members, what Durkheim calls the *conscience collective*" (pp. 132–33 passim). Luckmann's work is discussed in Chapter VI, pp. 312–17. For Durkheim's definition of "conscience collective," see p. 20.

[160]Habermas' concerns here are, as he recognizes, very close to those of many modern philosophers, including, notably, John Searle. See J. R. Searle, *Speech Acts* (Cambridge: Cambridge University Press, 1969).

[161]Anthony Giddens offers a similar analysis in his "structuration theory." See Chapter VII.

This is why Habermas argues that communicative action

> is not only a process of reaching understanding; . . . actors are at the same time taking part in interactions through which they develop, confirm and renew their memberships in social groups and their own identities. Communicative actions are not only processes of interpretation in which cultural knowledge is "tested against the world"; they are at the same time processes of social integration and of socialization.[162]

Lifeworld and System   In his earlier work on evolution (discussed above), Habermas emphasized the move from tribal to class societies, the emergence of state organizations, and the way in which the economy becomes self-regulated, with the state ensuring general conditions rather than directly involved. He has now reformulated this somewhat using the concept of lifeworld and the neo-Parsonian "system" framework of Niklas Luhmann.[163]

Habermas argues that, as social evolution progresses, there develops a "system" of institutions—markets "steered" by money and state organizations "steered" by power. It is then possible for more people to be involved with each other *without sharing meanings or the same lifeworld.* The social system becomes increasingly complex and differentiated; the lifeworld becomes increasingly rationalized; *and the two are uncoupled to a large degree.*[164] In tribal society, by contrast, system integration and social integration remain tightly interwoven because structures of "linguistically mediated, normatively guided interaction immediately constitute the supporting social structures."[165]

Within our contemporary state and market structures, one does not obey people (Weber's "traditional" authority) or even officeholders, but general principles and abstract laws. "Social relations are regulated only through money and power. Norm-conformative attitudes and identity-forming social memberships are made peripheral."[166] Lifeworlds get more provincial as the social system gets more complex. This means that "the burden of social integration [shifts] more and more from religiously anchored consensus to processes of consensus formation in language."[167]

---

[162]Habermas *Theory of Communicative Action*, Vol. II, p. 139.

[163]See Chapter II, pp. 71–73.

[164]See Chapter II for a discussion of Luhmann's work. We can relate Habermas' and Luhmann's work to Parsons' AGIL paradigm by noting that the "social system" corresponds to Parsons' *A* (the economy) and *G* (political institutions). The educational, family, and religious institutions which make up Parsons' *L* are also the level of the lifeworld and, as such, become progressively detached from *A* and *G*. Compare modern work patterns with those of previous societies, where the family home was also the work place, and the aristocratic home a center of political power.

[165]Habermas, *Theory of Communicative Action*, Vol. II, p. 156.

[166]Ibid., p. 154.

[167]Ibid., p. 180.

Only by explicit "rational" discussion do we agree on how things should be carried out—whether it is the way a course is graded or a major foreign policy decision.

Habermas' account is meant to make explicit what to Weber "was still self-evident," namely "the intrinsic (that is, not merely contingent) relationship between modernity and what he called 'Occidental rationalism.' "[168] However, what actually most interested Weber was the conditions for the emergence of modern industrial society. What this century has shown—most notably in the case of Japan and its East Asian neighbors—is that the countries in which modernity first develops may be very different indeed from those which modernize successfully thereafter. Habermas' analysis, by contrast, seems to imply that all modern societies will be similar in the lifeworlds that evolve.

Habermas' analysis also treats as basically self-evident the claim that a society must have one consistent legitimating set of norms accepted by its inhabitants—a very Parsonian view. However, as van den Berg has pointed out, Habermas does not actually provide any proof of this. It is thus quite possible to argue that "different value orientations can and do exist within the same system without any disastrous effects on its stability"[169]—that contradictions do not, necessarily, produce systemic change. At the same time, the values and opinions people have—in the West, but also and notably in "state socialist" countries such as the Soviet Union—call into question Habermas' belief that, in modern society, explicit, "rational" legitimation is necessary. In fact, many Soviet citizens seem to hold extremely traditional values, including passive acceptance of an autocratic state,[170] implying that a "modern" state may still be able to maintain its legitimacy on "old-fashioned" foundations.

Lifeworld and Crisis   Habermas also uses this communicative perspective on social evolution to elaborate on the development of crises. They are to be found, he argues, at the "seam," where lifeworld and system meet. Continuing rationalization can become pathological if it goes so far as to endanger the whole process of social integration and socialization by which society reproduces itself. For example, the competitive individualism of the marketplace may destroy family structures. The bureaucratic welfare state can be equally destructive. "The deformations of a lifeworld that is regulated, fragmented, monitored, and looked after are surely more subtle than the palpable forms of material exploitation and impoverishment; but inter-

---

[168]Jürgen Habermas, *The Philosophical Discourse of Modernity: Twelve Lectures*, trans. Frederick Lawrence (Cambridge, England: Polity Press, 1987), p. 1.

[169]See especially Axel van den Berg, "Critical Theory: Is There Still Hope?" *American Journal of Sociology*, 86, no. 3 (1980), 449–78, especially p. 465.

[170]Thompson and Held, *Habermas: Critical Debates*. See especially Chapter 10 (Held) and Chapter 11 (Andrew Arato).

Structural components \ Disturbances in the domain of	Culture	Society	Person
Cultural reproduction	**Loss of Meaning**	**Withdrawal of legitimation**	Crisis in orientation and education
Social Integration	Unsettling of collective identity	**Anomie**	**Alienation**
Socialisation	**Rupture of tradition**	Withdrawal of motivation	Psycho-pathologies

FIGURE 3-3   Manifestations of Crisis When Reproduction Processes Are Disturbed. (Adapted from fig. 22 in Habermas, *Theory of Communicative Action*, Vol. II: *Lifeworld and System* [Cambridge, England: Polity Press, 1988])

nalized social conflicts that have shifted from the corporeal to the psychic are not therefore less destructive."[171]

Figure 3-3 shows how Habermas has expanded his analysis of "legitimation crisis" to create a more general typology of crisis phenomena. Thus, a loss of meaning at the cultural level is reflected in the social system by withdrawal of legitimation. This may be connected, in turn, to disturbances in social integration, reflected in *social* anomie and *individual* alienation.

Reason and Rationalization   Habermas' analysis of "rationalization" is often very similar to Weber's. Yet he is not a "Weberian": this is a dialogue and argument, not an exegesis. In his approach to "reason" and to the pessimism of Weber's "Iron Cage," Habermas stands directly in a line that goes through the Frankfurt School to Marx.

The Frankfurt theorists believed in the possibility of a "rational," and not merely a "rationalized," society, and in the validity of critical theory compared to the products of other ideologically tainted theories. Marx, too, identified "ideologies" and argued that they were self-interested rather than true, while believing in the special status of his own theories. To sceptics[172] this has always seemed inconsistent, for if other people's beliefs

[171]Habermas, *Philosophical Discourse*, p. 362.
[172]See the discussion of Marcuse above pp. 121–22.

reflect self-interest and socialization, this must be equally true of "critical theorists." Moreover, the latter cannot *prove* that their values are the right ones. We can all discuss values and look at their empirical consequences, but they are not subject to proof. We accept them or we don't.

Habermas, however, in critical theory tradition, argues that you *can* provide grounding for the ultimate norms that govern our lives and thereby replace the void left by modernity's "disenchantment" of the world. He also attempts to show how, in a far more developed way than his Frankfurt School predecessors. His earlier work in this area centers on the concept of an "ideal-speech situation."[173] This is a situation in which everyone would have an equal chance to argue and question, without those who are more powerful, confident, or prestigious having an unequal say. True positions would prevail under these circumstances, because they are more rational.

The "theory of communicative action" further develops the argument. Communicative action, Habermas argues, is a distinctive type of social interaction because it is oriented to mutual understanding and not to success or "purposive" achievement of ends.[174] Thus,

> the goal of coming to an understanding is to bring about an agreement that terminates in the intersubjective mutuality of reciprocal understanding, shared knowledge, mutual trust and accord with one another. Agreement is based on recognition of the corresponding validity claims of comprehensibility, truth, truthfulness, and rightness.[175]

The claim that Habermas makes here is common to his earlier and later work. It is that people can, in principle, agree on correct ways of proceeding and arguing. If we do accept and follow such "procedural" norms, we will then reach substantive agreement, because the position of reason will win. More specifically, critical theory and its judgments will appear as objectively correct because they are based on less distorted communication than other approaches.

Is this really the case? As an illustration, take the proposition that it is *wrong* to exterminate any other species that shares the globe with us—not just unwise (because they might be useful one day) but actually wrong. If you believe this, it may be for religious reasons or simply because you are convinced that everything has a right to life. Alternatively, you may not believe the proposition at all. It is not obvious why rational communicative action would shift people's positions on this issue or on others, such as

---

[173] Habermas, *Legitimation Crisis* and *Knowledge and Human Interests.*

[174] There are echoes here of Aristotle's distinction between "techne," or the purposive action involved in making things, and "praxis," the distinctive human interaction exhibited in intersubjective communication. Cf., Marx's use of "praxis," above p. 89.

[175] Habermas, "What is Universal Pragmatics," in *Communication and the Evolution of Society,* p. 3.

abortion, divorce, defense expenditure, or the government's role in the economy. Habermas' critics and, indeed, most social scientists believe that value differences are ultimately irreconcilable.[176]

It is because of his belief in "reason" that Habermas does not consider the progressive "rationalization" of the world to be entirely negative. Because it demands that meaning and action be justified very explicitly, it *also* creates the potential for rational discourse and "noncoercive" argumentation. Whereas "purposive rationality" in the arena of the system indeed creates an Iron Cage, communicative rationality, Habermas argues, does not.[177]

Just as Marx saw the evils of capitalist society as creating the wealth required for communism, so Habermas sees the horrors of a "rationalized" uncoupled lifeworld as a precursor of genuine reason. It is because of this, he believes, that the new sorts of conflicts arising in our societies are about the "grammar of forms of life," for example, emancipatory feminism, and about lifeworld. "Again and again," Habermas asserts, this claim to reason "is silenced, and yet in fantasies and deeds it develops a stubbornly transcending power, because it is renewed with each moment of living together in solidarity, of successful individuation, and of saving emancipation."[178]

This may be true; but it is not obvious that Habermas has in any way proven it. He has not actually provided us with examples of the process at work in groups. Nor does he grapple with the potential for conflict in such situations, however "reasonable" the participants. How can we assume that people are equally able to conduct the required discourse? Or that people's desire to be fair and just will really overcome not simply individual ends but family ties, sexual jealousy, and the whole gamut of emotions from love to grief to hatred? Habermas' rejection of Weber's pessimistic conclusions seems as much a product of faith as argument.

This is not to imply that Habermas' concern with reason is a matter of academic philosophising. One reason why European sociologists are so concerned with people's ideas and concepts, and their relationship to social systems,[179] is that it is hard to explain the terrible history of the continent, especially in this century, in purely economic (or functionalist) terms. Habermas tells us that his own crucial formative experience was that of listening, as a German adolescent, to radio broadcasts of the Nuremberg trials of Nazi leaders and war criminals. Around him, his elders disputed the justice of the trials by referring to general principles of procedure and questions of who had jurisdiction. They used concepts which were the

---

[176]See, for example, van den Berg, "Critical Theory: Is There Still Hope?"

[177]See Pusey, *Jürgen Habermas,* p. 109.

[178]Habermas, "A Reply to my Critics," in his *Critical Debates,* p. 221.

[179]See, for example, the work of Lévi-Strauss and Foucault (Chapter VII).

product of rational modernity, he tells us, to close off the "collectively realized inhumanity" of Nazi Germany.

For a German of Habermas' generation, questions about social evolution must include questions about recent German history. Equally, "academic" discussion of the subject is not something in present-day Germany for amicable coffee-shop discussion (or, indeed, anything which looks much like ideal communicative action). In 1987 the intellectual and newspaper community was riven by the "historians' dispute" over whether or not fascism should be seen as a reaction to Bolshevism and Auschwitz and other death camps as rooted in the Russian Gulag. Predictably, Habermas was heavily involved in the attack on any such views.

Summary

Critical theory is consciously at odds with mainstream social science, not so much in its Marxist roots as in its emphasis on language and discourse and the way it looks to philosophical argument rather than supposedly "objective" data.[180] Critical theorists' analyses of the role of ideas and culture in social stability and change and their discussions of the evolution of modern society away from nineteenth-century capitalism are their most important contributions to social theory. However, many commentators have attacked their view of social science in general and Marcuse's view of modern culture in particular. As we shall see in the next section, many theorists—including other conflict theorists—also disagree with critical theory's continuing emphasis on the role of private property and profit, which both Habermas and the older Frankfurt theorists derive from Marx.

C. WRIGHT MILLS

Among American sociologists, C. Wright Mills (1916–1962) is the best-known modern theorist whose work combines a conflict perspective with a strong critique of the social order. Mills was born and raised in Texas; he never left the state until he was in his twenties, when he won a research fellowship to the University of Wisconsin. Most of his academic career was spent at Columbia, where he was a professor until he died of a heart condition while still in his mid forties.

Mills was subjected to a barrage of criticism, especially in his later years, when his writing became increasingly accusatory and polemical. He also had many admirers and was never quite the "lone wolf" he considered

---

[180] For a review of current approaches to the study of culture which reject "positivist" social science, see Robert Wuthnow, James Davison Hunter, Albert Bergesen, and Edith Kurzweil, *Cultural Analysis: The Work of Peter L. Berger, Mary Douglas, Michel Foucault and Jürgen Habermas* (Boston: Routledge and Kegan Paul, 1984).

himself. Mills was increasingly agonized and pessimistic about the immediate future. He believed that immorality was built into the American system,
and he never voted because he considered political parties to be manipulative and "irrational" organizations. He also bitterly attacked his fellow intellectuals for abdicating their social responsibilities and for putting themselves at the service of men of power while they hid behind a mask of
"value-free" analysis.

Mills thought that it was possible to create a "good society" on the basis
of knowledge and that men of knowledge must take responsibility for its
absence.[181] He believed in a libertarian socialism, and he supported the
Cuban revolution (and attacked the United States' reaction to it) because he
hoped that it would combine revolutionary socialism and freedom.[182] In his
sociology, his major themes were the relationship between bureaucracy and
alienation and the centralization of power in a "power élite." Both these
subjects were aspects of his attack on modern American society.

The Sociological Imagination

Mills argues that micro and macro levels of analysis can be linked by
the *sociological imagination*. As he describes it:

> The sociological imagination enables its possessor to understand the large
> historical scene in terms of its meaning for the inner life and the external
> career of a variety of individuals. It enables him to take into account how
> individuals, in the welter of their daily experience, often become falsely con-
> scious of their social positions. . . . By such means the personal uneasiness of
> individuals is focused upon explicit troubles and the indifference of publics is
> transformed into involvement with public issues.[183]

Mills contends that individuals can only understand their own experiences fully if they can locate themselves within their period of history. Then
they become aware of the life chances shared by all individuals in the same
circumstances. Thus, the sociological imagination enables us to "grasp history and biography and the relations between the two within society."

Mills makes an important distinction between *personal troubles* and
public issues. Personal troubles are those troubles which occur "within the
individual as a biographical entity and within the scope of his immediate
milieu" and relations with other people. Public issues are matters that have
to do with the "institutions of an historical society as a whole," with the
overlapping of various milieus which interpenetrate to "form the larger

---

[181]C. Wright Mills, *The Sociological Imagination* (New York: Oxford University Press,
1959).

[182]C. Wright Mills, *Listen Yankee: The Revolution in Cuba* (New York: McGraw-Hill, 1960).

[183]Mills, *The Sociological Imagination*, p. 5.

structures of social and historical life." To explain this distinction, Mills presents the example of unemployment. If only one person in a city of 100,000 is unemployed, then it is a personal trouble. But if 5 million people are unemployed in a nation of 50 million, that is a public issue.

Dobash and Dobash used Mills' approach in their study entitled *Violence Against Wives*. They analyzed the laws and ordinances which, throughout history, have legitimized the physical abuse of women, and they combined this study with an analysis of nearly a thousand police and court cases of assaults against wives and with hundreds of hours of in-depth interviews with battered women. This combination of biography and history shows how the private troubles of battered women constitute a public issue.[184]

Dobash and Dobash's analysis of laws from ancient Roman times to the present illustrated how the "patriarchal order" was enforced through the laws upholding the husband's right to beat his wife. They note that the "rule of thumb," allowing a husband to chastise his wife with a stick no thicker than his thumb, was only repealed in English law in 1829.[185] Not until 1871 was wife beating illegal within the United States, specifically with changes in Alabama and Massachusetts.[186] Even this, the authors point out, did not have an immediate effect. The husbands of battered wives were, by and large, dealt with leniently.[187] In modern times, the study of court cases and interviews provides a similar picture. According to the women interviewees, the typical response of the police was "refusing to arrest and treating the assault as a private and/or civil matter."[188]

Alienation and Bureaucracy

Mills argues that the material hardships of the workers of the past have been replaced today by a psychological malaise rooted in workers' alienation from what they make.[189] He sees white-collar workers as apathetic, frightened, and molded by mass culture. In modern society, he argues, "those who hold power have often come to exercise it in hidden ways: they have moved and are moving from authority to manipulation. . . . The rational systems hide their power so that no one sees their sources of authority or understands their calculation. For the bureaucracy . . . the world is an object to be manipulated."[190]

In a world of big business and big government, the ever-increasing

---

[184]R. Emerson Dobash and Russell Dobash, *Violence Against Wives: A Case Against the Patriarchy* (New York: The Free Press, 1979).

[185]Ibid., p. 63.

[186]Ibid., p. 63.

[187]Ibid., p. 74.

[188]Ibid., p. 214.

[189]C. Wright Mills, *White Collar: The American Middle Classes* (New York: Oxford University Press, 1951), pp. xvi–xvii.

[190]Ibid., pp. 110–11.

group of white-collar people lives not by making things, but by helping to turn what someone else has made into profits for yet another person. Fewer and fewer people own their own productive property and control their own working lives. Stable communities and traditional values, which "fixed" people into society, have disappeared, and their disappearance throws the whole system of prestige or status into flux. Like Veblen, Mills believes that status and self-esteem are closely linked, and the loss of traditional values, he argues, undermines people's self-esteem and embroils them in a status "panic."[191] In fact, Mills' concerns here are curiously like those of Durkheim and the functionalists, who see modern society as threatened by normlessness, or anomie. His critics argue that he ignores the freedom that the breakup of old and restrictive communities can offer.

Unlike Marx, Mills does not believe that work is necessarily the crucial expression of oneself, but he does condemn modern bureaucratic capitalism for alienating people from both the process and product of work. This is particularly clear, Mills argues, with white-collar workers like salespeople whose personalities become commodities to be sold and for whom friendliness and courtesy are part of the "impersonal means of livelihood."[192] Thus, he claims, "in all work involving the personality market, . . . one's personality and personal traits become part of the means of production . . . (which) has carried self and social alienation to explicit extremes."[193]

Mills' emphasis on alienation derives from his concern with the relationship between character and social structure. Salesmanship, he argues, estranges people from themselves and others because they view all relationships as manipulative.[194] Alienation from work makes people turn frenziedly to leisure, but the entertainment industry produces synthetic excitement, which offers no real release and establishes no deep common values.[195] Others aspects of social structure strengthen psychological tendencies that make modern societies liable to fascist or revolutionary totalitarian success.[196] People's fragmented working environments give them little understanding of how society works, and they believe that the interventionist government is responsible for insecurity and misfortune. An increasingly centralized structure with no remaining traditional beliefs and with permanently anxious people is, Mills argues, highly vulnerable.

[191]Ibid., pp. 237–58.
[192]Ibid., p. xvii.
[193]Ibid., p. 225.
[194]Ibid., p. 188.
[195]Ibid., p. xvii.
[196]Hans Gerth and C. Wright Mills, *Character and Social Structure* (New York: Harcourt Brace, 1953), pp. 460–72.

The Power Élite

Mills argues consistently that the growth of large structures has been accompanied by a centralization of power and that the men who head government, corporations, the armed forces, and the unions are very closely linked. He carries this part of his analysis the furthest in his discussion of the "power élite."[197]

Mills argues that America is ruled by a "power élite" made up of people who hold the dominant positions in political, military, and economic institutions. "Within the American society," he writes, "major national power now resides in the economic, the political and the military domains. . . . Within each of the big three, the typical institutional unit has become enlarged, has become administrative, and, in the power of its decisions, has become centralized. . . . [The] means of power at the disposal of centralized decision-making units have increased enormously."[198]

Mills argues, moreover, that the three domains are interlocked, so that "the leading men in each of the three domains of power—the warlords, the corporate chieftains, the political directorate—tend to come together to form the power élite of America: . . . The military capitalism of private corporations exists in a weakened and formal democratic system containing an already quite politicized military order."[199] Mills believed that power can be based on factors other than property. However, the unity of the élite's institutional interests brings them together and maintains a war economy.

Mills' analysis coincided with and reinforced an attitude toward American society that was apparent in Eisenhower's denunciation of the "military-industrial complex." Many nonradical sociologists agree that economic life is increasingly intertwined with the activities of the government.[200] However, they argue that it is not simply military expenditures that are important, but rather the increased involvement of government in *all* spheres of economic life. Those of us who live in Washington notice how, month by month, more and more industrial, trade, and labor associations set up headquarters in the city's burgeoning office blocks, close to the federal government and its power.

[197]Mills, *White Collar*, pp. 83 and 349; C. Wright Mills, *The New Men of Power* (New York: Harcourt Brace, 1945); C. Wright Mills, *The Power Élite* (New York: Oxford University Press, 1958); C. Wright Mills, "The Power Élite: Military, Economic and Political," in Arthur Kornhauser, ed., *Problems of Power in American Society* (Detroit: Wayne University Press, 1958).

[198]Mills, "The Power Élite," pp. 156–58.

[199]Ibid., p. 164.

[200]See, for example, William Kornhauser, " 'Power Élite' or 'Veto Groups'?" in Reinhard Bendix and Seymour Martin Lipset, eds., *Class, Status and Power* (New York: Free Press, 1966); William V. D'Antonio and Howard J. Ehrlich, eds., *Power and Democracy in America* (Notre Dame, Indiana: University of Notre Dame Press, 1961).

Moreover, critics frequently disagree with Mills' perception of a single "power élite" pursuing its united interest and excluding others from influence. They argue that powerful interests may—and frequently do—conflict with each other. "Business," for example, undoubtedly has power. It gets some of the measures it wants, and some firms and industries acquire a protected, semimonopolistic position from government regulators. For others, however, plans are delayed or demolished by decisions about environmental quality, prices are set at levels they oppose, or costs are raised by taxes, government paperwork, pollution requirements, and the like.

In general, Mills shares with Marxist sociology and the "élite theorists" a tendency to see a society as divided rather sharply and horizontally between the powerful and the powerless. He also shares Marxist and neo-Marxist theorists' concerns about alienation, the effects of social structure on the personality, and the "manipulation" of people by the mass media. At the same time, however, Mills clearly belongs to a distinctively American populist tradition, which does not regard property as such as the main source of evil in society. To Mills, small-scale property ownership and the class of independent entrepreneurs are the major safeguards of freedom and security, and he regrets the waning of the old American society of independent farmers and businessmen.[201]

Summary

Of all contemporary sociological theories, those which combine a conflict perspective with social critique are the most clearly associated with arguments current outside academic life, especially among the politically involved. The political importance of these theorists is consequently greater than that of any other group we describe. This is especially evident outside the United States, but it is also true within it, as we can see from the following excerpt from the Port Huron Statement of Students for a Democratic Society, a central document of the student New Left of the 1960s. We find echoes of Marx's economic analysis, Mills' condemnation of the power élite, critical theory's view that society is "administered" and manipulated, and the concern of all these theories with people's alienation in its statement:

> We regard *men* as infinitely precious and possessed of unfulfilled capacities for reason, freedom, and love. . . . We oppose the depersonalization that reduces human beings to the status of things. . . . We oppose, too, the doctrine of human incompetence because it rests essentially on the modern fact that men have been "competently" manipulated into incompetence. . . .
>
> The American political system . . . frustrates democracy by confusing the individual citizen . . . and consolidating the irresponsible power of military and business interests.
>
> We would replace power rooted in possession, privilege or circumstance by

[201]Mills, *White Collar*, pp. 7–12.

power and uniqueness rooted in love, reflectiveness, reason and creativity. As a *social system* we seek the establishment of a democracy of individual participation. . . . The economic sphere would have [among its] principles:

> that work should involve incentives worthier than money or survival . . .
>
> that the economic experience is so personally decisive that the individual must share in its full determination.

Major social institutions should be generally organized with the well being and dignity of men as the essential measure of success.[202]

As we shall see in the next section, analytic conflict theory shares many of the general orientations of the "critical" conflict perspectives. The belief in an ideal society and the combination of analysis and moral outrage that the Port Huron Statement embodies are, however, as foreign to it as they are central to the work of the "critical" theorists we have just discussed.

PART TWO
Conflict Theory and Analytic Sociology: The Legacy of Max Weber

---

Ralf Dahrendorf, Lewis Coser, and Randall Collins, the theorists discussed in this section, can be grouped as "analytic" conflict theorists because they share the belief that a conflict perspective is central to the development of an objective, or "scientific," sociology. However, they are different from critical theorists in three important respects. First, whereas critical theorists see social science as intrinsically a part of political action and deny that fact and value can or should be separated, analytic theorists consider such a separation to be essential. They argue that it may be difficult or impossible for analysts, particularly those concerned with human society, to frame their hypotheses independently of their own opinions and concerns. Nonetheless, those hypotheses have implications that can be observed and tested objectively with empirical measures. It follows that ideas are not automatically distortions of reality just because they are also the products of particular social circumstances or tend to favor the interests of a particular social group.

Second, analytic conflict theorists do not analyze all societies as stratified along a single dimension, with a ruling group opposed to the masses. Analytic theorists would agree that some societies are of this type. Yet they believe that many others have far more complex power and status distributions and interlocking patterns of stratification, which do not line up neatly.

---

[202]Students for a Democratic Society, *The Port Huron Statement* (Chicago: SDS, 1969). The Port Huron Statement, as will be obvious to the reader from its wording, predates the growth of the feminist movement.

This is true, they believe, because there is a number of different sources of power and position in society, and one particular set of institutions, such as that based on property, is not always paramount.

Third, the analytic theorists do not contrast the present with a rational or conflict-free ideal for the simple reason that they do not believe in one. On the contrary, they emphasize that conflict and its roots are permanent and that conflicts of interest are inevitable.

In all these respects, modern analytic theorists share Max Weber's approach, just as Marx was the primary influence on the critical approach. Weber believed in the vital importance of objective social science. As we saw earlier, he developed a typology of "class, status, and party" as important influences on people's lives, as opposed to Marx's emphasis on property classes alone. Furthermore, Weber considered that the conflicts these generate are permanent features of human society, and he saw modern society tending not toward a communist utopia but toward a bureaucratic society inimical to human freedom. This is not to say, however, that either he or the analytic conflict theorists he influenced are indifferent to political action. In general, conflict theory appeals to sociologists who hold strong political views, and a number of modern analytic theorists have been very involved in politics and social policy, often in direct opposition to the ideas of critical and Marxist theory.

RALF DAHRENDORF

Ralf Dahrendorf (b. 1929) has for many years been widely known and respected in both Europe and North America. As a teenager in Nazi Germany, he was sent to a concentration camp for his membership in a high-school group opposing the state, and he has continued to be deeply involved in political affairs. He has been a Free Democratic member of the Baden-Württemberg Landtag (Regional Parliament) and the West German Bundestag (Parliament). As a member of the Commission of the European Communities, he has been responsible for external relations and for education, science, and research.

Dahrendorf has worked as an academic in Germany, Great Britain, and the United States. From 1974 to 1984 he was Director of the London School of Economics, one of the most prestigious British institutions of higher education. In 1984 he returned to Germany for a while, as professor of sociology at the University of Constance. He is now in England once again, as Warden of St. Anthony's College, Oxford University.

Dahrendorf's work on conflict reveals two major concerns. The first is with what he himself describes as "theories of society"[203]—that is, with

[203]Dahrendorf, *Essays*, pp. vi–viii.

setting out the general principles of social explanation. Here, Dahrendorf stresses the primacy of power and the consequent inevitability of conflict. Like Marx, his second concern is with the determinants of active conflict—the ways social institutions systematically generate groups with conflicting interests and the circumstances in which such groups will become organized and active.

Power, Conflict, and Social Explanation

There is, Dahrendorf argues, an inherent tendency to conflict in society. Those groups with power will pursue their interests, and those without power will pursue theirs. The interests of the two are necessarily different. Sooner or later, he argues—and in some systems the powerful may be very thoroughly entrenched—the balance between power and opposition shifts, and society changes. Thus, conflict is "the great creative force of human history."[204]

Power   According to Dahrendorf's theory of society, the distribution of power is the crucial determinant of social structure. His definition of power is Weber's: "the probability that one actor within a social relationship will be in a position to carry out his own will despite resistance, regardless of the basis on which this probability rests."[205] In this view, the essence of power is the control of sanctions, which enables those who possess power to give orders and obtain what they want from the powerless. However, people dislike submission. Therefore, Dahrendorf argues, there is inevitably a conflict of interest and an impetus for the powerless to conflict with the powerful, the former in pursuit of power, the latter in defense of it. Power is a "lasting source of friction."[206]

This essentially coercive view of power, which is common to most conflict theorists, is very different from that of functionalism.[207] As we have seen, Parsons believes that power is embodied in political institutions that solve the "functional imperative" of goal attainment.[208] The ability power bestows to get what one wants at others' expense he regards as a "secondary and derived" phenomenon. Dahrendorf's view is the opposite. Power is necessary if large organizations are to achieve their goals; and at times, such

---

[204]Ralf Dahrendorf, *Conflict and Contract: Industrial Relations and the Political Community in Times of Crisis,* the Second Leverhulme Memorial Lecture (Liverpool: Liverpool University Press, 1975), p. 17.

[205]Ralf Dahrendorf, *Class and Class Conflict in Industrial Society* (Stanford, Calif.: University of Stanford Press), p. 166; quotation from Max Weber, *The Theory of Social and Economic Organization* (Stanford, Calif.: Stanford University Press, 1959).

[206]Dahrendorf, *Essays,* p. 138.

[207]This view also differs from that of exchange theory, which is that power is rooted in the exchange of scarce and valuable resources.

[208]See Chapter II.

as in a defensive war, the powerful may carry out very clearly the common aims of a group. However, what Parsons considers the secondary aspect of power, Dahrendorf considers primary: the powerful are not granted power by the community to carry out some "common will," but grasp and use that power for their own ends.

Dahrendorf does not see the struggle for power as the sum of social life, however. Weber's (and Dahrendorf's) definition of power includes actors "within a social relationship"—that is, in situations where other people's actions matter. But there are also times when people are free to do what they like without other people mattering at all. In his recent lectures on the current political situation in the West, Dahrendorf has discussed the factors that endow societies with more or less "liberty" in this sense—with what has been called "negative freedom."[209] In America, for example, you are "at liberty" to move from one city to another without anyone's permission. In China you are not, and whether you get the requisite permission and papers largely depends on your own "power" and influence.

Norms   Like other conflict theorists, Dahrendorf argues that societal norms do not define or emerge from social consensus. Conflict theory, he argues, perceives, unlike functionalism, that norms "are established and maintained . . . by power, and their substance may well be explained in terms of interests of the powerful."[210] This may be seen from the fact that norms are backed by sanctions. Vivid examples of what Dahrendorf means can be found in China, where dissidents risk prison or exile to the remote countryside, or in the pre–civil rights South, where so-called "uppity" blacks or nonconforming whites could lose their livelihoods or even their lives. In turn, sanctions involve the control and use of power, particularly the power of law and punishment.[211] "In the last analysis, established norms are nothing but ruling norms," he suggests.[212]

Social Stratification   Dahrendorf clearly distinguishes between two facts: first, that positions and jobs are different and demand different skills, and second, that different jobs are treated as "superior" or "inferior" to one

[209]Ralf Dahrendorf, *The New Liberty* (London: Routledge and Kegan Paul, 1975). Power and liberty are not, of course, entirely distinct concepts. Some of the most interesting discussions of the two concepts are Brian Barry, ed., *Power and Political Theory: Some European Perspectives* (New York: Wiley, 1976); Stephen Lukes, *Power: A Radical View* (London: Macmillan, 1974); Isaiah Berlin, *Four Essays on Liberty* (London: Oxford University Press, 1969); Friedrich von Hayek, *The Constitution of Liberty* (Chicago: Henry Regnery Company, 1972); John Rawls, *A Theory of Justice* (Oxford: Oxford University Press, 1972).

[210]Dahrendorf, *Essays*, p. 140.

[211]Ibid., p. 141.

[212]Ibid., p. 174.

another. There are both "*social differentiation* of positions . . . and *social stratification* based on reputation and wealth and expressed in a rank order of social status."[213] Social stratification is what makes college presidents more generally respected than bus drivers and lies behind claims that teachers "ought" to be paid more than maintenance men.

Stratification, Dahrendorf argues, is caused by norms, which categorize some things as desirable and others as not. In every group, norms defining how people should behave entail discrimination against those who do not comply. During the Vietnam War, for example, those who supported the war were ostracized on some campuses, those who opposed it on others. In some adolescent groups, drug use and criminal behavior may be the norm, while in others drug use is viewed as a sign of personal weakness. Moreover, every society has *general* norms, which define certain characteristics as good (such as being an aristocrat or having more education than average) and which therefore entail discrimination against those who do not or cannot conform. These norms, Dahrendorf argues, are the basis of social stratification, and they are themselves derived from and upheld by power. Once again, therefore, power is the central concept.

This is a very different explanation from that of functionalists, who argue that social stratification derives from society's need to attract talented people into important positions. The two may not be as totally irreconcilable as Dahrendorf implies, however. Dahrendorf does not explain how a group becomes powerful in the first place, but this will surely often depend, at least in part, on its offering skills and a type of social order that people value. Not all successful ruling groups are military invaders! It is precisely the existence of a relationship between power and general social values that functionalism addresses. Similarly, economics' statement that income differentials are a result of the market value of skills[214] has given rise to theories of stratification linking success with the provision of scarce services.[215] However, a group that gains a hold on power in this way will almost certainly strive to maintain and take advantage of its position, convince everyone of its legitimacy and importance, and prevent competition from groups with different potential power bases—and Dahrendorf's approach is far better suited than functionalism's to analyzing this process.

---

[213]Ibid., p. 154.

[214]A good discussion of differing theories of pay inequalities can be found in Henry Phelps Brown, *The Inequality of Pay* (Oxford: Oxford University Press, 1977). See also the review by H. A. Turner, *Times Higher Education Supplement*, January 6, 1978. Janet Chafetz synthesizes alternative theories in her analysis of gender-linked pay inequalities. See below pp. 163–65.

[215]We shall meet this approach when we discuss exchange theory, and it is also embodied in Schumpeter's argument that innovations bring new groups to power. See the earlier section on "Intellectual Roots." Schumpeter was, in fact, primarily an economist.

The Determinants of Conflict:
A Theory of Conflict Groups

In his best-known work, *Class and Class Conflict in Industrial Society,* Dahrendorf addresses the question of when inequalities and conflicting interests will actually produce conflicts. His central argument is that social conflicts will take place, systematically, among groups that differ in the authority they enjoy over others. By *authority,* Dahrendorf (again following Weber) means the sort of power that is attached to a social role or position, that is legitimate in the sense of being defined and delimited by social norms, and that is backed by sanctions up to (and no further than) these limits. A university, for example, has the authority to charge you for your courses, board, and lodging, but not to take all your money. A mugger has the power to do just that—but no authority at all to do so.

Dahrendorf's position is that the stable and recurrent patterns of institutional authority systematically give rise to social conflict between those who have some degree of authority and those who have none. In a departure from conventional "economic" usage, Dahrendorf labels these groups *classes.* He writes that "the term 'class' signifies conflict groups that are generated by the differential distribution of authority in imperatively co-ordinated associations":[216] that is, organizations in which orders are given and taken.

Dahrendorf's theory thus implies that authority is dichotomous: you have it or you do not, and your interests are formed accordingly. Critics have suggested that whether you have more or less authority may be equally important and thus that conflict may form around other groupings. But Dahrendorf affirms, with Marx, that conflict involves only two sides. On the other hand, all "classes" do not engage in active conflicts all the time. Dahrendorf therefore attempts to explain when people will actually mobilize.[217]

The Mobilization of Classes The *structural* requirements for people to form active "interest groups" are "technical," "political," and "social."[218] Technically, Dahrendorf argues, a group requires a founder and a charter or ideology to become active. Politically, the more liberal the state, the more likely is mobilization for active conflict; the more totalitarian the state, the less likely. Finally, three social factors are important. Group formation is more likely first, if potential members are fairly well-concentrated geographically; second, if they can communicate easily (as modern communications technology makes it easier for them to do); and third, if people who stand in

---

[216]Dahrendorf, *Class and Class Conflict,* p. 204.
[217]Ibid., pp. 184–93.
[218]Ibid., pp. 178–93.

the same relation to authority are recruited in similar ways and come, for example, from the same type of families or educational organizations.

The most important *psychological* requirements are, of course, that individuals identify with the interests associated with their position and that these interests seem important and "real" to them. Dahrendorf disagrees with Marx's argument that people's class positions (in either the "property" or the "authority" sense) determine the whole of their social life and behavior, but he does believe class interests will be more "real" to people who also share a culture. He also suggests that people are less likely to identify with their class's interests and to mobilize, the larger the number of associations to which they belong.[219] Finally, the greater people's personal chances of leaving their class—in other words, the greater the degree of "intragenerational mobility"[220]—the less likely they are to identify actively with it.

Dahrendorf's "structural" arguments are fairly convincing, although he pays surprisingly little attention to force. He tends to emphasize that if conflict is not to become explosive, there must be some degree of mobility and freedom to express opposition. But as tyrannies throughout history have shown, a sufficient degree of force can suppress conflict very effectively.

Dahrendorf's discussion of the "psychological" requirements for class action is less satisfactory. Especially in preindustrial societies, the poor have often shared a culture, led lives confined to the immediate community, had few opportunities for advancement, and yet accepted the existing order of things almost without question. Thus, Dahrendorf fails to explain satisfactorily how attitudes of opposition originate.

Chafetz and Dworkin had similarly mixed success in explaining the rise of women's movements using Dahrendorf's perspective.[221] The appearance and size of "ameliorative" movements, concerned simply with legal and educational reforms, can be related very clearly to the breakdown of geographical barriers and to ease of communication—Dahrendorf's structural requirements. What the authors call "second-wave" movements, however—such as U.S. feminism—challenge gender roles directly and are highly ideological. Chafetz and Dworkin are correspondingly less successful in explaining why such feminist ideologies have emerged more or less strongly in different industrialized countries.

The Violence and Intensity of Conflict   Dahrendorf also discusses at considerable length what affects the intensity and violence of class conflict when it occurs. He defines *violence* as "a matter of the weapons that are chosen" and

[219]Ibid., p. 191.

[220]Ibid., p. 220.

[221]Janet Saltzman Chafetz and Anthony Gary Dworkin, *Female Revolt: Women's Movements in World and Historical Perspective* (Totowa, N.J.: Rowman and Allanheld, 1986).

intensity as the "energy expenditure and degree of involvement of conflicting parties."[222]

Dahrendorf argues that there is one preeminent factor affecting the degree of violence. This is how far conflict is institutionalized, with mutually accepted "rules of the game"; "those who have agreed to carry on their disagreements by means of discussion do not usually engage in physical violence."[223] For example, the days of extreme violence in strike breaking and picketing in America predate the general acceptance of unions.

Dahrendorf also identifies three important factors influencing the intensity of a conflict. Of these, the first (which he also considers to be the most important[224]) is the degree to which those who are in positions of subjection in one association are in the same position in their other associations. The second and parallel factor is the degree to which authority in an organization is held by people who are also "on top" in other respects—in Dahrendorf's terms, whether positions are "pluralist" or "superimposed." Thus, if the managers of firms are also the owners and if they also use their wealth and position to control politics, one can expect particularly intense industrial conflicts.

Dahrendorf's third argument is that the greater the mobility between positions, the less intense the conflict will be. This is true not only when individuals themselves can move, but also when their children are mobile. This is partly because mobility makes it less likely that a class will have a common culture and partly because people are less inclined to attack a class their children may one day join. On the other hand, if there is little or no mobility, the struggle becomes more intense.

Dahrendorf's theory allows one to pinpoint potential areas of conflict within any given organization. As we have seen, however, it does not give enough attention to the role of brute force. Nor does it help us much in predicting which organizations (of the many in which people give or receive orders) are more likely to experience open conflict. One simple reason for the latter problem is that Dahrendorf does not discuss how important a given institution is to someone's life. In a society of "superimposed" positions, there is almost certain to be one major source of power and authority from which the others follow. When conflicts in totalitarian countries do break through, they center on the party's power and control of the state. In Western societies, since both the state and one's place of work are very important institutions, they are both far more likely to generate active conflict than an athletic or church social club. Dahrendorf's own discussion does in fact pay most attention to industrial enterprises and the state.

[222]Ibid., pp. 211–12.

[223]Ibid., p. 228.

[224]Ibid., p. 214, p. 317. See also the discussion of Blau's structuralist theory and, especially, his concept of consolidation in Chapter VII.

Conflict in Industry   During the last hundred years, there have been increasing numbers of "joint stock" companies, in which ownership by shareholders is divorced from management control. As we have seen, modern Marxist sociologists generally argue that the change is not very important, since the firms still represent and are run in the interests of the owners. Other writers, such as Burnham,[225] believe that it signifies a far-reaching change in social structure and the roots of power.

Dahrendorf argues that his approach demonstrates both what has really changed and what has not. He suggests that because nineteenth-century managers and owners were generally the same people, Marx mistakenly ascribed to property differences a conflict that actually centered on authority, although it was intensified by the "superimposition" of industrial authority, wealth, and political influence.[226] Today, he continues, industrial conflict will be less intense both because ownership and control are separate and because of industry's "institutional isolation"[227] (which means that one's position in industry has less to do with the rest of one's life than before). At the same time, the split in authority and the conflicts of interest it generates remain. Arguments that the divide between workers and management has blurred are quite mistaken.

A study with direct relevance to Darhrendorf's argument is *The Affluent Worker in the Class Structure*.[228] This intensive survey of affluent British industrial workers was largely aimed at determining whether there had been a breakdown of the old social divisions between the "working" and the "middle" classes. The results cast doubt on the degree to which industry is, as Dahrendorf suggests, "institutionally isolated." The workers' family-centered social life, for example, remained quite separate from that of white-collar families. However, although union organization was stronger in these plants than in many much less wealthy areas, these workers were only rarely committed to the "union movement" as a national "working-class" force; instead they were extremely involved in union affairs at the level of the workplace.[229] Only 8 percent attended union branch meetings often enough to vote regularly in branch elections, but 83 percent voted regularly for their shop stewards. In other words, they were closely involved in union organization at the level where they were given orders directly and where they grouped together, to face and face down the managers who gave them, but not in questions of union and economic policy or "class" politics at the national level.

---

[225]James Burnham, *The Managerial Revolution* (London: Putnam, 1942).

[226]Dahrendorf, *Class and Class Conflict*, p. 136.

[227]Ibid., p. 267.

[228]John H. Goldthorpe, David Lockwood, Frank Bechhofer, and Jennifer Platt, *The Affluent Worker in the Class Structure* (Cambridge: Cambridge University Press, 1969).

[229]Ibid., pp. 168–69.

Conflict and the State   Dahrendorf argues that in the state, as in industry, the crucial lines of conflict are between those who give and those who receive orders. The state is the most powerful association in society, and the "ruling class" is, in a sense, the élite group that holds the positions at the top of the state hierarchy. But the ruling class is not composed solely of this group. The bureaucracy, too, belongs to a chain of command, and this command of authority makes it part of the ruling class, even though it does not define the concerns and objectives of a bureaucratic state. Dahrendorf's argument helps explain the enormous stability of such bureaucratic states as Byzantium and the Egypt of the Pharaohs. The larger the authority-bearing class, the larger the group that will marshall against any threat to it from an organized conflict group of subordinates.[230]

Dahrendorf's argument also implies that the state and bureaucracy are together a separate institution, not simply a reflection of other social groupings, and that other powerful social groups will necessarily oppose the state's authority and try to influence it and restrict its control over them. Thus, in Washington, a building boom transformed the downtown area during the 1970s and 1980s. The new offices house thousands of registered lobbyists, as well as law firms that are expanding in response to more and more regulatory legislation. In Dahrendorf's own recent analyses of British politics,[231] he argues that "clearly there is today a conflict between government and industry"[232] in which the trade unions are the most visible protagonists but which also involves the giant companies.

A number of modern commentators echo Dahrendorf when they write that growing government activity will have consequences for the range and intensity of political conflict. For example, Christopher DeMuth, a faculty member at Harvard's Kennedy School of Government who formerly worked for Conrail, discussed in the *Wall Street Journal* the behavior of the huge Greyhound bus company. He described how Greyhound lobbies vigorously against the federal subsidies given to passenger trains, with which the buses must compete, while it attempts with equal vigor to stop the Interstate Commerce Commission from allowing new bus companies to start competing with Greyhound and tries to prevent any general deregulation of bus transport. DeMuth argues, "There is no reason to expect Greyhound or any other company to compete in the economic marketplace while abstaining from the political marketplace . . . [when government involvement] becomes . . . sufficiently large, it alters fundamentally the na-

---

[230]It also enabled one of the authors (to her own great satisfaction) to predict correctly during the 1970s power struggles in China that the bureaucrats, who favored stability and industrialization, would defeat the radicals, who favored "continuous revolution," Red Guard iconoclasm, and extreme egalitarianism.

[231]Dahrendorf, *The New Liberty* and *Conflict and Contract.*

[232]Dahrendorf, *Conflict and Contract,* p. 14.

ture of competition in the private part [of the economy]—increasing the
relative importance of political as opposed to economic competition."[233]

Summary

Dahrendorf provides an illuminating account of the close and permanent relationship between power, or authority, and conflict. He also presents a concrete theory of conflict group formation, which provides a good
starting point for explaining people's objectives and identifying potential
confrontations. He describes a number of the important factors that either
create mobilized conflict groups and intense conflicts or, correspondingly,
tend to reduce social conflict. However, his theory of conflict group mobilization fails to explain what makes people aware of themselves as a group
with common interests and common grievances. This crucial shift from
what Marx characterizes as a class "in itself" to a class "for itself" occupies
most conflict theorists,[234] and it is also addressed by the rational choice
perspective.[235] No one theorist provides a fully satisfactory answer, probably because both micro and macro psychological and sociological variables
are involved.

Dahrendorf also fails to specify precisely which institutions in a society
will be the ones in which conflict will actually occur. This makes it difficult
to "test" his basic proposition about conflict formation. Nevertheless his
general perspective has proven illuminating enough to suggest that the
polarization which Dahrendorf identifies between those with and without
authority is at least one important source of social conflict.

LEWIS COSER

Like many other conflict theorists, Lewis Coser (b. 1913) combines a distinguished academic career with a strong interest and involvement in social
policy and politics. He was born in Berlin into a Jewish family of bankers,
against whom he reacted strongly. Because of his involvement with the
socialist student movement, he left Germany when Hitler came to power.
There followed some miserable years in Paris, where, without a work permit, Coser survived at just above starvation level. However, enrollment at
the Sorbonne[236] was free, and Coser studied comparative literature. He
proposed a dissertation topic comparing nineteenth-century French, En-

[233]Christopher C. DeMuth, "Tubthumping in the Political Marketplace," *The Wall Street
Journal* (1977). See also Chapter IV passim.

[234]See above p. 94 and below p. 153 (Coser's analysis). See also Durkheim on the role of
religion and ritual in creating group identification.

[235]See below pp. 222–24.

[236]University of Paris.

glish, and German novels in terms of their countries' different social structures. "This is sociology, not comparative literature," a horrified professor exclaimed. So, Coser explains, "I switched to sociology and have been stuck with it ever since."[237]

On the outbreak of war, Coser was interned as an enemy alien.[238] Aided by a local socialist mayor, he managed to get a visa as a political refugee, and reached New York via Spain and Portugal.[239] After the war he taught at the University of Chicago for a while, before earning a Ph.D. at Columbia. He spent nearly twenty years at Brandeis University, and from 1968 to 1988 he was Distinguished Professor of Sociology at the State University of New York (SUNY) at Stony Brook. Since retirement in 1988, he has been Professor Emeritus of Sociology at SUNY at Stony Brook and Adjunct Professor of Sociology at Boston College.

Coser remains a socialist, though no longer a Marxist. His writings have always reflected his concern with politics and the links between ideas and the nature of society. With Irving Howe he founded *Dissent* "during the darkest years of the McCarthy nightmare, to dissent from the intolerance and cowardice of so many intellectual spokespersons that marked this dismal episode."[240] Coser has also contributed frequently to other serious nonspecialist journals, such as *Partisan Review* and *Commentary,* and is coauthor of a history of the American Communist Party dedicated to Milovan Djilas.[241]

Some of Coser's more recent work is about "greedy institutions" that demand total involvement from their members. Coser says that in the face of recent "indiscriminate" condemnations of the "differentiated, segmented and 'alienated' character of modern life,"[242] he felt bound to point out the threat to human freedom inherent in total involvement. "I wish it to be clearly understood," he writes, "that I consider it essential that an open society be preserved above all."[243]

Of the modern theorists discussed in this chapter, Coser is the closest to Simmel. He is the most concerned with the "web of conflict," or the cross-

---

[237]Lewis A. Coser, "Notes on a Double Career," in Matilda White Riley, ed., *Sociological Lives,* Vol. 2: *Social Change and the Life Course,* American Sociological Association Presidential Series (Newbury Park, Calif.: Sage, 1988).

[238]Fortunately the camp was in the Vichy zone, which was run by a collaborationist French regime after the defeat of France by Germany.

[239]On arrival he visited the International Relief Committee. The young woman handling his case, Rose Laub, herself a refugee, was to become his wife and fellow sociologist.

[240]Coser, *Notes on a Double Career,* p. 69.

[241]Irving Howe and Lewis Coser with the assistance of Julius Jacobson, *The American Communist Party: A Critical History 1919–1957* (Boston: Beacon Press, 1957). See above for a description of Djilas' critical analysis of Communist societies.

[242]Lewis Coser, *Greedy Institutions: Patterns of Undivided Commitments* (New York: The Free Press, 1974), p. 17.

[243]Ibid., p. 18.

cutting allegiances that can both bind a society together and generate struggles and confrontations. Indeed, Coser's major book on conflict theory, *The Functions of Social Conflict*,[244] is an exposition and development of Simmel's own rather fragmented insights. Coser emphasizes that conflict, although very important, is only one side of social life and no more "fundamental" than consensus.[245]

Coser's contributions to conflict theory are also distinctive in two other respects. First, he discusses social conflict as a result of factors other than opposing "group interests." Second, he is concerned with the *consequences* of conflict. As we have seen, Dahrendorf's major concern is with the origins of conflict, which, he argues, then creates social change. Coser has less to say about the institutional roots of conflict, but he distinguishes among its different possible consequences, which include greater social stability as well as change. His discussion of the conditions under which conflict is likely to be divisive or cohesive adds considerably to Dahrendorf's analysis of conflict's characteristics.

The Origins of Social Conflict

In his discussion of the origins of conflict, Coser pays far more attention than do most conflict theorists to the role played by people's emotions.[246] He agrees with Simmel that there are aggressive or hostile "impulses" in people, and he emphasizes that in close and intimate relationships both love and hatred are present. Close proximity, he points out, means that there are also ample opportunities for resentment to develop; hence, conflict and disagreement are integral parts of people's relationships, not necessarily signs of instability and breakup.

At the same time, Coser argues, the forms that hostility and conflict take and their relative frequency in different situations have to be explained in terms of social institutions and social roles. A good example of what Coser means is the differences among countries in how much children fight with their parents. This is the sort of "close" relationship in which some resentments are inevitable. However, there are also intercultural variations in the father's authority; whether the children have financial independence; whether the steps by which children assume well-defined adult roles are clearly laid down; and whether other family members provide practical and emotional support outside the nuclear family. Coser's own work ad-

---

[244]Coser, *The Functions of Social Conflict* (New York: The Free Press, 1956).

[245]Lewis Coser, *Continuities in the Study of Social Conflict* (New York: The Free Press, 1967), p. 139.

[246]The arguments of *The Functions of Social Conflict* are presented in the form of sixteen separate propositions. Coser's discussion of the origins of conflict can be found under propositions 3, 4, 5, and 8.

dresses the way such "structural" factors interact with people's underlying emotions.

Coser defines two basic types of conflict: "realistic" and "nonrealistic."[247] In realistic conflict, people or groups are simply using conflict as the most effective way of getting what they want; if they could get what they wanted without a fight, they would give up the conflict immediately. Coser's inclination is to see most kinds of social conflict as essentially "realistic," or rational—explicable in institutional terms. Thus, in the Los Angeles Watts riot of August 1965, Coser saw something other than the "insensate rage of destruction" described by the official McCone report. The path of the riot, he pointed out, led straight to City Hall; the riot was a way of getting the authorities' attention. Similarly, the Luddite machine smashers of the early nineteenth century were highly selective in their targets; they were, Coser argues, engaging in "collective bargaining by riot" at a time when more organized union channels were outlawed.[248]

Conflicts of this type are essentially the same as those that other conflict theorists analyze in terms of "self-interest." However, Coser argues, there are also nonrealistic conflicts, in which the conflict is the end in itself, whether or not this is admitted. Nonrealistic conflict serves as a way of releasing tension or affirming one's identity, and it embodies hostilities that actually derive from other sources. Blaming everything on a scapegoat is a classic example. So are cases where sacked employees react by holding fellow workers hostage at gunpoint or even murdering their boss.[249] Often, of course, a conflict contains both realistic and nonrealistic examples.

The Consequences and Functions of Conflict

In his analysis of the results of social conflict, Coser argues that conflict often leads to change.[250] For example, it can stimulate innovation[251] or, especially in war, increase centralization.[252] For the most part, however, Coser concentrates on conflict's role in maintaining group cohesion. This is, of course, the subject that most concerns functionalists. However, Coser is a "functionalist" only in the sense of sharing this interest. He does not

[247]Ibid., pp. 48–55.

[248]Lewis Coser, "Internal Violence as a Mechanism for Conflict Resolution." Paper presented to the Sixth World Congress of Sociology, Evian, France, 1966: reprinted in *Continuities*, pp. 93–110. See also Lewis Coser, "Some Social Functions of Violence," *The Annals*, 364 (March 1966); reprinted in *Continuities*, pp. 73–92.

[249]Both are 1988 Washington-area incidents. Example provided by Anne J. Kanour.

[250]See especially Coser, *Functions*, propositions 9, 13, 15, and 16.

[251]Coser suggests that conflict between employers and unions over wages was one of the forces encouraging innovation, because it gave employers a strong incentive to develop the labor-saving technology that increased the economy's productivity. Lewis Coser, "Social Conflict and the Theory of Social Change," *British Journal of Sociology*, VIII, no. 3 (1953); reprinted in *Continuities*, pp. 17–35.

[252]Coser, *Functions*, pp. 89–95.

imply that it is necessarily desirable for a group to survive and remain cohesive or that conflict occurs *because* it may be functional for the group. He sees cohesion as only one of conflict's possible results.

In this context, Coser distinguishes between conflicts that are external and conflicts that are internal to a group. Both types, he argues, can define a group, establish its identity, and maintain its stability and increase its cohesion.

External Conflict   In his most unqualified statement about the relationship between conflict and cohesion, Coser argues that external conflict is essential in establishing a group's identity. In this he is following not only Simmel but also Marx, who felt that only conflict makes a class self-aware. Coser states, with Simmel, that "conflict set boundaries between groups within a social system by strengthening group consciousness and awareness of separateness, thus establishing the identity of groups within the system."[253] However, he also distinguished expressly between hostile sentiments and actual conflict,[254] and we would suggest that it is hostile sentiments, rather than actual conflict, that are essential to group formation. A religious group or utopian agricultural settlement of the type common in American history may coexist with other parts of society without overt conflict.

Coser also argues that external conflict can often strengthen a group. It makes group members conscious of their identity by introducing a strong "negative reference group" to which they contrast themselves; it also increases their participation.[255] Nonetheless, the process is not inevitable. If internal cohesion before the outbreak of conflict is very low, the conflict may simply hasten disintegration. Coser contrasts the disruptive effects of the Second World War on French society with its unifying effects in Britain.[256] A less dramatic but similar example is America during the Vietnam and Second World Wars. However, since Coser offers no way of telling in advance which development is likely, his arguments here are not very useful in explaining actual conflicts.

Internal Conflict   Coser follows Durkheim, Mead, and even Marx in arguing that a group's opposition to and conflict with "deviants" makes apparent to group members what they ought to do.[257] In this sense, internal conflict is central to defining a group's identity, which is embodied in norms that define "correct" behavior.

[253]Ibid., p. 34.
[254]Ibid., p. 37.
[255]Ibid., p. 90.
[256]Ibid., p. 93.
[257]Lewis Coser, "Some Functions of Deviant Behavior and Normative Flexibility," *American Journal of Sociology*, LXVIII, no. 2 (1962); reprinted in *Continuities*, pp. 111–33.

Coser also argues that internal conflict can increase a group's survival, cohesion, and stability. He again follows Simmel when he argues that internal conflict is a crucial safety valve under "conditions of stress . . . preventing group dissolution through the withdrawal of hostile participants."[258] If opposition to one's associates were not possible, people would, in Simmel's words, "feel pushed to take desperate steps . . . opposition gives us inner satisfaction, distraction, relief."[259] Indeed this is one of the few occasions when Coser falls into the trap of implying that because something is functional it will automatically happen, and that because safety valves are important all societies will provide them.[260]

Coser's argument here seems to confuse a group's survival or stability with its cohesion. He implies that whatever promotes survival also promotes cohesion. However, if it uses brute force and terror to support imbalances of power, a society can survive and even remain stable in the face of a great deal of internal hostility: witness "Papa Doc's" Haiti or Stalin's Russia. Although conflict *may* help maintain a society by providing a safety valve, this pattern is hardly a necessary or universal one. On the other hand, Coser is probably correct in emphasizing the close links between internal conflict and group *cohesion*. In rigid social structures with no channels for expressing hostility, when conflict occurs it is disruptive and violent.

Finally, Coser argues that internal conflict can be important because "stability within a loosely structured society . . . can be viewed as partly a product of the continuous incidence of various conflicts crisscrossing it."[261] When people belong to many different groups, each of which pursues its own interests and is consequently involved in its own conflicts, they are less likely to devote all their energies to a single conflict that could break the society apart. Thus, Coser suggests, "one reason for the relative absence of 'class struggle' in this country is the fact that the American worker, far from restricting his allegiance to class-conflict groupings and associations, is a member of a number of associations and groupings . . . [and] the lines of conflict between all these groups do not converge."[262]

In this context, Coser admires Max Gluckman's work on the importance of cross-cutting conflicts in African tribes. Gluckman notes that "all over the world there are societies which have no governmental institutions. . . . Yet these societies have well-established and well-known codes of morals and law. . . . We know that some of them have existed over long

---

[258]Coser, *Functions*, p. 39. Coser also argues that violent conflicts, such as ghetto riots, serve the function of calling attention to neglected conditions. However, social stability would surely be better served if the discontented accepted their position. See *Continuities*, pp. 93–110.

[259]Georg Simmel, *Conflict*, trans. Kurt H. Wolff (Glencoe, Ill.: The Free Press, 1955). Quoted in Coser, *Functions*, p. 39.

[260]Coser, *Functions*, p. 48.

[261]Ibid., p. 77.

[262]Ibid.

periods with some kind of internal law and order, and have successfully defended themselves against attacks by others."[263]

These "feuding" societies rely on private vengeance instead of government. The process does not tear them apart, Gluckman argues, because they "are so organized into a series of groups and relationships that people who are friends on one basis are enemies on another. [For example,] a man needs help in herding his cattle: therefore he must be friends with neighbors with whom he may well quarrel over other matters. . . . And through his wife he strikes up alliances with relatives-in-law which are inimical to a wholehearted one-sided attachment to his own brothers and fellow-members of his clan. . . . A man's blood-kin are not always his neighbours: the ties of kinship and locality conflict. . . . These allegiances . . . create conflicts which inhibit the spread of dispute and fighting."[264]

Divisive Social Conflict

In discussing conflict's role in defining a group and maintaining its cohesion, Coser makes the proviso that internal conflict has this role only if it is not about basic values and principles. This, in turn, depends on the rigidity of a society and, once again, the degree to which its members are interdependent.

Coser argues, first, that an internal conflict is more likely to involve basic principles (and so be socially divisive) in a rigid society that allows little "expression of antagonistic claims."[265] We have already noted Coser's belief that some conflict is functional because it serves as a safety valve, without which social hostility would eventually erupt violently. Here, he suggests that when conflict emerges after having been suppressed for a long time, it will also split the group around basic issues and values.

Second, Coser returns to the theme of "cross-cutting" allegiances and argues that "interdependence checks basic cleavages."[266] Interdependence therefore makes divisive internal conflict much less likely and reduces the likelihood that external conflict will find a noncohesive group. As we have already discussed, the basic reason is that "interdependence" means that people with common interests in one respect are opposed in another, so that an overriding and polarizing issue is less likely. However, there is also a related psychological process involved. Conflicts are much more intense,

---

[263]Max Gluckman, *Custom and Conflict in Africa* (Oxford: Basil Blackwell, 1933), pp. 2–3.

[264]Ibid., pp. 4, 17–18. A situation of this type may not be stable. Marc Bloch suggests that the inability of people in medieval Europe to obtain reliable protection through kinship relations was important in creating the feudal system, under which the lords provided such protection. Differences in military technology and the inability of ordinary people to combat mounted swordsmen probably help explain the different outcomes in Europe and Africa. See Marc Bloch, *Feudal Society*, trans. L. A. Manyon (Chicago: University of Chicago Press, 1962).

[265]Coser, *Functions*, p. 45.

[266]Ibid., p. 76.

Coser argues, when they involve exclusive groups; this further increases the likelihood that divisive conflicts will occur in societies that have non-overlapping groups.

Such conflicts are intense because it is in close relationships that love and hate coexist. "The coexistence of union and opposition in such relationships makes for the peculiar sharpness of the conflict," Coser argues.[267] The fewer the groups people belong to, the more likely they are to become intensely involved in the ones they have. An intense involvement affects the nature of conflicts both within the group itself and between it and others. Although Coser, a sociologist, makes this point formally, the leaders of sects and the founders of revolutionary parties have always been aware that the more a person's relationships all lie within the group, the more his or her loyalties and energies will be at its disposal.[268]

The most dramatic and horrifying illustration of this principle in recent times occurred at Jonestown in Guyana in 1978. Jim Jones, leader of a community called the People's Temple, moved the community wholesale from California to a jungle site where members' isolation was total. There, one November day, 911 adults and children lined up to drink a lethal punch laced with cyanide. Its effects were clear to all but the very first drinkers; yet almost none resisted or attempted to escape from an agonizing death.

Coser and his wife, discussing the Jonestown horror, argue that, like other communes, the People's Temple was "an experiment in the total absorption of personality. Communes have an innate tendency to become . . . *greedy institutions.*"[269] Jones' means were classic ones. Members were isolated from any contact with the outside world. Before leaving the United States, they signed away all their possessions, leaving themselves no independence and nowhere else to go. A combination of promiscuity and enforced abstinence forced couples apart; people were submitted to public confessions, humiliations, and "catharsis." Jonestown "succeeded not merely in totally absorbing members within its boundaries but in reducing them to human pulp as well."[270] The final tragedy was precipitated by U.S. investigators, who posed a threat to Jones but had no quarrel with his followers. It was the nature of the group that made his conflicts theirs and left them incapable of resistance or escape.

Coser's arguments about interdependence follow reasoning similar to James Madison's in *The Federalist Papers.* One of Madison's reasons for urg-

---

[267]Ibid., p. 71.

[268]Coser also related violence to these factors. Violent conflict is most likely, he argues, when groups are *both* unorganized *and* involve people with few other relationships—for example, poor urban blacks. *Continuities,* pp. 93–110. See also Coser, *Greedy Institutions.*

[269]Rose Laub Coser and Lewis Coser, "Jonestown as a Perverse Utopia: A 'Greedy Institution' in the Jungle," *Dissent* (Spring 1979), 159.

[270]Ibid., p. 163.

ing voters to adopt the American Constitution was that the resulting union of states would be one of considerable size and diversity. This would reduce the likelihood of one "faction" trampling over its fellow citizens and of oppression of a minority by the majority. He argued:

> The smaller the society, the fewer probably will be the distinct parties and interests composing it; the fewer the distinct parties and interests, the more frequently will a majority be found of the same party; and the smaller the number of individuals composing a majority . . . the more easily will they concert and execute their plans of oppression. Extend the sphere, and you take in a greater variety of parties and interests; you make it less probable that a majority of the whole will have a common motive to invade the rights of other citizens.[271]

Finally, although Coser stresses the importance for divisive conflict of a society's rigidity and the degree of its members' interdependence, his arguments about the role of ideas in conflict are also relevant here. Coser suggests that conflicts will be more intense when those involved feel that they are fighting on behalf of the group and not just for themselves—when, in consequence, they feel that what they are doing is morally legitimate. They also then feel strengthened by power derived from the collectivity with which they have identified and which they embody.[272] This is why Coser argues that intellectuals increase the bitterness and the radicalism of conflicts between labor and management; in Mannheim's words, they transform "conflicts of interest into conflicts of ideas"[273] and provide just this moral impetus.

Summary

The major importance of Coser's conflict theory lies in its demonstration that conflict can often be neither socially divisive nor a source of change. This is especially clear in his comparison of societies with or without many independent and overlapping groups and of the differing natures and consequences of conflict within them. However, Coser's account is not fully satisfactory. Complex and interdependent societies that are not particularly "rigid" may experience conflicts that are highly divisive, and rigid, hierarchical societies may survive for centuries without explosive conflict. The recent history of political strife in Central America, Chile, and Argentina illustrate our first point; the thousand-year history of the Byzantine Empire our second. In addition, the abstract quality that Coser's work shares with Simmel's and the way it ignores the nature and bases of group

---

[271]*The Federalist,* with an introduction by Edward Mead Earle (New York: The Modern Library, n.d.), pp. 60–61.

[272]Coser, *Functions,* p. 118.

[273]Ibid., p. 116.

resources mean that on its own it explains very little about concrete social situations. Finally, Coser's emphasis on the functions of conflict, although a useful corrective, is one-sided. At the very beginning of his work, he described social conflict as a struggle in which opponents attempt "to neutralize, injure, or eliminate their rivals."[274] Thereafter, one looks in vain for him to pay much attention to such behavior or to recognize the stability of many situations based on force and oppression.

RANDALL COLLINS

Randall Collins (b. 1941), the last of the conflict theorists we shall discuss, is also the youngest, and his work exemplifies the growing interest among American sociologists in a conflict perspective. We noted earlier the renewed interest in Marxism and the discovery of the Frankfurt School by younger, left-wing sociologists, who see their sociology as inextricably entwined with their desire for social change. Many of their contemporaries, whose aim in their sociology is scientific explanation and not political action, also now believe that a conflict perspective is the most fruitful way to approach sociological analysis.[275]

Collins' work is the most far-reaching theoretical synthesis based on this approach to date. Unlike Marx's or Dahrendorf's, Collins' work is not a conflict theory in the sense of describing when social conflict will actually occur. Indeed, in many of the situations he describes there is no overt conflict at all. Rather, he sets out to show that one can explain a wide range of social phenomena on the basis of a general assumption of conflicting interests and an analysis of the resources and actions available to people in particular social situations.

Collins took a B.A. at Harvard, an M.A. at Stanford, and a Ph.D. at the University of California, Berkeley. While still a student working as a research assistant at the Institute of International Studies at Berkeley, he began publishing.[276] He taught at the University of California, San Diego, and at the University of Virginia in Charlottesville; he is currently at the University of California, Riverside.

Collins' work incorporates all the major elements of conflict theory: an emphasis on people's interests, a view of society as made up of competing groups whose relative resources give their members more or less power over each other, and an interest in ideas as a weapon of social conflict and

---

[274]Ibid., p. 8

[275]See, for example, Jonathan Kelley and Herbert S. Klein, "Revolution and the Rebirth of Inequality: A Theory of Stratification in Post-Revolutionary Society," *American Journal of Sociology*, 83, no. 1 (1977), 78–99.

[276]For example, J. Ben-David and R. Collins, "Social Factors in the Origins of a New Science: The Case of Psychology," *American Sociological Review*, 31 (1966), 451–65.

domination. As he acknowledges, Collins' major debts are to Marx, "the great originator of modern conflict theory,"[277] and above all to Weber,[278] whose analytic framework, comparative historical approach, and non-utopian outlook he adopts.

In addition, of all the conflict theorists we have discussed, Collins draws most on Durkheim, who is commonly seen as the father of functionalism. Collins has little good to say about functionalism, but he believes that Durkheim explains a great deal about the ways in which emotional bonds and loyalties are created among people. The most original aspect of Collins' work is the way he incorporates a theory of how social integration is achieved into a conflict approach. Unlike most conflict theorists, Collins also draws on the work of such theorists as Mead, Schutz, and Goffman, who are generally associated with such "micro-sociological" perspectives as symbolic interactionism and phenomenology. This is the result of his concern with exactly how individual loyalties and emotional bonds develop.

The Nature of Conflict Sociology

Collins' basic assumptions are that there are certain "goods," namely wealth, power, and prestige, that people will pursue in all societies,[279] and that everyone dislikes being ordered around and will always do his or her best to avoid it.[280] That is, he assumes that people have certain basic interests wherever they live and that they will act accordingly.

From this it follows that there will always be social conflict. This is true even though not everybody is equally greedy, simply because power, in particular, is inherently unequal: if I have a great deal of power, other people must necessarily have less, and they must obey me. "Since power and prestige are inherently scarce commodities and wealth is often contingent upon them, the ambition of even a small proportion of persons for more than equal shares of these goods sets up an implicit counter-struggle on the part of others to avoid subjection and disesteem," Collins concludes.[281] Such social conflict can take many forms, but at the very heart of it, he believes, lies direct coercion. Force is something people can always turn to, and some people always fare better at it than others. "Above all else, there is conflict because violent coercion is always a potential resource, and it is a zero-sum sort."[282]

[277]Randall Collins, *Conflict Sociology: Toward an Explanatory Science* (New York: Academic Press, 1975), p. 428.

[278]Ibid., pp. 58–59.

[279]Collins, "Functional and Conflict Theories of Educational Stratification," *American Sociological Review*, 36 (1971), 1009; and *Conflict Sociology*, Chapter 2.

[280]Collins, *Conflict Sociology*, p. 59.

[281]Collins, "Functional and Conflict Theories," p. 1009.

[282]Collins, *Conflict Sociology*, p. 59.

As part of his analysis of the determinants of social structure and change, Collins provides a typology of the resources people bring to this struggle. First are material and technical resources, which include not only property, tools, and such skills as literacy but also—very importantly—weapons. Second, he stresses the role that strength and physical attractiveness play in personal relationships. Third, he mentions the sheer numbers and types of people with whom individuals have contact and with whom, therefore, they have the possibility of negotiating for material goods and status.[283] Fourth, Collins emphasizes the resources people possess in their "store of cultural devices for invoking emotional solidarity."[284] By this he means their ability to create and maintain a shared view of how things are and should be, which also sustains the favored position of those promoting that view.

We can see what Collins is talking about if we compare the position of a rural Indian untouchable with that of, say, a nineteenth-century Hindu maharajah. The untouchable has almost no skills he could market in a city, for he is barred by the caste system from all but certain "unclean" jobs, such as curing hides or cleaning latrines. For him to work with caste Hindus would pollute them. His social contacts are extremely limited, so he knows very little about whether he has any alternatives; he is dirty and undernourished; and his religion, dominated by the priestly caste of the Brahmins, teaches him that his lot is the inevitable result of his conduct in previous lives and must be accepted as such. By contrast, the maharajah has enormous resources and breadth of opportunities and social contacts. Being better fed, he is almost certainly bigger and more attractive physically. Moreover, although he has little or no control over the conduct of the Hindu religion and the influence of its priests, his cosmopolitan contacts may well have weakened the priests' influence over him. Obviously the maharajah is in a position of enormous power compared to the untouchable, and he is in a position to achieve a much wider range of objectives. If you compare two very dissimilar people in America, such as a mother on welfare and a company president, you will find that there are again big differences—but also that they are less extreme. This is because the two societies distribute their resources very differently.

Collins follows Weber in suggesting that there are three main areas of life in which people obtain more or fewer resources and are more or less dominant or subjected. Together these create the patterns of "social stratification." They are first, people's occupations, where they can be grouped into different *classes;* second, the communities where people live, with their different *status groups,* including age, gender, ethnic, and educational groupings; and third, the political arena, where different *parties* seek political

---

[283]See exchange theory's discussion of "monopoly" in Chapter IV for a related analysis.
[284]Collins, *Conflict Sociology,* p. 60.

power.[285] In every case, what is crucial for social behavior is the degree to which people are in a position to control others and so obtain wealth, status, and overt deference. Collins does not regard one aspect of stratification as primary: people's overall position is simply the sum of their resources and positions in a number of different areas. In other words, Collins prefers Weber's pluralist model to Marx's unicausal one, arguing that "different orders of stratification do not line up neatly."[286]

The major part of Collins' work sets out propositions about the concrete ways in which the distribution and use of resources result in different sorts of social behavior and institutions. He also discusses in detail what creates a shared culture and a "legitimate" social order.

Social Institutions and the Balance of Resources

Some of Collins' most interesting arguments about the relationships among conflicting interests, the distribution of resources, and the nature of social institutions concern modern education, organizational theory, and the state. In each case, we shall find that his method is drawn from Weber: for the most part, he discusses general principles in terms of concrete historical settings and the balance of power within them.

Stratification by Education   Collins has always been interested in how educational qualifications have been used as a resource in the struggle for power, wealth, and prestige, and he has used a conflict perspective to carry out empirical research on the role of education in people's careers. He treats education as one important basis of status-group differences, a sort of "pseudo-ethnicity" that socializes people into a particular form of culture.[287] The educational élite, which shares a given culture, will use it as a criterion for employment in élite positions he argues. As educated people themselves, it is in their interests for educational institutions to serve a "gatekeeping" function, with only those who have passed through successfully allowed to proceed to the next level of the social hierarchy. Similarly the élite will try to instill respect for its culture in the society as a whole.[288]

Modern industrial societies have longer periods of formal education and require far higher educational credentials for jobs than preindustrial ones. The usual explanation given is that more jobs require more skills than in the past, but Collins argues that this is, at best, only a part of the truth. The evidence shows that education "is not associated with employee produc-

[285]Ibid., pp. 79–87.

[286]Ibid., p. 50.

[287]C.f. the work of Pierre Bourdieu, especially his *Homo Academicus*, trans. Peter Collier (Cambridge, England: Polity Press, 1988); Collins, *Conflict Sociology*, pp. 86–87.

[288]See Collins, "Functional and Conflict Theories of Educational Stratification," and Randall Collins, *The Credential Society: An Historical Sociology of Education and Stratification* (New York: Academic Press, 1979).

tivity on the individual level, and job skills are learned mainly through opportunities to practice them,"[289] and not at school at all. Differences among industrial countries are very marked, but not obviously related to technological progress. For example, in the postwar period, American education has, on average, gone on far longer than that of the Japanese or West Germans.[290] Moreover, Collins points out, engineers are the one professional group with real technical skills that industry needs. If the "technological" explanation of modern education were correct, one would expect the engineering schools to have the highest prestige on campus, and engineering training to dominate education. Nothing of the sort has occurred. Indeed, America, at the undergraduate level, has "the most massively nonvocational system of education in the modern world."[291]

The best way to understand the enormous growth of the "credential system" is to see education as a way of setting up entry requirements for jobs (and so limiting competition) and creating exclusive occupational cultures which are defined as prerequisites for doing a job. Thus, if you do not speak the same language (or jargon) as established workers, having learned it during "professional" training, then this provides evidence against your competence. This process can, quite quickly, create the sort of "credential inflation" which we have experienced in recent years. The highly educated set up job requirements that favor them; people recognize the importance of education as a route to success and acquire ever more of it; employers raise entry requirements yet further to screen out the flood of applicants—and so on.

Weber showed that the Chinese literati used education in just this way. Confucian education was essentially literary with no obvious relevance to political administration. However, senior administrative and advisory posts were monopolized by those who were successful in the grueling literary examinations. Collins identifies similar examples at work today. The most "educated" executive group is found not in the most rapidly developing high-technology companies, but in the "traditionalistic" financial and utilities firms.[292] It is difficult to see this pattern as a result of "technological imperatives."

Unlike many Marxist analysts,[293] Collins does not see anything specifically capitalist about the use of education to create and preserve social position. Rather, education is always a potentially important resource,

---

[289]Collins, *The Credential Society*, p. 48.

[290]Ibid., p. 92. Russian education is also longer, on average, than that of European countries.

[291]Ibid., p. 162. Industrial countries vary markedly in the relative status of engineers, with the French having created an engineering élite educated outside the universities, in the "grandes écoles."

[292]Collins, "Functional and Conflict Theories," pp. 1013–14, and *Credential Society*, Chapter 2 passim.

[293]E.g., Bowles and Gintis, *Schooling in Capitalist America*.

though societies will vary in the degree of success which educated groups achieve. The analysis also has echoes of Ivan Illich's famous diatribe against formal education, *Deschooling Society*. Illich argues that schools teach little. Their main purpose is to assign social rank. "School reserves instruction to those whose every step in learning fits previously approved measures of social control," Illich charges.[294]

Stratification by Gender   In all societies, one of the most important "status groups" for determining people's life chances has been their gender. In almost every case, women are markedly inferior to men in their access to wealth, power, autonomy and other valued resources; in no known case are they actually superior.[295]

Collins outlines a theory to explain both this general situation and the *variations* in the general status of women.[296] He argues that the generally lower status of women results ultimately from human beings' strong drive for sexual gratification and from the fact that males are for the most part larger and stronger. However, between societies there are great variations. For example, in strict Islamic societies, women are kept veiled, in purdah; whereas in hunting and gathering and technologically simple tribal societies, women may enjoy relative equality. These variations, Collins argue, are a result of two major factors: women's market position and the way coercion operates in a society. Women are relatively well off in subsistence economies and affluent market economies, but worse off in "surplus-producing" economies of an intermediate sort. They are better off in nation-states where the state has a monopoly on coercion, and worse off where individuals are able to use force with no legal recourse for their victims or where coercion is "delegated" to the household level.

A number of feminist theorists have disagreed with Collins' argument that male strength is at the root of women's lower status. Both Janet Saltzman Chafetz and Rae Lesser Blumberg argue that is is women's biological role as childbearers which is crucial. Its impact can be minimized but not eliminated.[297] All societies have found it to be more efficient for those who bear and nurse children to do the caretaking too. In no society do women "as a category . . . specialize solely in productive/public sector roles."[298]

Although they may reject his general explanation of women's lower

[294] Ivan Illich, *Deschooling Society* (New York: Harper and Row, 1971), p. 19.

[295] Rae Lesser Blumberg notes that the very few societies in which sexes appear to be equal are small and noncomplex. Rae Lesser Blumberg, *Stratification: Socioeconomic and Sexual Inequality* (Dubuque, Iowa: W. C. Brown, 1978).

[296] Chapter V passim.

[297] Janet Saltzman Chafetz, *Sex and Advantage: A Comparative, Macro-Structural Theory of Sex Stratification* (Totowa, N.J.: Rowman and Allanheld, 1984); Rae Lesser Blumberg, *Stratification: Socioeconomic and Sexual Inequality,* and "A General Theory of Gender Stratification," in Randall Collins, ed., *Sociological Theory 1984* (San Francisco: Jossey-Bass, 1984), pp. 23–101.

[298] Chafetz, *Sex and Advantage*, p. 21.

status, a number of feminist theories of sexual stratification share Collins' basic approach to explaining *variations* in women's circumstances. These theories too, relate women's position to structural variables which can be present in varying degrees and share Collins' desire to establish general propositions about social institutions and practices.

Chafetz's theory of sex stratification is very much of this type. She defines the degree of inequality between the sexes in terms of access to scarce and valued resources and argues that a large number of variables affect this inequality. Among them are the average percentage of the female life cycle devoted to childbearing, the distance between work and home, the ideological/religious support for sex inequality, and the degree of "threat" (and of more or less formal warfare). Thus, Chafetz argues, for example, that "the higher the average fertility rates in a society and the greater the distance between worksite and homesite, the less involved women will tend to be in productive activities."[299]

Factors like these affect not only the number of women involved in productive activities, but also the ways in which they are involved. And this is crucial, because "the greater the involvement of females in the most important (highly valued) productive roles in their societies, the less the degree of sex stratification will tend to be, and vice versa."[300]

Chafetz does not see property as central in the way that Marxist theorists do. However, she does believe that women's participation in production is absolutely central to their status,[301] and she analyzes their continuing low pay and low participation in high-status occupations.

Pay inequalities are a perennial topic of debate in the social sciences, as well as in national politics.[302] Chaftez notes that most explanations fall into one of two categories. "Human capital" theory argues that people's pay is a reflection of their skills along with employers' "tastes" or requirements. If women have the skills employers want, then, according to this theory, they will be hired. It would be unprofitable for them not to be. "Dual labor market" theorists reject this explanation as a conservative apologia for the market system. They argue instead that the labor market falls into two parts. The "primary" sector, dominated by men, has security and good wages. Women and minority groups are forced into the "secondary" sector, marked by insecurity, short-term employment, and low returns.[303]

However, Chafetz points out, the two theories are not really incompati-

[299]Ibid., p. 68.

[300]Ibid., p. 52.

[301]Chafetz discusses this in terms of the "nature of work organization."

[302]The low pay of women graduates in the U.S. is one of the themes to which we return throughout this text. See especially Chapters I and VIII.

[303]See the sections on Dahrendorf's theory, above pp. 141–43, and on Gerson's analysis of women's career paths, below pp. 233–34, for further discussions of this issue.

ble.[304] Many factors, including childbearing, home tasks, and "ideological" attitudes toward girls' education, may affect dramatically women's ability to offer what employers require. Equally, gender stereotypes will affect employers' "tastes" and hiring practices, at least for as long as a shortage of labor does not force them to change. It is also true that workers in high-status occupations have every incentive to protect their position by making it as hard as possible for them to be replaced by alternative workers (such as women.) Structuring jobs so that it is difficult for them to be done by people who cannot work at all and any hours or who take a break during early child-rearing years, is an obvious strategy. It protects one's interests as an occupational group and keeps one's income level high.

Organizational Theory   Collins' general approach to organizations is to view them as "arenas for struggle" in which superiors try to control their subordinates. He argues that, in consequence, one can best understand the structure of an organization by looking at the sanctions available to those in charge.

The three main types of sanction which can be used are coercion; material rewards given in return for appropriate activities and behavior; and normative control, which invokes people's loyalty to ideals. Each has distinctive consequences. People dislike and resist coercion, and subordinates in the organizations that rely on coercion resort to "dull compliance and passive resistance."[305] Forced labor camps are extremely unproductive, and slaves consistently appear stupid and irresponsible to their masters. Material rewards, Collins suggests, are less alienating, but they produce organizations where there are continual fights over pay and piece rates, where informal groups control the work pace and prevent people from working "too hard" and where people tend to do things only if and insofar as they are paid.[306]

Normative control is the most desirable for superiors, because if subordinates share superiors' goals, they will be far more motivated to cooperate, obey, and work hard.[307] However, it too has costs attached. One of the most effective ways to create normative control is to spread authority, because the more people give orders in an organization's name, the more they identify with it. Superiors can, for example, "co-opt members into responsible positions; a related method is to offer them a chance to be promoted."[308] Both these approaches, however, tend to reduce the superior's own centralized power.

[304]Chafetz, *Sex and Advantage*, pp. 74–76.
[305]Collins, *Conflict Sociology*, p. 299.
[306]Ibid., p. 300.
[307]Ibid., pp. 300–301.
[308]Ibid., p. 301.

An alternative tactic is to recruit members who have a feeling of solidarity or friendship. Nepotism, the recruitment of family members, is a traditional way of creating organizational loyalty,[309] and recruiting people with similar backgrounds also makes friendships and thus loyalty to the organization more likely.[310] Collins also argues that the more an organization emphasizes rituals, is isolated from the world, and feels itself to be in danger from outside,[311] the more it will reinforce identification and loyalty. A good example of how isolation increases people's loyalty to an organization is the landslide majority that white South Africans gave to the Nationalist Party, the architects of apartheid, in 1978, a time of strong public American pressure and criticism. Similarly, in discussing Jonestown, the community whose members died after taking cyanide *en masse*, we noted the importance of ritual and isolation.[312]

However, Collins points out, people who like each other tend to form strong informal groups, which may disagree and conflict with their leaders. Organizations that rely on normative control can expect continual conflicts about policy and factional fights about who is best able to implement the group's goals. "Astute organizational politicians, then, always attempt to mix normative incentives with material rewards and perhaps subtle coercive threats, since the latter can be administered much more routinely and kept under more stable control."[313] To transform the revolutionary Bolshevik party into the bureaucratic Communist Party, Stalin changed from the "normative control" of shared ideals, with its intense ideological disputes, to control by the material rewards available to party members and the underlying fear of the secret police.

The State   In using a conflict perspective to analyze the state, Collins again emphasizes that coercion is at the core of social life and social conflict. The state, he suggests, is a special sort of organization, because it is "the way in which violence is organized"[314] and "*is*, above all, the army and the police."[315] To analyze political systems, Collins suggests, one must ask how violence is organized and which interest groups control and influence the state's policy.

Collins argues that the resources enabling people to win control of the state include systems of belief, property, networks of communication, and military technology.[316] Indeed, of all the theorists discussed in this chapter

---

[309]Ibid., p. 303.
[310]Ibid., p. 305.
[311]Ibid., pp. 304–305.
[312]See the section on Coser, above pp. 155–56.
[313]Ibid., p. 315.
[314]Ibid., p. 351.
[315]Ibid., p. 352.
[316]Ibid., p. 353.

Collins is (after Schumpeter) the most sensitive to the effects of military technology and military organization on political and social life. A society in which a large proportion of households fight with their own cheap weapons will be far more democratic, he argues, than one in which a small group with expensive individual equipment, like the medieval knights, monopolizes warfare. Similarly, whether an army is supplied and paid from central stores, like the Roman army, or requisitions locally and takes conquered lands as its reward, is crucial in determining whether there is a centralized state or a loose-knit feudal order.

Unlike Collins' analysis of military force, his discussion of economic resources as a basis for political power is sketchy. Collins sees coercion and military power as primary, and in discussing economic underpinnings of political systems, he essentially restates Lenski's rather Marxian typology, in which techniques of production are the major causal factor.[317] Collins' discussion tends to neglect the effect of different forms of property and economic organization on political structure. He also ignores the different laws and systems of law in which these forms are rooted, although law is as essential a function of the state as is the use of force. Curiously enough, Weber, the greatest influence on Collins' work, gave considerable emphasis to economic organization and its legal basis. For example, he pointed to the historical and political consequences of the ability of European townsmen to own their own labor and property and to govern their towns, and he showed the consequences of the way the Chinese were legally tied to the village-based sibs or clans, while their towns had no rights to self-government.

Culture, Ideology, and Legitimation

In discussing Collins' analysis of social structure, we have noted the importance he attaches to the creation of legitimacy. This emphasis on the role of ideas is, of course, common to conflict theory; but Collins' distinctive contribution is to provide detailed discussions both of the actual process by which common beliefs are generated and of the general relationships between people's outlook and the way they experience conflict situations.

Collins is continually at pains to remind his readers that his subject is ultimately individual people. Writers in the tradition of "social phenomenology," such as Mead and Goffman, have, he believes, a great deal to tell us

---

[317]Hunting and gathering societies are seen as the most politically (and financially) equal, since there is not enough wealth to support a large group not directly involved in producing essential goods; horticultural and agrarian societies are far more unequal, since the greater wealth and concentration of population permit a military aristocracy or priests, ruling through religion and ritual, to extract more; industrial societies are less unequal because power must be dispersed to run complex organizations. Although Lenski sees technology as primary, he also lists a number of secondary factors that affect social structure, including the percentage of men involved in bearing arms, but his discussion of the influence of military factors is far less detailed and sensitive than Collins'. See Gerhard E. Lenski, *Power and Privilege: A Theory of Social Stratification* (New York: McGraw-Hill, 1966).

about social interaction, because they focus on individual experiences and recognize that these are not something given, fixed, and immutable.[318] Instead, our experiences are in large part a result of our own perceptions and values, so that "men live in self-constructed subjective worlds."[319] These worlds determine whether we see a photograph, for example, as harmless, as a way of stealing our souls, or as a transgression of God's commandment against graven images. They also affect whether we experience our societies as good and satisfactory or oppressive. Moreover, Collins argues, the sorts of perceptions we have are themselves subject to regular and identifiable influences. We can identify the sorts of individual experiences that make people view a social order as "real" and legitimate, and so alter the course of social conflict.

The experiences Collins identifies are first, and most important,[320] the giving and taking of orders; and second, the sorts of communications people have with others.[321] He argues that because of the nature of human psychology, those who *give orders* will tend to identify with the ideals of the organization in which they hold power and in whose name they justify their orders. Also, because of their experiences, they will be self-assured and generally formal in manner. By contrast, the more people *receive orders,* the more alienated from organizational ideals they are likely to be and the more fatalistic, subservient, concerned with extrinsic rewards, and distrustful of others they will be. Those in the middle of the authority hierarchy, who give *and* receive commands, tend to combine subservience with organizational identification, but they are little concerned with an organization's long-term objectives.

Collins' basic premise is that people wish to maximize the degree to which they give rather than receive orders. Hence, he argues, a mid-level official or bureaucrat "attempts to transform order-taking situations into orders that he passes on to others."[322] This explains the proverbial inflexibility of mid-level bureaucrats compared to their superiors, who see rules as a means to more distant ends. On the other hand, Collins' general emphasis on the relationship between one's outlook and whether one gives or receives orders implies a world in which everyone works in large organizations. In fact, if you think about people's occupations, you will find that many people—such as farmers, insurance salesmen, and many housewives—are not much involved with "orders" on a day-to-day basis at all.

The types of communication that people have with others are extremely important, Collins argues, because they may reinforce or (and this

---

[318]See Chapters V and VI for a full discussion of this approach.
[319]Collins, *Conflict Sociology*, p. 60.
[320]Ibid., p. 73.
[321]Ibid., pp. 75–76.
[322]Ibid., p. 74.

is crucial for social control) offset the effects of people's experiences of command. They, above all, are what determine the degree to which people accept as "real" the ideas and norms around which their society is organized. They determine whether people see the social order as legitimate. Collins points out that human beings, like all animals, have automatic emotional reactions to certain gestures, sounds, and signals, and he suggests that social ties are fundamentally based on shared reactions, which differ from those of animals because they involve symbols (such as flags or salutes) rather than genetically programmed sounds and gestures.[323] The strength of these reactions depends on two aspects of people's communications with each other: the amount of time people spend together, or their "mutual surveillance," and the diversity of their contacts. These, Collins argues, correspond to what Durkheim called "social density" in his analyses of how "society" creates loyalty and identification among its members.[324]

Social Density Collins argues that the greater the degree of *mutual surveillance*—the more people are in the physical presence of others—the more they accept the culture of the group and expect precise conformity in others.[325] Conversely, the less they are around others, the more their attitudes are explicitly individualistic and self-centered.[326] This is in large part because being physically together makes it more likely that "automatic, mutually reinforcing nonverbal sequences" will develop. These increase "emotional arousal," and "the stronger the emotional arousal, the more real and unquestioned the meanings of the symbols people think about during that experience."[327]

The *diversity* or *cosmopolitanism* of people's contacts similarly affects the way they think. Collins argues that the more different sorts of communication people are involved in, the more likely they are to start thinking in abstract terms and in terms of long-range consequences. On the other hand, the less varied people's contacts, the more likely they are to think only about particular people and particular things and to see the world outside their own familiar circle as alien and threatening. Thus, limited contact will tend to create shared, local views of reality and a feeling of identification with familiar local people vis-à-vis the outside world.[328]

Ritual Collins believes that mutual surveillance and limited communications counteract the effects of being on the receiving end of orders. They

[323]Ibid., pp. 152–53.
[324]Ibid., p. 76.
[325]Ibid.,p. 75.
[326]Ibid., p. 75.
[327]Ibid., p. 153.
[328]Ibid., pp. 75–76.

create emotional ties that bind a group together and make the way it is organized unquestionably "real." Thus, they strengthen the position of the dominant members of a group. In addition, Collins argues, *rituals* or "stereotyped sequences of gestures and sounds,"[329] can make people's emotional arousal more intense and so commit them more strongly to certain views of reality. Emotional arousal is also affected, he suggests, by the sheer number of people involved.[330] If we look at the ceremonies to which groups and societies attach great importance, we can see that they generally combine highly stereotyped rituals with large gatherings of people. Durkheim pointed this out in his discussion of aboriginal religious ceremonies and their role in "integrating" society;[331] Hitler's Nuremberg rallies, graduation ceremonies, and the use of particular songs and symbols at civil rights or antiwar demonstrations are also good examples.

Collins' arguments here complement Schumpeter's and Habermas' discussions of the declining legitimacy of the modern market economy.[332] The "rational attitudes" of such a society mean that we tend to find ritual increasingly distasteful: compare a president holding barbeques at the White House with a pharaoh or a medieval king holding court. Using Weber's terminology, Collins observes, "*Traditional authority* . . . uses highly stereotyped gestures and verbal formulas, with the result that the symbols of authority are highly reified and emotionally compelling. . . . [Under] *rational-legal authority* . . . little attention is paid to the surrounding postures, with the result that symbols are regarded as human enactments with little emotional compulsion."[333]

The empirical evidence gives Collins' arguments considerable but far from total support. Politics, about which Collins says surprisingly little, provide useful confirmation, because party activists often occupy a position in the party that is quite different from their day-to-day occupations in breadth of communication and power—and as Collins' theory would indicate, this affects their outlook substantially. Parents who are manual workers and who are active in politics and unionism tend to have upwardly mobile children who become managers and professionals.[334] The federal Office of Equal Opportunity was founded in the 1960s on just these assumptions; one of its objectives was to create, by involving poor people in "community action," a new set of attitudes toward the "authorities" and a new ability to deal with them.

Melvin Kohn's surveys of attitudes and values showed that "middle-

[329]Ibid., p. 153.

[330]Ibid.

[331]Durkheim, *The Elementary Forms of the Religious Life.*

[332]Collins, *Conflict Sociology*, pp. 384–85.

[333]Ibid., p. 155.

[334]Brian Jackson and Dennis Marsden, *Education and the Working Class* (London: Routledge and Kegan Paul, 1963).

class parents . . . are more likely to emphasize children's *self-direction,* and working-class parents to emphasize their *conformity to external authority.*"[335] Kohn argued that this can be explained for the most part by differences in whether the fathers' occupations allow self-direction or require them to receive and obey directions from others.[336]

On the other hand, evidence on working-class union militancy and the development of revolutionary ideologies suggests that Collins' analysis is too simple. His account of how "ritual communities" are created would lead one to expect that military, revolutionary doctrines, and a commitment to "working-class solidarity" are most likely to develop among isolated, homogeneous groups of workers with their own tight-knit communities. For a number of years, sociologists have argued that this is indeed the case, citing the study by Kerr and Siegel which argued that "isolated masses" of workers are more militant and strike-prone.[337] More recently, however, this view has been challenged by a new research group interested in strikes and political violence and, in particular, by the work of Shorter and Tilly. Their study of France during the period 1830–1968 shows that militancy was a characteristic of the metropolis, not the isolated enclave—and of the relatively cosmopolitan skilled worker at that.[338] It is similarly true, we might add, that tightknit, fanatical, revolutionary political parties of the right and left have been born in heterogeneous cities, not in small, cohesive communities.

This suggests a serious imbalance in Collins' treatment of ideas. In his emphasis on the way ideas can be used to support the ruling order, he neglects the origins of ideas and beliefs that oppose it. Indeed, his arguments sometimes leave one wondering why all ruling groups have not been able to assure themselves of permanent legitimacy by manipulating ritual! Tribal societies seem almost never to generate ideas of "revolution" (changing the entire order) as opposed to "rebellion" against individual leaders,[339] but in Europe and America such ideas have been a part of social life for many centuries, and they are held with quite as much passion and conviction of their "reality" as the beliefs of a tribal "ritual community." A full account of the origins of beliefs and world views needs to explain this process, too, and indeed, "conflict sociology" in general, needs to take more

[335]Melvin L. Kohn, *Class and Conformity: A Study of Values* (Homewood, Ill.: The Dorsey Press, 1969), p. 34.

[336]Ibid., p. 163. Bourdieu makes similar points in his discussion of the "habitus," or system of perceptions common to a class. See above pp. 98–101. See also the discussion of the sociology of the emotions in Chapter V.

[337]Clark Kerr and Abraham Siegel, "The Interindustry Propensity to Strike," in Arthur Kornhauser, Robert Dubin, and Arthur M. Ross, eds., *Industrial Conflict* (New York: McGraw-Hill, 1954). Dahrendorf's arguments about mobilization are also along these lines.

[338]Edward Shorter and Charles Tilly, *Strikes in France 1830–1968* (London: Cambridge University Press, 1974). See also David Snyder and Charles Tilly, "Hardship and Collective Violence in France 1830–1960," *American Sociological Review,* 37 (1972), 320–32.

[339]Max Gluckman, *Custom and Conflict,* p. 28.

account of the origin and force of ideas as tools of opposition as well as domination.

Summary

Collins provides an excellent exposition of the basic assumptions of "analytic" conflict theory. His work is also important because it provides a large number of concrete propositions that relate institutional structure to the resources available to different groups. Further, it incorporates the insights of "micro-sociological" perspectives, especially in its account of how social experiences affect people's outlooks and hence the nature of social behavior, conflict, and change.

Not surprisingly, Collins' major weaknesses are the weaknesses of conflict theory as a whole. The most important are, we would suggest, an overemphasis on the "zero-sum" aspects of social interaction; too mechanistic a view of ideas as an offshoot of the existing social structure; and an inadequate account of the nature of the state. It is to these general weaknesses of conflict theory, as well as its major strengths, that we now turn briefly in conclusion.

CONCLUSION

Conflict theory's major strength lies in the way it relates social and organizational structure to group interests and the balance of resources. This analytical framework is often very productive. Moreover, whereas functionalism never really identifies a mechanism of change, conflict theory does, when it points to shifts in resource distribution and power. Conflict theory insists fruitfully that values and ideas must be related to their social environment and not treated as autonomous. Finally, it avoids "explaining" things simply in terms of their results. By tracing social behavior back to individuals' interests and the purposive way they pursue them, it shows how changes may actually occur.

However, conflict theory also has important weaknesses. Its insistence that power is people's main objective and the primary feature of social relationships is too limited. One can hardly account for the behavior of the Pilgrim Fathers in terms of "self-interest" or the search for power, as conflict theory commonly uses those terms. Moreover, the way in which they define and discuss power leads many conflict theorists to imply that the whole of social life is essentially "zero-sum": that is, that one man's gain is by definition made up from others' equal loss.[340] In fact, this is not necessarily the case.

---

[340]Some of Dahrendorf's recent work, notably *Conflict and Contract*, observes that situations may be "positive-sum" but does not address fully what this implies for his theories of power and the state.

Suppose that we take a hypothetical self-interested ruler who wishes to get as much money out of his subjects as possible. He can either seize whatever he can find by brute force, or he can set up a well-defined tax system in which people know in advance exactly how much they will owe— and that nothing more will be demanded. In the latter case, it is still ultimately the ruler's ability to coerce which ensures that his subjects pay up. However, they will also find it far more worthwhile to work hard, save, invest, and create economic growth than they will if anything they produce is liable to arbitrary confiscation. For that reason, the ruler may well, ultimately, do better for himself by choosing the less arbitrary course. Certainly, his subjects will fare much better if he does.[341]

Of course, no ruler ever has a completely free hand to choose one alternative or the other. However, societies can and do vary systematically in how far they provide the sort of environment which gives people security, encourages economic growth, or creates some degree of the "positive-sum" in their affairs. Contemporary conflict theory tends to ignore such important differences in how state power is exercised and in how far it provides people with a secure and predictable framework for their actions.[342] Consequently, it also tends to produce an inadequate theory of the state and to treat laws—the product of the state—oversimplistically, as though they were merely a reflection of group interest rather than systems with their own dynamic and influence.[343]

The same oversimplification is apparent in conflict theory's treatment of values and ideas. It is important to analyze the degree to which ideas are rooted in a social order and the ways laws and "ideologies" reflect people's interests; but it is also important to be aware—as functionalism is—that they have a degree of autonomy. Conflict theorists tend to treat ideas as though they were simply a reflection of the interests of the powerful, but narrow self-interest is often not a full explanation of events. Self-interest would have suggested the total extermination of the Native Americans. That this did not happen was largely the result of notions of justice and morality which, however compromised, were universal in their application.

Similarly, conflict theory tends to emphasize how ideas maintain stability, when in fact the ideas in a given society often criticize and undermine

[341]These arguments over the nature of society and the rule of law derive essentially from Thomas Hobbes (*Leviathan*) and John Locke (*The Second Treatise of Civil Government* and *A Letter Concerning Toleration*).

[342]It is important to note that none of this requires altruistic behavior "for the good of the people" or implies that systems of law and government exist which are equally good for everyone.

[343]By contrast, Weber pays a great deal of attention to differing legal systems. See p. 167. For an elaboration of this argument, see Douglass C. North, *Structure and Change in Economic History*, Chapter III (New York: W.W. Norton, 1981). North argues that (p. 21) "one cannot develop a useful analysis of the state divorced from property rights," and treats the state as essentially wealth-maximizing (on its own behalf).

the current order.[344] For example, Christianity produced figures like St. Francis and Luther whose teachings created massive social upheavals; and the Kremlin suppressed Russian dissidents brutally for decades because it feared their ideas so much.

Finally, although conflict theory specifies a mechanism of change, it does not provide an entirely satisfactory account of it. This is because conflict theory is far better at explaining how a group maintains power than it is at showing how it acquired it in the first place. Collins, for example, argues that educational qualifications are an important source of privilege without saying very much about why they are now a more significant resource than they were in the past. Yet groups do not acquire resources and power at random, and we had occasion to suggest earlier in the chapter that the origins of a group's power can often be explained by the services they provided. Educational qualifications may be used to protect and strengthen an élite group's position, but they are a more effective weapon now than in the past *because* education is also necessary to provide the technical skills on which modern wealth depends. The way social life involves the exchange of such goods and services, as well as values and coercive power, is emphasized by exchange theory.

---

[344]This is not universally true, as Schumpeter and Habermas show.

IV

THEORIES OF
RATIONAL CHOICE

INTRODUCTION

Theories of rational choice are guided by the assumption that people are rational and base their actions on what they perceive to be the most effective means to their goals. In a world of scarce resources this means constantly weighing up alternative means to alternative ends and choosing between them: hence the term rational *choice.*

Theories of this type are most closely associated with economics. Indeed, the approach can be expressed through the commonplace phrase that "there is a price for everything and everything has its price." This is not to imply, however, that conventional economic affairs—production, employment, and the sale of goods—are the only truly important facts in explaining social behavior. Rather, what rational choice theorists are suggesting is that the way to understand much of how people behave toward each other is by seeing them as rational decision makers in a world of scarcity.[1]

We can give a good example of how this perspective works by examining the rise in the divorce rate in recent years. Commentators have suggested a number of possible influences: affluence, changing moral values, and legal changes that make the process of divorce easier. Social scientists using a rational choice perspective start, instead, with the fact that all divorces involve individuals making choices about whether or not to stay married. They then ask what it is that makes many more people than in the past choose divorce.

John Scanzoni, for example, uses this approach to argue that an urban economy, rising salaries, and increased job openings for women are crucial because they make divorce an increasingly practicable option for women financially.[2] We can see what Scanzoni means if we imagine two women in their late thirties, the first a farmer's wife in the nineteenth-century American Midwest and the second a contemporary woman in Los Angeles or Paris. The first is almost bound to stay with her husband, even if he is frequently drunk and violent. In her area there are almost no jobs open to single women, let alone divorced women with children. The whole family, adults and children, must work to gain a livelihood on the farm.

The modern woman, by contrast, probably has at least secretarial skills. She could, for example, get a job as a medical secretary, take a small apartment in a modern high-rise building, and support both herself and her children on her salary alone. Because of the development of modern contraceptives, she need not even resign herself to celibacy. If she finds that her relationship with her husband is very unsatisfactory, let alone if he

---

[1]And of uncertainty. The fact that I cannot predict the future does not mean that I have to act at random and cannot adopt perfectly rational strategies based on what I do know. See pp. 192–93.

[2]John Scanzoni, *Power Politics in the American Marriage* (Englewood Cliffs, N.J.: Prentice-Hall, Inc., 1972).

actively maltreats her, the choice of divorce is therefore a much more attractive one. You can probably think of several people you know who have made that choice. What exchange theory does is to approach divorce and a wide range of other social behavior in terms of people's choices and the considerations that enter into them.

In sociology, the best-known examples of rational choice approaches have been those associated with "exchange theory." Exchange theorists conceptualize social interaction as an exchange of tangible or intangible goods and services, ranging from food and shelter to social approval or sympathy. People choose whether to participate in an exchange after they have examined the costs and the rewards of alternative courses of action, and have chosen the most attractive. In Simmel's words, "all contacts among men rest on the schema of giving and returning the equivalence."[3]

The best-known works on exchange theory were written in the 1960s, after which, for a number of years, interest in a rational choice perspective declined among sociologists. In other disciplines the opposite was true. Political scientists are increasingly concerned with "public choice," or the application of the rational choice perspective to the public goods with which political science is concerned. Thus, topics such as voting behavior or union membership have been analyzed in terms of the exchange of votes or membership for specific rewards.[4] In social psychology, Thibault and Kelley's analysis of groups is based on the premise that whether people choose to have anything to do with each other depends on whether they get more out of the relationship than they would from alternatives. "Interdependence matrices" are used to specify how attractive various combinations of behaviors are to group participants, and the authors then analyze how people control each other's behavior in terms of these matrices.[5] Much recent work in biology and, especially, sociobiology, similarly starts from a rational choice perspective.[6]

Perhaps because the approach seems so productive in other disciplines, the 1980s saw a renewed interest in rational choice among sociologists. Work directly concerned with "social exchange" is growing in volume, especially in analyses concerned with individual and small group behavior. A growing number of works concerned with institutional or "structural" questions also starts explicitly from a rational choice perspective. Small

[3]Georg Simmel, *The Sociology of Georg Simmel* (Glencoe, Ill.: The Free Press, 1950).

[4]Key texts include Anthony Downs, *An Economic Theory of Democracy* (New York: Harper and Row, 1957), and Mancur Olson, *The Logic of Collective Action: Public Goods and the Theory of Groups* (Cambridge: Harvard University Press, 1965). See pp. 211–31, for a discussion of the rational choice perspective on "macrosociological" concerns.

[5]Harold H. Kelley and John W. Thibault, *Interpersonal Relations: A Theory of Interdependence* (New York: John Wiley, 1978). See also John W. Thibault and Harold H. Kelley, *The Social Psychology of Groups* (New York: John Wiley, 1959).

[6]See Chapter VII.

group analysis is most strongly associated with the theories of George Homans, and institutional analysis with the exchange theory of Peter Blau.
This chapter discusses the work of both theorists in some detail. However,
in looking first at the individual/small group and then the institutional
level, it also considers the work of other theorists, including Richard Emerson, and the importance of some of the recent general propositions used by
rational choice theorists working in the field as a whole.

INTELLECTUAL ROOTS

Exchange theory's stress on people's rationality bears a strong resemblance
to the outlook of many nineteenth-century thinkers. The nineteenth century was a period when both economists and many philosophers emphasized individual activity and choice. The utilitarians, for example, described
people as "self-interested" in the sense of desiring pleasure, being averse
only to pain, and actively pursuing their desires. They also argued that
behavior was more or less moral according to the amount of "utility" it
bestowed on numbers of individuals. Economics built upon the work of
Adam Smith and retained his emphasis on understanding economic activity
as the result of individuals' myriad choices and decisions.[7]

Early sociologists, by contrast, showed little interest in an exchange
perspective. The sole major exception was Georg Simmel, who, as we have
seen,[8] was interested in identifying universal characteristics of human behavior. He was particularly concerned with why and how people move from
isolation to different forms of contact with each other.[9] Like modern social
exchange theorists, he argued that their motive was to satisfy needs and
pursue individual goals. Simmel also suggested that although the returns
people receive may not be equal, their interactions are always characterized
by some form of reciprocity and should therefore be viewed as kinds of
exchange. Blau, in particular, makes use of Simmel's work.

However, Simmel's concept of interaction as exchange was not elaborated or much used by the succeeding generation of sociologists. The major
intellectual influences on those sociologists who have adopted a rational
choice perspective are found instead in other areas of social science: anthropology, economics, psychology, and, more recently, public choice theory in
political science and the theory of games.

---

[7]Welfare economics, the normative part of mainstream economics, assumes, with the
utilitarians, that courses of action should be judged according to the total amount of utility
they bestow on individuals.

[8]Chapter III, "Intellectual Roots."

[9]D. Levine, E. Carter and E. Miller, "Simmel's Influence on American Sociology II,"
American Journal of Sociology, 81 (1976), 112–32.

Anthropology and the Importance of the Gift

Many of the great twentieth-century anthropologists have been concerned with the central role exchange plays in social life. One of the most important was Bronislaw Malinowski (1884–1942), whose emphasis on long periods of field work and intimate acquaintance with a particular culture played a crucial role in the development of modern anthropology. He spent many years among the Trobriand Islanders of the Melanesian Islands, where he concluded that mutual exchange is the basis of social cohesion.

> Trobriand society is founded on the principle of legal status . . . [involving] well-balanced chains of reciprocal services. The whole division into totemic clans, clans of a local nature and into village communities, is characterized by . . . a game of give and take. . . . [Moreover] reciprocity, the give-and-take principle, reigns supreme also . . . within the nearest groups of kinsmen. . . . [The] most unselfish relation, that between a man and his sister, [is] founded on mutuality and the repayment of services.[10]

The Gift   In examining exchange, we can draw a distinction between, on the one hand, institutions that have no independent purpose outside of exchanging or "gift giving" and, on the other, "instrumental" exchange, which characterizes interactions that take place primarily so that people may obtain things they want. Although Malinowski's discussion of reciprocal services covers both kinds, anthropology has paid special attention to the former.

Among the best-known examples of institutionalized, reciprocal gift giving is the Kula, a Trobriand ceremony that fascinated Malinowski. At regular intervals, the men from an island community would row out toward another island, meet its inhabitants, and exchange bracelets for necklaces of shells. These bracelets and necklaces were highly prized, but they had no obvious use. Instead they were kept until the next exchange and then passed on again, so that the same ceremonial jewelry traveled year after year around the "Kula Ring."

Anthropologists and exchange theorists argue that a crucial aspect of such exchanges is the way they bind society together through mutual obligations and so increase "social cohesion." It is not difficult to find other examples. Homer's Greek kings exchanged gifts continually,[11] and so do modern Americans—Christmas is unlikely to be uncommercialized in a hurry. Indeed, the role of gifts in establishing friendly relations is demonstrated every time we offer a visitor coffee. The reciprocal friendly gesture

---

[10]Bronislaw Malinowski, *Crime and Custom in Savage Society* (London: Routledge and Kegan Paul, 1926), pp. 46–48. See also Chapter II, p. 25.

[11]M. I. Finley, *The World of Odysseus*, rev. ed. (Harmondsworth, Middlesex: Penguin Books, 1972).

of accepting makes endless cups of tepid liquid an occupational hazard for social workers or the clergy.

Anthropologists have argued that there are also less obvious exchanges of a similar kind: the exchanges of marriage partners. Tribal societies generally have very complex and precise rules about marriage—for example, that a girl should always (or never) marry a father's sister's son and a boy, conversely, a mother's brother's daughter. Claude Lévi-Strauss, the famous French anthropologist, attempted to make sense of these rules by analyzing kinship groups and marriages as a system of alliances. From this viewpoint, wives are the most valuable gifts of all and hence the most effective exchange with which to cement an alliance and ensure social cohesion.[12]

Anthropologists are also aware of the relationship between power and the exchange of gifts. In his book *The Gift*, Marcel Mauss (1872–1950) emphasized the "obligatory and interested" nature of gifts and other forms of exchange.[13] Gifts, he argued, are intrinsically bound up with the way power and precedence are determined in a society, for *receivers of gifts are at a disadvantage* vis-à-vis the donor unless they can discharge their obligations by making an equal return. This concern with the role of exchanges in creating power relationships has been adopted by exchange theorists, especially Peter Blau.

A characteristic of some sociological variants of rational choice theory—and particularly exchange theory—is their concern with the existence of recurrent generalized norms governing social exchange.[14] Most often cited is the existence of a binding *norm of reciprocity*, and for this, too, the debt is to anthropology. Mauss, for example, argues that one must make return or incur hostility or loss of status from people other than those directly involved.[15] Reciprocity is a rule enforced by society. Malinowski is somewhat less precise, but he too implies the existence of a socially enforced *obligation* to reciprocate.

Economics, Profit, and Price

The central corpus of economic theory developed by such great economists as Adam Smith, David Ricardo, and Carl Menger rests on certain premises about individual psychology and its implications for people's behavior in the marketplace. Rational choice theorists similarly start with

---

[12]Claude Lévi-Strauss, *The Elementary Structures of Kinship*, rev. ed. (London: Eyre and Spottiswoode, 1969); Robin Fox, *Kinship and Marriage* (Harmondsworth, Middlesex, Penguin Books, 1967). See also Chapter VII, pp. 322–26.

[13]Marcel Mauss, *The Gift* (Glencoe, Ill.: The Free Press, 1954), p. 1.

[14]This is especially striking because, on the whole, rational choice theorists do not like "normative" explanations.

[15]See Alvin Gouldner, "The Norm of Reciprocity: A Preliminary Statement," *American Sociological Review*, 25 (1960), 161–78.

individual psychology[16] and apply the same premises to behavior that does not involve the exchange of material goods for money, the production of goods for sale, or the workings of the "economy." Like economists, they emphasize how important it is that we live in a world of scarcity, where we cannot have all the goods, or status, or emotional support we might like. Rational choice theorists adopt four of the basic propositions of economics:

1. Individuals are rational profit-maximizers, making decisions on the basis of their tastes and preferences.
2. The more of something an individual has, the less interested he or she will be in yet more of it.
3. The prices at which goods and services will be sold in a free market are determined directly by the tastes of prospective buyers and sellers. The greater the demand for a good, the more "valuable" it will be and the higher will be its price. The greater the supply, the less valuable it will be and the lower will be its price.
4. Goods will generally be more expensive if they are supplied by a monopolist than if they are supplied by a number of firms in competition with each other.

The first two propositions are assumptions about people's basic psychological makeup. For all their apparent simplicity, they can be used to make some very concrete predictions about behavior. They are, moreover, far from universally accepted. For example, for many years people have debated whether there exists a "cycle of poverty" in which people are trapped, largely by their own values and actions, for generation after generation. Some proponents of this view have argued that one reason for the continuing poverty of the underdeveloped nations is that peasants in these countries are too conservative and wedded to tradition to adopt new farming techniques.

This argument implies a sort of irrationality in human behavior; after all, what is at stake is not some esoteric objective but a universal human desire for material comfort and security. It is also an argument that economists and rational choice theorists find inadequate. They assume that peasants are as interested in increasing their profits (or "utility") as anyone else, and they are mistrustful of "culture" or the "weight of tradition" as an explanation of behavior. Thus, throughout the world, peasants tend to farm several scattered plots of land, even though, on average, consolidating these plots and strips could raise output by at least 10 percent. For people who are often close to starvation, this seems quite irrational, until you realize that scattered plots make any *particular* family less at risk from

---

[16]This is most explicit in the case of George Homans' theories of "elementary social behavior."

"local" disasters, such as mildew, flooding, or wandering animals. The village community has no way of insuring people against the risks of consolidation, so peasants, quite rationally, stick with an "individual-level, safety-first" strategy.[17]

Economists tend to concentrate on situations in which they can compare the financial benefits of alternative courses of action. They can predict with considerable success that shifts in "pay-offs" will produce shifts in people's choices; for example, there seems to be a definite link between the number of people enrolling in college and the financial benefits of a degree.[18] Sociology rarely deals with situations where there is a convenient measure of price or profit.[19] However, rational choice theorists, sharing the same basic orientation, do believe that one can often compare the relative pay-offs of different actions quite clearly. Therefore, one can explain or predict people's actions accurately even without being able to put an exact value on each possibility.

The second of the propositions above, which is also a statement about human psychology, is the law of "diminishing marginal utility." This law declares that as the amount of a good consumed increases, its marginal utility (that is, the extra utility that one gains by consuming another unit of it) tends to decrease and so, therefore, does the amount people will pay for it. For example, if it is a very hot day and you are very thirsty, you will be prepared to pay a lot for a first cold drink. A second drink, however, will be worth considerably less, and you may well forgo it if you can get it only for a lot of money.

If you think back to high school dating, you can see this same process at work. At first you probably valued any proof that you were not unattractive, and so you dated people in whom you were only mildly interested or who made great demands on you. But every relationship that made you more self-confident correspondingly made a date as such less valuable. You could hold out for more or be prepared to give less, and you could end a relationship that in the past might have been important enough to you to continue. Homans in particular draws on this proposition in his analyses of interpersonal and small group behavior.

The third and fourth of the propositions which rational choice theo-

---

[17]Samuel L. Popkin, *The Rational Peasant: The Political Economy of Rural Society in Vietnam* (Berkeley: University of California Press, 1979). See especially pp. 49–51. Strictly speaking, the problem with consolidation is that it produces *greater variance* in yields from year to year.

[18]Of course, they are not predicting the behavior of every individual. Rational choice theorists would agree with symbolic interactionists that an enormous number of factors influence an individual's decision to go to college. However, shifts in the importance a degree makes to one's earnings make a difference "at the margin"; that is, they tip the scales one way or another for some individuals and so affect the *total* size of enrollments.

[19]Richard Emerson made some attempts to provide a theory of "value" in social exchange: see pp. 191–92. For a discussion of whether "utility maximization" is a testable proposition or a tautology, see pp. 192–93.

rists share with economists concern the price at which people will exchange things. Again, sociologists extend these propositions beyond the market-place and argue that other forms of social interaction or "exchange" also involve prices that are determined by supply, demand, and the degree to which would-be buyers can get what they want only from a single, monopo-listic supplier. For example, theorists analyzing the "marriage market" in these terms would point out that it is successful and wealthy men who, on the average, have the prettiest wives. They explain this by the fact that success (or power) and female beauty are both valued and scarce qualities, each of which can therefore command a high price.

An individual who monopolizes valued qualities and powers is in an even better position. A pre-twentieth-century monarch, for example, could obtain as casual mistresses women who would hold out for marriage with any other men. Recent work in the rational choice tradition has focused increasingly on the importance of complete or partial monopolies as a way of analyzing power and dependence.

While anthropology contributes a view of society as a network of exchanges regulated by the norm of reciprocity, it is from economics that rational choice theorists draw most of the basic propositions used to explain particular phenomena. Consequently, their approach also shares econom-ics' limitations. Its users are generally not concerned with explaining the origins of people's beliefs, values, and tastes but take them as given and address themselves to the behavior that follows. Fortunately, this is not as restrictive as it sounds, since there are a good number of basic and universal human desires. Assuming no more than that people value money, power, social esteem, and, of course, survival, they can build up quite detailed theories about friendship, status differences, and social discontent—just as very similar assumptions about what makes up "self-interest" underlie con-flict theorists' detailed analyses of inequality, conflict, and change.

Behaviorist Psychology and the Theory of Games

Especially in analyses of individual behavior and its consequences, there are two final but important influences on the rational choice ap-proach. They share a concern for formal deductive argument, and, once again, both are from outside sociology proper. Behaviorist psychology was very important for the development of exchange theory, although, in more recent years, concepts and models drawn from the theory of games have increasingly been adopted for sociological analysis.[20]

In formulating his version of exchange theory, George Homans

[20]The theory of games has itself reached a wider audience because its approach is used by many of the most influential writers on public choice. The way in which rational choice theories cross disciplinary boundaries is encapsulated in the award of a Nobel Prize for Eco-nomics to James Buchanan, whose work on public choice has had an enormous effect on political science.

turned to the behavioral school of experimental psychology founded by his friend B. F. Skinner. He wanted direct evidence of the validity of propositions that economists tend to treat as assumptions. Behavioral psychology takes the position that in studying behavior, one can avoid hypotheses about unobservable phenomena. Experimental psychologists of this school try to avoid making statements about the "black box" of a human (or animal) mind that cannot be directly tested or falsified. Instead, they attempt to construct a satisfactory theory of behavior that deals only with the overt responses that result from observable stimuli—not with the thoughts or feelings that lead people or animals to react to stimuli in a particular way. Mead and the symbolic interactionists argue against this theory vehemently, stressing instead the importance of internal and unobservable perceptions and meanings.

In fact, exchange theory, in common with rational choice theories as a whole, does make statements about unobservable phenomena, especially about people's values. For exchange theory the importance of behavioral psychology's propositions is that they are consistent with economics; thus Richard Emerson, too, uses the vocabulary of operant conditioning in much of his exchange theory. The congruence of economics and psychology strengthens exchange theory's argument that these principles apply to all areas of social life. Thus, Homans writes, "We believe that the propositions of behavioral psychology are the general explanatory propositions of all the social sciences. Accordingly, they are the general propositions of economics."[21]

Psychology is also an important influence in the area in which sociological variants of rational choice theory are most distinct: their concern with the "morality of social exchange."[22] Either economic man does not recognize the existence of a raw deal—or a "fair price"—or he takes what comes to him in silence. This hardly describes the people we know (and are), full of ideas and disagreements about what is our due or what we "ought" to pay or get. The more the issue in question affects our daily lives, the more vehement our concern with what is right or fair. The debate about the division of property after a divorce (and the justification for "palimony") offers a very fruitful hunting ground for those in search of conflicting notions of justice.

Although experimental psychologists are not concerned with justice per se, they are interested in what happens when expectations are not fulfilled—for example, when a looked-for reward fails to materialize. Their

[21]George C. Homans, *Social Behavior: Its Elementary Forms*, rev. ed. (New York: Harcourt Brace Jovanovich, 1974), p. 67. © 1974 by Harcourt Brace Jovanovich, Inc. Reprinted by permission of the publishers. See also George C. Homans, "Fundamental Social Processes," in Neil J. Smelser, ed., *Sociology* (New York: John Wiley, 1967), pp. 27–78.

[22]Anthony Heath, *Rational Choice and Social Exchange* (Cambridge: Cambridge University Press, 1976). In discussing the distinction between the rational and the moral elements in social exchange, as well as for his numerous other perceptive remarks, we are indebted to Anthony Heath's analyses of exchange theory.

evidence on the way people and animals react is the basis of much of Homans' discussion of "distributive justice."

The theory of games, by comparison, is concerned very much with particular sets of choices and alternatives and with identifying recurrent dilemmas and strategies. In discussing conflict theory, we noted that it tends to see social life as a "zero-sum game," in which one person's gain is necessarily another's loss. However, games theory as a whole is concerned with a far wider range of situations than this. Its best-known example is the "Prisoner's Dilemma,"[23] but the theory's value and interest to sociologists lies not in the range of different possible "games" devised but in the number of social situations which can be seen as examples of one or another type. Sociologists interested in phenomena as diverse as the expansion of higher education, the lobbying success of the Sierra Club, and the prospects of peace between the superpowers have discovered that finding the underlying "game structure" helps them to analyse both past events and likely developments.

Most of the perspectives discussed in this text concentrate on either the micro *or* the macro level. Although this division applies to most individual theorists working in the rational choice tradition, it is not true of the perspective as a whole. While some of the best-known work covered here— and especially that associated with exchange theory—is very much focused on small group behavior, other theorists are expressly concerned with structural and institutional analysis.

Part One of this chapter covers theory and research work that is concerned predominantly with individual actions and behavior. It looks first at the basic propositions associated with exchange theory, especially the work of George Homans, and then at the implications of assumptions about individual rationality for the analysis of a wide range of social phenomena. Part Two looks at rational choice perspectives on social structure. The exchange theory of Peter Blau is described in detail, as are some recent works on social cohesion. This section assesses the contribution of the rational choice perspective to answering the fundamental sociologist's question: What creates social order?

PART ONE
Rational Choice and Individual Behavior

GEORGE HOMANS: ELEMENTARY SOCIAL BEHAVIOR

Modern social exchange theory is associated primarily with two sociologists: George Caspar Homans and Peter M. Blau. George Homans (1910–89) was

---

[23]See pp. 203–4.

a Boston Brahmin, born—most unusually for a sociologist—into one of the city's great Yankee families.[24] In his autobiography Homans notes,

> To use words that now provoke scorn, the Brahmins were gentlemen and ladies. Other people were not. . . . We were not able to muster up "pride in our port, defiance in our eye"—whom were we going to defy?—and seldom talked about class. Nevertheless we were class conscious. By profession all sociologists are class conscious but usually about other persons' classes, not their own.[25]

At Harvard, Homans studied English, not sociology. Nonetheless, he maintained,

> "If I learned no theoretical, I learned much practical sociology. One of the routes by which a person gets interested in this subject is by living in an environment in which people are highly conscious of social relations. This rule holds good more often of micro-sociologists like me, who are concerned with the face-to-face interactions of persons, than of macrosociologists, concerned with the characteristics of whole societies. For us microsociologists the laws of sociology are the laws of snobbery, and an undergraduate of my background found Harvard to a high degree "socially conscious"—in the bad sense of the phrase.[26]

The "final clubs" were at the core of prewar Harvard, and membership depended on a mixture of qualities—personal as well as those related to class, religion, and ethnic background. (Homans himself, intellectual and rather sardonic, was by no means the "right" sort of person.) The structure of small groups and the way in which social approval is engendered—the core, in fact, of Homans' later theory—are indeed typified in the operation of "final clubs," fraternities and sororities.

Homans spent his whole academic career at Harvard, interrupted only by four and a half years in the wartime Navy. He came to sociology "because I had nothing better to do" when a postgraduation newspaper job disappeared with the Depression. Unemployed and in Cambridge, he accepted an invitation to attend a seminar on Pareto, whose sociology was then almost unknown in America. Homans ended up collaborating with Charles Curtis on *An Introduction to Pareto* and soon thereafter was elected to the Harvard Society of Fellows as a sociologist. Homans, who never earned—or studied for—a doctorate, was a president of the American Sociological Association, and in 1988, while Professor Emeritus at Harvard, he was awarded the association's Distinguished Scholarship Award.

---

[24]Homans' mother was a niece of Henry Adams.

[25]George Caspar Homans, *Coming to My Senses: The Autobiography of a Sociologist* (New Brunswick, N.J.: Transaction Books, 1984).

[26]Ibid., p. 9.

The influence of Pareto remains clear in Homans' later work, notably in his concern with the basic laws of psychology that underpin human behavior, his receptiveness to concepts generally associated with economics, and his desire to establish full "deductive" theories or explanations. However, Homans' work was also always stimulated by his wide range of friends working in other disciplines and involved both anthropology and English history, in which he taught a course for many years.

The results of Homans' interest in small group research were synthesized first in *The Human Group*.[27] He then turned to the basic principles of human activity which he came to see as underlying small group behavior. These he set out in his most important book on what has come to be known as exchange theory, *Social Behavior: Its Elementary Forms*.[28]

By "elementary social behavior" Homans means behavior that appears and reappears whether or not people plan on its doing so. Homans believed elementary social behavior can be explained by basic propositions about individual psychology and motivation. He argued consistently that satisfactory explanations of social phenomena must ultimately be "psychological" explanations; that psychological principles are the basic building blocks of explanation in all the social sciences; and, indeed, that there are no such things as purely "sociological" explanations—something, he points out, that is also true of history without apparently causing historians much discomfort.[29]

Presidents of the American Sociological Association frequently have used the presidential address to make controversial statements about the state of sociology. In 1964, Homans employed his to argue that because functionalism had rejected psychological propositions, it had been unable to generate explanations. "Let us get men back in, and let us put some blood in them," he argued;[30] his theory is a worked-out statement of this position.

The general statements which Homans presents are accepted, more or less intact, by other social exchange theorists and sociologists in the rational choice tradition. However, Homans' work sets them out most clearly as an interlocking deductive system. As most recently stated, they are:

[27]George C. Homans, *The Human Group* (New York: Harcourt Brace Jovanovich, 1950).

[28]George C. Homans, *Social Behavior: Its Elementary Forms* (Harcourt Brace and World, 1961). Reprinted by permission of the publishers. References in this chapter are mostly to the 1974 revised edition, which incorporates substantial changes in Homans' theories.

[29]George C. Homans, "A Life of Synthesis," in Irving L. Horowitz, ed., *Sociological Self-Images: A Collective Portrait* (Beverly Hills, Calif.: Sage, 1969).

[30]George C. Homans, "Bringing Men Back In," *American Sociological Review*, 29, no.5 (December 1964), 809–18.

1. *The success proposition.* For all actions taken by persons, the more often a particular action of a person is rewarded, the more likely the person is to perform that action.

2. *The stimulus proposition.* If in the past the occurrence of a particular stimulus, or set of stimuli, has been the occasion on which a person's action has been rewarded, then the more similar the present stimuli are to the past ones, the more likely the person is to perform the action, or some similar action, now.

3. *The value proposition.* The more valuable to a person is the result of his action, the more likely he is to perform the action.

   The rationality proposition (combining 1 through 3). In choosing between alternative actions, a person will choose that one for which, as perceived by him at the time, the value, V, of the result, multiplied by the probability, p, of getting the result, is the greater.

4. *The deprivation-satiation proposition.* The more often in the recent past a person has received a particular reward, the less valuable any further unit of that reward becomes for him.

5. *The aggression-approval proposition.*
   a. When a person's action does not receive the reward he expected, or receives punishment he did not expect, he will be angry; he becomes more likely to perform aggressive behavior, and results of such behavior become more valuable to him (the frustration-aggression hypothesis).
   b. When a person's action receives the reward he expected, especially a greater reward then he expected, or does not receive punishment he expected, he will be pleased; he becomes more likely to perform approving behavior, and the results of such behavior become more valuable to him.[31]

We noted above that Homans is known as a major exchange theorist, but in these propositions, the term nowhere appears. This is because Homans is not talking about a particular sort of exchanging behavior but about universal principles, applying to all forms of social activity. In doing so, he envisages "social behavior as an exchange of activity . . . between at least two persons."[32] He sees his main task as explaining "the repeated exchanges of rewards between men which we shall refer to as interpersonal relationships."[33] However, Homans actually disliked the way "my theory . . . got stuck with the name of 'exchange theory'. . . . This was too bad . . .

---

[31]Homans, *Social Behavior,* rev. ed., pp. 16–50 passim.

[32]Homans, *Social Behavior,* 1st ed., p. 13.

[33]Homans, *Social Behavior,* rev. ed., p. 51.

because it suggested that the theory was a special kind of theory, whereas it is a general behavioral psychology."[34] This emphasis on general principles of human action lies at the core of all theories of rational choice.

The Principle of Rationality

The first three principles of human behavior that Homans advances are essentially a statement of human rationality. To argue that people repeat rewarding actions, respond to stimuli associated with such rewards, and act on the basis of the "values" they attach to things is, in fact, to state that they are rational—though *not* to say that they are always right about what the most rewarding or rational choice would be.

This sounds tame and obvious enough, but it is not necessarily either. Criminology draws on this principle when examining the deterrent effects of arrest rates and sentencing. A principle of rational behavior implies that, other things being equal, the more often crimes succeed, the more people will commit them. The evidence is largely consistent with this argument and the obverse is also true.[35]

In 1988 the Washington, D.C. area saw the start of a murder epidemic, involving, for the most part, young men buying and selling drugs (especially crack). Interviewed at the end of that year, the city's Assistant Chief of Police made the point that, given the dealers' values and opportunities, what we were seeing was purely rational behavior.

> Something has changed to produce the kids that I see. Let me give you an example. Not long ago, I went with the homicide squad to arrest a kid who was 18 years old. This kid had a hardworking mother who is doing her best . . . a working family that is trying to give him the benefit of a good value system. And yet this kid . . . is defining himself in terms of material things— not in terms of his mother's values. . . . He's got to have it all, right now. He's got to have a 4 × 4 truck, he's got to have a big car, he's got to have the most expensive jewelry, he's got to have designer clothes. . . . He's got to get what he wants, right now.

> I went back to my alma mater, Eastern High School, a couple of years ago, and talked to some students about drugs and money. One kid said to me, "Chief Fulwood, you're full of bullshit. Why should I go and make $3.50 or $4.25 an hour at a regular job? I can make that in one minute on the street. . . . How much do you make, Chief?" I told him . . . He smiled. "I can

[34]Homans, *Coming to My Senses*, p. 338.

[35]See, for example, Isaac Erlich, "Participation in Illegal Activities. A Theoretical and Empirical Investigation," *Journal of Political Economy*, 81 (May–June 1973), 521–65 and "The Deterrent Effect of Capital Punishment: A Question of Life and Death," *American Economic Review*, LXV, no. 3 (June 1975), 397–417. Another area in which the principle of rationality has proven very fruitful is the analysis of fertility. See Geoffrey Hawthorn, *The Sociology of Fertility* (London: Collier-Macmillan Ltd., 1970).

make more than that." *Those kids can make as much money as they're willing to take risks.*[36]

The rational choice approach proves similarly useful in looking at another of our cities' enduring problems: the poor education so many children obtain in inner-city schools and the overt war between teacher and pupils that characterizes many inner-city classrooms. If people are basically rational, those pupils who are most involved in warfare and disruption and least interested in studying and cooperating with the teacher, presumably find studying less valuable than its alternatives. Leaving aside for the moment the reasons for their choice, this implies that if you increase the rewards of studying and thereby alter the relative value of pupils' alternatives, you will also increase the number who choose cooperation over war.

George Richmond taught in just such a New York elementary school, where both his arguments and pleas for cooperation and his threats and punishments failed. Looking for some way out of the impasse, he came to see the traditional school room as a feudal society, where students were "tied to the land—to room 308," having no private property and requiring his permission to exercise their most basic liberties. His response was to devise what he called the "micro-economy game" and to use it in the classroom, as he describes here:

> The next morning I arrived in 308 with a plan, and with some materials. I immediately began a discussion that eventually altered everything. . . .
>
> "From now on, I'm going to buy compositions with this." I held up a bundle of paper money that I had mimeographed the day before. "These are soul dollars. They come in ones, fives, twenties, hundreds, and five hundreds. You'll also get a dollar for each point that you score on a spelling or a math test."
>
> "Hey, Mr. Richmond," Sandoval called. "You expect us to get rich off that phony stuff? Man, if I take that phony-baloney down to the candy store all it gonna buy me is a kick in the ass."
>
> "Patience, Sandoval, patience. You want to know what you get for this money, right?"
>
> "Yeah," they chorused.
>
> "At the end of each month, I'm going to bring books, brownies, cookies, soda, and other things to school and auction them off to the highest bidder. That means that the people with the most of this phony-baloney get what they want."
>
> "You mean this money buys things, real things?"
>
> "Yes. . . . Your parents work, right?"
>
> A couple of kids shook their heads.

[36]Extracted from the transcript of an interview with Isaac Fulwood, Jr., assistant chief of police for field operations, Washington, D.C. *Washington Post* (Outlook section), January 1, 1989). Italics ours.

"Well, some of them do. They trade their work for dollars. Then they trade their dollars for food that somebody else's work produced. Well, you work too, but in school. And I'm going to pay you for your work because it's valuable to me. Then I'm going to bring stuff—candy, soda, and other things—and you'll trade your work for food just the way your parents do."[37]

Students could also be paid for classroom jobs, and those who wanted them found them. The results were spectacular. "Those who took jobs performed enthusiastically. Students doubled their academic output."[38]

Although we do not know for sure how the quality of their work changed, it is worth comparing these results with those of the federal government's ill-fated performance contracting experiments. These paid outside firms to come into the schools and teach disadvantaged students basic skills, but the students showed no clear improvement over their performance in the regular program. Since the students themselves received no direct reward, introducing payments tied to the *teachers'* success made little difference to the value of *pupils'* options.[39]

In spite of its apparent usefulness in explanation, the idea of rationality, especially the idea that people choose courses of action on the basis of their potential value, has come under more attack than any other part of exchange theory. This is partly because Homans originally advanced the "value proposition" as an empirically verifiable proposition.[40] Many of his critics argued that it was a tautology and so true by definition; or, as a matter of fact, untestable; or, in some cases, both at once! More recently, the late Richard Emerson attempted to develop a theory of value in social exchange. He argued that because sociology is concerned with the "interpersonal comparison of benefits from exchange," it also needs a "concept of subjective value or utility possessing a nonarbitrary origin and unit of measure."[41] In other words, we need a way of measuring the value of things to people that goes beyond saying that "we know she prefers a business career to helping people *because* she took these particular courses." (If we had such an independent measure we could, of course, test the value proposition directly.)

Emerson did not succeed in establishing an independent measure of subjective value. We would question whether this is or was ever a viable

[37]George Richmond, *The Micro-Society School: A Real World in Miniature* (New York: Harper and Row, 1973), specified excerpts from pp. 15, 24–26, 31, 33–35. Copyright © 1973 by George Richmond. Reprinted by permission of John Hawkins & Associates, Inc. The micro-economy game, described fully in Richmond's book, was rather more complicated and closer to Monopoly than this excerpt implies.

[38]Ibid., p. 31.

[39]Edward M. Gramlich and Patricia P. Koshel, *Educational Performance Contracting: An Evaluation of an Experiment* (Washington, D.C.: Brookings Institution, 1975).

[40]Homans, *Social Behavior*, 1st ed., p. 43.

[41]Richard M. Emerson, "Toward a Theory of Value in Social Exchange," in Karen S. Cook, ed., *Social Exchange Theory* (Newbury Park, Calif.: Sage, 1987), p. 12.

proposition. The meanings and values which people attach to things vary enormously within, as well as between, societies—hence the consistently micro focus of a perspective such as symbolic interactionism. Economics deals with the problem by focusing almost entirely on transactions where money is involved and where there is consequently a shared and commonly understood metric. Thus, we can assume, within the utility maximization framework, that people will almost always value more money and pursue profit; then we can examine whether they do in fact follow the most profitable course of action.

To the extent that sociologists wish to go beyond the transactions of the marketplace, they are faced with values and preferences which cannot be measured precisely. However, this does not mean that the value proposition, let alone the whole perspective, is useless. Sociologists in the rational choice or exchange theory tradition can plausibly assume—like conflict theorists—that people value survival, approval, and power. Rational choice theory can then predict behavior accordingly. Assumptions are in any case *not* arbitrary. They stand or fall by whether theories incorporating them produce the goods, and here the value proposition does rather well.[42]

What *is* true is that the value proposition on its own is often an inadequate explanation of—or guide to—behavior. On many occasions, people are in a situation of uncertainty or risk, where they cannot be sure of the outcomes of their actions or, therefore, which is the most "valuable" alternative. It is a great strength of Homans, as compared to Blau, that he addresses this point. His "rationality proposition," which is based on the first three propositions we quoted, states that people will multiply the value of an action's possible reward by the probability of it actually materializing and then choose on the basis of these results.[43]

As stated, the principle sounds extremely complicated, and, of course, no one is suggesting that we stand around with calculators all the time. However, much of people's behavior does seem to be explained by their making approximate comparisons of this kind. When you make decisions

[42]Those interested in following up the debate are referred to R. Maris, "The Logical Adequacy of Homans' Social Theory," *American Sociological Review*, 35 (1970), 1069–81; Morton Deutsch, "Homans in the Skinner Box," in H. Turk and R. L. Simpson, eds., *Institutions and Social Exchange: The Sociologies of Talcott Parsons and George C. Homans*, (Indianapolis: Bobbs-Merrill, 1971); Stephen Turner, "The Logical Adequacy of 'The Logical Adequacy of Homans' Social Theory,'" *American Sociological Review*, 36 (1971), 706; Anthony Heath, *Rational Choice and Social Exchange;* and Homans, *Social Behavior*, rev. ed., pp. 33–37. Neither Homans nor a number of his critics seem to distinguish clearly between an untestable proposition and a strictly tautologous one. However, in either case, the proof of the pudding lies in the hypotheses it can generate.

[43]In economics, the "rationality" proposition is discussed in terms of "maximizing expected utility." Actually, both Blau (*Exchange and Power*, p. 18) and Homans (*Social Behavior*, rev. ed., p. 33) suggest, rather curiously, that people's preferences are not necessarily "transitive" or consistent; in other words, the fact that they prefer A to B and B to C does not necessarily imply that they prefer A to C. Neither makes much of this, but if true, it would make much of people's behavior indeterminate or unpredictable and undermine their whole approach. In fact, there is some evidence, described by Heath, that people's preferences *are* transitive and thus that one of the basic assumptions of utility theory is justified.

about what to major in or what career to choose, your estimates of the probable rewards are among the things you take into account. The enormous rise in house prices in recent years is partly the result of people estimating that inflation is likely to remain high or get worse—in other words, that the probable reward of putting your money into housing is higher than the probable reward of investing in stocks or depositing your money in a savings account. Again, the rationality principle can perfectly well accommodate people's use of "rules of thumb"—short cuts to decision making which work most of the time and which we use rather than incur the very real costs of working out, on the basis of inadequate evidence, exactly what the "best" option is likely to be.

The Deprivation-Satiation Proposition

The deprivation-satiation proposition is a straightforward counterpart of the economists' principle of declining marginal utility, which we described above. Blau, in particular, presents it in economists' language. It states that if you have recently received something you value, you will be decreasingly interested in more of the same, at least in the short term. Economists accept this proposition because and insofar as it produces correct predictions, and exchange theory's position is basically the same.[44]

Declining marginal utility plays a central role in the economic theory of price. Correspondingly, the deprivation-satiation proposition is central to exchange theory's discussion of how exchange rates are set and exchange relationships entered into and left. Obviously, rational individuals will do something only if its value to them is greater than what they give up to get it, in either direct costs or foregone opportunities (in other words, if they make a net profit). However, because the first "unit" of something is worth more to people than the second, and the second is worth more than the third, they may quickly reach a situation where it is no longer worthwhile to go on paying up. At that point the exchange relationship is likely to come to an end.

Aggression and Approval

Homans expresses his fifth basic proposition in behavioral psychology's terms. It states that if people's expectations are disappointed, they become angry and often aggressive, whereas if their expectations are fulfilled or exceeded, they are pleased. The proposition is important for sociology because many of people's expectations are rooted in customs and social norms, which define what ought to happen and what is right and just. This fifth proposition moves well beyond the concerns of economics to questions of norms and the morality of social exchange and, indeed, is the distinguish-

---

[44]In his earlier work, Homans included some discussion of laboratory pigeons in this context. George C. Homans, "Social Behavior as Exchange," *American Journal of Sociology*, LXII (1958), 597–606.

ing characteristic of those variants of rational choice theory associated with the term "exchange theory."

Homans proposes an actual rule of distributive justice, *which applies in all societies.* It states that what matters to people is that "reward should be proportional to investment and contribution."[45] Peter Blau, whose application of exchange theory to macro-sociology is discussed below, similarly argues that "people compare themselves in terms of their investments as well as in terms of their rewards, and expect differences in the rewards to correspond to differences in the investments."[46]

Both within and between societies and groups, there are big variations in what "contributions" and "investments" (or background characteristics) are considered relevant, and how they are valued. Most whites and most men, for example, used to believe that race and sex were relevant investments and that whites and men should therefore be paid more than blacks and women. Many societies, unlike our own, have accorded high value and respect to old age. In their analyses of particular situations, social exchange theorists, like other rational choice theorists, take these valuations—and values—as givens: the stage set within which the action is played out. In discussing justice, however, they argue that there is a general, substantive norm which affects people's actions in all societies, irrespective of what other particular values they may hold.[47]

An area of social life in which notions of justice can be seen to affect behavior directly and obviously is wage bargaining. Often a group of workers demands parity with or higher pay than another group on the basis of what they consider to be fair. In recent years there has been a number of big cases involving gender-linked pay differences which were perceived as "unfair." Similarly, Homans describes a research study which showed that supermarket workers did not like to "bundle" (pack a shopper's goods into bags) for cashiers whose status was lower than theirs. They felt, for example, that a part-time worker attending college ought not to bundle for one still in high school. Supermarkets where status and job relationships were generally "congruent" were also noticeably more efficient and profitable.[48]

Approval and Social Conformity   In Homans' analyses, social approval's role is comparable to that of money in economics and market exchanges. Social approval is not as ideal a unit of exchange, of course; it cannot easily be measured or counted, banked, lent, and passed from hand to hand. Nonetheless, it is the one thing that can be offered in almost any exchange situation, on the assumption that everyone finds it a desirable commodity,

[45]Homans, *Social Behavior*, rev. ed., p. 250.
[46]Peter M. Blau, *Exchange and Power in Social Life* (New York: John Wiley, 1964) p. 156. Copyright © 1964 by John Wiley and Sons. Reprinted by permission of John Wiley and Sons, Inc.
[47]See pp. 180, 201–2, 216.
[48]Homans, *Social Behavior*, rev. ed., pp. 202–8.

and it can also be used by one side or other to balance an exchange. We can see how this works in Homans' favorite example, in which one person requests and receives advice from another. The individuals concerned, "Person" and "Other," work in the same office.

> Person is new to the work and unskilled at it. . . . Other seems to be experienced in the job and he has time to spare. . . . Therefore, Person seeks out Other and asks him for advice about a problem he has run into in his work. Other does give him help and in return Person gives Other approval in the form of heartfelt thanks.[49]

Homans uses the assumption that people value approval to explain how conformity is created and maintained in informal groups. Group members can supply each other with social approval, he argues. They will therefore have good reason to behave in a way their friends approve and to "conform" with their wishes, in order to obtain approval and esteem.

In support of his case, Homans cites a study of married students living in Westgate, a housing project at M.I.T.[50] The buildings in Westgate were built in clusters facing grass courts, although a few corner buildings faced in the other direction with doors on the street. When the investigators examined attitudes toward the tenants' organization, they found that a majority of the couples in each court shared the same attitude but, at the same time, that attitude differed from court to court. The way housing assignments were made could not explain this. It was a group norm.

The investigators then looked at friendship patterns within Westgate. They found that the more "cohesive" a court—that is, the more couples selected their friends from among their neighbors—the smaller the number deviating from the group norm. Within each court, moreover, deviates consistently received fewer friendship choices than did conformers. Finally, deviates were especially likely to live in the corner houses that faced away from the court center.

Homans suggests that couples whose houses faced onto the court were likely to see each other often and therefore to establish friendships. This, in turn, set up the process (the feedback loop) by which conformity could be established and maintained. People wanted to continue being friends and therefore had a motive for conforming; moreover, conforming would bring them yet more approval and strengthen the friendship. Couples in the corner houses, by contrast, saw less of the others. They were less likely to have friends there, and consequently the group had less hold on them. If people have little to lose, they also have little reason to change their opinions; and, of course, if they do not, the group will hardly be more welcom-

---

[49]Homans, *Social Behavior*, rev. ed., p. 54.

[50]Leon Festinger, Stanley Schachter, and Kurt Back, *Social Pressures in Informal Groups* (New York: Harper, 1950).

ing than before. Other forces, Homans notes, must also have affected friendships and opinions. Nonetheless, because of its effect on the frequency of their interaction with others, a couple's geographical position " 'caused' its social acceptance and its social acceptance in turn 'caused' its conformity to the court norm . . . if, moreover, social acceptance 'caused' conformity, conformity also 'caused' social acceptance."[51]

What Homans advances is a convincing account of the dynamics of friendship and conformity in small groups. However, it is not an adequate explanation of "social integration" in the wider sense. Conformity to the norms of a large society requires more than people's desire for companionship and approval; many different groups at odds with each other could form, and each could have strong and distinctive internal norms and no interest in the approval of outsiders. In this respect, Homans' version of exchange theory is a theory of small groups, not social institutions—a point we shall also have occasion to make in discussing other of his explanations of behavior.

Power

In discussing friendship and conformity, Homans identifies social approval as the good people offer when they have nothing else desirable to exchange. This same situation of imbalance—when one party or other has relatively little to offer—is at the root of exchange theory's analysis of power.

Homans defines power as the ability to provide valuable rewards. His analysis explains someone's potential power in exactly the same way that economists explain something's price:

> Power depends on an ability to provide rewards that are valuable because they are scarce. . . . Yet the objective scarcity of the reward is not what counts. The ability to whistle well may be scarce, but probably no one has ever acquired power through the ability to whistle well. Only if a large number of persons found it valuable to listen to concert whistling would the ability to whistle be a basis for power—a means, for instance, of getting people to pay money. What determines the scarcity value of a reward is the relation between the supply of it and the demand for it.[52]

---

[51]Homans, *Social Behavior*, rev. ed., p. 152.
[52]Homans, *Fundamental Processes*, p. 571. Put more succinctly:

> The end is easily foretold.
> When every blessed thing you hold
> Is made of silver or of gold
> You long for simple pewter
> When you have nothing else to wear
> But cloth of gold and satins rare
> For cloth of gold you cease to care
> Up goes the price of shoddy.
>
> (Gilbert and Sullivan, *The Gondoliers*)

Thus, power is seen as reflected in the price people can get for their services. This price may be paid in the form of some concrete exchange, such as money, or in a more generalized form, such as obedience to orders. However, having resources that are generally valuable does not necessarily give someone power over any given individual. For that there has to be some imbalance: the other must have nothing that you want as badly or that is as valuable, at least to you, as what you already have.

Homans' conception of power can be applied to coercive power, which depends on the ability to punish, and to noncoercive power, in which both sides obtain some degree of extra reward. In a mugging, victims generally believe their choice to be between losing life (and thus money too) or just losing money; they perceive muggers as unlikely to be caught and therefore willing to take the additional small risk of a murder charge. The victim's potential reward is therefore greater than the mugger's. "If the withdrawal of a punishment is a reward, as indeed it is, and if the capacity to kill is also the capacity to spare, then the capacity to kill is also the capacity to reward."[53] However, Homans argues, noncoercive power is not only more common, it is also more effective. Carrots are more reliable than sticks.[54] Threats of punishment often stir rebellion, and they may not elicit the behavior you want unless all other routes are blocked.

An example of the process Homans describes is given by George Richmond in his account of the "micro-economy" game from which we have already quoted. As part of the Monopoly-like game, players were allowed to borrow money, either to pay off debts they had not done enough work to cover immediately or because they had an eye on profitable investments. The change in the rewards available to pupils, and therefore in the resources and skills they valued, shifted the distribution of power.

> Ramon became 308's banker. . . . Frankly, I would never have predicted that Ramon, of all people, would get the job. When I first began teaching in P.S. 484, he caused me so little trouble that I barely knew him. Ramon was quiet, well-mannered, but uncoordinated; he played only a nominal role in the daily skirmishes that claimed our energies. In the order of selection for a punchball team, Ramon was often the last to be chosen. Sometimes team captains refused to let him play.
>
> In one respect, Ramon's passivity was an effective strategy for survival. As every hack in the schoolhouse knows, if you keep to yourself and take few gambles, teachers and other students don't bother you. No one was threatened by Ramon. He made no challenges, so few calls were made for him to defend himself in the brutal infighting that went on in 308. At least, this description fitted Ramon until we started playing Micro-Economy.
>
> After I introduced money to the classroom, all that multiplying, adding

---

[53]Homans, *Social Behavior,* rev. ed., p. 80.
[54]Homans, *Fundamental Processes,* p. 571.

and subtracting began to make sense, and Ramon's life began to change. He was unanimously chosen to be banker, not for his popularity, only possibly for his anonymity or his prosperity, but chiefly because he could add, subtract, and multiply better than anyone else. He became rich by getting a hundred on his math tests, and after I began paying for points on spelling tests, he scored perfectly there too. . . . Instinctively entrepreneurial, Ramon turned a part of his cash holdings into property; the rest he loaned to his classmates. Both investments earned him enviable returns.

As Ramon got richer and richer, he began to pay a price for his success. The cloak of anonymity came off; he became important and powerful; his advice, previously ignored, was now sought by other children. . . . His natural business head and his common sense were important ingredients in a new social order. The fiefdom was breaking down in favor of commercial baronies, and whether he liked it or not, Ramon was 5-308's first commercial baron. . . .

Intellect was now competing with muscle for dominance. It came as no great shock to anyone when Ramon hired Raoul, the strongest kid in the class, to protect his interests, to collect his debts, to run his errands. No one but me saw the significance of that seemingly inconsequential reversal of the student hierarchy. Muscle had surrendered to commerce. . . . There were other signs of change. The first indication of Ramon's emergence had been a line of children waiting to see him with their financial problems. The second sign, however, shook me just a little. Ramon was now among the first to be chosen for punchball.[55]

What happened in Richmond's classroom is that a shift in what the children valued made Ramon the source of scarce "rewards" for which, within the context of the game, the others had relatively little to offer in return. As a way of balancing things, his classmates altered other parts of their behavior in ways that Ramon would like. Ramon, that is, acquired the power to affect their behavior in a noncoercive way.

Homans' analysis of power is very different from both conflict theory's view of power (the ability to coerce on the basis of one's command of resources) and from functionalism's (the means by which society organizes and implements decisions). In our earlier discussions, we criticized other perspectives for ignoring the relationship between power and individuals' provision of valued services. Homans' account introduces just this element. At the same time, however, it also explains only so much about the origins of power. Homans takes values as given; he says nothing about the institutional bases of power, the circumstances that make particular goods and services valuable, or the means by which groups acquire or monopolize valued resources and leave others with nothing to bargain with. Once again, his concern is with the underlying continuities of behavior, not the institutional structure of particular societies.

[55]Richmond, *The Micro-Society School*, pp. 33–35.

Distributive Justice, Anger, and Guilt

As we have noted, the fifth of Homans' basic propositions concerns the ways in which people react to having their expectations disappointed, met, or exceeded. Exchange theorists use this proposition to explain situations that involve "distributive justice," meaning the social norms about what is due to people by right. Homans' own work in the Customers' Accounting Division of the "Eastern Utilities Company" provides a good example of how people's behavior can be explained by shared notions of distributive justice.

In this office, there were three main groups of workers, all women. One group consisted of the address file workers, who kept customers' addresses up to date; another of the cash posters, who recorded how much customers had paid on their bills; and the third of the ledger clerks, who did everything else necessary to keep the accounts up to date. The address file workers were young women who had the most boring and worst paid jobs. Among the other workers the clerks tended to be older and to have more seniority and more varied and responsible work. However, they received no more pay. Moreover, because the managers felt that cash posting had to be kept up to date, some of the clerks were set to work helping the posters in the afternoon.

Homans found that the address file workers, although they grumbled about the dreariness of their jobs, did not compare their situation unfavorably with the others. Rather, it was the ledger clerks who complained constantly about being paid the same as the cash posters and about being "taken off their own jobs and put down to work on posting." Homans interprets these results in terms of distributive justice:

> The investments of the ledger clerks were greater than those of the cash posters: they had put in more time in the company; they had learned to do a more responsible job, one that the cash posters could not do. Distributive justice accordingly demanded that their rewards should be greater than the posters' and some of them were: their work was more varied and interesting. But not all were: they got the same pay as the cash posters, and they were allowed even less autonomy—whereas the bosses left the posters alone, they took the ledger clerks off their "own" job and put them "down" on posting. Apparently distributive justice demands not just that higher investment should receive higher reward in one respect but that it should do so in all.[56]

The address file workers, by contrast, complained about the nature of their job but not about its relative rewards. It was a far worse job: its costs were high in terms of monotony, isolation, and lack of autonomy, and its rewards were low. However, Homans argues, these workers had few

---

[56]Homans, *Social Behavior,* 1st ed., p. 240.

"investments"—they were young, with little seniority—and so did not feel there was anything unjust about their situation.

In a direct study of distributive justice at work, Adams and Jacobsen paid people to do an identical proofreading job. On the basis of a "test," they told some of the readers that they were qualified for a full rate and others that they were not qualified but would be paid the full rate anyway.[57] The result was that the "unqualified" group found more errors and marked more nonerrors, such as lighter type. Apparently they felt guilty at being overpaid and thus morally obligated to redress the balance by working hard.

Homans originally suggested that people recognized some very precise rules governing the relationship between rewards, costs, and investments.[58] More recently he argued simply that people believe the relative amount they put into something—including costs, contributions, and investments—should be in line with the relative amount they get out. "The condition of distributive justice is satisfied when the ratio of the measures of the persons is equal to the ratio of the measures of their respective rewards. That is, if the two persons are equal, they should, in justice, receive equal rewards; if one is better than the other, he should receive the larger reward."[59] If we look back to the Eastern Utilities Company or Adams and Jacobsen's proofreaders, we find their attitudes compatible with this rule.

However, such a rule is also little more than a general statement that costs and investments also matter in social exchange. Societies may differ greatly not just in what they classify as an investment or a cost, but also in the weight they attach to each. Heath notes that there is evidence that a concern with rights (or investments) "will be greatest in a traditional or feudal society where there is . . . little concern with individual autonomy" and that an emphasis on deserts (or contributions) will tend to characterize an "open, mobile society" such as America.[60]

Power and Equity: The "Social" Mix   We have stressed at a number of points in this chapter that what most distinguishes sociologists' versions of "rational choice" theory is their insistence on a moral or normative dimension to social exchange. This is especially evident in recent theoretical work on social exchange theory, notably in the work of Richard Emerson, Karen Cook, and their collaborators.[61]

---

[57]J. Stacy Adams and Patricia R. Jacobsen, "Effects of Wage Inequities on Work Quality," *Journal of Abnormal and Social Psychology*, 69 (1964), 19–25.

[58]Homans, *Social Behavior*, 1st ed., pp. 234–45 passim, and Heath, *Rational Choice*.

[59]Homans, *Social Behavior*, rev. ed., p. 249.

[60]Heath, *Rational Choice*, p. 143.

[61]For an overview of this work, see especially Karen S. Cook, Jodi O'Brien, and Peter Kollock, "Exchange Theory: A Blueprint for Structure and Progress," in George Ritzer, ed., *Frontiers of Social Theory: The New Synthesis* (New York: Columbia University Press, 1990) pp. 158–81, and Cook, *Social Exchange Theory*.

In his formulations of exchange theory, Emerson emphasizes the concepts of dependence and of the alternatives available to people—very much on the lines of Thibault and Kelley's analyses in social psychology. The dependence of individual or group A on individual or group B is analyzed as a function of how much A values the resources to be obtained from an exchange with B, and how many alternative sources exist for that same resource. The power (P) of B over A, Emerson states, is the mirror image of the dependence (D) of A on B:

$$P_{ba} = D_{ab}$$

The greater your power in an exchange relationship, the greater your potential for profit: "the existence of alternatives is the key factor in defining dependence."[62] So far, this accords with the economists' theory that monopolies will raise the price of goods. However, social exchange theorists argue, the existence of notions of equity and justice actually feed directly into power relations, *constraining the use which people make of their power.*

Cook and Emerson illustrated this directly through laboratory studies of exchange relationships.[63] People were recruited to take part in a study of trading relationships and were paid according to the profits they made during "trading" sessions. Trading was conducted via computers, through which they could receive and send messages to trading partners. However, some participants were in a far more favorable situation to make profits than others—their potential rewards from a deal were greater and their alternatives more numerous.

At first, participants had no idea what situation their partners were in and, therefore, had no reason to do anything but maximize their own profits—that is, take advantage of their potential power and the others' dependence. They duly did so. However, when the situation was changed, so that participants knew not only what their own earnings would be from a deal but also how their partners would fare, their behavior changed. Constrained by concerns for equity, *those in potentially powerful positions ceased to make full use of their power.*

In demonstrating the interaction of power and equity (or justice), the empirical studies of Emerson, Cook, and others have extended Homans' formulations and underlined the distinctive characteristics of *social* exchange. Moreover, while there are no really fundamental differences in Homans' and Emerson's conceptions of power, Emerson's focus on what he calls the "exchange domain"—the continuing series of actual and possible

[62]Karen S. Cook, "Emerson's Contributions to Social Exchange Theory," in Cook, *Social Exchange Theory*, p. 215. See also below, pp. 218–20.

[63]See especially Karen S. Cook and Richard M. Emerson, "Power, Equity and Commitment in Exchange Networks," *American Sociological Review*, 43 (1978), 721–39.

transactions with different partners—highlights the crucial fact that social relationships may exist over long periods of time. Thus, in the study described above, participants' concern for equity was related to the fact that they developed longer-term relationships with—and commitments to—trading partners. In the following section, we will discuss at greater length the way in which rational choice theorists, by studying relationships over time, have contributed to our understanding of such social characteristics as interpersonal trust and group norms—generally regarded as outside the domain of their theories.

Summary

Homans' work on justice is particularly applicable to explaining behavior in "small group" situations. In general, it is characteristic of Homans' approach to exchange theory that his analyses concern interpersonal relationships and informal groups in which values are taken as given. Within these limits, Homans is quite successful in producing satisfactory deductive explanations. However, the work described in the following section, while maintaining an emphasis on individual perceptions and relationships, is concerned with their consequences for society at large.

THE CONSEQUENCES OF INDIVIDUAL CHOICE: RATIONALITY APPLIED

In discussing the intellectual roots of sociological theories of rational choice, we mentioned the growing influence of game theory and the public choice writings of economists and political scientists.[64] Sociologists' own renewed interest in a rational choice perspective is apparent in the launching in 1989 of the new journal *Rationality and Society*. The journal is edited by James Coleman, whose work is discussed below; but among its early contributors are eminent sociologists more often associated with other perspectives, including the functionalist Robert K. Merton.

This section looks in more detail at the way in which theories of games and public choice, taken together with the general model of rationality advanced by Homans, have been applied to sociological questions. In particular, we discuss the "prisoner's dilemma" and its application to modern education; coalition building; the emergence of norms and trust; and the market for "lemons."

---

[64]For an excellent review of the current state of "public choice" theory, see Iain McLean, "Review Article: Some Recent Work in Public Choice," *British Journal of Political Science*, 16 (1989), 377–94.

Prisoner's Dilemma and Perverse Effects:
Raymond Boudon

The *prisoner's dilemma* is the best known of all "games." This is partly because in the original "one-off," or one-occasion, formulation there is a wonderfully inevitable awfulness to its outcome. However, it is also because the parallels with many social situations can be grasped very easily.

In the classic version of the game, two prisoners have committed a crime together. They are both under arrest and unable to communicate with each other. In order to force a confession, the authorities offer each prisoner, *separately*, the following deal:

> If you confess and your companion does not, he will get nine years, and you will be let off scot-free.
> If you both confess, you will get five years each.
> If neither of you confesses, you will get two years each.

Figure 4-1 summarizes the choices facing each prisoner. Each quadrant show the consequences of given actions for each prisoner separately and the combined number of years in prison which will follow. The box in the upper left corner shows the consequences if both confess. It is clearly the third worst choice for each individual—and the worst of all in terms of the *total* number of years' imprisonment which it implies. Yet this is, quite inevitably, the choice that their dilemma will lead them to make. Why?— because each prisoner will, in isolation, reason this way:

> If I don't confess, and the other guy doesn't either, we will only get two years each.
> But it is also quite possible that I'll keep quiet and then find the other guy has confessed. I'll then end up with nine years in prison. So not confessing is really risky.
> On the other hand, if I do confess, I may strike lucky—he may stay silent, and I'll get off completely. At worst, I'll get five years, which is better than nine. I'll confess.

The paradox which makes the prisoner's dilemma so intriguing is that both participants end up defecting even though they both know that they would be better off cooperating. Raymond Boudon, one of the foremost contemporary French sociologists, believes that the unintended consequences of social action, especially what he calls "perverse effects," can very often be understood as variants of a prisoner's dilemma or other game.

Boudon defines perverse effects as "individual and collective effects that result from the juxtaposition of individual behaviours and yet were not

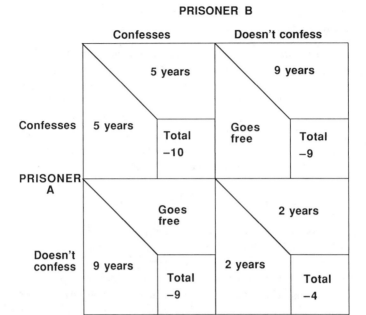

FIGURE 4-1 The Prisoner's Dilemma

included in the actors' explicit objectives."[65] Some such effects may be bene-ficial,[66] but the "perverse mechanisms that are most significant socially are those that end up producing *undesirable* effects, those that are in everyday parlance called perverse."[67]

Boudon's major interest is in one of the recurrent themes of this text: the role of formal education in modern industrial societies. In France, as in the United States and Great Britain, the expansion of higher education has been seen as a way of increasing opportunities for children from poorer and lower-class homes. In France, as in other countries, these hopes have largely been disappointed, while at the same time people experience the kind of "certification spiral" analyzed by conflict theorists such as Randall Collins.[68] Boudon's contribution is to argue that the structure of individual options and choices makes such outcomes quite inevitable. We will do far better, he

[65]Raymond Boudon, *The Unintended Consequences of Social Action* (London: Macmillan, 1982), p. 5.

[66]The most influential work on unintended beneficial effects is that of Adam Smith, who pointed out that "it is not from the benevolence of the butcher, the brewer, or the baker, that we expect our dinner, but from their regard to their own interest." Adam Smith, *An Inquiry into the Nature and Causes of the Wealth of Nations*, Edwin Cannan edition (London: Methuen, 1904), Vol. I, bk. 1, ch. 2, p. 18.

[67]Boudon, *Unintended Consequences*, p. 5.

[68]See Chapter III.

argues, to look at the "paradoxes arising from the aggregation of individual decisions than [at] cultural explanations" for what has occurred.[69]

As an example, Boudon takes the French government's decision to create Institutes of Technology offering two-year degrees in technical subjects.[70] Since 1945, higher education in France has been marked by big increases in numbers of students and in the average length of time for which people study. Most students, moreover, take rather general degrees—arts and social sciences rather than science and technology. Boudon rejects the idea that people are studying longer because of some large increase in the body of knowledge they need to acquire. Rather, it is that

> economic and social remuneration tends to vary positively, on average, with a person's amount of education. Each student, therefore, seeks to obtain the largest possible amount of education for himself. If everyone pursues the same strategy, this results in a rise in the demand for education; the supply of educated persons increases beyond the demand for particular skills in the labour market. This in turn leads to underemployment, with its attendant devaluation of qualifications, and this gives a further twist to the spiral by again increasing the demand for education.[71]

France's technical institutes (IUTs) were a conscious attempt to break this cycle by offering students the chance to acquire technical skills in intensive two-year courses, using newer teaching methods and with closer ties to industry, commerce, and the job market. Students would spend fewer years obtaining a degree; it would cost them less; and in the eyes of the government, the IUTs would provide an education closer to "the aspirations of contemporary youth and the demands of the modern world." French students complain regularly about the amount of time they have to spend studying and about the costs—directly and in income forgone. The government correspondingly forecast that within eight years of their establishment, the institutes would be educating 21 percent of all students in higher education. In fact, it was a bare 7 percent. What went wrong?

Looking at the incomes of French university graduates at first makes this even more puzzling. The *average* salary of graduates from "long" university and "short" institute courses is the same. However, the pattern of salaries is very different. Institute salaries are more clustered together. Some university graduates earn considerably less than institute ones, but some earn considerably more. This gives Boudon his clue to solving the problem, which he does by casting it in the form of a game. Each high

---

[69]Ibid., p. 101. Boudon takes issue here with fellow French sociologist Pierre Bourdieu, who emphasizes class-related cultural factors and whose work is discussed in Chapter III, pp. 98–101.

[70]Raymond Boudon, "Educational Institutions and Perverse Effects: Short-Cycle Higher Education," in Boudon, *Unintended Consequences*, pp. 77–104.

[71]Ibid., p. 83.

school graduate can be seen as choosing, *in isolation,* a strategy which will maximize his or her chances of a high payoff from higher education.

Suppose you are a French student. You don't *want* to spend many years in crowded, expensive lecture halls and classrooms. If you and your peers could get together and quit the universities for the institutes *en masse,* then all employers would have to accept your institute degrees as adequate qualifications. You would be able to compete for any jobs, and your costs would be considerably lower than those of current students.

However, at present, the best jobs in France go not to IUT graduates, but to university ones—even though there are too many of them and some end up worse off than the technically qualified institute students.[72] This means that you, as an individual student, would like *other* people to go to the institutes, while *you* attend university and get an increased chance of one of the plum jobs. Conversely, you dare not risk going to one of the institutes while your peers all go to the university. If that happens, they will shoulder you out of the market for the jobs you want and think you have a chance of getting.

With every potential student weighing possible choices or strategies in this way, one quickly ends up, as Figure 4-2 shows, with something very close to the classic prisoner's dilemma. People choose the long university courses even though they know that if they all agree to "cooperate" and choose the short institute courses, they would all be better off. The French, inevitably, according to Boudon, find their institutes a failure. Comparable processes are at work elsewhere. Americans grit their teeth and proceed to endless graduate degrees. The British government finds it impossible to persuade students to take "socially important" engineering degrees, because in the United Kingdom, it is generalists, not technical graduates, who get a crack at the very best jobs.

Boudon argues that his model of rational choice and perverse effects can "serve as an analytical instrument for assessing the likely success of certain institutional changes."[73] What is crucial, in his view, is that it takes account of the paradoxical effects of multiple individual decisions, rather than looking for cultural factors such as the "devaluation of technical training."[74] However, one must also emphasize that educational developments reflect the prisoner's dilemma so well because the individual actors concerned are making once-and-for-all choices in isolation from each other. Skeptics have queried the use of a rational choice perspective to analyze groups and institutions which operate and cooperate over time. The following sections review briefly work which attempts just such an analysis.

[72]In fact, the very best jobs in France go to graduates not of the big universities but of the very small and highly selective grandes écoles. However, the general argument holds, both for France and for other countries.

[73]Boudon, *Unintended Consequences,* p. 103.

[74]Ibid., p. 101.

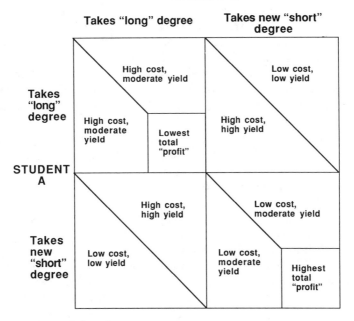

FIGURE 4-2 The Student's Dilemma

Coalition Building

James Coleman, professor of sociology at the University of Chicago, is one of the best-known American sociologists currently working in the rational choice tradition. Like Raymond Boudon, he is especially interested in the way individual decisions, aggregated, produce what are often unanticipated social effects. In particular, he argues that "collective decisions," such as the votes of Congress or Parliament, can be better understood if they are seen in terms of individuals maximizing utility. People care very much about some issues, he suggests, and relatively little about others. They therefore try to do as well for themselves as possible by trading or exchanging their partial control over some matters for greater control over others. For example, members of Congress vote with a colleague on a piece of legislation in return for that colleague's support in receiving an assignment to a particular committee.[75]

Coleman tested some of his theories about coalition building by devising a game in which players played the role of legislators whose constituen-

---

[75]See especially James S. Coleman, "Foundations for a Theory of Collective Decisions," *American Journal of Sociology,* LXXI (1966), pp. 615–27; James S. Coleman, *The Mathematics of Collective Action* (Chicago: Aldine Publishing, 1973). See also Olson, *The Logic of Collective Action.*

cies were more or less interested in various issues.[76] Over the period of the game, different issues would come to a vote, and, as predicted, players always formed coalitions, trading "useless" for "useful" power according to their degree of constituency interest. Moreover, the *more issues there were to negotiate*—that is, the more possible exchanges—*the easier it was for players to put together winning coalitions* on the particular issues they cared about.

Situations like this differ crucially from the prisoner's dilemma examples given earlier. Coleman's players were not involved in once-and-for-all decisions but rather in relationships that extended over a long period. Coleman found that as the game continued, all players became trustworthy—that is, if they promised to deliver a vote in a given way, they kept their word.[77] Moreover, players who early on had been tempted into reneging on deals, found their reputation for unreliability a handicap. They therefore attempted to restore confidence by making exchanges which were less favorable to themselves than they might be—not as in the Cook and Emerson example quoted above,[78] because they believed in equity, but because it was rationally self-interested of them to do so.

This sort of analysis, based on individuals' preferences and decisions, obviously works best in situations where people are fairly autonomous. Thus, contemporary American congressmen can and do behave not dissimilarly to Coleman's players because they must cultivate their own local political bases. In most other Western democracies, legislators are elected as members of a political party that controls very strictly the way they vote. However, here, too, we can apply a theory of coalitions based on rational choice principles. Instead of dealing with individual legislators' *votes*, it applies to the combinations of *policies* that politicians stitch together.

Such a theory starts from the fact that politicians are in business to win elections. In order to do so, they build coalitions of voters—groups such as farmers, pensioners, and teachers whose interests they promise to advance. If one party persistently loses, then its politicians will try to find issues with which to break up their opponents' winning coalition and attract enough of its voters over to their side.[79]

American coalitions are very easy to study because there have always been two, and only two, parties fighting for power at national level.[80] At the time of independence, the conflicts were between the Federalists, represent-

---

[76]James S. Coleman, *Individual Interests and Collective Action: Selected Essays* (Cambridge, England: Cambridge University Press, 1986). See also James S. Coleman, "Free Riders and Zealots," in Cook, ed., *Social Exchange Theory.*

[77]See Chapter VII for sociobiology's discussion of altruistic behavior, which overlaps in many ways that offered by rational choice theorists.

[78]See pp. 201–2.

[79]The discussion of coalition theory draws heavily on Iain McLean, *Public Choice: An Introduction* (Oxford: Basil Blackwell Ltd., 1987), especially chapter 6, "Winning Elections and Winning Power: The Theory of Political Coalitions."

[80]Or, to be more specific, only two with any real chance of winning.

ing the interests of the Northern manufacturers, and the agricultural coalition, which became the Democratic party. However, between 1816 and the eve of the Civil War there was effectively one-party rule. The Democrats' coalition, representing both slave-owning and non-slave-owning farmers from the South and West, was so effective that the cities and Northeast could never win.

Rational choice theorists argue that in this situation the obvious thing for the minority to do was to find a coalition-splitting issue. After failing to split the Democratic coalition over immigration and the role of Freemasons, they hit on a winner—slavery.[81] "A number of northern politicians took up the slavery issue for reasons which their opponents saw as pure expediency. . . . Raising the issue of slavery did break up the Jacksonian coalition and it (also destroyed) the Union."[82] While disgust at slavery had to exist for the maneuver to be workable, rational choice theorists would argue that it took "rational," or self-seeking, actors pursuing votes to translate this into the Civil War.

Trust and the Formation of Group Norms

Rational choice perspectives are frequently contrasted—by proponents and critics alike—with "sociological" explanations that use "group norms" to explain behavior. The argument is that rational choice perspectives are suitable for explaining individual behavior within a framework of given norms and values, but they cannot provide an explanation of how groups and societies develop norms in the first place.

In fact, as we saw earlier, sociological variants of rational choice theory are distinguished by their concern with the "morality of social exchange" and particularly by the argument that there exist general social principles of distributive justice and equity.[83] Homans argues that the explanation for such norms is to be found ultimately in aspects of human psychology. However, Coleman's legislative game, described above, suggests another approach—namely, that group norms emerge naturally in the course of "rational" interaction among group members.

Thus, in Coleman's game players kept their words and behaved in a trustworthy fashion; if they did not, they soon learned that it would be in their interests to do so. The development of "good behavior" of this type is obviously more likely the longer people are going to spend together and the more they depend on each other. In describing Boudon's work, we saw how students' once-and-for-all choices could be modeled using a two-person, prisoner's dilemma-type game. However, many longer-term rela-

---

[81]See especially W. H. Riker, *Liberalism Against Populism: A Confrontation Between the Theory of Democracy and the Theory of Social Choice* (San Francisco: W. H. Freeman, 1982).

[82]McLean, *Public Choice*, p. 107.

[83]See pp. 193–94.

tionships can also "be modelled as two-person encounters. If I co-operate with the other person now, there is a fair chance that she will co-operate with me next time, if there is a next time. . . . [This] is clearly likeliest to work when we both value the future relatively highly and are likely to meet again."[84]

An obvious rational strategy to adopt in this situation is "Tit for Tat." This means that I will cooperate in the first game (or encounter), but after that, I will do exactly what you did the time before. Hence, if you cheat on me, I will cheat right back, and if you cooperate, I will too. Simple as it is, "Tit for Tat" can be an extremely successful strategy for winning games and, by analogy, for creating stable and cooperative social groups.[85]

Rational choice theorists have taken the analysis furthest in discussing the market for "lemons." Suppose that I am a small used-car salesman and that some of my cars are lemons. If you come in off the street, planning to buy a car, I know that this is probably the only sale I will ever make to you. (I am also a bit mistrustful of you myself and not convinced that your credit is all that good.) Obviously, I have no incentive to tell you that the car you like is one of the lemons. If I can unload on you a car that I wish I'd never bought, so much the better.

Unfortunately, of course, the customer is as aware of this situation as I am. The effect of lemons in the marketplace is actually to shift our behavior—and cost us all money. In the case of secondhand cars, for example, the cheapest way to buy a car is from another individual; the second-cheapest from a small used-car salesman; and by far the most expensive, from a large established dealership. So why do any of us go to the dealer? Answer: because of the "lemon" problem. A big dealer is going to be around for a long time, values his reputation, and hopes some day to sell us new cars as well. Therefore, we reason, we are less likely to get a lemon. Instead of getting just the car we want from an individual on the next block, we pay more for another, and quite possibly worse one, from the dealer.

What these analyses emphasize is the crucial difference between one-time and continuing relationships. The former, which include house sales as well as used-car sales, are in fact notorious for producing cheating or attempted cheating. Moreover, the people who attempt to cheat in these

[84]McLean, "Some Recent Work in Public Choice," p. 383.

[85]See especially Robert Axelrod, "The Emergence of Co-operation among Egoists," *American Political Science Review*, LXXV (1981), 306–18, and *The Evolution of Cooperation* (New York: Basic Books, 1984); and J. Maynard Smith, *Evolution and the Theory of Games* (Cambridge: Cambridge University Press, 1982). Sociobiology is a major source of insights in this area, because of its analysis of reciprocal altruism in animals (see Chapter VII below). Richard Dawkins provides an excellent introduction to the implications of different "strategies" among animals: notably in his analysis of the benefits accruing to "Suckers" (who always help), "Cheats" (who never do), and "Grudgers" (who always help the first time, but then bear a grudge against anyone who doesn't reciprocate). Richard Dawkins, *The Selfish Gene* (Oxford: Oxford University Press, 1976), ch. 10.

situations often would not dream of doing so at other times. In other words, whether or not people follow, as well as develop, norms will depend on the "rational" choices facing them—what they can get away with and how much they hope to gain.

These developing theories of cooperation are fully consistent with Homans' arguments that group norms could emerge easily in small groups because conformity would bring friendship and approval.[86] What remains less clear is whether this approach can explain the development of general social norms that cannot depend on the face-to-face enforcement mechanisms of small groups. In the next section, therefore, we look at rational choice theory's approach to the analysis of social structure and, in particular, the work of Peter Blau.

PART TWO
Rational Choice and the Analysis of Social Structure

The work described in the previous section focuses on the origins and nature of individual choices and does so almost entirely within a small group setting. However, among the major sociological perspectives, rational choice theory is notable for encompassing both macro- and microsociologists. In the following section we review their contributions. We look first at the work of Peter Blau on social integration; then at analyses of power, notably those of Blau and Emerson; and finally at recent "macro" analyses concerned with institutional structure and the "problem of collective action."

PETER BLAU: EXCHANGE AND SOCIAL INTEGRATION

Peter Blau and George Homans are the two sociologists most responsible for establishing exchange theory and alerting sociologists to the potential of a rational choice approach. However, of the two, Peter Blau has been closer to the mainstream of American sociology. Born in Vienna in 1918, he received his sociology degrees from Elmhurst College and Columbia University. After teaching at Wayne State, Cornell, and then, for many years, at the University of Chicago, he became professor of sociology at Columbia in 1970. In 1964, Blau became president of the American Sociological Association. He has been largely concerned with the analysis of bureaucracies,

[86]See pp. 194–96.

from federal regulatory agencies to the modern university, and with the general characteristics of social structure and established social institutions, rather than with small or informal groups. His writings are particularly notable for their combination of original empirical research with general or "theoretical" propositions.

Blau's interest in social structure is common to both his theories of social exchange and his later work, in which he is no longer directly concerned with exchange per se. Thus, in a discussion of structural analysis, he emphasizes his concern with occupational variation (the division of labor) as compared to particular individuals' occupations and with "the distribution of incomes in a society which reflects income inequality" rather than with "the income of individuals."[87] Whereas Homans believes that such properties are ultimately to be explained by psychological factors, Blau argues that distinctively social factors are involved as well. Nonetheless, he also believes that the study of the "simpler processes that pervade the daily intercourse among individuals"[88] is crucial to understanding complex social structures. Social exchange is such a process.

Exchange and Power in Social Life is Blau's only direct contribution to exchange theory. Its analysis of the origins and principles governing exchange behavior is very close to Homans'. However, Homans is essentially concerned with setting out a deductive theory of behavior in general. By contrast, Blau sees exchange as one particular aspect of most social behavior. He deals with all "voluntary actions of individuals that are motivated by the returns they are expected to bring,"[89] but does not see these as comprising all social activity. Correspondingly, his analyses include more suggestive remarks about how an exchange perspective can provide explanation and less strict deduction and exposition.

Blau extends Homans' analyses of interpersonal relationships with a more explicit discussion of price mechanisms in social exchange and an analysis of people's general objectives in friendship and love. His major contributions to exchange theory, however, concern the relationship between exchange and the integration of society at large, and the exchange basis of power in large institutions as well as small groups. In describing Blau's exchange theory, we shall also refer to his own empirical studies of bureaucracy, which are among the best analyses of exchange processes in institutional settings.[90]

---

[87]Peter M. Blau, ed., *Approaches to the Study of Social Structure* (New York: The Free Press, 1975), p. 14. See Chapter VII below for a discussion of Blau's structuralist theory.

[88]Blau, *Exchange and Power,* p. 2.

[89]Blau, *Exchange and Power,* p. 91.

[90]See especially Peter M. Blau, *The Dynamics of Bureaucracy: A Study of Interpersonal Relationships in Two Government Agencies* (Chicago: The University of Chicago Press, 1955).

The Distinctive Nature of Social Exchange

Like the anthropologists we discussed above, Blau believes that social exchange is extremely important in social integration. He also argues that one of the two general functions of social—as compared to economic—exchange is the creation of bonds of friendship. The other function is to establish subordination or domination. Blau argues that exchanges increase social integration by creating trust, encouraging differentiation, enforcing conformity with group norms, and developing collective values.

Blau clarifies some of the distinctive social factors that affect "price" in noneconomic exchanges. For example, he points out that some social associations are intrinsically valuable. "It is not what lovers do together but their doing it together that is the distinctive source of their special satisfaction," he argues.[91] This aspect of exchange means that what we ask in return for a given service is likely to vary depending on who is involved; we will require a smaller return from a friend than from a stranger. Because there is no unit of account (like money), it is harder for social exchange theory to compare the value of alternative actions than it is for economics. The importance of the intrinsic elements of social exchange reduces exchange theory's precision even further.

Blau also emphasizes the importance in social exchange of "impression management," or how people present themselves to others. People want to be seen in two ways—as associates who promise rewarding "extrinsic" benefits and can therefore command favorable returns and as companions whose presence is intrinsically rewarding. Impressions are therefore crucially important to the "prices" at which social exchange is conducted.[92] Blau draws here on the work of Erving Goffman, an important contributor to symbolic interactionism, who emphasizes the creative aspects of human behavior. Goffman's work on how people control their images includes, for example, the concept of "role distance"—how people impress others by distancing themselves from a task and demonstrating how easily they can perform it.[93]

Blau believes that role distance is especially relevant to social exchange, where people wish to demonstrate how skilled they are and thus how valuable their services must be.[94] In his analysis of a federal agency enforcing regulations for business, Blau noted how agents would sometimes attempt to conceal requests for help by presenting them in the guise of discussions of an interesting problem[95]—a maneuver you will probably

[91]Blau, *Exchange and Power,* p. 15.

[92]Ibid., pp. 34–43.

[93]Erving Goffman, *Encounters* (Indianapolis: Bobbs-Merrill, 1961). See Chapter V of this text for a full discussion of Goffman's work.

[94]Blau, *Exchange and Power,* pp.40–41.

[95]Blau, *Dynamics of Bureaucracy,* p.112.

recognize as common from grade school on! "Impression management" also further distinguishes social from economic exchange and makes the nature of social exchange more difficult to predict.

Blau also discusses the determinants of friendship and love. He starts with the assumption that people value status; he defines status as the common *recognition* by others of the amount of esteem and friendship that someone receives.[96] This, he argues, implies, first, that "sociable" intercourse and friendship generally occur among people whose social standing is roughly equal; and *second*, that relationships between unequals are *less* strained when the inequality is clear and marked.

The first of these points is easily explained. Quite apart from the fact that people in different social positions are less likely to have interests and life-styles in common, status requires that inferiors cannot be allowed to get away with ignoring the deference they owe to superiors. A situation in which people are worried that "subordinates" might be perceived as "equals" clearly impedes easy socializing.

Blau argues that the second proposition holds because people whose status is not very secure are most threatened by being seen with lower-status people, especially lower-status people who may not even recognize themselves as such! By contrast, people whose status is very firmly established are unaffected by such exposure. In a modern office, one often finds that supervisors are much more relaxed with their secretaries than with immediate subordinates, who, they fear, may make claims of friendship and equality. Similarly, modern social scientists infer correctly that overt racial prejudice is strongest among those whites whose own status is least secure.

Blau argues that exchange considerations also apply to the most romantic of "love relationships" and that equality of status is as important to lovers' relationships as to friends'. Although much of what lovers exchange, such as affection and companionship, is intrinsic to the relationship, very few people are entirely indifferent to conventional valuations of looks, potential career success, athletic ability, and the like. Successful men tend to have beautiful wives and are able to attract and marry such women well into old age.

Blau discusses the effect on love relationships of an imbalance such that one partner contributes more than she or he receives and finds the relationship less important and valuable than does the other. Like Homans, Blau considers an exchange imbalance of this type to be the essence of power. He cites Willard Waller's "principle of least interest," whereby the partner who is less involved in a relationship is in an advantageous position.

> Costly possessions are most precious, in love as elsewhere.... A woman whose love is in great demand among men is not likely to make firm commit-

---

[96]Blau, *Exchange and Power*, p. 70. Blau's analysis of status is close to Homans'.

ments quickly, because she has so many attractive alternatives to weigh before she does. . . . A woman who readily gives proof of her affection to a man, therefore, provides presumptive evidence of her lack of popularity and thus tends to depreciate the value of her affection for him.[97]

In this context it is worth comparing Blau's analysis with those of some economists who have recently been paying increasing attention to "sociological" topics. Gary Becker, for example, starts an analysis of marriage with the statement that "persons marrying . . . can be assumed to expect to raise their utility level above what it would be were they to remain single."[98] However, because of "declining marginal utility,"[99] a man or woman gains less additional utility from a second spouse than from the first. The total gain in utility from three monogamous unions will therefore be greater than it would be if one man married three women and two men were left single, or vice versa. Equally, if "one's own children" are one of the major incentives to marry, then marriages in which the children's parentage is clear will be preferred to those in which it is not. In polyandry the mother of a child is unlikely to be in doubt, but the father will not always be known. It follows that monogamy will be the most common form of marriage, and polyandry the least, as indeed is the case.[100]

Exchange, Trust, and Reciprocity   Blau argues that social exchange is different from economic exchange because it creates trust between people and integrates individuals into social groups. Because it is so difficult for anyone precisely to measure and value what they are exchanging, exchanges tend to start small and evolve slowly. This tendency is strengthened, according to Blau, by the fact that in social exchange obligations cannot be specified and stipulated in advance, and one has no formal recourse against freeloaders. Reciprocation and expanded exchange are "accompanied by a parallel growth of mutual trust. Hence, processes of social exchange, which may originate in pure self-interest, generate trust in social relations through their recurrent and gradually expanding character."[101]

Blau's own studies of bureaucracy again provide a good illustration. In his analyses of the federal enforcement agency and of a state employment agency, Blau found that a work group's "social cohesion," as shown by whether they lunched or spent rest periods together, was directly related to

[97]Ibid., pp. 78–79.

[98]Gary S. Becker, "A Theory of Marriage Part I," *Journal of Political Economy*, 81 (July/August 1973), 813–46. It is important to note that Becker's argument does not imply anything about the *absolute level* of utility that people enjoy either before or after marriage. For either or both sexes it may be very low (or very high). What he is saying is that the institution of marriage implies that utility is expected to be *relatively* higher for married people.

[99]See pp. 182 and 193.

[100]See Chapter VII, pp. 353–56, for sociobiology's approach to polygamy.

[101]Blau, *Exchange and Power*, p. 94.

whether they cooperated in their work. The more they exchanged advice or services, the more they liked each other. By contrast, workers who competed head-on did not seek each other's company away from their desks.[102] In the employment agency, this was apparent in the case of staff members who tried to maximize the number of unemployed workers they placed by concealing vacancies from their colleagues.

Underlying this process of social exchange, in Blau's view, is the fundamental *social norm* of reciprocity. As we discussed earlier, anthropology stressed the existence of such a norm, and Blau, in turn, argues that the "need to reciprocate for benefits received in order to continue receiving them serves as a 'starting mechanism' of social interactions."[103] Group norms, "including the fundamental and ubiquitous norm of reciprocity," regulate exchange transactions, and a known failure to reciprocate brings with it group sanctions. At the same time, social exchange differs from economic exchange in that the nature of the return cannot be bargained over, and social exchange (unlike economic exchange) entails "unspecified obligations . . . while there is a general expectation of some future return, its exact nature is definitely not stipulated in advance."[104]

Blau provides a convincing account of how trust and social integration can be promoted by social exchange. It may even be possible to account for the emergence of a generalized norm of reciprocity in this way—either instead of, or alongside, Homans' psychological account of people's desire for "justice." However, Blau tends to overstate the difference between economic and social exchange. In the previous section, we saw how purely self-interested quasi-economic exchanges can also generate trust. You may have little formal recourse against a freeloader on a specific, isolated occasion, but failure to reciprocate will often deprive the culprits of services they may want in the future, because of social disapproval and reluctance to trade with them. In situations like this, the balance of chance and sanctions is not so different from the balance in economic exchange.

Social Conformity and the Development of Collective Values

In using an exchange perspective to explain conformity in the wider society, Blau points out that one distinguishing characteristic of large institutions is that exchange is increasingly indirect. Rewards come to you in a roundabout fashion, often from someone who does not even know the individual who received your services. Blau believes that this type of indirect exchange depends on the strength and internalization of social norms,

---

[102]Blau, *Dynamics of Bureaucracy*, pp. 61–62 and 132–36.
[103]Blau, *Exchange and Power*, p. 92.
[104]Ibid., p. 93.

which in turn depend on the fact that people receive approval in exchange for their conformity.

> The condemnation of rate busters in factories, of apple polishers and teacher's pets in schools, of traitors to their country, of stool pigeons and informers in groups of any kind—all these reflect social norms designed to suppress conduct that advances the individual's interest by harming the collective interest. . . .
>
> Social norms substitute indirect exchange for direct transactions between individuals. The members of the group receive social approval in exchange for conformity. . . . By adhering to . . . moral principles, individuals establish a good reputation which stands them in good stead in subsequent social interaction . . . [and] is like a good credit rating.[105]

Blau's analysis here is very similar to that of Homans, who, although he deals largely with direct exchange, also sees social approval as the main force creating conformity. However, while approval and disapproval may work well enough in small groups, it seems unlikely that people will know enough about each other's actions for this to create and maintain conformist behavior in larger institutions. In fact, as the final section of this chapter discusses, rational choice theorists have other ideas about how large institutions maintain conformity, suggesting that approval and disapproval are only one possible mechanism.

The Development of Collective Values   Blau also proposes an "emergent process" by which shared experiences actually produce group norms and values. The mechanism is not direct exchange, but rather people's dislike for the psychological state of *cognitive dissonance.* This term is used by social psychologists to describe a situation in which either some of the facts that someone faces are in conflict with others, or someone's experiences are not in line with what "ought" to be happening. Leon Festinger, who coined the term, suggests that people dislike this dissonance and try to avoid and reduce it, for example, by denying or arguing away the facts and opinions behind it.[106]

Blau suggests that when this happens in a group context, individual responses and rationalizations can be strengthened and transformed into common values and norms. People who find themselves in the same situation of cognitive dissonance are likely to discuss it with each other and to seek and get support for their arguments. In the course of such mutual discussion, individual rationalizations are transformed into social consensus and, indeed, social norms. In his empirical analyses of bureaucracy, for

[105]Ibid., pp. 257–59.
[106]Leon Festinger, *A Theory of Cognitive Dissonance* (Evanston, Ill.: Row, Peterson, 1957).

example, Blau describes how interviewers in the state employment agency would commonly discuss troublesome cases and decisions *after* the event in order to elicit colleagues' assent and approval and to allay their own doubts.[107] More generally, Blau believes that intensive group discussion and interaction create shared values. Those employment agency interviewers who had trained together at a period when intensive consultation and counseling were emphasized had developed a common code of cooperation, which they maintained by the usual mechanisms of approval, disapproval, and withholding help from deviants.

The process Blau describes here goes beyond the basic approach of exchange theory. That people discuss situations of dissonance because they want reassurance can be fully accounted for by the idea of rational choice. However, Blau suggests, emerging from this process are new, shared values and norms whose origins lie not in individual utility maximization but in some aspect of group psychology. Blau's account of the process is somewhat sketchy and far from conclusive, but it does seem plausible that rational choice alone cannot explain the development—as opposed to the consequences—of our values.

EXCHANGE AND POWER: BLAU AND EMERSON

The Nature of Power   Richard Emerson and Peter Blau have both offered analyses of power differentials which root them in exchange relationships but also look beyond individual (or "dyadic") relationships to larger structural settings. Both see power as originating when valued services are provided as part of an unbalanced exchange, so that one party places a higher value on the outcome than the other. The approach is also that adopted by Homans in his more recent work.

The crucial notion here is that one partner in exchange is *dependent on the other* for services and values those services more than the other values anything he can offer.[108] This is the argument Blau uses in discussing the balance of power in love relationships, which we discussed earlier. However, it can be extended to include the coercive aspects of power and the fact that someone who is in a position of power has the potential to secure submission and compliance.[109]

Thus, in a much-cited article which appeared in 1962,[110] Richard

---

[107]Blau, *Dynamics of Bureaucracy*, pp. 89–90. Lewis Coser argues that conflict may similarly give rise to new norms because it encourages people to discuss ideas very explicitly and refine these ideas—and because it creates new social formations. Lewis Coser, *The Functions of Social Conflict* (Glencoe, Ill.: The Free Press, 1956), p. 125.

[108]See above pp. 200–202.

[109]Homans' work generally emphasizes power's noncoercive aspects—the fact that someone may pay a high price but nevertheless obtain something he or she wants.

[110]Richard M. Emerson, "Power-Dependence Relations," *American Sociological Review*, 27 (1962), 31–41.

Emerson listed the conditions determining the extent to which the supplier of a good or service (such as weekly wages or companionship) exerts power over those receiving the supplies. The supplier's power is greater the more it is true that (1) the individual who wants a service has nothing the supplier needs that he or she can offer in return; (2) the recipient has no alternative to turn to; (3) the recipient cannot use direct coercion to extract the services he or she needs; and (4) the recipient cannot resign himself or herself to doing without the services or find a substitute. The second and fourth conditions echo the conditions economists use to describe monopoly. However, in economic exchange the result is simply that the buyer pays more, whereas in social exchange the supplier can make general demands and secure compliance.

Blau's account of power follows on from Emerson's, as, indeed, has much of the more recent empirical work on exchange and power.[111] Blau defines power as:

> the ability of persons or groups to impose their will on others despite resistance through deterrence either in the form of withholding regularly supplied rewards or in the form of punishment, inasmuch as the former as well as the latter constitute, in effect, a negative sanction. . . . If [a person] regularly renders needed services [others] cannot readily obtain elsewhere . . . their unilateral dependence obligates them to comply with his requests lest he cease to continue to meet their needs.[112]

Emerson's work is more formal than Blau's, and, in elaborating his conception of power, he pays particular attention to the existence of alternatives for actors. With Karen Cook and others, Emerson conducted empirical studies in laboratory settings which examined the way in which patterns of exchange relations among actors, and their relative degrees of dependence and valuation of outcomes, create power advantages. Current work in this tradition is increasingly concerned with power relations in exchange *networks* rather than in dyadic relationships.[113] Cook in particular emphasizes that "networks, as social structures, affect exchange transactions that occur within these structures. Certainly they determine the nature of the

---

[111]See, for example, R. L. Burgess and J. M. Nielsen, "An Experimental Analysis of Some Structural Determinants of Equitable and Inequitable Exchange Relationships," *American Sociological Review*, 39 (1974), 427–43; K. S. Cook, M. R. Gillmore, and T. Yamagishi, "The Distribution of Power in Exchange Networks: Theory and Experimental Results," *American Journal of Sociology*, 89 (1983), 275–305; L. D. Molm "The Conversion of Power Imbalance to Power Use," *Social Psychology Quarterly*, 44 (1981), 42–48, and "Linking Power Structure and Power Use," in Cook, ed., *Social Exchange Theory.*

[112]Blau, *Exchange and Power*, pp. 117–18.

[113]See especially Karen S. Cook and Richard M. Emerson, "Power, Equity and Commitment in Exchange Networks," *American Sociological Review*, 43 (1978), 721–39. See Chapter VII, pp. 335–38, for a general discussion of network analysis.

distribution of exchange opportunities and thus structurally determine dependence and power."[114]

As does Homans', this approach has both similarities to, and differences from, those of functionalism and conflict theory. Conflict theorists' major interest is in the conditions that support what rational choice theorists might call monopolies—in other words, in the ways groups establish and maintain a position of control over scarce and valued resources. In considerably greater detail than Emerson or Blau, conflict theorists analyze the particular institutional conditions under which groups can increase the degree to which the four conditions of power hold. For example, in the case of the Communist Party in communist states, they identify ways in which the party may monopolize services that are essential to people through centralized socialism and bureaucratic organization (the second and fourth conditions again), or they examine the party's efforts to ensure control of the army and the means of coercion (the third condition).

By contrast, Blau and Emerson emphasize the exchange relationship at the core of inequality. Unlike most conflict theorists, they note the independent importance of the fourth condition—that the recipients of services are not prepared to do without them. At the same time, Blau, in particular, pays far more attention to the coercive and monopolistic aspects of power and its resulting inequalities than do most functionalists. The functionalist theory of social stratification, for example, argues that higher rewards for some occupations than for others are "functional" in that they induce people with rare talents and skills to fill those occupations. The exchange perspective similarly identifies a link between power and exchange of goods or services and relates the value of a service to the price its supplier can command. However, functionalism pays little attention to the fact that groups may, in effect, distort the "market"—for example, by introducing barriers to social mobility and by maintaining a form of society in which people cannot choose whom to turn to as employer, landlord, or physical protector. Exchange theory's discussion of coercive power recognizes the importance of "distortions," and it also anchors power relationships in myriad individual actions, not "society" in the abstract.

Normative Factors in Social Exchange.   The basic account of power offered by Blau and Emerson is essentially an economic one, and as such it is very much in the mainline of rational choice analysis. However, Blau also offers a rather different account of power, which, like his discussion of social integration, implies a distinctive moral element in social exchange. He argues that power may also be based on people's *normative obligations.* This theory bears very little resemblance to either the "economic" approach

---

[114]Cook et al., "Exchange Theory," in Ritzer, *Sociological Theory.* The University of Washington is the center of empirical work of this type.

or to conflict and functionalist analyses. It seems to owe most to Marcel Mauss' discussion of the status competition inherent in gift giving, and it derives from the norm of reciprocity. Blau argues that any service one person supplies to another, including a gift, carries with it obligations that cannot simply be discharged, as Homans implies, by "payment" in the form of social approval. Rather, an "individual who supplies rewarding services to another obligates him. To discharge this obligation, the second must furnish benefits to the first in turn."[115] If he or she cannot, the donor has achieved a concrete source of power and can cash in on the accumulated obligations by directing those concerned to do what he wants.

Although we know of no studies that directly compare these two accounts of power, there is considerable evidence to support a general link between relative power and the supply of services. Of particular note is Blood and Wolfe's study of the balance of power between husbands and wives.[116] Blood and Wolfe argue that the more crucial the husband's skills to the family's survival and well-being and the more complete his control of its wealth and resources the more patriarchal the family. They suggest that this is because the husband's or wife's say in decisions is a direct result of what each contributes—not through some conscious calculation of relative power but because the partner who receives more than he or she gives feels both indebted for the past and dependent on future contributions. In a study of decision making in over 700 contemporary Detroit families,[117] Blood and Wolfe found evidence of just this pattern at work:

> Although society no longer insists upon a particular balance of power in marriage, the larger community still affects husband-wife relationships. Today, the more successful the husband is in the eyes of the community, the more dominant his part in marital decision-making . . . [although the] husband's earnings are an even more sensitive indicator of his power than his occupation. . . . Bringing home the bacon is a prime example of contributing a resource to marriage. That top-income-bracket husbands should be most

[115]Blau, *Exchange in Power*, p. 89.

[116]Robert O. Blood, Jr., and Donald M. Wolfe, *Husbands and Wives: The Dynamics of Married Living* (New York: The Free Press, 1960). For similar analyses and findings, see Scanzoni, *Power Politics;* and M. Anderson, *Family Structure in Nineteenth Century Lancashire* (Cambridge: Cambridge University Press, 1971). While later replications of Blood and Wolfe's account have not always found such clear patterns as they report, the general findings stand. See C. Safilios-Rothschild, "The Study of Family Power Structure, A Review 1960–1969," *Journal of Marriage and the Family*, 32 (1970), 539–52. The developments of the 1960s and 1970s, including the women's movement and the greater numbers of working mothers, may be presumed to have changed the average distribution of power within marriages, though not the underlying relationships between power and services.

[117]The decisions studied were: (1) what job the husband should take; (2) what car to get; (3) whether or not to buy life insurance; (4) where to go on a vacation; (5) what house or apartment to take; (6) whether or not the wife should go to work or quit work; (7) what doctor to have when someone was sick; and (8) how much money the family could afford to spend per week on food. See Blood and Wolfe, *Husbands and Wives*, p. 19.

influential in marriage reflects the magnitude of their contribution to the family exchequer. By contrast, where the total income of the family (rather than the husband's alone) is taken into consideration, the balance of power is altered in the wife's direction. . . . So, high-income husbands are most powerful *if* their wives contribute no income.

. . . [Another] index of individual resources is the couple's stage in the family-life cycle. . . . Having a young child creates needs for the wife which lead her to depend more on her husband for help, financial support, and making decisions. . . . Childlessness allows a continuation of the honeymoon state of mutual emotional and financial interdependence with the husband. [By contrast] the mother of a new baby . . . gives up her job and is confined to her home by the heavy demands of child-care. Not only is she cut off from contact with her fellow workers but even the opportunity to participate in recreational activities and organizational meetings is impaired by her babysitting responsibilities. . . . It is no wonder, therefore, that the wife's dependence increases.[118]

Blood and Wolfe tend to emphasize the relationship between power and obligations, but their results are also consistent with theories emphasizing normative factors. Indeed, it may be that power can rest on either basis. In families where the wife is the major breadwinner there is a tendency for the women to cede *some* of their financial power to their husbands. A study by David Morley of family television viewing habits in Great Britain showed that, when either men *or children* were at home, women almost invariably deferred to them in their choice of program. The women felt that they "ought" to be the peacemakers in the family, giving other members power to choose by default.[119]

Power, Legitimacy, and Opposition.   A major theme of this chapter has been the ability of rational choice theories to explain the emergence of norms that hold beyond the confines of a small group. Blau, whose own interest is in large-scale social structures, offers an exchange analysis of just such a process: the development of legitimate institutional power.[120]

Blau argues that the major determinant of legitimacy is found in the exchange aspect of power—namely, whether or not subordinates feel that power is being exercised not merely fairly but generously. "If the benefits followers derive . . . exceed their expectations of a fair return for the costs they have incurred . . . their collective approval of [the] leadership legitimates it," he states.[121] Legitimacy transforms power into *authority* because legitimacy makes it right and proper to obey; in other words, the group

[118]Blood and Wolfe, *Husbands and Wives*, pp. 30–32 and 41–43 passim.

[119]Peggy Stamp, "Research Note: Balance of Financial Power in Marriage: An Exploratory Study of Breadwinning Wives," *The Sociological Review*, 33 (1985), 546–57; David Morley, *Family Television: Cultural Power and Domestic Leisure* (London: Comedia, 1986).

[120]See Chapter III, especially the sections on Weber and Habermas, for discussions of legitimacy and authority.

[121]Blau, *Exchange and Power*, p. 202.

develops norms, which help to enforce members' obedience. By contrast, superiors who perform their tasks well or even make major contributions to the achievement of common goals, will command respect and power but not necessarily legitimation and authority.

The mechanism is the one we described earlier. People find that deference and submission create costs of a substantial order and will question whether they should comply with others' commands. To resolve their state of "cognitive dissonance" in situations involving deference or obedience, they will discuss and seek support for their opinions from others. From this, social consensus and group norms will emerge. When power is exercised generously, Blau argues, individual rationalizations of obedience will be transformed into a collective norm that mandates obedience to legitimate authority. The development of opposition ideologies follows a parallel course. When subordinates experience collectively the unfair exercise of power, their collective disapproval generates opposition movements based on appropriate values.[122]

Blau's argument is an interesting one, but there is unfortunately very little evidence to either support or contradict it. In his own work on a federal enforcement agency, Blau describes a situation in which the agents all accepted the general legitimacy of their bureaucratic superiors' positions, but their degree of willing obedience also depended on an individual superior's behavior. The supervisor in the office Blau studied did have personal influence and "authority," yet he was also generous in the way he allowed agents to break minor rules and in his efforts to get them promotions.[123] This is certainly consistent with Blau's interpretation, but it is impossible to be sure whether the important factor was generous use of power or something else, such as the agents' perception that their supervisor was advancing their interests directly.

Blau's arguments, therefore, remain suggestive rather than conclusive. Indeed, this is generally true of his attempts to use exchange theory to explain social structure and "emergent processes." In the next section, we examine some more recent attempts to apply a rational choice perspective to institutional analysis, with particular reference to the emergence and enforcement of social norms and values.

INSTITUTIONAL STRUCTURES AND THE "PROBLEM OF COLLECTIVE ACTION"

In recent years, Blau has rejected exchange theory on the grounds that a perspective rooted in individual choice is, after all, inadequate to deal with

---

[122]Ibid., p. 230.

[123]Blau, *Dynamics of Bureaucracy*, pp. 171–76.

social structure. However, while Blau has been arguing for a distinctively "structuralist" approach, other social scientists, have continued to develop analyses rooted in individuals' "rational choices." Michael Hechter, for example, argues that such a perspective is far superior to its traditional alternatives.[124] "Structuralist" explanations, among which he includes variants of conflict theory, and "normative" explanations, such as functionalism, must both be found wanting.

Normative theories explain the fact that we behave in particular ways, cooperate, and carry out social "roles" by referring to the internalization of social norms. However, Hechter argues, such a theory fails completely to explain why we only obey norms sometimes and why norms change over time. Why, for example, if little girls are so well socialized in "feminine" ways, did the contemporary women's movement emerge?

Structuralist explanations, by contrast, look to the conditions and restraints shared by different groups to explain both action and inaction. "Oppressed" classes are quiescent, in their view, because they are effectively coerced; equally, we should expect that groups with "common interests" will act in common to pursue these. But if that is the case, retort the rational choice theorists, how come groups that could act often *don't*? Why is it, in Marx's terms, that a "class in itself" only rarely mobilizes as a "class for itself"? And does the implicit claim of the structuralists[125]—that when people share the same social position, individual differences wash out—really hold up? If women are so alike in their class position, why do we find that the majority of the most committed activists on *both* sides of the abortion debate are women?

Rational choice theory is as concerned as any of the other macro perspectives with the question of what holds societies together and explains group behavior. However, by starting from the viewpoint of a rational individual, it recasts the question and also makes it apparent just how difficult it is to explain both social order and group, or "collective," action. In the previous sections of this chapter, we have observed that rational choice explanations seem to work best for small group situations, and even their advocates admit that, so far, the perspective has "done a better job of posing this question [of collective action] than of resolving it."[126] Nonetheless, we can, increasingly, find theories rooted in individual rationality which do explain institutional and group phenomena.

---

[124]Michael Hechter, *Principles of Group Solidarity* (Berkeley, Calif.: University of California Press, 1987.)

[125]See, for example, the discussion of Blau's structuralism in Chapter VII.

[126]Hechter, *Principles of Group Solidarity*, p. 9.

Collective Action and the Problem of "Free Riders"

Rational choice theory's distinctive approach to macrosociology can best be introduced by looking at the types of question that it poses. Take, for example, its best-known puzzle: Why do people turn out to vote?[127]

Imagine that it is the morning of an election day. Our rational individuals, if they decide to vote, will have to take time to do so—perhaps get up early, or go out in the evening after supper, or miss a favorite TV program . . . Why should they?

In his classic analysis of voting behavior, Anthony Downs assumed that everybody is aware of (can calculate) their "party differential." This is a measure of how much better off they will be if one party or candidate wins rather than another—or of how much they care about the result. However, even if someone's party differential is very high, he should also, rationally, take into account whether his vote is likely to make a difference. Thus, he may much prefer one candidate over another, but what are the chances that his vote, and his alone, will decide the issue? Even in a school board election, the odds are fairly low, "and in an electorate of millions this probability is so small that the value of voting will be infinitesmal, even for someone who has a large party differential. Thus, it seems to follow that rational citizens would not vote if there are costs involved—and it always takes time and energy to cast a vote."[128] If you calculate your party differential and *then multiply it by the odds that your vote will be the crucial one*, the result is likely to be less than the cost in shoe-leather of walking to the polls.[129]

Of course, the fact is that large numbers of people do vote; in the U.S. about half the eligible population does so. Some critics have taken this to prove that the rational choice perspective has to be abandoned and that we need to revert to an explanation in terms of norms—people believe they "ought" to vote, and so they do. However, it is equally the case that a lot of people *don't* vote, when, according to normative explanations, they should. Moreover, the people who do—or don't—aren't always the same, so it cannot simply be a question of good (or failed) internalization.

Rational choice theory, by contrast, can easily explain why in an election where you don't much care who wins, a rainstorm may well tip the balance.[130] Equally, it can suggest why people vote more in presidential

---

[127]See especially Anthony Downs, *An Economic Theory of Democracy* (New York: Harper and Row, 1957); Brian Barry, *Sociologists, Economists and Democracy* (London: Collier-Macmillan, 1970); and Howard Margolis, *Selfishness, Altruism and Rationality* (Cambridge: Cambridge University Press, 1982).

[128]Barry, *Sociologists, Economists and Democracy*, p. 15.

[129]See McLean, *Public Choice*, p. 46.

[130]Rational choice theories as a whole share with economics an emphasis on what happens "at the margin". Thus, the point is not that a rainstorm will make everybody stay at home: but that those to whom voting was only marginally worthwhile on a dry day will find it (marginally!) unworthwhile on a wet one. See pp. 182 and 189–90.

elections, where their vote really can hardly matter, than in school board or parish council ones, where it might. The theory points out that people's party differential is generally greater in the former than in the latter case. However, we are still left with the question of why anyone votes at all.[131]

A common response of people, when asked why they—or anyone else—votes is "Well, what if everyone stopped voting?" The implication is that they are, in fact, being rational, helping to maintain a system that benefits them in the long-term. Unfortunately, there is a difference here between what seems "rational" in a small group and "rational" in a large one. In the previous section, we described how a rational choice perspective can explain cooperative behavior and trust quite well in small groups: because those who do not cooperate and keep their word are quickly identified and repaid in kind. In a large group, this isn't true. It is quite possible, and apparently rational, to *free ride:* Let everyone else vote and keep the system going, while I go to the movies.

Blau got around this problem by invoking a general "norm of reciprocity," but there are other, more fully worked out answers to the voting puzzle, to which we turn below. Before doing so, however, one should emphasize that, while it remains puzzling that anyone does vote, or collect for charity, or write to their senator,

> the logic of collective action is overwhelmingly successful in predicting negligible voluntary activity in many realms such as, say, the contemporary environmental movement. Then what about the Sierra Club and other environmental organizations? The answer is that environmentalists contribute woefully little to their cause given the enormous value to them of success and given the repeated survey results that show high commitment by a large percentage of Americans to that cause. Environmentalists annually spend less on their apparently great cause than 25,000 two-pack-a-day smokers spend on cigarettes. . . . One could go on to note even more embarrassing statistics on how little Americans have spent on such honored causes as civil rights, the contemporary women's movement, gun control (as opposed to anti-control) and so forth. . . .[132]

Rational Choice and Group Solidarity   In their explanations of collective behavior, rational choice theorists emphasize the differences between public goods and selective benefits. With *public goods,* there is no way of stopping noncontributors from benefiting. Thus, in the voting example given above, if most people vote and in doing so preserve a democratic system,

---

[131]A further twist is added by those people who, having had a vague feeling that they "ought" to vote, gave up doing so with a clear conscience once they knew about public choice theory.

[132]Brian Barry and Russell Hardin, eds., *Rational Man and Irrational Society? An Introduction and Source Book* (Beverly Hills, Calif.: Sage, 1982), p. 21.

there is no way of stopping the nonvoters from enjoying its (presumed) benefits.

By contrast, *selective benefits* can be kept for group members who pay their dues.[133] Take a very common form of organized group, a trade union to which members pay regular dues. If a union negotiates with management and obtains a pay increase or change in working conditions, all workers in a plant or industry benefit, regardless of whether or not they are union members. Why, then, should anyone ever join a union?

Rational choice theory suggests that much of the answer lies in the selective benefits which only members receive. Thus, if a union member is involved in a dispute with management, the union officials will get involved on his or her behalf. The union may provide legal advice and representation and may also offer other benefits, such as low-cost insurance packages. Selective benefits of this type can be very substantial. For example, in Great Britain, the cost of joining the Association of University Teachers is about the same as the reduction in automobile insurance you can receive as an AUT member.

The benefits of legal staff and negotiated insurance packages are not something which individuals can obtain on their own: they are essentially collective goods, produced by groups.[134] Michael Hechter argues that this situation can provide us with a satisfactory rational choice theory of group formation and solidarity.

> The starting point of this theory is the assumption that actors initially form groups, or join existing ones, in order to consume various *excludable jointly produced* goods—goods whose attainment involves the cooperation of at least two (but usually far more) individual producers. The survival of any group therefore hinges on the continuous production of such goods. But this is a highly problematic outcome. It requires the establishment of several different kinds of rules—rules about how to make rules, rules that serve to coordinate members' productive activities and rules that govern each member's access to those goods once they have been attained.[135]

In many cases, people will obey the rules of the group because, and only insofar as, they are compensated for doing so. People's "rule-abiding" behavior at work is very much related to direct compensation, in the form of money now and/or the prospect of promotion in the future. If something better offers itself,[136] people quit. Rational choice theory can obviously account for this sort of group membership. But what about "solidaristic" groups—the

[133]This point was made most forcibly by Olson in *The Logic of Collective Action*.

[134]Selective incentives don't on their own explain the emergence of "public-interest" groups. See the following section.

[135]Hechter, *Principles of Group Solidarity*, p. 10.

[136]Allowing for exit costs.

sort of tight-knit group with shared patterns of living associated with Durkheim's concept of "mechanical solidarity" or Toennies' *gemeinschaft?* Why do people conform with their often very pervasive demands?

Hechter defines solidarity as "compliance in the absence of compensation" and agrees that, in varying degrees, it characterizes many groups whose members act in accordance with group norms, many of them very demanding and restrictive. However, rather than explaining this in terms of "internalization" or "identification" with the group, he argues that "individual compliance and group solidarity can be attained only by the combined effects of dependence and control."[137]

Hechter's notion of dependence is the same as that used by Emerson and Cook.[138] It is a function of how much someone wants the joint good produced by the group *and of how many alternative sources exist.* The more dependent someone is, the more compliance for the less compensation the group can extract. In effect, the "more dependent people are, the more tax they must pay for access to the same quantity of a given good."[139] The economists' formulation, quoted at the beginning of this chapter, is only slightly different: Goods will generally be more expensive if they are supplied by a monopolist than by a number of firms in competition.

Compare, Hechter suggests, the extent of the group obligations incurred by Orthodox and Reform Jews in return for group membership and support. "When the bulk of Eastern European Jews were confined to the shtetl, they subscribed to a religion with extensive obligations. Once individual Jews were granted full citizenship and became less dependent upon their coreligionists for their life chances, Reform Judaism began to supplant the Orthodox variety."[140] More and more Jews abandoned the strict dietary laws, restrictions on Sabbath activities, and requirements for daily prayer.

At the same time, dependence is not enough to ensure that people meet the obligations the group demands. The reason it is not—especially in larger groups—is the same: the incentive to free ride. The larger the group, the more it must rely on formal controls and sanctions for noncompliance. This is true, Hechter argues, however great the members' dependence and however much the group is one which offers "community" and support, rather than the material goods.

Hechter argues his point by an analysis of "intentional" communities, where people who are not kin live together—places such as the communes of the 1960s or monastic and semimonastic communities (such as the Shakers). They are "quintessential obligatory groups whose members seek to provide joint goods—like a sense of community, friendship, love, and the

---

[137]Hechter, *Principles of Group Solidarity,* p. 11.
[138]See pp. 201 and 219.
[139]Hechter, *Principles of Group Solidarity,* p. 46.
[140]Ibid., p. 57.

feeling of security—all of which flow from the existence of social har-mony."[141] They also survive *to the degree that they use exactly the sort of compli-ance mechanisms that succeed elsewhere.*

Communities that reject hierarchy, do not make their members highly dependent on the group for food and shelter, and do not enforce specific obligations rarely last long. Conversely, those which are able to monitor members' actions in great detail—for example, through communal living quarters and regular, ritualized meetings; which impose very high costs on leaving; and which make all rewards collective, notably by insisting on communal property, are also those which survive in the long term. Hechter concludes, "The *Gemeinschaft* is more solidary than the *Gesellschaft*, not be-cause it entails more extensive normative internalization or promotes greater commitment, but because its institutional arrangements permit members' behavior to be controlled more economically."[142]

Altruists and Zealots

We emphasized earlier that rational choice theory is valuable for hav-ing shown that certain taken-for-granted behavior is actually very puzzling: for example, voting, donating blood, or participating in Sierra Club or Greenpeace volunteer activities. Some of this behavior may be explained in Hechter's terms; namely, people belong to groups on which they are very dependent and which can therefore extract a very high behavioral "tax" from them. Much of the behavior, however, cannot be explained in this way. For example, in Great Britain blood supplies are provided entirely through voluntary contributions, and in neither the United States nor Western Eu-rope are there any penalties for failing to vote.

Public choice theory does, in fact, offer some explanations of why people behave like this and, by analogy, of why "public interest" groups may emerge in the first place. James Coleman provides a formulation which is very close to that of the "conventional" model of rationality and to Homans' exchange theory. Coleman argues that if your actions benefit others, then those others have an incentive to provide rewards—in the form, say, of social approval.

> Thus, one's efforts [may] directly help to satisfy one's interests (even if not enough to outweigh the costs of those efforts) and . . . also bring rewards from others for helping to satisfy their interests. In some cases the combina-tion of these two benefits is far greater than the costs of the activity to the person. This is the rationality of the zealot.[143]

---

[141]Ibid., p. 148.

[142]Ibid., p. 167. See the section on Coser in Chapter III for a complementary analysis of "greedy institutions."

[143]Coleman "Free Riders and Zealots," in Cook, ed., *Social Exchange Theory*, p. 63.

An explanation of this type works quite well for small groups. Often, however, the sort of behavior we are dealing with is effectively invisible. Who knows that we vote, give blood, or give to charity, let alone rewards us for doing so? Rational choice theory thus has to admit that truly "altruistic" behavior exists and has to account for it.

Margolis, for example, suggests that most of us are altruistic in two ways.[144] The first is that we want people to have things; this is "goods altruism." We therefore tell the polls that we approve of government doing things for people; give (a bit) to charity; and may take into account not just what we will gain from our party's winning but also what other people will.[145] We also act on the basis of a second "participation altruism"—that is, we get a good feeling from actually taking part in things for what we feel are nonselfish reasons. Many blood donors express this feeling when asked why they volunteer.[146]

An alternative formulation involves the "norm of reciprocity" invoked by anthropologists and by exchange theorists such as Blau and Homans. Because people feel it is morally unacceptable to free ride, they feel guilty when they do and assuage their guilt when they don't.[147]

However, although doing something because of our altruistic or moral feelings may be perfectly rational, critics may also feel, quite reasonably, that this isn't much of an explanation. The theorists seem to be importing factors to fill necessary gaps without really explaining *why* human beings behave in this moral or altruistic way.

Homans' argument that laws of social behavior must be ultimately psychological would certainly seem to apply to any explanations of human altruism. One possible approach is that taken by sociobiology,[148] which looks at the reproductive advantage which certain behavior—such as moderate degrees of altruism—might bestow on a species. However, some recent sociological work suggests that we can also learn a lot by combining a rational choice perspective with the way microsociology—such as symbolic interactionism or phenomenology—views human identity.

Kristin Luker studied women activists on both sides of the abortion debate: women who gave considerable amounts of their time either to the pro-life movement or to pro-choice activism.[149] She concluded that the

---

[144]Margolis, *Selfishness, Altruism, and Rationality*.

[145]As McLean points out, this changes the whole arithmetic of voting decisions. Even if my "party differential" is minuscule, the combined differential of all supporters is huge. Multiply $50,000,000 rather than $2,500 by even the minuscule chance that my vote will make a difference, and you will get quite a respectable sum of money.

[146]See R. M. Titmuss, *The Gift Relationship* (London: Allen and Unwin, 1970).

[147]Iain McLean and Jo Poulton, "Good Blood, Bad Blood, and the Market: *The Gift Relationship* Revisited," *Journal of Public Policy*, 6, no. 4 (1988), 431–45.

[148]See Chapter VII.

[149]Kristin Luker, *Abortion and the Politics of Motherhood* (Berkeley, California: University of California Press, 1984).

activities of both groups were bound up with the way they defined not only their individual identity, but their whole world view. Participating in a political movement was a way of having both of these validated and made more real by other people.

Pro-life people, Luker found, see the world as inherently divided into a male and female sphere. Abortion on demand, for them, breaks up a whole set of social relationships in which women and children are protected, and everyone loses out. A pro-life doctor told Luker that

> I think women's lib is on the wrong track. . . . The women have been the superior people. They're more civilized, they're more unselfish by nature, but now they want to compete with men at being selfish. And so there's nobody to give an example, and what happens is that men become *more* selfish.[150]

Pro-life people also feel that there is a lot of anti-child feeling in modern society, and that this is encapsulated in the cultural norm of small families and the idea that births should be timed to fit in with adults' career plans. Their own position is the opposite. They value traditional roles and believe that if you take on the responsibilities of marriage and parenthood, other parts of your life should be subordinated to these. Most pro-life activists are, themselves, wives and mothers for whom these roles are the most important in their lives.

Taking an active part in the pro-life movement enables these people to defend and reinforce their whole world view and self-concept. Being among others who share their values and attitudes is a crucial part of the process, and provides a strong, if unconscious, motive for their behavior. Exactly the same holds for pro-choice activists, although their world view is, obviously enough, a very different one.

Thus, Luker ties collective and altruistic behavior to the process by which people get their chosen selves "confirmed" and approved. In the chapters on symbolic interactionism and phenomenology, this text discusses in detail the essentially social way in which we develop a "self" and experience our world as real and substantial.[151] The rational choice tradition generally stands apart from these micro perspectives, but by linking the two, Kristin Luker provides a fuller explanation of collective behavior.

CONCLUSION

Rational choice theorists tend to adopt their perspective in self-conscious rejection of other prevailing theories. Its greatest strength is summarized by James Coleman:

[150]Ibid., p. 163.
[151]See Chapters V and VI. See also the section on Giddens in Chapter VII.

Rational action of individuals has a unique attractiveness as the basis for social theory. If an institution or a social process can be accounted for in terms of the rational actions of individuals, then and only then can we say that it has been "explained." The very concept of rational action is a conception of action that is "understandable," action that we need ask no more questions about . . .[152]

However, as one might expect, such a perspective tends to be most successful when used to analyze behavior in small group situations. Homans, for example, focuses entirely on "elementary social behavior." Although Emerson and Cook argue that their work on exchange relations can be generalized to larger groups, their work in fact deals almost entirely with small groups rather than institutions. Blau's exchange-based analyses of love and friendship and of the interpersonal imbalances at the root of power are generally more satisfactory than his attempts to explain the origin of collective values, legitimacy, or opposition movements. He, indeed, has come to believe that the approach is intrinsically suited only to "face-to-face relations . . . and must be complemented by other theoretical principles that focus on complex structures."[153]

In fact, as the last part of this chapter described, there is now a growing body of work which applies the rational choice perspective to structural issues, notably the problem of collective action. This work tends to support theorists such as Coleman and Homans in their contention that psychological propositions underlie all sociological explanation. Nonetheless, it seems likely that most sociologists concerned with social institutions will continue, for good reason, to discuss their subject matter in terms of structural variables, such as class structures or legitimacy, rather than individuals' decisions and reactions.

We can see why from Homans' response to the challenge to reduce to psychological principles the finding that a society's degree of literacy is positively correlated with its level of industrialization.[154] He did so by suggesting that because a higher proportion of industrial jobs reward literacy and industrial societies are wealthier, the latter have more people trying to acquire literacy and a more widespread ability to pay for schooling. This is

---

[152]Coleman, *Individual Interests and Collective Action*, p. 1.

[153]Peter M. Blau, "Interaction IV: Social Exchange," in David L. Sillo, ed., *International Encyclopedia of the Social Sciences*, Vol. 7 (New York: The Free Press, 1968), p. 457.

[154]Robert R. Blain, "On Homans' Psychological Reductionism," *Sociological Inquiry*, 41 (Winter 1971), 3–25: George C. Homans, "Reply to Blain," *Sociological Inquiry*, 41 (Winter 1971). Homans has been criticized for not explaining why wealth is greater in industrial societies or when, exactly, literacy is rewarded. [Jonathan H. Turner, *The Structure of Sociological Theory* (Homewood, Ill.: The Dorsey Press, 1974), pp. 243–47.] This seems to us very unfair, since Homans was challenged to recast "Golden's Law" in psychological terms, not to undertake a massive research program to explain definitively something the original "Law" did not. What is true is that the reformulation adds little.

perfectly acceptable as far as it goes, but it is not obvious that recasting the propositions in this way actually adds very much to the explanation.

As rational choice theory nowhere denies, people live in a social world that involves social institutions and social creations, such as laws, schools, and job markets. Although the ultimate constituents of this world are individuals whose actions create, maintain, and change it, they (or we) look at the world, act, and choose on the basis of thoughts and perceptions to which social concepts (such as literacy) are central. Turning all propositions that employ abstract or "collective" terms (such as the "Industrial Revolution" or a "totalitarian state") into statements about individuals' beliefs, actions, and resources may be either impossible in practical—as opposed to logical—terms or pointless.

In this respect, it is instructive to look back at the conflict sociology of Randall Collins. Like Homans, Collins emphasizes the importance of remembering that we are dealing with "real people" and of analyzing social institutions in terms of individuals' motives, experiences, and actions. Nonetheless, many of his propositions refer to such constructs as "bureaucratization" or "classes." In other words, in analyzing regularities among societies, Collins uses a "structural" vocabulary.

Where a rational choice perspective *is* especially valuable is in explaining people's actions when the institutional setting is largely given and the details of individual behavior are of special interest. It is also valuable in explaining people's reactions to institutional changes when we can assume that their values remain much the same. Cases with a given institutional setting include the informal groups on which Homans concentrates but also Blau's discussion of modern love and Richmond's experience with the micro-economy game.

Our final example of rational choice analysis is given as an example of the type of situation to which this perspective is particularly well suited. Gender and the role of women in society is one of the themes running through this text. Kathleen Gerson studied in detail the way that a sample of women aged 25 to 34 made decisions about "work, career and motherhood."[155] Like so many of the other sociologists whose work has been cited in this chapter, she looked at theories which emphasized the role of childhood socialization in forming women's lives and found them wanting;[156] she also examined theories couched in terms of "structural coercion" and found them wanting also.

What Gerson stresses is that home backgrounds and expectations as young people *do not allow us to predict with any confidence how individuals will behave in adult life.* Thus, of her sample, she found that:

[155]Kathleen Gerson, *Hard Choices: How Women Decide about Work, Career and Motherhood* (Berkeley: University of California Press, 1985).

[156]Among those rejected explicitly is the work of Nancy Chodorow. See p. 286.

> about half expected, as teenagers, to lead a "domestic" lifestyle
> a third of these women did so
> two-thirds did not

Similarly,

> about half expected, as teenagers, to follow "nondomestic" careers
> a third of these women did so
> two-thirds did not

Thus, some women, happily childless and/or unmarried and successful in their careers, had fully expected to follow their mothers into full-time domesticity. Others, though, reared by parents who encouraged education and ambition, have turned toward home and children in preference to paid employment.

Gerson's in-depth analysis of her subjects' life histories bring out vividly how important individual—albeit recurring—experiences are in explaining this two-way switch around. From the individual woman's point of view, "change is a dominant motif. . . . even the most carefully calculated choices had unintended consequences that led in unanticipated directions."[157] For the group as a whole, however, certain themes emerge. For many, the crucial decision is that they value a personal relationship more than their career. "It was more desirable to live with Don than to be a customs inspector," one woman explained. For others, what matter are blocked workplace opportunities or a dislike of work: "I hated my job," "I . . . think of teaching in terms of nightmares." For others, "triggering events"—unstable relations with men, unexpected workplace opportunities, or an economic squeeze—direct them, against their childhood expectations, into nondomestic, career-oriented lives.

In Gerson's view, the important point is that while we can identify various paths through life which modern women follow, these can only be understood in terms of individual choices, made in response to individual, unpredictable sets of events and opportunities. We may find common sets of "parameters," but the explanatory factor is the *individual's* values and decisions. That perspective encapsulates theories of "rational choice."

[157]Gerson, *Hard Choices*, pp. 191–92.

V

SYMBOLIC INTERACTIONISM

INTRODUCTION

The term *symbolic interactionism* originated with Herbert Blumer, who describes it as "a somewhat barbaric neologism that I coined in an offhand way in an article written in *Man and Society*. The term somehow caught on and is now in general use."[1]

Man and Society was designed to survey the field of the social sciences and to serve as an "introduction to the spirit, the methods and the subject matter of each of the social sciences."[2] Herbert Blumer, invited to write the chapter on social psychology, coined the term *symbolic interactionism* in an attempt to clarify how social psychologists differed in their views of human nature. Blumer explained that social psychology was largely interested in the social development of the individual and that its central task was to study how the individual develops socially as a result of participating in group life.

To study the social development of the individual, Blumer proposed, it is necessary to consider the "nature of the equipment with which the human infant begins life."[3] First he discussed two views of original nature with which he disagreed: instinct psychology, which emphasizes the importance of unreasoned natural impulses, and the stimulus-response approach, which sees behavior as acquired but essentially involuntary responses to external stimuli.[4] Blumer contrasted these with the position he held, explaining that his approach pictures the newborn infant as unorganized and dependent on adults for direction and survival. According to his view,

> the development of the infant into childhood and adulthood is fundamentally a matter of forming organized or concerted activity in place of its previous random activity, and of channelizing its impulses and giving them goals or objectives. This view, then, . . . recognizes original nature to be important, but not determinative of its subsequent development. It emphasizes the active nature of the child, the plasticity of this nature, and the importance of the unformed impulse. It is substantially the view taken by the group of social psychologists who may be conveniently labeled "symbolic interactionists."[5]

Thus the term was born. However, for all his later remarks, Blumer's use of the word *symbolic* reflects an important theoretical viewpoint, not the

[1] Herbert Blumer, *Symbolic Interactionism: Perspective and Method* (Englewood Cliffs, N.J.: Prentice-Hall, Inc., 1969), p. 1. © 1969. Reprinted by permission of Prentice-Hall, Inc.

[2] Emerson P. Schmidt, ed., *Man and Society* (Englewood Cliffs, N.J.: Prentice-Hall, Inc., 1937), p. v.

[3] Ibid., pp. 146–47.

[4] See Chapter IV, where we discuss the stimulus-response approach in relation to the work of George C. Homans.

[5] Schmidt, *Man and Society*, pp. 151–52.

offhand labeling of a perspective. In *Man and Society*, Blumer identifies the cornerstone of symbolic interactionism: a common set of symbols and understandings possessed by people in a group.[6] Symbolic interactionists assume that the key elements in children's milieus are the symbols and understandings that guide the individuals around them. This common set of symbols and understandings which make a child's social environment symbolic are given great prominence by this perspective.

Symbolic interactionism, then, is essentially a social-psychological perspective; its primary focuses are on the individual "with a self" and on the interaction between a person's internal thoughts and emotions and his or her social behavior. Most of the analysis is of small-scale interpersonal relationships. Individuals are viewed as active constructors of their own conduct who interpret, evaluate, define, and map out their own action, rather than as passive beings who are impinged upon by outside forces.[7] Symbolic interactionism also stresses the processes by which the individual makes decisions and forms opinions.

According to symbolic interactionists, the form interaction takes emerges from the particular situation concerned. This is in contrast to what Blumer calls the "straitjacket" approach of functionalists, whose stress on norms implies that most interaction is fixed in advance. Although symbolic interactionists admit the influence of social rules, these are not their primary concern, and neither are the "average" behavior and the general shape of institutions, which other theorists concentrate on.[8] Rather, they are primarily concerned with fully explaining individuals' particular decisions and actions and with demonstrating the impossibility of explaining these by predetermined rules and external forces.

INTELLECTUAL ROOTS: THE INFLUENCE OF MAX WEBER AND GEORG SIMMEL

The forerunners of and direct contributors to the symbolic interactionist perspective include Georg Simmel, Robert Park, William Isaac Thomas, Charles Horton Cooley, John Dewey, and George Herbert Mead.[9] Max Weber should also be cited, for in his definition of sociology, he emphasized

---

[6]Ibid., p. 159.

[7]Anthony Giddens, whose work on structuration theory is discussed in Chapter VII, borrows from symbolic interactionism the role of human agency, the view that social life is an active accomplishment of purposive, knowledgeable actors. See Anthony Giddens, *Central Problems in Social Theory* (Berkeley: University of California Press, 1979), p. 50.

[8]See, for example, "Conflict Theory" (Chapter III).

[9]In addition, Blumer mentions E. W. Burgess, Florian Znaniecki, Ellsworth Faris, James Mickel Williams, and William James. See Blumer, *Symbolic Interactionism*, p. 78.

the importance of *verstehen* (interpretive understanding or "subjective meaning"):

> Sociology is a science which attempts the *interpretive* understanding of social action in order thereby to arrive at a causal explanation of its course and effects. In "action" is included all human behavior when and insofar as the *acting individual* attaches a *subjective meaning* to it. Action in this sense may be either overt or purely inward or subjective; it may consist of positive intervention in a situation, or of deliberately refraining from such intervention or passively acquiescing in the situation. Action is social insofar as, by virtue of the *subjective meaning* attached to it by the *acting individual* (or individuals) it takes account of the behavior of others and is thereby oriented in its course.[10]

Weber's action theory, with an emphasis on the individual's interpretation of a situation and on the importance of subjective meaning, was influential in the emergence of symbolic interactionism. Earlier in the text we highlighted Weber's contribution to conflict theory.[11] His significance to the symbolic interactionist perspective is an illustration of the breadth of his theoretical contributions and, in particular, his ability to "bridge" macro and micro perspectives.

Georg Simmel, Robert Park's intellectual mentor, was also of central importance to the development of this perspective. We can understand Simmel's influence on the early symbolic interactionists by examining his defense of many of the tenets of this approach to sociological analysis:

> To confine ourselves to the large social formations resembles the older science of anatomy with its limitation to the major, definitely circumscribed organs such as heart, liver, lungs, and stomach, and with its neglect of the innumerable, popularly unnamed or unknown tissues. Yet without these, the more obvious organs could never constitute a living organism.

Similarly, Simmel says, society is pieced together by "countless minor syntheses." He describes some of these human linkages:

> That people look at one another and are jealous of one another; that they exchange letters or dine together; . . . that gratitude for altruistic acts makes for inseparable union; that one asks another man after a certain street, and that people dress and adorn themselves for one another—the whole gamut of relations that play from one person to another and that may be momentary or permanent, conscious or unconscious, ephemeral or of grave consequence, . . . all these incessantly tie men together. Here are the interactions among the

[10]Max Weber, *The Theory of Social and Economic Organization,* trans. and eds. A. M. Henderson and Talcott Parsons (New York: Oxford University Press, 1964), p. 88. Emphasis ours. Copyright © 1947, 1975 by Talcott Parsons. Reprinted by permissions of The Free Press, a division of Macmillan, Inc.
[11]See Chapter III.

atoms of society. They account for all the toughness and elasticity, all the color and consistency of social life, that is so striking and yet so mysterious.[12]

Simmel's words are encouraging for sociologists who are interested in analyzing individual behavior, as contrasted with those whose interests lie in analyzing social systems. This is so not only because the details of individual behavior are themselves of interest, but because some crucial decisions are made on the individual level, among the "atoms of society," which can cause reverberations throughout an entire nation. These decisions help us, as Simmel puts it, "to piece together the real life of society as we encounter it in our experience." One dramatic example is a decision made by Frank Wills, a security guard at the Watergate complex, who noticed some tape on the lock of a door on the evening of June 17, 1972. On his first round of inspection, he simply removed the tape. On the second round, when he saw the same door taped again, he reinterpreted the situation and decided to phone the police. Some sociologists are interested in analyzing behavior like this, which triggered a series of events leading to the resignation of President Nixon and to changes in party structure, such as campaign financing limitations. For many of them, the inspiration for such analysis is supplied by Georg Simmel, and Simmel's formal sociology, the "geometry of social space," has become a blueprint.[13]

Two of Simmel's key concepts are the *dyad* and the *triad*. In stressing the significance of numbers for social life, Simmel argues that in a dyadic relationship, each of the two participants is confronted by only one other. Hence, neither can deny responsibility by shifting it to the group. Because a dyad depends on only two participants, a withdrawal of one will destroy the whole.[14] The transformation of a dyad into a triad, however, causes a major qualitative change. In a triadic relationship the individual participant is confronted with the possibility of being outvoted by the majority. Thus the triad can impose its will upon one member through the formation of a coalition by the other two. Three types of strategy are open to the third participant: playing the role of mediator between the other two, helping to keep the group intact; turning a disagreement between the other two to his own advantage; or intentionally creating conflicts between the others for his own advantage. Simmel's microsociological examples of triadic relationships include the competition of two men for one woman. Other examples of a triad would be the addition of a third roommate in a college dorm or an aged parent moving in with a married couple.

[12]Kurt H. Wolff, ed. and trans., *The Sociology of Georg Simmel* (New York: The Free Press, 1950), pp. 1–10. Copyright © 1950, 1978 by The Free Press, a division of Macmillan, Inc. Reprinted by permission of the publisher.

[13]See Lewis A. Coser, *Masters of Sociological Thought* (New York: Harcourt Brace Jovanovich, 1977), p. 215.

[14]Wolff, *The Sociology of Georg Simmel*, p. 124.

The link from Georg Simmel in Germany to a group of social psychologists at the University of Chicago was forged when Robert Park spent one semester in Simmel's classroom. "It was from Simmel," Park wrote, "that I finally gained a fundamental point of view for the study of the newspaper and society."[15]

Simmel's conception of society as a system of interaction, his interest in the geometry of social space, and his stress on social process were adopted by Park and passed on to his students and colleagues at the University of Chicago, which became the birthplace of symbolic interactionism.

A significant theoretical contribution to symbolic interactionism is William Isaac Thomas' notion of the "definition of the situation." Thomas believed that individuals have the power to ignore a stimulus which they responded to at an earlier time and that "preliminary to any self-determined act of behavior there is always a stage of examination and deliberation which we may call the definition of the situation."[16] Even more important is Thomas' belief that people's definitions of the situation have behavioral consequences. Thomas' theorem was stated this way: "If men [sic] define situations as real, they are real in their consequences."[17] Thomas argued that unless researchers pay attention to subjective meanings or definitions of the situation, they cannot understand human activity.

In our own everyday life we know that women and men, younger and older people, upper and lower class, will often present different definitions of the same situation. Witness the various ways people interpret and evaluate news items, episodes in a movie, segments of sports events, even common cultural objects, like a flag, a dishwasher, or a computer. Young children, for instance, often create an imaginary playmate. The playmate, who is real for the child, may have consequences for other family members as well. They may interact with the playmate, even to the point of setting an extra place at the dinner table.

Together with Thomas, Park encouraged students to study various aspects of the social processes in their own city. Rather than examining social structure with a camera producing "still" pictures of social life, Park's students used the "moving camera" of the naturalistic approach to catch life as it was happening. The Chicago School produced Thomas and Znaniecki's classic piece of research on the adjustment of first-generation Polish immigrants, *The Polish Peasant in Europe and America;* Frederick M. Thrasher's research on juvenile delinquency, *The Gang;* Louis Wirth's investigation of the densely populated district where most of Chicago's first-generation Jews lived, *The Ghetto;* and Harvey W. Zorbaugh's analysis of

---

[15]Paul J. Baker, "The Life Histories of W. I. Thomas and Robert E. Park, with an Introduction by Paul J. Baker," *American Journal of Sociology,* 79 (1973), 256.

[16]William I. Thomas, *The Unadjusted Girl* (Boston: Little, Brown, 1923), p. 41.

[17]William I. Thomas (with Dorothy Swaine Thomas), *The Child in America* (New York: Alfred A. Knopf, 1928).

the juxtaposition of affluent and slum sections of Chicago, *The Gold Coast and the Slum.*[18]

Charles Horton Cooley, who taught all his life at his alma mater, the University of Michigan at Ann Arbor, was also a forerunner of symbolic interactionism. One of his important contributions is his conception of the "looking-glass self"—that is, the self you understand as a result of the information reflected back at you in the judgments of others with whom you interact. Cooley's three elements of the looking-glass self are "the imagination of our appearance to the other person; the imagination of his judgment of that appearance; and some sort of self-feeling, such as pride or mortification."[19]

As Cooley points out, the looking-glass does not suggest the imagination of the other's judgment of our appearance, but he sees this as an essential element. In fact, Cooley states, "the imaginations which people have of one another are the solid facts of society, and to observe and interpret these must be the chief aim of sociology."[20] In other words, both the larger social structure and such constructs as "industrial organizations" and "political parties" ultimately rest on these "solid facts."

However, symbolic interactionism was systematized not by these forerunners but by two major theorists, George Herbert Mead and Herbert Blumer. Although Blumer is the intellectual leader of symbolic interactionism among social theorists, he owes a great deal to his teacher, George Herbert Mead. Most of the elements of symbolic interactionism are Meadian in origin, and Blumer acknowledges Mead as the most important influence on his thinking.

PART ONE
George Herbert Mead: The Self

It has been said of George Herbert Mead (1863–1931) that "he may now well be reckoned as one among a handful of American thinkers who have helped to shape the character of modern social science."[21] Mead's

[18]See Faris' description of the "golden era" of Chicago sociology. R. E. L. Faris, *Chicago Sociology 1920–1932* (Chicago: University of Chicago Press, 1970). Mary Jo Deegan, "Symbolic Interaction and the Study of Women: An Introduction," in Mary Jo Deegan and Michael Hill, eds., *Women and Symbolic Interaction.* (Boston: Allen and Unwin, 1987), pp. 3–15, has suggested that Jane Addams, who described the world of Chicago during the founding years of the Chicago School of Symbolic Interaction, should be listed as a major figure of this school. See Jane Addams, *Twenty Years at Hull-House* (New York: Macmillan, 1910). See also Mary Jo Deegan, *Jane Addams and the Men of the Chicago School: 1890–1918* (New Brunswick, N.J.: Transaction Press, 1986), for an analysis of Addams' relation to the work of Mead and Thomas.

[19]Charles Horton Cooley, *Human Nature and the Social Order* (New York: Charles Scribner's Sons, 1902), p. 184.

[20]Ibid., p. 121.

[21]Coser, *Masters of Sociological Thought,* p. 347.

father was a Puritan clergyman who taught homiletics at Oberlin, where Mead received a B.A. in 1883. His mother was president of Mount Holyoke College after her husband's death. After one year of additional study in philosophy and Greek, Mead received a second B.A. at Harvard in 1888.[22] While at Harvard, Mead studied under Josiah Royce and was converted to pragmatic philosophy. In Europe he did graduate studies under Wilhelm Wundt at Leipzig, where he also met G. Stanley Hall; he later studied at Berlin, but never completed his doctorate. On returning home, Mead taught for two years at the University of Michigan, Ann Arbor, where he met and became friends with John Dewey and Charles Horton Cooley. When Dewey moved to the University of Chicago, Mead decided to follow him, and he taught in the philosophy department there until his death in 1931.

Mead's forte was teaching. He published a number of articles, but his books were published posthumously, taken from the lecture notes of his students who gathered them for publication. The most famous, *Mind, Self and Society*, will be one of our chief sources for the basic components of Mead's theory. The four elements we have chosen to highlight are the self, self-interaction, the development of the self, and symbolic meaning.

THE SELF

Mead's view of the self is central to symbolic interactionism. He sees the self as an acting organism, not as a passive receptacle that simply receives and responds to stimuli. Blumer explains:

> For Mead, the self is far more than an "internalization of components of social structure and culture." It is more centrally a *social process*, a process of self-interaction in which the human actor indicates to himself matters that confront him in the situations in which he acts, and organizes his action through his interpretation of such matters. The actor engages in this social interaction with himself, according to Mead, by taking the roles of others, addressing himself through these roles, and responding to these approaches. This conception of self-interaction in which the actor is pointing out things to himself lies at the basis of Mead's scheme of social psychology.[23]

The self, then, is active and creative; there are no such ingredients as social, cultural, or psychological variables that "determine" the actions of the self. Blumer often depicted social scientists' different views of the self in

---

[22]We wish to thank Professor Harold L. Orbach for supplying us with a copy of a page from the 1908–09 Annual Register from the University of Chicago, listing Mead's educational background (p. 26).

[23]Herbert Blumer, "Comments on 'Parsons as a Symbolic Interactionist'," *Sociological Inquiry,* 45 (1975), 68.

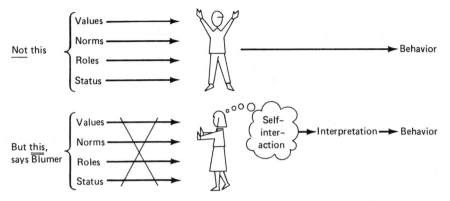

FIGURE 5-1   Blumer's View of the Individual.

his own classroom teaching by means of a drawing like Figure 5-1, as he enthusiastically transmitted Mead's ideas to his students. Here one can see what the symbolic interactionists are rejecting in the functionalists' view of self. Functionalists like Parsons tend to look at the individual as a passive agent impinged upon by social and psychological forces. According to Blumer, "the process of self-indication by means of which human action is formed cannot be accounted for by factors which precede the act."[24] In Blumer's estimation, social exchange theorists like George Homans share this passive view of human beings. Blumer writes:

> The self, or indeed human being, is not brought into the picture merely by introducing psychological elements, such as motives and interests, alongside of societal elements. Such additions merely compound the error of the omission. This is the flaw in George Homans' presidential address on "Bringing Men Back In."[25]

In contrast to this passive view of the individual, Mead stresses people's ability, through the mechanism of self-interaction, to form and guide their own conduct. Mead's position is that individuals act on their own environment, and in so doing they create the objects that people it. He distinguishes between "things," or stimuli that exist prior to and independent of the individual, and "objects," which exist only in relation to acts. "Things" are converted to "objects" through the acts of individuals.[26] A tomato, for instance, serves as an object of nutrition when it is eaten and as an object of an expression of anger when it is thrown. The individual, by acting on it, designates the

[24]Blumer, *Symbolic Interactionism*, p. 82.
[25]Ibid., p. 64. We discuss Homans' address in Chapter IV, p. 187.
[26]See George J. McCall and J. L. Simmons, *Identities and Interactions* (New York: The Free Press, 1966), pp. 50–51.

tomato as food in one instance and as a weapon in another. The tomato is not intrinsically either of these; it is simply a "thing" before the individual acts on it. Thus, Mead's "person" is more active and more creative than is social exchange and functional theorists' "person" or "ego."

Symbolic interactionism avoids a deterministic stance by refusing to treat the self as something that is undifferentiated. Specifically, Mead outlines two "phases" of the self. One phase is the "I," which Mead sees as the unorganized response of the organism to the attitudes of others, the spontaneous disposition or impulse to act. The other is the "me," a set of organized attitudes of others that the individual himself assumes in turn; that is, those perspectives on oneself that the individual has learned from others.[27] Mead says, "The attitudes of the others constitute the organized 'me,' and then one reacts toward that as an 'I,' "[28] The "me" guides the behavior of the socialized person, and this aspect of the self brings the influence of others into the individual's consciousness. On the other hand, the incalculable spontaneity of the "I" allows for a certain degree of innovation and creativity as well as a degree of freedom from control by others.[29] As Mead puts it:

> The "I," then, in this relation of the "I" and the "me," is something that is, so to speak, responding to a social situation which is within the experience of the individual. It is the answer which the individual makes to the attitude which others take toward him when he assumes an attitude toward them. Now, the attitudes he is taking toward them will contain a novel element. The "I" gives the sense of freedom, of initiative.[30]

The self, then, consists of the acting "I" when the self is the subject and of the acted upon "me" when the self is the object. Mead concludes:

> The self is essentially a social process going on with these two distinguishable phases. If it did not have these two phases there could not be conscious responsibility, and there would be nothing novel in experience.[31]

SELF-INTERACTION

Because he makes room for what is "novel in experience," Mead offers social scientists a perspective that enables them to analyze behavior that is

[27]See the discussion in McCall and Simmons, ibid., p. 55.

[28]George Herbert Mead, *Mind, Self and Society* (Chicago: University of Chicago Press, 1934), p. 175. Copyright 1934 by The University of Chicago Press. Reprinted by permission.

[29]By contrast, functionalism allows only for the "me"; the "I" is Mead's addition to the view of the self. See Chapter II. In our estimation, the "I" disappears in the work of Kuhn's "Iowa School" of symbolic interactionism, which is one reason we omitted it in this text.

[30]Mead, *Mind, Self and Society*, p. 177.

[31]Ibid., p. 178.

"unstructured" and not affected by previously established conventions. For instance, symbolic interactionists would be interested in analyzing Roentgen's accidental discovery of X-rays. According to Thomas Kuhn,

> The physicist Roentgen interrupted a normal investigation of cathode rays because he had noticed that a barium platinocyanide screen at some distance from his shielded apparatus glowed when the discharge was in process. Further investigations—they required seven hectic weeks during which Roentgen rarely left the laboratory—indicated that the cause of the glow came in straight lines from the cathode ray tube, that the radiation cast shadows, could not be deflected by a magnet, and much else besides. Before announcing his discovery, Roentgen had convinced himself that his effect was not due to cathode rays but to an agent with at least some similarity to light.[32]

Kuhn adds that this discovery was greeted with surprise and shock, principally because X-rays violated deeply entrenched expectations.[33]

As Kuhn explains it, a discovery like Roentgen's necessitates "paradigm change" and changes in expectations and laboratory procedures. He defines *paradigms* as "universally recognized scientific achievements that for a time provide model problems and solutions to a community of practitioners," and he stresses that changes meet considerable resistance at all times.[34]

Why is it so rare for an investigator like Roentgen to make such an accidental discovery—to perceive that something has happened that his paradigm has not prepared him to perceive and cannot explain? According to Kuhn, such a discovery goes against the idea of normal science, which does not aim at novelties of fact or theory. Rather than abandon the theories and ideas they use to perceive and "understand" the world, people will try to explain away anomalous findings, to show that they do not really disprove the current paradigm. So Kuhn suggests that a discovery that commences with an awareness of anomaly must continue with a more or less extended exploration of the area of the anomaly, which then results in an adjustment of paradigm theory.[35]

In analyzing why Roentgen continued investigating and discovered X-rays instead of explaining them away, Mead would emphasize Roentgen's self-interaction. What did Roentgen "say to himself" during those fateful days before he was finally convinced that he had made a discovery? First of all, he had to persuade himself that in spite of the existing paradigm he had indeed seen the glow, that it was not a figment of his imagination, a mirage

---

[32]Thomas S. Kuhn, *The Structure of Scientific Revolutions* (Chicago: University of Chicago Press, 1970), p. 57. © 1962, 1970 by The University of Chicago, Press. Reprinted by permission.

[33]Ibid., p. 59.

[34]Ibid., p. viii.

[35]Ibid., pp. 52–53.

caused by his own fatigue, or an inconsequential oddity. During those seven weeks in the laboratory, Roentgen must have been asking himself, over and over again, how the phenomenon happened, where it came from, what produced the glow, under what conditions, and why it occurred. Through this kind of self-interaction, combined with repeated experimentation, Roentgen finally convinced himself of his discovery; and the nature of this dialogue determined whether or not he did so.

The "internal conversations" one has with oneself are an essential part of the Meadian perspective, because they are the means by which human beings take things into account and organize themselves for action. Self-interaction is also the basis for role taking, which is at the heart of Mead's conception of the human act.

Mead explains that communication is a process whereby each person "takes the role of the other"; that is, each person "assumes the attitude of the other individual as well as calling it out in the other," which would be impossible without self-interaction. Mead's description of role taking under-lines the importance of individuals' "putting themselves in the other's shoes." As he puts it:

> He himself is in the role of the other person whom he is so exciting and influencing. It is through taking this role of the other that he is able to come back on himself and so direct his own process of communication. This taking the role of the other, an expression I have so often used, is not simply of passing importance. . . . The immediate effect of such role-taking lies in the control which the individual is able to exercise over his own response.[36]

One of the attractions of the Meadian conception of self-interaction is that it "makes sense" in terms of one's daily experiences. If you think back to the last time you walked somewhere by yourself (on the way to class for example), there are probably things you can remember "talking to your-self" about—reminding yourself to do or to refrain from doing something, making a phone call, stopping at the grocery store, going to the library. Again, people need not think back very far to find a time when they "talked to themselves" about how to approach a certain situation or whether or not to confront someone and how to do it. In such a situation you are, in a sense, "rehearsing" for future action and organizing yourself by an internal conversation, which prepares you to "take the role" of others. For instance, people who have been through the anxiety of preparing themselves for an encounter with a friend who has recently lost a loved one will recognize that the more they "talked to themselves" about what to say and how to ap-proach their friend, the more able they were to "take the role of the other" and the more effective the interaction was. If we assess the resulting action and ask ourselves whether or not the "internal conversation" affected the

[36]Mead, *Mind, Self and Society*, p. 254.

interaction, we can see that Mead's conception of the human act probably does make sense.

Blumer summarizes Mead's idea of the human act like this:

> The human act is formed through self-interaction, in the course of which the actor may note and assess any feature of the situation, or any feature of his involvement in the act. The act is constructed through this process of self-interaction, irrespective of whether the construction is done intelligently or stupidly. . . . The subjection of the act to the process of self-interaction imparts a career to the act—the act may be stopped, restrained, abandoned, resurrected, postponed, intensified, concealed, transformed or redirected.[37]

THE DEVELOPMENT OF THE SELF

Mead outlines the stages by which the self develops in his writings on the play, the game, and the generalized other. The first stage of self-development, the "preplay" stage at about age two, is marked by meaningless, imitative acts. In Meadian vocabulary, the word *meaning* appears regularly and has a unique connotation:

> Meaning as such, i.e., the object of thought, arises in experience through the individual stimulating himself to take the attitude of the other in his reaction toward the object. Meaning is that which can be indicated to others while it is by the same process indicated to the indicating individual.[38]

· In other words, when individuals share symbolic interpretations, the act is meaningful to them. They are "speaking the same language" or "looking through the same eyeglasses." Meaning is, then, the wedding of different attitudes and the use of significant symbols that have the same import for all concerned.

The reason Mead labels acts in the preplay stage "meaningless" is that the child at that age lacks the ability to "take the attitude of the other." As Mead outlines it, this ability gradually evolves as the child develops a self. The second stage, the "play" stage, which appears later in childhood, is the stage when the child can put himself in the position of another person but cannot relate the roles of the other players. The connection between play, on the one hand, and the development of the "me" and the ability to take the role of the other, on the other hand, is particularly apparent when small children scold their toys for being bad or warn them that they are getting dirty or doing something dangerous. Similarly, children at this stage act out others' parts in simple role-taking, such as "playing teacher," and games,

[37]Blumer, "Comments on 'Parsons as a Symbolic Interactionist,' " p. 60.
[38]Mead, *Mind, Self and Society*, p. 89.

such as hide-and-seek or tic-tac-toe, that involve only one or two roles and particpants. At the play stage, the player had only one alternative role in mind at a time. Nevertheless, this is the time, according to Mead, when the child begins to form a self by taking the roles of other people.

At the game stage, several players are in action together. This happens in complex, organized games in which the team member must anticipate the responses of the others in the game and must, therefore, have in mind all the attitudes and roles of all the other players. The person playing first base in a baseball game, for instance, must have a generalized knowledge of what the other team members will do in a given situation. At the game stage, the relevant "other" is an organization of the attitudes of all involved in the game, so that what the person on first base does is controlled by everyone else on the team. In a wider context, this generalized other includes the organized attitudes of the whole community. As Mead puts it, "the mature self arises when a generalized other is internalized so that the community exercises control over the conduct of its individuals. . . . The structure, then, on which the self is built is this response which is common to all, for one has to be a member of a community to be a self."[39]

Critics of Mead have reevaluated the concept "generalized other" and argue that it is somewhat like Parsons' definition of socialization, because it means that individuals internalize the norms and values generated by the dominant institutions. Feminists point out that the generalized other incorporates the existing distribution of power in society within the individual.[40] In short, it is the people in power—males, upper classes, educational élites—who define the generalized other.

In a study of sex differences in children's games, Janet Lever found that boys played outdoors more, played more in larger groups, played in more age-heterogeneous groups, and played more often in competitive games than girls.[41] Lever suggests that boys' games teach them to take the role of the generalized other, thus preparing them for successful performance in a wide variety of work settings. By contrast, girls learn the role of the "particular" other in their play groups, preparing them for their roles as wives and mothers in the private sphere of the home. Thus, the way children's play is organized serves to protect the traditional gender-role divisions in our society.

Lever reports that boys, who were more involved in playing competitive games, learned that emotional discipline and self-control were necessary for team goals. Girls, who were more involved in play that involved

[39]Ibid., p. 163.

[40]Kathy E. Ferguson, *Self, Society, and Womankind* (Westport, Conn.: Greenwood Press, 1980), p. 56.

[41]Janet Lever, "Sex Differences in the Games Children Play," *Social Problems*, 24 (April, 1976), 478–87.

turn-taking rather than competition, also showed affection to their best friends more often. Lever states:

> Most girls interviewed said they had a single "best" friend with whom they played nearly every day. They learn to know that person and her moods so well that through non-verbal cues alone, a girl understands whether her playmate is hurt, sad, happy, bored, and so on. There is usually an open show of affection between these little girls—both physically in the form of hand-holding and verbally through "love notes" that reaffirm how special each is to the other.[42]

SYMBOLIC MEANING

The meaning of *symbol* is derived from Mead's definition of *gesture,* which is not only the first element of an act but also a sign for the whole act. For instance, when a smoker reaches for a pack of cigarettes, that gesture can be enough to prompt a nonsmoker to leave the room, to open windows, to request that smoking be prohibited, or to engage in other kinds of behavior to avoid what the nonsmoker knows will follow. In this situation the gesture, the first component of the act, can be enough for the nonsmoker, who does not have to wait to see the rest of the act. Thus, reaching for a pack of cigarettes is not only a gesture; it becomes a significant symbol, because the gesture calls out in the nonsmoker the meaning of the entire act and signals the beginning of his or her adjustments to it. As Mead puts it, "Gestures thus internalized are significant symbols because they have the same meaning for all individual members of a given society or social group, i.e., they respectively arouse the same attitudes in the individuals making them that they arouse in the individuals responding to them."[43]

Mead defines a symbol as "the stimulus whose response is given in advance." Consider the situation in which a person threatens you and you knock him down. Mead says that in doing this you are taking the attitude of the community and responding to it in a conversation of gestures. Mead explains how an insulting word is a symbol:

> There is a word, and a blow. The blow is the historical antecedent of the word, but if the word means an insult, the response is one now involved in the word, something given in the very stimulus itself. That is all that is meant by a symbol. Now, if that response can be given in terms of an attitude utilized for the further control of action, then the relation of that stimulus and attitude is what we mean by a significant symbol.
>
> Our thinking that goes on, as we say, inside of us, is a play of symbols in the

[42]Ibid., p. 484.
[43]Mead, *Mind, Self and Society,* p. 47.

above sense. Through gestures responses are called out in our own attitudes, and as soon as they are called out they evoke, in turn, other attitudes.[44]

A key element is the meaning of the word (in this case, an insult). It becomes "the stimulus whose response is given in advance," because in the community in question, the connotations of that word and the intentions implied by its use evoke a blow as the "appropriate" response from the person so addressed. Another crucial element is the self-interaction that is going on in this process, the "conversation of gestures" that is going on in the mind of the individual. Mead explains:

> We often act with reference to objects in what we call an intelligent fashion, although we can act without the meaning of the object being present in our experience. One can start to dress for dinner, as they tell of the absent-minded college professor, and find himself in his pajamas in bed. A certain process of undressing was started and carried out mechanically; he did not recognize the meaning of what he was doing. He intended to go to dinner and found he had gone to bed. The meaning involved in his action was not present. The steps in this case were all intelligent steps which controlled his conduct with reference to later action, but he did not think about what he was doing. The later action was not a stimulus to his response, but just carried itself out when it was once started.[45]

Why was this *not* a case of symbolic interaction? Obviously, some crucial elements are missing. The individual did *not* recognize the meaning of what he was doing. The act does not include, in Mead's words, "the adjustive response of one organism to the gesture of another."[46] Since the professor was not interpreting his gestures (he was not going to bed because it was late or because he was sick), there was no meaning in the gestures of the act.

In addition, the professor did *not* think about what he was doing; he was *not* "talking to himself" about what he was doing. Significant symbols, according to Mead, are gestures (such as the smoker reaching for the pack of cigarettes) that possess meaning. A significant symbol is that part of the act that calls out the response of the other. This assumes interpretation of the symbol, as in the case of the insult.

The relationship between significant symbols and the self becomes clearer when Mead considers the case of Helen Keller, who recognized that it was "not until she could get into communication with other persons through symbols which could arouse in herself the responses they arouse in

[44]Ibid., p. 181.
[45]Ibid., p. 72.
[46]Ibid., p. 78.

other people that she could get what we term a mental content, or a self."[47] Let us recall the scene in Helen Keller's life in which her teacher and friend, Annie Sullivan, is pumping water, and Helen, feeling the running water, realizes that water has a name, the very name Annie is finger-spelling in the palm of her hand. She finally understands what the gesture for "water" means. The water episode is a dramatic example of the beginning of the process of symbolic meaning through communication. For Keller, this moment marked the beginning of her acquisition of a set of common symbols.[48]

The Keller case is an illustration of all the components of George Herbert Mead's theory, for once Helen Keller was capable of symbolic interaction, she not only possessed a "me" as well as an "I," but she could also "take the role of the other" and could internalize the "generalized other." This means that she could possess a social self.

PART TWO
Herbert Blumer: Interpretation and Methodology

Herbert Blumer (1900–1987) was on the sociology faculty at the University of Chicago from 1927 to 1952, having finished his doctoral dissertation in 1928 under the direction of Ellsworth Faris, whom Blumer describes as a "profound and faithful disciple" of George Herbert Mead. Blumer studied under Mead as a regular student and auditor in several of his graduate courses.[49] Mead manifested his confidence in Blumer's interpretation of his thought shortly after the beginning of Mead's last quarter of instruction at the University of Chicago, when he had to withdraw because of illness. On that occasion Mead asked Blumer to take over his major course, "Advanced Social Psychology."[50]

Blumer carried on Mead's tradition for twenty-five years at the University of Chicago and for another twenty-five years at the University of California at Berkeley, where he taught until his retirement. During his "Chicago era," Blumer was involved in such diverse activities as playing professional football, serving as a mediator in labor disputes, and interviewing under-

[47]Ibid., p. 149.

[48]See Helen Keller, *The Story of My Life* (New York: Doubleday and Company, 1902).

[49]Blumer has stated that he was "tremendously influenced at the University of Chicago by George H. Mead." He also "worked closely with Professor Robert E. Park," whom he regards as "the best sociological research scholar produced in the United States." (Personal communication, 1976).

[50]See Herbert Blumer, "Going Astray with a Logical Scheme," *Symbolic Interaction*, 6 (1983), 127–37.

world figures from the Al Capone gang. Blumer's stature in the profession and the profound respect he commands are indicated by his editorship of the *American Journal of Sociology* from 1941 to 1952, his presidency of the American Sociological Association in 1956; the festschrift in his honor,[51] and several memorial sessions at professional meetings after his death on April 15, 1987.

Blumer's chief contributions to the symbolic interactionist perspective are his work on interpretation, the three basic premises of symbolic interactionism, structure and process, and methodology. We will discuss each of these contributions in turn.

INTERPRETATION

Blumer's discussion of interpretation is an elaboration of Mead's argument against Watsonian behaviorism or any mechanical "stimulus-response" approach.[52] Like Mead, Blumer argues for the necessity of including subjective experience, or covert behavior, as well as observable behavior in scientific explanations of human interaction. This argument logically follows from the importance symbolic interactionism places on understanding things from the point of view of the actor.

In Blumer's estimation interaction involves something more than simple stimulus-response. Blumer explains that symbolic interactionism inserts a middle term into the stimulus-response couplet so that it becomes stimulus-interpretation-response. "Thus," he says, "A acts; B perceives this action and seeks to ascertain its meaning, that is, seeks to ascertain A's intention; B responds according to what meaning or interpretation he has attached to A's act; in turn, A responds according to the meaning which he sees in B's response."[53] Thus, the stimulus alone cannot account for B's action or A's response to it.

As Figure 5-1 showed, symbolic interactionism views the process of self-indication as essential to interpretation. Blumer rejects behaviorism because it leaves out interpretation and thus reduces the individual to responding to environmental stimuli.

Blumer explains that in the process of self-indication, individuals point out certain stimuli to themselves and then interpret the appearance of the stimuli to themselves. For instance, people may note that certain

[51]See Tamotsu Shibutani, ed., *Human Nature and Collective Behavior: Papers in Honor of Herbert Blumer* (Englewood Cliffs, N.J.: Prentice-Hall, Inc., 1970). This festschrift includes papers by many of Blumer's former students, as well as a complete bibliography of Blumer's work up to 1970.

[52]See Mead, *Mind, Self and Society*, pp. 4–5. Also see Chapter IV, where we discuss Skinner's behaviorism in relation to exchange theory.

[53]In Schmidt, *Man and Society*, p. 171.

social demands are being made on them, that they are hungry, that they want to purchase something, that they are eating with people they despise. In all these examples, Blumer pictures people as acting, not being acted upon. He concludes:

> By virtue of indicating such things to himself, he places himself over against them and is able to act back against them, accepting them, rejecting them, or transforming them in accordance with how he defines or interprets them.[54]

Comic strip artists frequently employ self-indication in their depiction of their characters. Sometimes they differentiate the conversation between two individuals from the conversation an individual is having with himself by drawing a different link or boundary between the character and the words; for instance,

is often used to illustrate self-indications, as opposed to

Gestures are a key element in the interpretation process. Earlier we discussed Mead's definition of gestures, which are significant symbols because they have the same meaning for all concerned, such as the smoker reaching for a pack of cigarettes. To interpret and understand the meaning of the interaction, each of the parties must "take the role of the other"; in other words, each must "get into the other's shoes." Instead of merely reacting to each other's actions in an automatic way, human beings interpret or define each other's actions, and they perform this interpretation on the basis of symbols. Thus the stimulus-interpretation-response process could be translated as a process of "meaningful interaction."

When people from different societies wish to understand and communicate with each other, the process of interpretation can be a doubtful and difficult one. Indeed, governments employ full-time experts to help them interpret the meaning of other societies' gestures and symbols.

A study by two symbolic interactionists that illustrates the process of interpretation is *Awareness of Dying*, by Glaser and Strauss. They have docu-

---

[54]Blumer, *Symbolic Interaction*, p. 81.

mented some rather painful and moving examples of a situation in which the ability to pick up on even very subtle cues is crucial—interaction between nurse and dying patients at the time when mutual pretense about the patient's true condition changes to open awareness. The following describes an actual conversation between a dying patient, in great pain and obvious bodily deterioration, and her nurse, Mary.

> There was a long silence. Then the patient asked, "After I get home from the nursing home will you visit me?" I asked if she wanted me to. "Yes, Mary, you know we could go on long drives together . . ." She had a far-away look in her eyes as if day-dreaming about all the things we could do together. This continued for some time. Then I asked, "Do you think you will be able to drive your car again?" She looked at me, "Mary, I know I am day-dreaming; I know I am going to die." Then she cried, and said, "This is terrible, I never thought I would be this way."[55]

The nurse in this scene recognized a gesture that was a significant symbol; she correctly interpreted the patient's daydreaming gesture, the "far-away look in her eyes." One could speculate that the nurse's second question precipitated the breaking of the pretense. From that moment on, the patient was no longer hanging onto a semblance of her former physically healthy self; she was admitting that she was a dying person. This is a good illustration of the relationship between the interpretation of symbolic gestures and the change in the patient's self-image.

By contrast, nonsymbolic interaction occurs when an individual responds directly to the action of another without interpreting that action. An example of nonsymbolic interaction would be a dog fight, in which the "gestures" of one dog have no "meaning" for the other angry participants but are simply attacks to be beaten off in the cause of survival. If the dog were interpreting the meaning of the action, then it would be devising all sorts of different responses. Similarly, human beings in a moment of anger or in self-defense are engaging in nonsymbolic interaction.

Now that we have looked at Blumer's elaboration of the interpretative process in symbolic interaction, let us examine his synthesis of the perspective—what he calls the three basic premises of symbolic interactionism.

THE THREE BASIC PREMISES

Blumer's three premises address the importance of meaning in human action, the source of meaning, and the role of meaning in interpretation.

[55]Barney G. Glaser and Anselm L. Strauss, *Awareness of Dying* (Chicago: Aldine, 1965), p. 75.

1. Human beings act toward things on the basis of the meanings that the things have for them.

As Blumer explains it, consciousness is a key element in understanding meaningful action:

> Anything of which a human being is conscious is something which he is indicating to himself—the ticking of a clock, a knock at the door, the appearance of a friend, the remark made by a companion, a recognition that he has a cold. . . . To indicate something is to extricate it from its setting, to hold it apart, to give it a meaning. . . . In any of his countless acts—whether minor, like dressing himself, or major, like organizing himself for a professional career—the individual is designating different objects to himself, giving them meaning, juding their suitability to his action, and making decisions on the basis of the judgment. This is what is meant by interpretation or acting on the basis of symbols.[56]

An illustration of Blumer's first premise was provided by one of our students, who was traveling by plane and talking to himself. When observed by another passenger, the student explained that he was "boning up" on aspects of the termite control business, attempting to memorize the essentials and putting himself in the "shoes" of potential customers, so that he would be successful in selling people on termite control. His greatest anxiety, he explained, was the health of his older brother, who had two small children and was the new owner and manager of a termite control business. This older brother lay gravely ill in the intensive care unit of a hospital. The younger brother had been enlisted to "fill in" and aid the floundering business; he had just taken a semester's leave from college, and he was frantically trying to "learn the ropes" of a business that heretofore had been almost totally unfamiliar to him.

The student in the above illustration, aware that he had a formidable task ahead of him, was so conscious of every aspect of the termite business, which now had considerable meaning for him, that he was not even conscious that his internal conversation was being "overheard" until he was so informed by his fellow passenger. Everything he had been indicating to himself was related to his success in keeping the business going; thus, he was guiding his future behavior. He was enabling himself to act toward things (aspects of termite control) on the basis of the meanings that the things had for him, because in this process he was giving meaning to, or making himself conscious of, the essential aspects of the business.

Another example, this time from Glaser and Strauss, will also illustrate Blumer's first premise. In the study of the situation of dying, the researchers observed various strategies nurses used to avoid the later stages

[56]Blumer, *Symbolic Interactionism*, p. 80.

of the dying scene: avoiding the night shift on wards where many patients die, taking vacation time, or getting sick themselves at the crucial moment. They explain the avoidance strategies thus: "Nurses find the death scene upsetting; the threat to the sentimental order of the ward increases with the number of deaths and the number of nurses who must witness them."[57] Through interviews with these nurses, the researchers discovered the meaning that the death scene had for them. Because they defined it as upsetting, some of the nurses "act toward" the death scene by avoiding it if at all possible.

> **2. The meaning of things arises out of the social interaction one has with one's fellows.**

Meaning is a social product; it is created, not "inherent in things"; it is not a given. Blumer elaborates, "The meaning of a thing for a person grows out of the ways in which other persons act toward the person with regard to the thing. Their actions operate to define the thing for the person."[58]

An example of this would be the meaning of a baseball bat to an American teenager as compared to its meaning to a member of a pygmy tribe in Africa, who has never seen a baseball game.[59] Another example is the meaning of the molimo, an instrument for song, to a member of the pygmy tribe as compared to its meaning to an American. Through interaction with others of their culture, individuals learn the very different uses of their implements, one for the purpose of sport and the other for religious festivals. The baseball bat would be no more puzzling to the pygmy youth than the molimo would be to the American, who has never witnessed the sacred ritual of which it is an integral part. Both are important cultural implements, and the meaning of both arises out of interaction with others in the society.

In his study of a boys' grammar school in an industrial town in England, Colin Lacey found two striking examples of meaning in interaction processes.[60] On the one hand, he observed the first-year boys in the process of becoming committed to the school, so much so that they would engage in rivalry among themselves. For instance,

> First-year boys adhere rigidly to school uniforms; caps and blazers are proudly displayed, and they attend school functions and clubs in disproportionate numbers. Their behavior in the classroom is characterized by eager-

---

[57]Glaser and Strauss, *Time for Dying*, p. 202.

[58]Blumer, *Symbolic Interactionism*, p. 4.

[59]See the excellent anthropological study of the BaMbuti by Colin Turnbull, *The Forest People* (New York: Doubleday, 1962).

[60]Colin Lacey, *Hightown Grammar: The School as a Social System* (Manchester: Manchester University Press, 1970). A "grammar school" is an academic high school.

ness, cooperation with the teacher and competition among themselves. "Please sir, Willy Brown is copying my sums" is a remark that could only come from a first-year boy.[61]

On the other hand, Lacey found that the teachers stereotyped working-class children as a "bad lot" or "lazy." Their consequent estimation of them as "harder to teach and more difficult to control within the classroom situation" resulted in a situation wherein working-class children would "escalate downward" or drop out.[62]

In both these examples, the meaning of things for the students, whether school loyalty or a negative label, arose out of the social interaction among students and school staff. In the case of the working-class children, the interaction with teachers, how they interpreted each others' words and actions, and the way they behaved on the basis of these interpretations, were crucial because they tended to result in students' failure or their dropping out of the system.

3. *The meanings of things are handled in and modified through an interpretative process used by the person in dealing with the things he encounters.*

How does this work? Blumer says that a person communicates and handles meanings through a process of "talking to himself." Someone who gives an account of personal worries and anxieties is interpreting what is disturbing to him or her; and Blumer says that it is in the process of "making indications to oneself" that someone arrives at such an account.

Blumer uses the example of a situation in which a checker at a grocery store is confronted by a (student) customer who tries to bargain for a lower price.[63] In examining and explaining what takes place, symbolic interactionists would focus on the indications the clerk is making to herself, or what she is "saying to herself" as she comes to a decision about how to interact with this customer.

Suppose, for instance, that the clerk rejected the idea of asking the manager for help in dealing with the customer. To explain why she did so, one would have to understand the "world" of the clerk. This particular clerk may have had an argument with the manager recently and may therefore avoid asking for help. The clerk's decision may also have depended on whether she could afford the time to bargain with the customer, and this, too, must enter the explanation. Indeed, the answer depends on a number of things—the size and physical strength of both parties, for example, and the financial resources of the clerk, who may decide that the simplest thing

[61]Lacey, *Hightown Grammar,* p. 5.

[62]Ibid., p. 181.

[63]This is the same example used by Garfinkel in his student experiments. See Chapter VI. Blumer used this example in a personal interview, 1975.

to do is to let the customer have the item for the lower price and make up the rest out of her own pocket.

The interpretative process, Blumer would point out, would also include indications the clerk is making to herself about the other people who are touched by this situation; thus to understand what goes on, we must know the "history" of the particular clerk concerned. Has this ever happened to her before? If so, what solutions did she come up with then? Were these solutions successful? Together, the basic premises of symbolic interactionism stress the ways human interaction emerges from an individual's ability to confer meaning to a situation.

STRUCTURE AND PROCESS

Blumer often refers to structure as a "straitjacket." Like Mead, he views people as ever active, ever striving, ever adjustable beings, and he sees a "drastic" difference between Mead's conception of society and the "widespread sociological conception of it as a structure." On the other hand, Blumer explains that Mead's view does not involve a rejection of the existence of structure in society. In fact Blumer points to the importance of such structures as "social roles, status positions, rank orders, bureaucratic organizations, relations between institutions, differential authority relations, and the like." Though admitting that such structures are very important, Blumer argues that they do not determine behavior:

> It is ridiculous, for instance, to assert, as a number of eminent sociologists have done, that social interaction is an interaction between social roles. Social interaction is obviously an interaction between *people* and not between roles; the needs of the participants are to interpret and handle what confronts them—such as a topic of conversation or a problem—and not give expression to their roles. It is only in highly ritualistic relations that the direction and content of conduct can be explained by roles. Usually, the direction and content are fashioned out of what people in interaction have to deal with. That roles affect in varying degree phases of the direction and content of action is true but is a matter of determination in given cases. This is a far cry from asserting action to be a product of roles. The observation I have made in this brief discussion of social roles applies with equal validity to all other structural matters.[64]

For further clarification, consider the difference between "interactive roles" and "social roles," as discussed by McCall and Simmons. When symbolic interactionists speak of role, they do not mean a social role that is specified by the culture; rather they mean something more flexible and

[64]Blumer, *Symbolic Interactionism*, p. 75.

capable of improvisation. What they call an "interactive role" is "a plausible line of action characteristic and expressive of the particular personality that happens to occupy the given position and represents that person's mode of coming to grips with the general expectations held toward someone in his position."[65]

Erving Goffman, an important contributor to the symbolic interactionist perspective,[66] illustrates the meaning of interactive role in his work on role distance, which he defines as "denying not the role but the virtual self that is implied in the role for all accepting performers"; that is, "actions which effectively convey some disdainful detachment of the performer from a role he is performing."[67]

Using a merry-go-round as the situation, Goffman shows that riders on the merry-go-round at age three or four throw themselves into the role in a serious way and play the role with verve and an admitted engagement of all their faculties. But this is changed at age five, when the riders exhibit a detachment from the role. Goffman describes the resulting role distance:

> To be a merry-go-round horse rider is now apparently not enough, and this fact must be demonstrated out of dutiful regard for one's own character. Parents are not likely to be allowed to ride along, and the strap for preventing falls is often disdained. One rider may keep time to the music by clapping his feet or a hand against the horse, an early sign of utter control. Another may make a wary stab at standing on the saddle or changing horses without touching the platform. Still another may hold onto the post with one hand and lean back as far as possible while looking up to the sky in a challenge to dizziness.[68]

To Goffman, the five-year-old rider is apologizing for the entire role and withdrawing from it by actively manipulating the situation. As children grow older, they increase the distance between themselves and the role; at ages seven and eight they dissociate themselves self-consciously by riding no-hands, and at ages eleven and twelve they "define the whole undertaking as a lark, a situation for mockery."[69]

The important point here is that the clues to role distance are the immediate audience as well as the age of the rider. Since the strategies of the merry-go-round riders were directly influenced by the immediate audience,

[65]McCall and Simmons, *Identities and Interactions*, p. 67.

[66]In Part Three we discuss Goffman's contributions in more detail. See other important contributors to this perspective in the following: Jerome G. Manis and Bernard N. Meltzer, ed., *Symbolic Interaction: A Reader in Social Psychology* (Boston: Allyn and Bacon, 1972); Nicholas C. Mullins, *Theories and Theory Groups in Contemporary American Sociology* (New York: Harper and Row, 1973); and the book festschrift by Shibutani mentioned previously, *Human Nature and Collective Behavior.*

[67]Goffman, *Encounters*, pp. 108–10.

[68]Ibid., p. 107.

[69]Ibid., pp. 108–09.

one could say that the riders were "taking them into account." One could, for instance, expect a considerable amount of role distance to be exhibited by teenagers if their peers were in the audience. At the same time, the concept "interactive role" allows for many improvisations in the execution of role distance, since it takes into account one's particular personality.

Blumer does not deny the existence of structure; what he decries is the overemphasis on the importance of structural matters in determining people's conduct. In their view of human nature, symbolic interactionists believe the human being possesses a self, which is an object to itself. This means that the individual can act toward himself as he confronts the world. Action is pieced together as the individual takes the setting of the act into account in making decisions. As acting human beings, people do not simply respond to others in a structured manner. Blumer says that human action is preceded by the individual briefly sketching out plans and intentions. Human action, for the most part, is constructed by people making indications to themselves of what confronts them.

"For the most part" is an important qualifier, however. We have seen that neither Blumer nor Mead totally denies structured action or defined situations. After all, human behavior would be far too complicated and would have too many potentially disastrous opportunities for mutual misunderstanding if every activity had to be defined from scratch! What the symbolic interactionist perspective points out is that there are many unstructured or undefined situations in which human beings must devise their own conduct. Further, even situations in which much is defined in advance include action that is not.

Problematic situations or situations that demand new interpretations are the focuses of analysis for symbolic interactionism, whereas some other perspectives tend to deny, sidestep, or acknowledge them without elaboration or substantive analysis. Blumer cites specific examples of such situations. For instance, he points to playful situations where sentiments play a major role—highly personal and informal situations, such as infectious humor or dancing crowds; and adversary relations, such as quarrels and conflicts.

This last category of problematic situations, adversary relations, is the one Blumer uses most often, and he suggests that only symbolic interactionism has the tools for analyzing it. Blumer often brings in the example of a football game, in which the emphasis is placed on ingenuity at winning or gaining the advantage.[70] Although most football plays can be predefined and precharted, when the ball is intercepted the situation becomes undefined, and self-indication and interpretation are necessary.

Other adversary relations involving undefined situations are crises,

---

[70]One suspects that this example stems from Blumer's own experience as a professional football player.

dilemmas, droughts, wars, riots, lynchings, and panics. How, asks Blumer, could the social scientist analyze such situations without examining self-indication and interpretation?

It is precisely because Blumer sees cultural structure and social structure as constraints or "straitjackets" that he chooses to focus on process in his analysis. He is especially adamant regarding the inability of structural analysis to explain anything about problematic situations. For instance, he acknowledges that Parsons' use of the pattern variables does assume some degree of self-interaction, but Blumer sees this as a very restricting form of self-interaction, since the "either-or" choice has been decided beforehand.

We will recall that each pattern variable represents a dilemma that must be solved by the actor before action can take place. As an illustration for one of the pattern variables, we presented the case of the employer who is expected to choose achievement over ascription when making a decision about a potential employee.[71] Parsons' position is that there is an appropriate choice to be made by the actor; the decision is not arbitrary but related to the norms and values of the employer's society. Blumer, on the other hand, likes to point out that many situations are unprecedented, and appropriate behavior cannot be spelled out beforehand. He has also recently remarked, with respect to the pattern variables:

> If human beings had to stop and choose between each of the alternatives in each of the five variables before they could interpret and act in each and every one of their situations, they would become paralyzed and human group life would come to a halt.[72]

The more unstructured the situation, Blumer argues, the more likely it is that symbolic interactionist analysis is indispensable to its understanding.

Given his position on structure, how does Blumer move from an analysis of the individual with a self to the group? Translating Mead's term *social act* into *joint action*, Blumer describes it as:

> the larger collective form of action that is constituted by the fitting together of the lines of behavior of the separate participants. Illustrations of joint action are a trading transaction, a family dinner, a marriage ceremony, a shopping expedition, a game, a convivial party, a debate, a court trial, or a war. . . . Each participant necessarily occupies a different position, acts from that position, and engages in a separate and distinct act. It is a fitting together of these acts and not their commonality that constitutes joint action.[73]

[71]See Chapter II.
[72]Blumer, "Comments on 'Parsons as a Symbolic Interactionist,' " p. 59.
[73]Blumer, *Symbolic Interactionism*, p. 70.

Blumer then states that each joint action has a career, or history, which is "orderly, fixed and repetitious" because of its common definition by the participants:

> Such common definitions serve, above everything else, to account for the regularity, stability and repetitiveness of joint action in vast areas of group life; they are the sources of the established and regulated social behavior that are envisioned in the concept of culture.[74]

At this point it seems that Blumer may be admitting that there is a great deal of "structured" social action. However, he quickly points to "many possibilities of uncertainty" in the career of joint actions. First, joint actions have to be initiated; then, once started, they may be interrupted, abandoned, or transformed; the participants may not make a common definition of the joint action; and, finally, new situations may arise in the joint act. As we would expect, Blumer's emphasis is on the "uncertainty, contingency and transformation," which are "part and parcel of the process of joint action."[75]

Blumer contrasts himself with those sociologists (functionalists or conflict theorists) who stress the importance of social structure in explaining behavior. His discussion of joint action does include some references to rather structured role interaction; and if we examine his examples of joint action, we can find some in which (although far from being highly ritualistic) much can be explained by roles. For instance, a "trading transaction" could be the grocery clerk who is confronted by the bartering customer. Blumer would have to admit that her role as a grocery clerk could explain at least some of her behavior. Nevertheless, the importance of roles in determining behavior is never central to his mode of analysis; rather, he sees

> the joint act as primarily an "organizing" action instead of an "organization" of action; it is an "organization" only in retrospect. A joint act represents the effort of the participants to work out their lines of action in the light of what they observe each other to be doing or about to do. Thus, the coordination of lines of action (which is the mark of social organization) is something to be achieved in and through the interaction instead of being merely an expression of systemic factors underlying such interaction.[76]

The statement graphically illustrates how Blumer uses a quite different kind of lens from the one a structural theorist such as Parsons would use when looking at the social world. Blumer's is a telescopic lens, which he

[74]Ibid., p. 71.
[75]Ibid., p. 72.
[76]Blumer, "Comments on 'Parsons as a Symbolic Interactionist,' " p. 59–60.

uses because he wants a magnified view of the interaction process between individuals.

During the rallies of the Free Speech Movement at Berkeley, for example, Blumer could be observed mingling with the crowds, observing from an upper level window, and later talking at length with students involved. As a symbolic interactionist, his approach to explaining students' involvement was to find out how individuals perceived and interpreted events and how they had made the decision to become involved. An illuminating contrast can be found in the work of sociologists such as Etzioni, who are more concerned with "social structure." They approach such an event not by looking at individual decisions and actions that went into making up the Free Speech Movement, but by looking for general social phenomena that explain why the sixties was a period of campus turmoil. Etzioni, for example, emphasizes the fact that young people numbered more and were a higher proportion of the population than before or since. In contrast, Blumer's "telescopic lens" gives us a "close-up" of the action, so that we can witness the individuals involved in "organizing" it.

METHODOLOGY

One of Herbert Blumer's chief contributions to symbolic interactionism has been his elaboration on the methodology of this perspective. In 1983, Blumer received the American Sociological Association Award for a Career of Distinguished Scholarship. The citation stated that Blumer's discussion of methodological issues deeply affected "the adoption and diffusion of field methods, ethnography and qualitative sociology."[77] As early as 1937, Blumer discussed the techniques researchers used in analyzing the "inner career of action." He said:

> One would expect that starting from such a view, actual study and research would use methods and techniques that aim to penetrate into the area of inner experience. Such is the case. We find that much use is made, in social psychology, of such devices as the life history, the interview, the autobiography, the case method, diaries, and letters. These devices are employed for three purposes. First, to gain a picture of the inner and private experience of the individual that seems to constitute the background for the emergence and existence of a given form of conduct. Thus the account given by a delinquent of his life history is held to reveal the texture of personal happenings, which presumably has given rise to, and which sustains, his delinquency. Second, to show the nature of the individual's subjective slant on life—the world as he views it, the values and meanings which different objects have for him, his "definitions" with which he seems to meet situations, his stock of attitudes,

[77] American Sociological Association, *Footnotes*, 2 no. 7 (October 1983), 1.

and the way in which he views himself. Third, to throw light on the life and operation of the imaginative process: fantasying, evading, planning, deciding, and the different ways in which, in his imagination, he meets difficulties, frustrations, and problematic situations.[78]

Inductive Approach

In a statement made thirty-eight years later, Blumer reveals the consistency of his position when he explains that symbolic interactionism is committed to an inductive approach to the understanding of human behavior, in which understanding or explanations are "induced" from data with which the investigator has become thoroughly familiar. Again he compares his position to functionalism. He explains that the scientific approach of symbolic interactionism starts with a problem regarding the empirical world, and it seeks to clarify the problem by examining that empirical world. He concludes:

> The isolation of relations, the development of propositions, the formulation of typologies, and the construction of theories are viewed as emerging out of what is found through constant observation of that world instead of being formed in an *a priori* fashion through deductive reasoning from a set of theoretical premises.[79]

Blumer shows that unlike functionalism, symbolic interactionism is not a deductive theory that begins with a set of hypotheses. Because its methodological approach precludes much of what is considered to be "proper research activity," symbolic interactionists run into difficulty when it comes to funding and/or publishing their research.[80]

Blumer discusses this problem in his major explication of symbolic interactionism:

> See how far one gets in submitting proposals for exploratory studies to fund-granting agencies with their professional boards of consultants, or as doctoral dissertations in our advanced graduate departments of sociology and psychology! Witness the barrage of questions that arise: Where is your research design? What is your model? What is your guiding hypothesis? How are you operationalizing the hypothesis? What are your independent and dependent variables? What standard instruments are you going to use to get the data for your variables? What is your sample? What is your control group? And so on. Such questions presume in advance that the student has the first-hand knowledge that the exploratory study seeks to secure. Since he

---

[78] In Schmidt, *Man and Society*, pp. 193–94.

[79] Blumer, "Comment on 'Parsons as a Symbolic Interactionist,' " p. 62.

[80] Some new journals have emerged to help solve this problem, like *Symbolic Interaction* and *Journal of Contemporary Ethnography*.

doesn't have it the protocolized research procedure becomes the substitute for getting it![81]

By contrast, the method advocated by symbolic interactionism is to look at the processes by which individuals define the world from the inside and at the same time identify their world of objects.

How this works in practice can be illustrated by those aspects of a lawyer's role that demand the use of a symbolic interactionist perspective. For instance, a criminal lawyer in the process of defending a client is likely to utilize many of Mead's insights. When Clarence Darrow defended Thomas Massie on charges of fatally shooting the man who had beaten and raped Massie's wife, central to Darrow's defense was the jury's ability to "take the role" of Massie. Darrow is speaking:

> We contend that for months Massie's mind had been affected by all that was borne upon him: grief, sorrow, trouble, day after day, week after week, and month after month. What do you think would have happened to any one of you under the same condition? We measure other people by ourselves. We place ourselves in their place and say, "How would we have acted?" We have no further way of telling, except perhaps from the conditions of the life in which we live.
>
> . . . No man can judge another unless he places himself in the position of the other before he pronounces the verdict.
>
> If you can put yourself in his place, if you can think of his raped wife, of his months of suffering and mental anguish; if you can confront the unjust, cruel fate that unrolled before him, then you can judge—but you cannot judge any man otherwise.
>
> If you put yourself in Tommy Massie's place, what would you have done? I don't know about you, or you, or you, or you—but at least ten out of twelve men would have done just what poor Tommy Massie did. The thing for which you are asked to send him to prison for the rest of his life.[82]

Darrow thus eloquently communicates his client's definition of the situation to the members of the jury, and he cleverly attempts to get the jury to take the role of the other when he pleads with them to "put yourself in his place." Without identifying it as such, Darrow adopts the methodology of symbolic interactionism.[83]

Modes of Inquiry

For social scientists who attempt to gather data from this perspective, Blumer had clarified its methodology. He sketches the two modes of in-

[81]Blumer, *Symbolic Interactionism*, p. 37.

[82]See Arthur Weinberg, ed., *Attorney for the Damned* (New York: Simon and Schuster, 1970), pp. 104–17.

[83]Another profession illustrating the "lay use" of this perspective is acting.

quiry by means of which the researcher will be able to get "close to the empirical social world'and dig deeply into it." Blumer refers to these modes as the "direct naturalistic examination of the empirical social world," and he terms one "exploration" and the other "inspection."

Exploration   The exploratory phase has a twofold purpose: first, to provide the researcher with a "close and comprehensive acquaintance with a sphere of social life which is unfamiliar and hence unknown to him"; and second, to develop, focus, and sharpen the researcher's investigation so that the research problem—what is noticed and what is ignored, what are recognized as data, and the way the data are interpreted and analyzed—will be grounded in the empirical world.

Blumer defines exploration as a flexible procedure

> in which the scholar shifts from one to another line of inquiry, adopts new points of observation as his study progresses, moves in new directions previously unthought of, and changes his recognition of what are relevant data as he acquires more information and better understanding. In these respects, exploratory study stands in contrast to the prescribed and circumscribed procedure demanded by current scientific protocol. The flexibility of exploratory procedure does not mean that there is no direction to the inquiry; it means that the focus is originally broad but becomes progressively sharpened as the inquiry proceeds.[84]

The various techniques utilized in this phase are: directly observing, interviewing people, listening to conversations and to radio and television, reading local newspapers and journals, securing life-history accounts, reading letters and diaries, and consulting public records.

For example, in her study of skid-row alcoholics, Jacqueline Wiseman combined direct observation, both participant and nonparticipant, with the examination of records and unstructured depth interviews to attain a close and full familiarity with the world she was examining.[85] Her developmental stages are a good illustration of the flexibility of this approach, because she was able to shift the lines of inquiry during the exploratory phase. When words like, "I never worry when a friend of mine is missing [from skid row]; I know he's out making the loop and will be back," kept recurring in the interviews, she discovered the importance of "making the loop." Although it had not occurred to her before she began interviewing, she soon found that "making the loop"—going to one or more institutions or stations in the skid-row environment to "make it better"—was a means of survival

---

[84]Blumer, *Symbolic Interactionism*, p. 40.

[85]For an excellent explanation of symbolic interactionist research methods, as well as a frank discussion of decisions made in the field, see Wiseman's "Methodology Appendix" in her *Stations of the Lost* (Englewood Cliffs, N. J.: Prentice-Hall, Inc., 1970).

on skid row. The analysis of these "stations" in the loop became the main focus of her study.

Blumer also urges the researcher to find experts or "participants in the sphere of life who are acute observers and who are well informed" in the exploratory phase. Arranging discussion groups of a small number of these experts is another technique that Blumer feels is "more valuable many times over than any representative sample."[86] Blumer consistently used the "panel of experts" in his own research efforts. For instance, in his study of a drug rehabilitation program in Oakland, California, Blumer and his associates sought to "form a core of youthful drug users, enjoying prestige and respect among their peers."[87] Over a period of time, Blumer claims that his staff "established excellent rapport with these central figures, gaining their confidence and respect and working in close relation with them." In the following excerpt, Blumer explains how these central figures influenced him in his decision to change the focus of the study:

> We were able to have continuing group meetings with them (the central figures), as well as close personal association—and we sought through both of these channels to form a nucleus group committed to abstinence. Our line of attack was to have full and frank discussions of their drug use and to seek to make them aware of the hazards to their careers that were set by drug use.[88]

However, the tables were turned on the research staff when they discovered that the central figures "were so well anchored in drug use and well fortified in their beliefs against all of the 'dangers' of drug use" that a program of abstinence was impossible. The research staff, thus faced with such opposition, decided to shift from the proposed abstinence program to a study of the world of youthful drug use, which would enable the researchers to "see how it was woven into the life style of drug using youths." The staff's reasoning was that if they were to hope to do anything effective regarding juvenile drug use, they would first have to "understand realistically the world of such drug use."[89]

Although this incident illustrates one of the advantages of the exploratory phase—namely, a flexibility that allows the researcher to shift the focus of the study—it also reveals a possible drawback of the use of a panel of experts. The experts can give the researcher an overconfidence that he or she has an edge on the "truth" about the phenomenon under study.

[86]Blumer, *Symbolic Interactionism*, p. 41.

[87]Blumer, "The World of Youthful Drug Use" (Manuscript, University of California, Berkeley, School of Criminology, 1967), p. i.

[88]Ibid., pp. i–ii.

[89]Ibid., p. 11.

Inspection   If, as Blumer predicts, the exploratory phase succeeds in providing a comprehensive and accurate picture of the area of study, then the researcher is ready to move to the next procedure, inspection:[90]

> By "inspection" I mean an intensive focused examination of the empirical content of whatever analytical elements are used for purposes of analysis, and this same kind of examination of the empirical nature of the relations between such elements.[91]

To elaborate, Blumer introduces the term *sensitizing concepts*. In his view, the progression from the exploratory phase to the inspection stage is a movement from description to analysis, when sensitizing concepts are crucial. Blumer contrasts a sensitizing concept with a *definitive concept*, which is a clear definition of attributes and which identifies the individual instance of a class of objects. A sensitizing concept, on the other hand, lacks such a specification of attributes, and it "does not enable the user to move directly to the instance and its relevant content." It does give the user "a general sense of reference and guidance in approaching empirical instances." In summing up this discussion, Blumer says, "Whereas definitive concepts provide prescriptions of what to see, sensitizing concepts merely suggest directions along which to look."[92]

In developing their theory of the awareness of dying, Glaser and Strauss employed sensitizing concepts, which, they reported, enabled medical and nursing personnel to grasp the theory in terms of their own experience. As they explain it:

> For example, our categories of "death expectations," "nothing more to do," "lingering," and "social loss" designate general properties of dying patients that unquestionably are vividly sensitizing or meaningful to hospital personnel; at the same time, they are abstract enough to designate properties of concrete entities, not entities themselves. Further, these concepts provide a necessary bridge between the theoretical thinking of sociologists and the practical thinking of people concerned with the substantive area, so that both may understand and apply the theory. The sociologist finds that he has "a feeling for" the everyday realities of the situation, while the person in the situation finds he can master and manage the theory.[93]

Another illustration of the inspection stage is provided by Howard Becker's "Becoming a Marihuana User," which has become a classic example

[90]See William F. Whyte's *Street Corner Society* (Chicago: University of Chicago Press, 1943) for examples of inspection.

[91]Blumer, *Symbolic Interactionism*, p. 43.

[92]Ibid., pp. 148–49.

[93]Barney G. Glaser and Anselm L. Strauss, *The Discovery of Grounded Theory: Strategies for Qualitative Research* (Chicago: Aldine, 1967), pp. 240–41.

of symbolic interactionist research. From the data he obtained in personal interviews with fifty individuals, Becker arrived at a career model of marihuana users. This model, which was composed of sequences of changes in attitudes and experiences, guided Becker's analysis. He describes the career model thus:

> In summary, an individual will be able to use marihuana for pleasure only when he goes through a process of learning to conceive of it as an object which can be used in this way. No one becomes a user without (1) learning to smoke the drug in a way which will produce real effects; (2) learning to recognize the effects and connect them with drug use (learning, in other words, to get high); and (3) learning to enjoy the sensations he perceives. In the course of this process he develops a disposition or motivation to use marihuana which was not and could not have been present when he began use, for it involves and depends on conceptions of the drug which could only grow out of the kind of actual experience detailed above. On completion of this process he is willing and able to use marihuana for pleasure.[94]

Qualitative Analysis   Becker's study illuminates the analytic procedure involved in the inspection stage, but it would be a mistake to assume that the two stages, exploration and inspection, are mutually exclusive. Qualitative researchers, who believe that the two phases overlap, use the term *naturalistic inquiry* to embrace both phases. Wiseman, for instance, describes the interconnections of the stages as a "web" in her article "The Research Web":

> This constant interplay of data gathering and analysis is at the heart of qualitative research. It is therefore difficult indeed to discuss coding, processing, analysis, and writing without also discussing planning and data gathering, for in no other approach is the interrelatedness of all portions of the research act quite so obvious. For me, with the possible exception of the early planning stages, all aspects of the research act are going on almost simultaneously. Early fragments of analysis and of conceptual insights make their appearance both in the organization or coding of material and in the most current decisions I make about what field material to gather in the future.[95]

As Wiseman explains, when the researcher makes a decision about which data will be the primary foci of the study and which will serve as background, this decision paves the way for the next consideration. That consideration, the general design or model, becomes the "organizing

---

[94]Howard S. Becker, "Becoming a Marihuana User," *American Journal of Sociology*, 59 (1953), 41–58.

[95]These excerpts from "The Research Web" by Jacqueline P. Wiseman are reprinted from *Urban Life and Culture*, 3, no. 3 (Oct. 1974), 317 and 321. By permission of the publisher, Sage Publications, Inc.

scheme of the analysis." Even at this point, exploration and inspection are going on simultaneously, for the model "comes out of the data already gathered" and it also aids in the "collecting and categorization of data yet to come."

Wiseman describes several models of behavior used by qualitative researchers. These are,

1. the time order or careers model, in which everything has a natural history with a beginning, a middle, and an end;

2. the cyclical model, which suggests a "constant renewal and replay of the phenomenon, often resulting in acceleration," like her own "loops";

3. the social types model, "a description of the various types of people that populate a setting and interact within it," like Blumer's different types of drug users;

4. the social actions and interactions model, used in comparing behavioral variations, such as the awareness contexts used by Glaser and Strauss; and

5. the social settings or scenes model, which focuses on behavior settings and includes descriptions of the special culture and activities that take place in these social "subscenes."[96]

Blumer rates naturalistic inquiry superior to other modes of inquiry because it directly examines the empirical world and its natural, ongoing activity, rather than abstracted and quantified data. Nonetheless, Blumer recognizes that his call for a direct examination of the empirical social world is not likely to make sense to most social scientists, who are committed to quantitative analysis. He says:

> They would hold that they are examining the empirical world directly when they do such things as collect and analyze various kinds of census data, make social surveys, secure declarations from people through questionnaires, use polls, undertake discriminating clinical examination, employ scales and refined measuring instruments, bring social action into controlled laboratory situations, undertake careful computer simulation of social life, and use crucial empirical data to test hypotheses.[97]

Obviously this is not what Blumer sees as a direct examination of the empirical social world. What Blumer wants is a "close and reasonably full familiarity with the area of life under study."[98] This involves none of the

[96]Ibid., p. 321.
[97]Blumer, *Symbolic Interactionism*, p. 34.
[98]Ibid., p. 87.

above-mentioned techniques, but rather a free exploration in the area, "getting close to the people involved in it, seeing it in a variety of situations they meet, noting their problems and observing how they handle them, being party to their conversations, and watching their life as it flows along." Blumer's position puts him at variance with the social scientists he mentions, who advocate collecting "hard" rather than what they term "soft" data.

In one of his most graphic arguments against the quantitative approach, Blumer attacks the I.Q. test. He asks how a given intelligence test can yield a satisfactory picture of intelligence, which is present in such varied forms as:

> the ingenious exploitation of a market situation by a business entrepreneur, effective methods of survival by a disadvantaged slum dweller, the clever meeting of the problems of his world by a peasant or a primitive tribesman, . . . and the construction of a telling verse by a poet.[99]

Blumer's objection to the I.Q. test is that such formal, out-of-context instruments cannot measure satisfactorily the kind of contextually rooted behavior he describes. He questions the value of the quantitative approach:

> The basic criticism usually made of the experimental approach, and of the objective, quantitative approach in the form of questionnaires, schedules, and tests, is that they fail to catch the "meanings" which mediate and determine the way in which the individuals respond to objects and situations. The items on a questionnaire, on a schedule and on a test may be clear and precise; and, the individual may answer in the categorical and definite way that is needed for the quantitative treatment of the responses. But the point is made that the responses to these items do not tell what is the meaning of these items to the individual; hence, the investigator is not in a position to state what are the individual's attitudes or to know what would be his likely behavior if he were actually to act toward the objects to which the items refer.[100]

For example, a female-headed family of six with an annual income of $7,500 may correctly be classified as in the "under $10,000 a year" category of families. For many researchers, interested in (for example) the statistical relationship between the percentage of poor homes in an area and the average achievement of schoolchildren, these data are enough. Researchers like Blumer, however, are interested in different questions. They want to know what that $7,500 income means to the mother in terms of how she behaves toward her children or makes decisions about looking for work, or how creative she is in stretching her budget to put food on the table three

---

[99]Ibid., p. 30.
[100]In Schmidt, *Man and Society*, p. 194.

times a day. Symbolic interactionists do not deny the usefulness of a quantitative national census; but for the research questions they want to ask, census questions and response are inadequate. Their approach and emphasis on meaning are simply not conducive to quantitative methods.

However, to us it seems unnecessary to select one approach at the expense of another. Qualitative research can contribute to quantitative research. It can generate fruitful hypotheses and uncover heretofore unknown areas of needed research, and it can provide necessary typologies. We want to argue that these two research approaches should cooperate rather than compete with each other.

Microsociology

In speaking of the limitations of the symbolic interactionists' microsociological approach, Skidmore says, "Research with this perspective tends to be the elaboration of ever-different situations and activities, with a consequent lack of emphasis on relating these works into a coherent view of whole societies."[101]

However, in a response to Jonathan Turner's article "Parsons as a Symbolic Interactionist," Blumer denies the charge that the methodology of the symbolic interactionists "emphasizes microinteractive processes." Blumer argues that the symbolic interactionist approach is capable of studying large organizations, and he refers the reader to his article, "Sociological Theory in Industrial Relations."[102]

A perusal of Blumer's article is a little disconcerting, for it fails to set forth a clear and complete methodology. Blumer states:

> The observations necessary to sharpen and fill in this vague perspective must meet the two requirements of intimate familiarity and broad imaginative grasp. . . . It is unfortunate that observation in the field of industrial relations has to be made in the form of large intricate patterns—but it has to be, in order to be realistic. In a way, the necessities of observation in industrial relations are quite similar to those required in modern warfare. The individual soldier in his single observation post, regardless of how competent he may be as an observer, can understand little of what is taking place over the broad area of a campaign. A sociological investigator making observations in a single factory suffers, I believe, from a corresponding limitation. Effective observation requires the observer to sense the movement in the field, to take many varied roles, to size up a variety of different situations and in doing so to perform the difficult task of fitting such things into somewhat of an inte-

[101]William Skidmore, *Theoretical Thinking in Sociology* (New York: Cambridge University Press, 1975), p. 236.

[102]Blumer, "Comment on 'Parsons as a Symbolic Interactionist'," 61. See also Blumer's article, "Sociological Theory in Industrial Relations," *American Sociological Review*, 12 (1947), 271–78.

grated pattern. This type of observation, whether we like it or not, requires a high degree of imaginative judgment in order to be accurate.[103]

As he concludes the article, Blumer says that we need a scheme of treatment that is suited to the analysis of collective and mass interaction—but that sociologists have not begun this task. Thus, what Blumer calls an article that will clarify symbolic interactionism's capability of studying the interaction among macro organizations is not that at all. Though he sets forth some "blurred outlines," readers are left not much further along in their understanding of how symbolic interactionists go about the study of groups at the macro level.[104] Microsociology is, after all, "home base" for symbolic interactionists. We turn now to Blumer's student, Erving Goffman, who specialized in face-to-face interaction.

PART THREE
Erving Goffman: Dramaturgy and the Interaction Order

BACKGROUND

In this section we will take a systematic look at Goffman's theoretical contributions. His work has influenced several theorists outside the symbolic interactionist perspective. Peter Blau, for instance, applied Goffman's concepts of impression management and role distance to his social exchange theory. Goffman's work has also been an inspiration for ethnomethodologists,[105] and Randall Collins incorporated many of Goffman's ideas into his book *Conflict Sociology*.[106] In fact, it was Collins who paid the highest tribute to Goffman when he argued that Robert Merton was "the best known figure in professional American sociology during the middle of the twentieth century," C. Wright Mills had "the greatest political impact," and Talcott Parsons was the "major comprehensive theorist," but Erving Goffman was the sociologist who "contributed most to intellectual progress."[107]

Born in Mannville, Alberta, in 1922, Goffman earned his B.A. at the University of Toronto in 1945 and his M.A. and Ph.D. at the University of

[103]Blumer, "Sociological Theory in Industrial Relations," p. 277.

[104]For a well-documented argument to the contrary, see David Maines, "Myth, Text, and Interactionist Complicity in the Neglect of Blumer's Macrosociology," *Symbolic Interaction*, XI (1988), pp. 43–57. Maines argues that the analysis of society-wide organizations was a major concern of Blumer's.

[105]See Paul Attewell's "Ethnomethodology Since Garfinkel," *Theory and Society*, I (1974), pp. 179–210.

[106]See pp. 159 and 167.

[107]Randall Collins, *Sociology Since Midcentury* (New York: Academic Press, 1981), p. 297.

Chicago in 1949 and 1953. Shortly after completing his dissertation, Goffman joined his former teacher Herbert Blumer at the University of California, Berkeley, where he taught until 1969.[108] He then accepted a position as Benjamin Franklin Professor of Anthropology and Sociology at the University of Pennsylvania, where he taught until his untimely death in 1982.[109]

Like Blumer, Goffman was most influenced by Mead, and this is evident in his focus on the self, particularly in his first book, *The Presentation of Self in Everyday Life*, which informed much of his later work. In true Meadian fashion, Goffman treats human beings as active and knowledgeable. In *Stigma* he illumines for us the creativity of deviants or stigmatized persons who manage to preserve a sense of self when the cards are stacked against them. His keen observations in a mental institution in *Asylums* led him to create the concept *total institution,* "a place of residence and work where a large number of like-situated individuals, cut off from the wider society for an appreciable period of time, together lead an enclosed, formally administered round of life."[110] He found that inmates invented many ingenious strategies to preserve their own selfhood rather than surrender to an acceptance of the role and the self that the institution prescribes—and this takes place in a very "structured" institution. He gives many examples in his discussion of "secondary adjustments," which he defines as "any habitual arrangement by which a member of an organization employs unauthorized means, or obtains unauthorized ends, or both, thus getting around the organization's assumptions as to what he should do and get and hence what he should be."[111]

Some of the secondary adjustments were "make-do's" (converting a bathroom sink and radiator to a private laundry system) and "free places" (a patch of woods behind the hospital used as a cover for drinking or the shade of a large tree near the center of the hospital grounds used as a cover for poker games). These secondary adjustments illustrate ways in which human beings meet situations and devise their own conduct. Furthermore, Goffman says:

> The practice of reserving something of oneself from the clutch of an institution is very visible in mental hospitals and prisons but can be found in more benign and less totalistic institutions, too. I want to argue that this recalci-

---

[108]While at Berkeley, Goffman became interested in the work of Harold Garfinkel, and he encouraged his students to read Garfinkel's published and unpublished work. Some of Goffman's students traveled from Berkeley to Los Angeles in the late 1960s to attend Garfinkel's seminars.

[109]His key publications include *The Presentation of Self in Everyday Life, Asylums, Encounters, Behavior in Public Places, Stigma, Interaction Ritual, Relations in Public, Strategic Interaction,* and *Gender Advertisements.* (See the bibliography.)

[110]Erving Goffman, *Asylums: Essays on the Social Situation of Mental Patients and Other Inmates* (New York: Doubleday, 1961), p. xii.

[111]Ibid., p. 189.

trance is not an incidental mechanism of defense but rather an essential constituent of the self. . . . Our sense of being a person can come from being drawn into a wider social unit; our sense of selfhood can rise through the little ways we resist the pull. Our status is backed by the solid buildings of the world, while our sense of personal identity often resides in the cracks.[112]

Goffman's research revealed an underlife in a mental hospital where inmates resisted every effort to strip away the "old self." His work, which is informed to a large extent by Mead's "I," is replete with analyses of situations in which individuals are "resisting the pull" and "residing in the cracks."

In his work Goffman combined several methods used by symbolic interactionists: participant observation supplemented by data from case histories, autobiographies, and letters. He describes his approach in *Asylums* as a "symbolic-interaction framework for considering the fate of the self."[113] Mead's concept of the self is, in fact, a central theme in much of Goffman's work.[114]

Durkheim's writings, in particular his analysis of ritual in *The Elementary Forms of the Religious Life,* fascinated Goffman. Not only did he publish a book on the topic (*Interaction Ritual*), but the theme of ritual appears in several of his works. For example, he cites Durkheim in *Asylums* when he discusses the ceremonial practices in a total institution like shows, sports events, and dances. As Goffman puts it, "These ceremonial practices are well suited to a Durkheimian analysis: a society dangerously split into inmates and staff can through these ceremonies hold itself together."[115]

While it may be true that Goffman self-consciously adopted a Durkheimian perspective in some of his early works,[116] this was neither permanent nor all-inclusive. The aerial view of large social structures was not for Goffman; his focus was on the "countless minor syntheses" of Simmel which we described at the beginning of this chapter, the human linkages which Simmel labeled the "atoms of society." Goffman's great interest in the forms of interaction and his ingenuity in fleshing out sociological concepts in his descriptions of face-to-face interaction were indeed reminiscent of Georg Simmel.

However, some of Goffman's later work, in particular *Frame Analysis,* represented a shift toward a variant of structuralism. We turn now to a discussion of two of Goffman's chief contributions to the symbolic interac-

---

[112]Ibid., pp. 319–20.

[113]Ibid., p. 47.

[114]Goffman did not approve of classifying scholars by their membership in "schools" of thought. He called this practice "a case of guilt by pigeonholing." See Erving Goffman, "Reply," *Contemporary Sociology,* X (January 1981), 61.

[115]Ibid., p. 109.

[116]Whitney Pope and Barclay D. Johnson, "Inside Organic Solidarity," *American Sociological Review,* 48 (October 1983), 691.

tionist perspective: his dramaturgical ideas and what he calls the "interaction order."

DRAMATURGY AND EVERYDAY LIFE

Webster defines dramaturgy as "the art of dramatic composition and theatrical representation."[117] In his early and often-cited work *The Presentation of Self in Everyday Life*, Goffman takes the familiar sociological concept, role, and puts it "back on stage" by placing the analysis of human behavior in a theatrical setting. He takes the dramatic situation of actors and actresses on stage and applies this theatrical representation to the everyday lives of ordinary women and men who are acting out their roles in the real world.

Goffman looks at the ways individuals in their everyday lives present themselves and their activities to others; in particular, he focuses on *impression management*, the ways in which the individual guides and controls the impressions others form of him or her. Two additional dramaturgical concepts are the "front" and "back" regions. The front is "that part of the individuals' performance which regularly functions in a general and fixed fashion to define the situation for those who observe the performance."[118] Front includes setting (furniture and other items supplying the scenery and stage props) and "personal front"—items of "expressive equipment," like insignia of office or rank, clothing, sex, age, racial characteristics, size, posture, speech patterns, facial expressions, and body gestures.[119]

Goffman makes the point that the standards which women are obliged to maintain regarding a disarray of personal front (clothing and appearance) are stricter than for men. "After all," Goffman says, "for a woman to appear in public with her costume disarrayed can be taken as a sign of accessibility and looseness of morals."[120]

Ask yourself, for instance, when you last carried a briefcase. You may have needed it to carry your books, but you may also have used it to impress a job interviewer, the dean of your college, or even your sociology professor. You may also recall how, in that situation, you carefully articulated each sentence and how you used other aspects of your personal front, like your clothing, posture, facial expressions, and body gestures, to present yourself

[117]*Webster's New Collegiate Dictionary* (Springfield, Mass.: Merriam, 1961), p. 250.

[118]Erving Goffman, *The Presentation of Self in Everyday Life* (Garden City, New York: Doubleday, 1959), p. 22.

[119]Ibid., p. 24.

[120]Erving Goffman, "The Arrangement Between the Sexes," *Theory and Society*, 4 (Fall 1977), 329. Giddens applauds Goffman's analysis of spatial divisions, a major feature of class differentiation. The front/back region contrast demonstrates how the setting is controlled, and Giddens argues that the capability to control settings is one of the major prerogatives of power. See Anthony Giddens, *Central Problems in Social Theory* (Berkeley: University of California Press, 1983), pp. 206–9.

in the best light. The front region, then, includes anything observed by the audience while the actor is on front stage which makes for a successful performance. The front region is the place where the actor is seriously playing out the script of impression management. In the front region the actor avoids anything that is inappropriate according to the script. Such behavior brings to mind Parson's pattern variables where the actor also carefully makes the appropriate choices. Goffman's actors are not improvising when they are on front stage.

What happens in the front region, then, is an attempt to manipulate the audience. An article in a London newspaper concerning a "scripted system" of selling cars describes this manipulation as it occurs in the automobile industry. The article explains that salespersons are taught a script which they must follow "like an actor has to learn his part in a play." One of the best scripts cited is entitled "Playing Harris": (Speaking to customer) "I've got Mr. Harris on the phone wanting to know if the car has been sold. Shall I say yes?"[121]

The front stage performance above would work best if the telephone rang at the strategic moment (prop) and if the script were delivered in a convincing tone of voice (personal front). The front would then have a better chance of defining the situation for the potential customer, who then quickly would answer, "Yes."

The back region, by contrast, is the place closed to and hidden from the audience where the techniques of impression management are practiced. Many forms of assistance to the actors are given in the backstage region, for example, adjustment of costumes and prompting. It is also a place where the performer can relax. As Goffman puts it, "He can drop his front, forego speaking his lines, and step out of character."[122] Backstage is where the actors do not need to engage in impression management; they can be themselves.

In a study of social interaction at the laundromat, Kenen used Goffman's concept of the front region to analyze some of the activity she was observing. She found customers engaged in "behind the scenes work" in a front stage setting as they attempted to conceal some of the items they were washing. As she put it, "Padded bras, torn underwear, stained garments, or even designer bedsheets can reveal too much about one's habits and tastes to a stranger, and may contradict the intended presentation of self."[123] While laundromats and automobile salesrooms may seem to be a far cry from the theater, keep in mind that Goffman's dramaturgy is con-

[121]*The Daily Telegraph* (London), April 5, 1984, p. 7.

[122]Goffman, *Presentation of Self in Everyday Life*, p. 112.

[123]See Regina Kenen, "Soapsuds, Space and Sociability: A Participant Observation of the Laundromat," *Urban Life*, 11, no. 2 (July 1982), 178.

cerned with the lives of ordinary women and men as they act out their daily roles on the stage of life.

By drawing our attention to the backstage region, Goffman helps us to understand all of the hidden work involved in accomplishing successful presentations of self in public. He shows us how, in the drama of everyday life, individuals manage to look good when they present themselves to others at home, school, work, neighborhood, and in other microinteractive settings.

Randall Collins uses Goffman's dramaturgical concepts to analyze organizational politics, which at the lower levels involve "presenting a united front to the supervisor, appearing to comply with the supervisor's demands while giving the workers a breathing space in which to control their own work pace." These encounters with authority are front stage. The workers on their own are backstage, engaging in conversation about such things as "how the boss was fooled, how a member of the team almost blew its cover; jokes are made and anecdotes are exchanged, creating an entire conversational culture of a particular backstage world."[124]

Here Collins, a sociologist, is consciously applying Goffman's ideas to an organizational structure. How does a nonsociologist use them? In a newspaper article on the on-and off-the-record statements of politicians, a journalist writes: "What we call the record often tends to be the precise opposite of a record. It is, rather, the artifice, the cooked-up part, the image that the politician, with our connivance, hopes to convey and generally does. The off-the-record part is where the reality and the authenticity are to be found and where they are generally supposed to remain forever obscure."[125] This journalist is alerting the reader to two important dramaturgical points: first, that on-the-record is, for the politician, front stage, where, as she puts it, "little tricks and big deceptions are being practiced." Second, the real record is in the backstage region, where the politicians speak candidly about what they *really* think. She is alerting us, the audience, to the attempt on the part of politicians to define the situation for us by their front-stage performances.

What happens when front and back stage activities are not well coordinated is that the actor does not perform well, and the performance is less successful, in varying degrees. In some cases the "goof" may be relatively minor, as when a prompter fails to act quickly enough to supply a forgotten line or when a portion of the costume or other props come crashing down on the stage. Such minor "hitches" can be covered up, and the performance completed. But what happens when back stage *becomes* front stage, when the audience suddenly sees all the hitherto hidden backstage activity?

[124]Collins, *Conflict Sociology*, p. 118.

[125]Meg Greenfield, "Must Reality be off the Record?" *Washington Post*, April 11, 1984, p. A21. Thanks to William Sandmeyer for drawing our attention to this article.

Goffman's analysis of fatefulness is illuminating on this point. In *Interaction Ritual,* he argues that in situations where coordination and concealment are vital, "a whole range of minor unanticipated hitches lose their usual quality of correctability and become fateful." He presents the following story as illustration:

> Three robbers who completely botched what was supposed to be a simple little bank robbery in Rodeo were sentenced in Federal Court here yesterday. . . .
>
> All three were nabbed by some 40 police officers Jan. 7 as they struggled to make off with $7710 stuffed into a laundry sack they had just taken out of the United California Bank, the only bank in Rodeo. . . .
>
> Pugh walked in with a sawed off shotgun and lined up the 13 employees and two customers, while Fleming, carrying a pistol, went to the vault and started filling the laundry bag with currency and, alas, coins.
>
> "The coins can't be traced," he said cleverly. He kept piling in coins until the bag weighed about 200 pounds. Then he dragged the bag across the floor to the door—and the frayed rope snapped.
>
> Both men then lugged the bag through the door, but it caught and ripped a hole, letting coins trail behind them as they dragged the bag to the get-away car, with Duren at the wheel.
>
> Duren, though, had parked too close to the high curb, so the three could not open the door to get the loot inside. Finally, they did, by moving the car, and raced away—around the corner. There the car stopped when the three saw the clutter of sheriff, Highway Patrol and police cars.[126]

Here a strategic prop (laundry sack) breaks down, and backstage assistance fails to come through on time. As Goffman explains, this is fateful for the individuals involved because the criminal enterprise has a much narrower reserve for correctability. A high price must be paid for bad breaks or goofs, situations in which backstage assistance is inadequate. Here the tables are turned, for the actors have the situation defined for them by the audience.

Goffman's dramaturgical ideas help us to examine those countless instances when we have used all the equipment of our front and back regions to create the best possible impressions of ourselves. His basic question to us is, "Aren't we all con artists after all?" There is no doubt that we use impression management in our own everyday lives when we, for example, succeed in "acing" a job interview, when we regale a group of strangers at a social gathering, when we convince the person we love to be our spouse, or when we do our best to be the "Rock of Gibraltar" for other family members at the funeral of a close relative. In each of these examples we want to be the one who defines the situation for the other individuals present, and Goffman's ideas show how this is possible.

[126]*San Francisco Chronicle,* March 10, 1966, in Erving Goffman, *Interaction Ritual* (Garden City, New York: Doubleday, 1967), pp. 165–66.

In a more recent book Goffman presents 500 magazine advertisements and analyzes the often unspoken social assumptions about gender conveyed by these pictures. Assuming that the ads represent advertiser's views of how women and men can be profitably pictured, Goffman's analysis could be described as focusing on the "front stage."

One of the themes emerging from Goffman's analysis, for instance, was "function ranking," the male performing the executive role both within and outside occupational specialization. Goffman asks the reader to examine how males are

> pictured when in the domains of the traditional authority and competency of females—the kitchen, the nursery and the living room when it is being cleaned. One answer, borrowed from life and possibly underrepresented, is to picture the male engaged in no contributing role at all, in this way avoiding either subordination or contamination with a "female" task. Another answer, I think, is to present the man as ludicrous or child-like, unrealistically so, as if perhaps in making him candidly unreal the competency image of real males could be preserved. A subtler technique is to allow the male to pursue the alien activity under the direct scrutiny of she who can do the deed properly, as though the doing were itself by way of being a lark or a dare, a smile on the face of the doer or the watcher attesting to the essentially unserious essayed character of the undertaking.[127]

In the next section we turn to Goffman's analysis of the interaction order, his final legacy to sociology.

THE INTERACTION ORDER

When Erving Goffman developed cancer in the summer of 1982, he was preparing the address he was scheduled to deliver as president of the American Sociological Association at the annual meeting in September. Although he could not give the address, he did complete the paper before his death on November 19, 1982. The title of this final work, "The Interaction Order," which was published in the *American Sociological Review,* is the label Goffman gives to his focus over his entire career, the domain of face-to-face social interaction, "where two or more individuals are physically in one another's presence."[128] As John Lofland puts it, "He showed us with a detail and poignancy no one had before how our sense of ourselves, of what is real, and how we feel is bound up in—is inextricably knotted to—the ever-moving microdynamics of the immediate interaction order in end-

[127]Erving Goffman, *Gender Advertisements* (New York: Harper and Row, 1979), pp. 36–37.

[128]Erving Goffman, "The Interaction Order," *American Sociological Review,* 48 (February 1983), 8.

lessly complicated ways of which we are not aware." Goffman was fascinated with discrepancies between appearances and realities and with "deception and manipulation."[129]

Goffman's presidential address, which sums up his life's work, is his attempt to make the case that the interaction order should be treated as a substantive domain in its own right. It outlines some of the basic units and recurrent structures and processes of the interaction order, from the smallest to the largest: (1) *persons,* whether single, couples, files, processions, or queues; (2) *contacts,* either through physical co-presence, telephone conversation, or letter exchange; (3) *encounters,* or arrangements in which persons come together into a small physical circle as participants in a consciously shared, interdependent undertaking (for example, card games, meals, lovemaking, and service transactions); (4) *platform performances,* where activity is set before an audience (for instance, a talk, a contest, a formal meeting, a play, a musical offering); (5) *celebrative social occasions,* gatherings of individuals in honor of some jointly appreciated circumstance where participants arrive and leave in a coordinated way. This last unit is the largest interactional one Goffman mentions, one which can be engineered to extend over a number of days.

Although the persons, contacts, encounters, performances, and celebrations outlined above are essentially microscopic, Goffman argues that the interaction order has direct bearing on the macroscopic order. We presented an instance of such a repercussion earlier in this chapter in the Watergate example, where the phone call to the police made by Frank Wills led to the resignation of President Nixon. Goffman states that a good deal of organizational work is done face-to-face, and he suggests, for example, that complex organizations are so dependent on particular personnel, especially those in governing roles, that they are extremely vulnerable when key personnel are abducted or injured. At such a time an organization may make every effort to conceal the absence of the administrator in order to keep the system operating. The question "Who is in charge?" raised at the time of serious illnesses of heads of state, like that of Yuri Andropov in the U.S.S.R. or Woodrow Wilson in the U.S., are cases in point. Another example is the disorder experienced (or created) by elementary school students when a substitute teacher takes over during the illness of the regular teacher. Reverberations reach beyond the classroom to other parts of the school, including supervision of playground and lunchroom activities and the policing of bus lines and hallway traffic.

Another element of the interaction order which has a direct effect on a person's life chances is what Goffman labels "processing encounters." These include interviews conducted by school counselors, personnel depart-

---

[129]John Lofland, "Erving Goffman's Sociological Legacies," *Urban Life,* 13 (April 1984), 7 and 22.

ment staff in business organizations, psychologists, and courtroom officials. These processing encounters can affect the relevant social institution as well as the person involved. How an individual performs on a job interview, for instance, affects her or his occupational future, but also the type of people who are processed successfully can change the institution itself. For example, consider the effects of increasing numbers of women students on institutions like the Naval Academy at Annapolis. Goffman also points to the importance of first impressions for friendship relationships and marital bonds. In fact, he suggests that such close bonds often "can be traced back to an occasion in which something more was made of an incidental contact than need have been made."[130] One need only read the February 14 (Valentine's Day) issue of a newspaper for some "love at first sight" stories to illustrate Goffman's point here.

In his final article Goffman also attempted to synthesize symbolic interactionism. His examples of the small-scale linkages recommended to our attention by Simmel are found in the interaction order, which consists of persons, contacts, encounters, platform performances, and celebrations. Goffman also claims that forms of face-to-face life, because they are constantly repeated, are more open to systematic analysis than many macroscopic entities. This article represents his final argument for the significance of the microinteractional level for sociology.

However, Goffman's analysis, for the most part, leaves out an important ingredient of the symbolic interactionist perspective, that is, self-interaction. He pays lip service to it when he states that these face-to-face forms are "anchored in subjective feelings and thus allow an appreciable role for empathy."[131] Here he is reiterating the value of taking the role of the other, which is at the core of symbolic interactionism. Goffman's own work, nonetheless, reveals much more about face-to-face interaction than about subjective feelings. He obviously believes in the central premise of symbolic interactionism, that actors interpret, map out, evaluate, and then act; that is, that human beings are active, not passive. However, while Goffman has enriched sociology with a number of important concepts based on his keen observations, his chief interest is not in what actors are saying to themselves as they map out their actions, but in how they succeed in manipulating the definition of the situation. Though his data do include sources for subjective meaning, for example, letters and autobiographies, these data are not central to his analysis. He has chosen a narrower focus than that of Blumer, but the depth of his analysis compensates for this.

Goffman's legacy to sociology emerges at the conclusion of his presidential address in the form of advocating a new direction for research on the interaction order. He who spent a substantial part of his career studying

---

[130]Goffman, "The Interaction Order," p. 8.
[131]Ibid., p. 9.

the "underdog," focusing on people in subordinate positions and on disenfranchised or discredited groups, recommends something different. Goffman suggests that sociologists pursue "unsponsored analyses of the social arrangements enjoyed by those with institutional authority—police, generals, government leaders, parents, males, whites, nationals, media operators, and all those well-placed persons who are in a position to give official imprint to versions of reality."[132]

Here we see Goffman addressing the realm of power and the management of social reality. In order to understand the recurrent patterns of interaction between subordinate and superordinate individuals, Goffman directs the attention of sociologists to the world of the latter. In his recommendation for an all-out effort to examine people in positions of power in our society, he is forcing microsociological researchers to deal with a key concept of conflict theorists, power relationships. In the last analysis this could be an important effort toward bridging the micro and macro levels of sociological analysis.

PART FOUR
Toward a New Social Theory of Emotion

PREVIOUS WORK

Many social theorists tend to overlook, ignore, or dismiss people's emotions as irrelevant. "What," they ask, "do individual feelings have to do with explaining the social world?" However, because symbolic interactionists focus on subjective meaning, we should expect that they will also take the emotions more seriously than any other theorists and supply us with many of the ingredients for a social theory of emotion. If we briefly review the material presented thus far in this chapter, we can detect a number of references to emotionality, some explicit and some implicit.

Weber's discussion of the importance of subjective meaning in his definition of sociology allows for the relationship between individual emotions and social interaction, without making it explicit. We would argue that the subjective meaning that an active individual ascribes to a situation includes an emotional element. The feelings people have toward those with whom they come in contact is a factor which can and does enter into the individual's definition of the situation, and this, in turn, influences people's decisions about whether to interact, to withdraw, or, as Weber puts it, to "passively acquiesce" in the situation.[133]

[132]Ibid., p. 17.
[133]See p. 238 in this text.

Taking another look at Simmel's description of human linkages, we discover that he explicitly includes two emotions—jealousy and gratitude—as examples of the "countless minor syntheses" that incessantly tie people together.[134] Likewise Cooley, defining the looking-glass-self, explicitly mentions "self-feeling, such as pride or mortification," which results from how we imagine the other to be judging our appearance.[135]

Blumer's discussion of the role of self-indication in the interpretation process also includes implicit mention of the emotions. As we explained earlier,[136] someone who gives an account of personal worries and anxieties is interpreting what is disturbing to him or her.[137] Examples of emotional self-interactions range from a young child who tells himself "I'm scared!" when he experiences a thunderstorm for the first time, to the adult who says to herself "I can hardly wait to see him!" as her train pulls into the station. Worries, anxieties, jealousy, pride, love, contempt—a whole array of emotions—are often included in the conversations people have with themselves. Thus what people are feeling and their self-indications about those feelings help them to devise or "map out" their conduct. In short, human beings often choose one behavior over another because it "feels good."

Two other theorists who include emotional elements are Goffman and Collins. Goffman's "impression management" is essentially a strategy for avoiding embarrassment or shame and is inspired by pride, a desire to "look good." When Goffman asks, "Aren't we all con artists, after all?" this points to one of the reasons why we want to control others' impressions of us—to avoid being embarrassed.

Collins discusses how rituals can intensify emotional arousal and commit participants more strongly to certain views, and how, as a consequence, these rituals tend to strengthen and legitimize a given social order.[138] More recently, Collins, influenced by Goffman as well as by Durkheim's work on rituals, has inserted emotional energy as an essential ingredient in his model of "the interaction ritual chain." He argues that the most basic ingredient in interactions is "a minimal tone of positive sentiment toward the other." Thus the individual who is accepted into a conversation, for instance, not only acquires an increment of positive emotional energy from that experience, but also additional emotional resources (confidence, warmth, enthusiasm) with which to negotiate successfully in the next interaction. Such chains, Collins says, "extend throughout every person's lifetime."[139]

[134]Ibid.

[135]Ibid., p. 241.

[136]Ibid., p. 257.

[137]In a personal interview (1975) Blumer suggested, as a teaching device which might help students to understand the importance of the symbolic interactionist perspective, that one might ask students about their own immediate worries, anxieties, and fears, and how those feelings, in turn, affect their behavior.

[138]See Chapter II, p. 170.

[139]Randall Collins, *Sociology Since Midcentury: Essays in Theory Cumulation* (New York: Academic Press, 1981), pp. 276–81.

ARLIE RUSSELL HOCHSCHILD: EMOTION WORK

When it turned the spotlight on gender and women's concerns, the contemporary women's movement helped sociologists to uncover new research topics and new concepts, thus enlarging the horizons of sociological theory. Among those feminists who have done serious theoretical work on emotionality, Arlie Russell Hochschild is a dominant figure. Her book *The Managed Heart: Commercialization of Human Feeling* is the pioneering work.

Although neither Mead nor Blumer developed a theory of emotion, this new social theory is, in part, an expansion of the symbolic interactionist perspective. Hochschild draws from a number of theorists, including Dewey, Goffman, and Freud. Hochschild makes the point that Goffman and Freud each provide a limited view of the emotions, for Goffman specialized in studying embarrassment and shame, while Freud specialized in analyzing anxiety.[140] By contrast, Hochschild's theory encompasses a whole range of emotions, including grief, depression, frustration, anger, fear, contempt, guilt, anguish, envy, jealousy, love, compassion, embarrassment, shame, and anxiety.

Hochschild focuses specifically on *emotional labor,* which she defines thus:

> I use the term *emotional labor* to mean the management of feeling to create a publicly observable facial and bodily display; emotional labor is sold for a wage and therefore has *exchange value.* I use the synonymous terms *emotion work* or *emotion management* to refer to these same acts done in a private context where they have *use value.*[141]

Hochschild researched the emotional labor required by two occupations: flight attendants (mostly women) and bill collectors (mostly men). She found that the flight attendants were asked to "feel sympathy, trust, and good will," whereas the bill collectors were asked to "feel distrust and sometimes positive bad will."[142]

The following is an illustration from an interview with a flight attendant:

> Even though I'm a very honest person, I have learned not to allow my face to mirror my alarm or fright. I feel very protective of my passengers. Above all, I don't want them to be frightened. If we were going down, if we were going to make a ditching in water; the chances of our surviving are slim, even though we (the flight attendants) know exactly what to do. *But I think I would*

---

[140]Arlie Russell Hochschild, *The Managed Heart: Commercialization of Human Feeling* (Berkeley: University of California Press, 1983), p. 216. See also Hochschild's *The Second Shift: Working Parents and the Revolution at Home* (New York: Viking Penguin, 1989).

[141]Ibid., p. 7.

[142]Ibid., p. 137.

probably—and I think I can say this for most of my fellow flight attendants—*be able to keep them from being too worried about it.* I mean my voice might quiver a little during the announcements, but somehow I feel we could get them to believe . . . the best.[143]

Hochschild learned that the struggle to maintain a difference between feeling and feigning led to a strain for the people in occupations calling for emotional labor, a strain which she labeled "emotive dissonance." She states, "We try to reduce this strain by changing what we feel or by changing what we feign."[144] The emotive dissonance involved in the management of feelings which Hochschild discovered in her research resulted in what Merton would call a "recasting" of the theory of cognitive dissonance, extending its margins to include emotive dissonance as well.[145]

OTHER CONTRIBUTIONS

Another feminist who has made an important contribution to the sociology of the emotions is Nancy Chodorow. In her book *The Reproduction of Mothering*, Chodorow, drawing on and expanding Freud's psychoanalytic theory, argues that male children see themselves as unlike the mothers with whom they have had their first emotional relationship, and they learn to repress and deny female qualities in order to accomplish their individuated male identity. Thus males grow up with an underdeveloped relational capacity, and they tend to see the feminine as inferior. Female children, on the other hand, strongly and continuously identify with the mother, accept their emotions, and develop a high relational capacity.[146]

In her participant-observation study of boys and girls in a grammar school environment, Raphaela Best found many examples of how children learn the meaning of gender through interaction. She observed the girls bustling around the classroom, busy with helping and housekeeping chores, while the boys were typically the passive recipients of this help. On occasion the boys would defy the teacher (a woman), insisting on repeatedly going to the bathroom or claiming to have turned work in when they hadn't. Both in the classroom and outside, the girls would openly express emotions, crying, hugging, and comforting each other, whereas the boys kept a tight lid on emotions and expressed affection only in rough play. Younger boys were often engaged in creating various "clubs," from which

---

[143]Ibid., p. 107.

[144]Ibid., p. 90. See Chapter IV for a discussion of Leon Festinger's theory of cognitive dissonance.

[145]Robert K. Merton, *On Theoretical Sociology* (New York: Free Press, 1967), p. 162.

[146]See Nancy Chodorow, *The Reproduction of Mothering* (Berkeley: University of California Press, 1978), and her *Feminism and Psychoanalysis* (New Haven: Yale University Press, 1989).

boys perceived as sissies, crybabies, mama's boys, and teacher's helpers were excluded.[147]

Why have male social theorists, until recently, tended to remain silent on the question of emotionality? One would expect that the sociology of the emotions would be an appropriate topic for symbolic interactionists who take self-interaction and subjective interpretation very seriously or for critical conflict theorists, who are interested in the relationship between personality and social structure and who often draw heavily on Freudian theory.

Meisenhelder's recent analysis of Habermas and feminism can shed some light on this question. He argues that although Habermas, like other critical theorists, holds that a core characteristic of the human being is the potential to reason, it does not occur to him to investigate human experiences of emotionality—such as the caring, affect, and solidarity within the private sphere of the family. Meisenhelder states:

> Habermas admits moral and aesthetic values into the totality of human reason but not feelings. In the end he never frees himself from the presumptive dualities of patriarchal thought. . . . His conception of reason remains formal and fails to adequately represent the experience of really existing men *and* women.[148]

Lillian Rubin, in her study of working-class families, quotes from one of her interviews which reveals the male denial of feelings and a husband's view of his wife's emotionality:

> She's like a kid sometimes, so emotional. I'm always having to reason with her, to explain things to her. If it weren't for me, nothing would happen very rational around here.[149]

Rubin then presents her analysis:

> This equation of emotional with nonrational, this inability to apprehend the logic of emotions lies at the root of much of the discontent between the sexes, and helps to make marriage the most difficult of all relationships.
>
> Her lifetime training prepares her to handle the affective, expressive side in human affairs; his, to handle the nonaffective, instrumental side. Tears, he has been taught, are for sissies; feelings, for women. A *real* man is the strong, silent type of the folklore—a guy who needs nothing from anyone, who ignores feelings and pain, who can take it on the chin without a whimper. For a

[147]Raphaela Best, *We've All Got Scars: What Boys and Girls Learn in Elementary School* (Bloomington: University of Indiana Press, 1983).

[148]See Thomas Meisenhelder, "Habermas and Feminism: The Future of Critical Theory," in Wallace, *Feminism and Sociological Theory*, p. 125.

[149]Lillian Breslow Rubin, *Worlds of Pain: Life in the Working Class Family* (New York: Basic Books, 1976), p. 117.

lifetime, much of his energy has gone into molding himself in that image—into denying his feelings, refusing to admit they exist. Without warning or preparation, he finds himself facing a wife who pleads, "Tell me your feelings." He responds with bewilderment. "What is there to tell?"[150]

The work of Hochschild and others[151] on the emotions has enormous implications for what Goffman described as the "interaction order," for when "two or more individuals are physically in another's presence" the feelings they have toward each other will have consequences for the behavior that ensues. What implications this work has for the macrosociological order has yet to be determined.

CONCLUSION

In this chapter we have discussed the basic premises and assumptions of the symbolic interactionist perspective as introduced by George Herbert Mead and his forerunners and as elaborated more recently by Herbert Blumer and Erving Goffman. The perspective's views of the self, especially Mead's stress on the "I," and discussions of self-interaction, taking the role of the other, interpretation, gestures, and symbolic meaning, lead to an emphasis on studying processes of interaction between individuals and a methodology that is primarily inductive, qualitative, and geared toward microsociological analysis. Given the interests of symbolic interactionists and the types of questions arising from these interests, we can see that the perspective is basically a social-psychological one, which focuses on Simmel's interactions among the "atoms of society." The result could be described as a "moving picture" rather than a "still" photograph of human behavior.

Symbolic interactionism, with its negative view of social structure, is certainly not considered to be in the "mainstream" of sociology. However, it has experienced a resurgence recently, with the founding of the Society for the Study of Symbolic Interactionism and the publication of a new journal, *Symbolic Interaction*. A perspective that places a primary value on subjective meaning and on process as opposed to structure, combined with a methodology that takes great pains to capture the "world of the other" as seen by that other, asks important sociological questions that cannot be answered by mainstream sociology. Symbolic interactionism can be seen as an alternative perspective providing theoretical tools which are missing in other perspectives. It therefore deserves recognition as an approach that makes important and distinctive contributions to sociology.

[150]Ibid., p. 117.

[151]See also Norman Denzin, *On Understanding Emotion* (San Francisco: Jossey-Bass, 1984), and Theodore Kemper, *A Social Interactional Theory of the Emotions* (New York: John Wiley, 1978).

VI

PHENOMENOLOGY

INTRODUCTION

Compared to the other sociological perspectives we discussed in this book, phenomenology has emerged most recently. The term "phenomenological sociology," like conflict theory, encompasses several types of sociological analysis; however, we will limit ourselves to a discussion of the two most prominent, Harold Garfinkel's ethnomethodology and Peter Berger's social reality construction.

The word *phenomenon* derives from the Greek meaning "appearance." *The Encyclopedia of Sociology* defines phenomenology as "a method in philosophy that begins with the individual and his own conscious experience and tries to avoid prior assumptions, prejudices and philosophical dogmas. Phenomenology thus examines phenomena as they are apprehended in their 'immediacy' by the social actor."[1] Suppose someone walked over to you now as you are reading this book and asked you how the object which you are reading appears to you. You would most likely label it an absurd question, because everyone knows what a book looks like. We arrive at the notion of a book through socialization, the process whereby we learn how to perceive and how to interpret the world, or as phenomenologists put it, "how to *be* in the world." If the person who asked you the absurd question had just arrived from outer space, you would probably take the question seriously and proceed to explain clearly the meaning of the term "book." Why would you respond in this way? You would do so because you would know that the visitor's social world differed from yours and you would want to help such a person learn how to *be* in your world.

Phenomenology asks us *not* to take the notions we have learned for granted, but to question them instead, to question our way of looking at and our way of being in the world. In short, this perspective asks us to assume the role of a stranger, like an extraterrestrial visitor. Phenomenological sociologists study how people define their social situations once they have suspended or "bracketed" their learned cultural notions. The basic proposition states that everyday reality is a socially constructed system of ideas which has accumulated over time and is taken for granted by group members. This perspective takes a critical stance with regard to the social order, and, in contrast to functionalism, it challenges our culturally learned ideas.

For example, phenomenologists would view the realities of woman's nature, needs, role, and place in society as systems of ideas constructed in past interactions and sustained by present on-going interaction.[2] Phenomenologists would ask, "Is it 'natural' that women, in addition to bearing children,

[1] *The Encyclopedia of Sociology* (Guilford, Connecticut: Duskin Publishing, 1974), p. 210.
[2] See Patricia M. Lengermann, Katherine M. Marconi, and Ruth A. Wallace, "Sociological Theory in Teaching Sex Roles: Marxism, Functionalism and Phenomenology," *Women's Studies International Quarterly*, 1, no. 4 (1978), 375–85.

children, also take sole responsibility for nurturing and rearing them?" "Do they have a natural 'need' to be rooted in the private sphere of the home while men's 'needs' are in the public sphere of wage work?" Contemporary feminism not only challenged these taken-for-granted ideas, but it also interjected alternative definitions of female identity and proposed other "realities" for women.[3] People who question the way their world is ordered or who find themselves in a subordinate position will acquire many insights into their situation if they put on the "lens" of this perspective.

INTELLECTUAL ROOTS: THE INFLUENCE OF EDMUND HUSSERL AND ALFRED SCHUTZ

The roots of the "youngest" of the sociological perspectives are primarily in European phenomenological philosophy, especially in the work of the German philosopher Edmund Husserl (1859–1938), who was the first to use the term *phenomenology*. Husserl defined phenomenology as interest in those things that can be directly apprehended by one's senses. This is the essential point about phenomenology: It denies that we can ever know more about things than what we experience directly through our senses. All our knowledge comes directly from these sensory "phenomena." Anything else is speculation, and Husserl argued that we should not even try to speculate.

Phenomenological sociologists consequently see the task of sociology as describing precisely how we see the world, although they emphasize that our perceptions are molded intrinsically by our concepts. They also examine the ways we come to have similar perceptions to those of others—how we put together the phenomena we experience in such a way that we all construct a similar or shared "everyday world." The most important influence on their approach, however, is less Husserl's work directly than Alfred Schutz's (1899–1959) developments of his arguments. Schutz was a social philosopher who left Germany in 1939 to escape the Nazis, took a daytime position in a New York bank to support himself, and began to teach evening courses in social philosophy at the New School for Social Research in 1943.[4] He became professor of sociology and philosophy in 1952 and taught at the New School until his death in 1959. Schutz introduced phenomenology to American sociology.

What precipitated the emergence of phenomenology? As we have

---

[3]See Dorothy Smith, *The Everyday World As Problematic: A Feminist Sociology* (Boston: Northeastern University Press, 1987). Smith's approach, a sociology based on women's experience, combines the materialist method developed by Marx and Engels with Garfinkel's ethnomethodology.

[4]See Nicholas C. Mullins, *Theories and Theory Groups in Contemporary American Sociology* (New York: Harper and Row, 1973), p. 186.

seen, Edmund Husserl wrote in the shadow of Nazism in Germany and Alfred Schutz came to the United States in order to escape the Nazi regime. Subsequently, the major American theorists, Harold Garfinkel and Peter Berger, wrote their major works during a period of social unrest in America in the 1960s, in the wake of the civil rights movement, the antiwar movement, and the contemporary women's movement. It is not surprising that a great deal of questioning about our way of looking at the world would coincide with these events. The "bracketing" or suspending of taken-for-granted assumptions by oppressed groups makes sense in such situations, and the time was ripe for the emergence of a new perspective with the conceptual tools to analyze these situations.

In his attempt to adapt Husserl's philosophy to sociology, Schutz incorporated Weber's concept of *verstehen* ('subjective understanding').[5] For Schutz, the meaning that the individual imparts to situations in everyday life is of prime importance; he puts the spotlight on the individual's own definition of the situation.

For Schutz, the definition of the situation includes the assumption that individuals draw on a common "stock of knowledge," that is, social recipes or conceptions of appropriate behavior which enable them to think of the world as made up of "types" of things like books, cars, houses, clothing, etc. Schutz' idea of the stock of knowledge is similar to Mead's "generalized other." Schutz thus views individuals as constructing a world by using the typifications (or ideal types) passed on to them by their social group.

Schutz illustrates the typification process in his discussion of the assumptions involved in mailing a letter.[6] He explains that in the mailing of a letter one takes for granted that there will be types of persons involved in processing the letter, like postal carriers, sorters, and deliverers. People who mail letters, by means of a process of self-typification, see themselves cooperating with postal workers, even though they do not know them personally. By using such "recipes" individuals are able to see the work of their everyday world as orderly, especially when the process is successful, as, for example, when the letter reaches the desired destination.

In addition, Schutz believes that the meaning one imparts to the interaction situation may be shared by the person with whom one is interacting; he calls this the "reciprocity of perspectives." For example, because the musicians in an orchestra share their meanings of the situation with the conductor, the musicians could exchange positions with the conductor and

[5]See p. 238 for a discussion of *verstehen*.

[6]Alfred Schutz, *Collected Papers I: The Problem of Social Reality* (The Hague: Martinus Nijhoff, 1962), p. 17. Schutz also corresponded with Talcott Parsons on their different points of view on a number of topics, including subjectivity. These letters provide an insight into the divergence between functionalism and phenomenology. See Richard Grathoff, ed., *The Theory of Social Action* (Bloomington: Indiana University Press, 1978).

experience the situation in the way the conductor did. In Schutz's scheme, then, shared meanings may be both assumed and experienced in the interaction situation.

Schutz says that in these situations people are acting on the basis of taken-for-granted assumptions about reality. They suspend doubts that things might be otherwise, and interaction proceeds on the assumption of the reciprocity of perspectives. Here we can detect some similarity to Mead's concept of "taking the role of the other," which Schutz also incorporated into his framework.[7] Thus, Schutz's thinking was heavily influenced by Husserl, but he was also responsible for introducing some of Weber's and Mead's ideas into phenomenological sociology.

In this chapter we will introduce two types of phenomenological sociology, both founded by students of Schutz. The first is Harold Garfinkel's ethnomethodology, and the second is Peter Berger's social construction of reality.

PART ONE
Harold Garfinkel: The Founder of Ethnomethodology

Of the current phenomenological approaches in sociology, ethnomethodology is the most prominent and the most unified.[8] Harold Garfinkel is recognized as its leading figure; since the publication in 1967 of his book *Studies in Ethnomethodology*, we have seen a proliferation in the number of sociologists who consider themselves ethnomethodologists.[9] Although it can by no means be considered a "mainstream" perspective, ethnomethodology has been influential enough to be the subject of attack in a recent presidential address of the American Sociological Association,

[7]See Chapter V.

[8]Helmut R. Wagner, "Sociologists of Phenomenological Orientations: Their Place in American Sociology," *The American Sociologist*, 10 (1975), 181. Randall Collins, for instance, classifies Talcott Parsons' work on voluntarism as the "far right" of the phenomenological world and the work of Harvey Sacks on linguistics and that of Berger and Luckmann as on the "right"; Garfinkel, Blum, McHugh, Zimmerman, and Pollner are "left." We consider the classification ambiguous, incomplete, and rather strained. Any further discussion of phenomenological categorizations is probably premature, and it would certainly distract from the aim of this chapter. (Collins, *Conflict Sociology: Toward an Explanatory Science* [New York: Academic Press, 1975], pp. 106–9.)

[9]We are aware that there are other interpretations of this perspective by ethnomethodologists, but we have decided to sidestep a discussion of the various directions and controversies among ethnomethodologists and to restrict our attention to an explication of Harold Garfinkel's ethnomethodology. See Harold Garfinkel, *Studies in Ethnomethodology* (Englewood Cliffs, N.J.: Prentice-Hall, Inc., 1967).

and this is another reason we should attempt to understand the perspective better.[10]

BACKGROUND

Born in 1917, Garfinkel completed his Ph.D. at Harvard in 1952. Aside from two years of teaching at Ohio State and a brief interim on a research project at the University of Chicago (the jury deliberation project), Garfinkel has spent his entire career at the University of California at Los Angeles, where he currently holds the title of professor emeritus. Because of Garfinkel's leadership, UCLA became a training center for ethnomethodologists. Both the University of California at Santa Barbara and the University of California at San Diego could be labeled its "branches" because of the presence of such ethnomethodologists as Aaron Cicourel, an important student of Garfinkel who was at UCSB from 1966 to 1971 and has been at UCSD since 1971. Garfinkel spent 1975–76 at the Center for Advanced Studies in the Behavioral Sciences at Stanford University, where he put together a manual of ethnomethodological studies that have been published since 1967, when his *Studies in Ethnomethodology* appeared.[11]

Garfinkel names four persons whose "writings have provided me with inexhaustible directives into the world of everyday activities."[12] They are Talcott Parsons, under whom he studied at Harvard; Alfred Schutz, whom he visited and studied under at the New School for Social Research; and the phenomenological philosophers Aron Gurwitsch and Edmund Husserl.[13] *Studies in Ethnomethodology* is replete with references to Schutz, and Garfinkel says that his own work is heavily indebted to him.

Garfinkel wanted to construct a perspective that would fill in one aspect of Parsons' theory of action, the motivated actor. He wanted to "remedy the sketchy treatment of the actor's knowledge and understanding within the voluntaristic theory."[14] Garfinkel himself attests to Parsons' influence, stating that ethnomethodology had its origins in Parsons' four-volume *Structure of Social Action*. Garfinkel says that ethnomethodology's "earliest initiatives were taken from these texts."[15] Parsons' influence relates

[10]Lewis Coser, "Presidential Address: Two Methods in Search of a Substance," *American Sociological Review*, 40, no. 6 (December 1975).

[11]Personal interview, September 1975. This book, *Ethnomethodological Studies of Work in the Discovering Sciences*, is forthcoming (London: Routledge and Kegan Paul).

[12]Garfinkel, *Studies in Ethnomethodology*, pp. ix and 31–37.

[13]Mullins, *Theories and Theory Groups*, p. 185.

[14]John Heritage, *Garfinkel and Ethnomethodology* (Cambridge, England: Polity Press, 1984), p. 9.

[15]Harold Garfinkel, "Evidence for Locally Produced, Naturally Accountable Phenomena of Order,* Logic, Reason, Meaning, Method, etc. in and as of the Essential Quiddity of Immortal Ordinary Society (I of IV): An Announcement of Studies," *Sociological Theory*, 6 (1988), 103–9.

to a point that is fundamental to both functionalism and ethnomethodology: an underlying trust as the basis of human behavior. As we will see in the following section, Garfinkel wants to break the taboo on questioning the social order and uncover the "taken-for-granted assumptions" or "myths" that are operating in the interaction situation.[16]

ETHNOMETHODOLOGY DEFINED

The beginnings of "ethnomethodology" can be traced to Harold Garfinkel's analysis of tapes of jury deliberations, which he conducted in 1945. It was when he was writing up the materials on these deliberations that he "dreamed up the notion underlying the term 'ethnomethodology.' "[17] What interested Garfinkel about the data was "how the jurors knew what they were doing in doing the work of jurors"; in other words, he was interested in "such things as jurors' use of some kind of knowledge of the way in which the organized affairs of the society operated—knowledge that they drew on easily, that they required of each other"[18] in doing the work of jurors. This is the concern underlying the practice of ethnomethodology.

The term itself was coined when, working with the Yale cross-cultural files, Garfinkel came to a section entitled "ethnobotany, ethnophysiology, ethnophysics." It occurred to him that on the jury deliberation project he was "faced with jurors who were doing methodology," and he decided that the label that seemed adequate to convey the notion was *ethnomethodology*, because "ethno" refers to the "availability to a member of common-sense knowledge of his society as common-sense knowledge of the 'whatever.' "[19] In the case of the jurors, it was their use of available commonsense (as opposed to scientific) knowledge of what was expected of jurors, as a result of which they were able to be jurors, that interested Garfinkel. -

If we translate the "ethno" part of the term as "members" (of a group) or "folk" or "people," then ethnomethodology can be defined as members' methods of making sense of their social world. Ethnomethodology's interest is in how people make sense of everyday activities. Obviously a lot of everyday activity is normally taken for granted, so the question of "making sense" of it is not even raised. Indeed, if people take reality for granted, why should they attempt to make sense of it? Garfinkel's approach, by contrast, is to treat as problematic what is taken for granted in order to understand the commonsense everyday world.

Suppose you were sitting in a classroom in the middle of a semester,

[16]See Collins, *Conflict Sociology*, pp. 106–7 for a discussion of Parsons and Garfinkel.
[17]See Roy Turner, ed., *Ethnomethodology: Selected Readings* (Baltimore: Penguin Books, 1974), p. 16.
[18]Ibid.
[19]Ibid.

waiting for class to begin as usual. The professor entered the room and, without speaking, proceeded to perform some seemingly nonsensical actions, such as placing sheets of newspaper on the floor, drawing obscure symbols on the blackboard, raising and lowering the window shades repeatedly and unnecessarily, and the like.[20] How would you and other students describe the professor's actions? No doubt many students would attempt to "make sense of" this highly unusual situation. In other words, students would look for ways to describe this behavior as an unusual example of behavior that is recognized as normal and familiar to Americans, in the way that placing pieces of paper on desks is quickly interpreted as meaning that a test is on the way.

In fact, this was the result in a number of experiments conducted by one of the authors. Some students suggested that the professor was "doing free form" or "attempting to evoke reactions"; one student said the professor was "performing mysterious rituals."

What the professor was doing was making the taken-for-granted situation of coming into class very obviously problematic; she was shattering the social world of the students. What the students were doing was "assembling the appearance of social order" in that situation; they were attempting to "put it all back together." It is to this process that ethnomethodology directs its attention. It puts the taken-for-granted everyday world on center stage and asks, "How do people present to others an orderly social scene?" or "How do people render scenes or situations intelligible or reasonable?"

From the classroom experiment we can see that the students interpreted the rather bizarre behavior of the professor in ways that gave meaning to the situation for them. They devised interpretations that illustrated some underlying order, interpretations that made it clear to themselves and others that what they experienced was comprehensible and in line with the underlying rules and conventions they shared with each other about a professor's behavior. Ethnomethodology examines the methods by which people do this. By "making sense" of events in terms of a preconceived order for society, people create a world that is indeed ordered.

Ethnomethodology is not simply a new methodology that can solve problems raised by traditional theoretical perspectives. It is a theoretical perspective that focuses on a completely different set of problems from those of most sociological inquiry. In setting out to understand these problems, ethnomethodologists use some methods that are similar to those used by other perspectives and some that are different.

Garfinkel disagrees with Durkheim's view that social facts, the subject matter of sociology for Durkheim, have objective reality, are *sui generis*, and are "out there somewhere." Instead, Garfinkel says, ethnomethodology sees the objective reality of social facts as an "ongoing accomplishment of

---

[20]We are indebted to Robert Moran for this idea.

the concerted activities of everyday life."[21] By this he means that in everyday situations individuals invoke or recognize social facts, such as taken-for-granted norms or values, that interpret the meaning of the situation for them. When they "make sense" of the situation by recognizing implicit social norms, individuals are constructing the social reality. In other words, they are ordering their experiences so that they are in line with what we consider the everyday social world to be like. Garfinkel proclaims that ethnomethodological studies "analyze everyday activities as members' methods for making those same activities visibly-rational-and-reportable-for-all-practical-purposes, that is, 'accountable' as organizations of commonplace everyday activities."[22]

What Garfinkel is saying, essentially, is that ethnomethodology denies the functionalists' suggestion that social facts have a reality of their own that impinges on the individual. Suppose we take as an example the "role expectations" of a professor. Functionalists believe these include preparing and giving lectures, reading and grading exams and papers, engaging in research, and publishing books and articles. These expectations "impinge on" the professor.

By contrast, ethnomethodologists do not treat order as "out there somewhere," created by society independently of the individual experiencing and living within it. Neither does ethnomethodology study how role expectations are created in the interaction process, as does symbolic interactionism. Instead, ethnomethodology studies the process by which people invoke certain taken-for-granted rules about behavior with which they interpret an interaction situation and make it meaningful. To ethnomethodology, in fact, the interpretive process itself is a phenomenon for investigation. In the professor's case, ethnomethodology would be concerned with which rules professors invoke as they go about doing the work of professors. Thus, for functionalists, norms and values are explicit and "out there" acting on the individual; for symbolic interactionists, norms and values emerge from the interaction process; but for ethnomethodologists, the origin of norms and values is not of primary interest. Instead, their interest is in the process by which human beings interact and prove to each other that they are following norms and values.

Schutz's essay on the "stranger" may help to clarify the area of social life that is of interest for ethnomethodology. Schutz discusses:

> the typical situation in which a stranger finds himself in his attempt to interpret the cultural pattern of a social group which he approaches and to orient himself within it. For our present purposes the term "stranger" shall mean an adult individual of our times and civilization who tries to be permanently

---

[21]Garfinkel, *Studies in Ethnomethodology*, p. vii. See also Warren Handel, *Ethnomethodology: How People Make Sense* (Englewood Cliffs, N.J.: Prentice-Hall, Inc., 1982).

[22]Ibid.

accepted or at least tolerated by the group which he approaches. The out-standing example for the social situation under scrutiny is that of the immi-grant, and the following analyses are, as a matter of convenience, worked out with this instance in view. But by no means is their validity restricted to this special case. The applicant for membership in a closed club, the prospective bridegroom who wants to be admitted to the girl's family, the farmer's son who enters college, the city-dweller who settles in a rural environment, the "selectee" who joins the army, the family of the war worker who moves into a boom town—all are strangers according to the definition just given, although in these cases the typical "crisis" that the immigrant undergoes may assume milder forms or even be entirely absent.[23]

Later, Schutz says that the stranger becomes "essentially the man who has to place in question nearly everything that seems to be unquestionable to the members of the approached group." Thus the situation of the stranger is one that is ripe for ethnomethodological analysis; it is the per-fect "problematic" situation.[24]

Schutz's work on the existence of "seen but unnoticed background experiences" or the "taken-for-granted world" is, as we have noted, the cornerstone of ethnomethodology. He wondered how these background expectancies, or implicit rules, could be brought to light. His suggestion was that somehow one must take the role of a stranger, a foreigner, someone who is unfamiliar with the "taken-for-granted" aspects of everyday life, so that those aspects become problematic. Similarly, Garfinkel's aim is to un-derstand commonsense everyday situations by treating them as problem-atic. Following Schutz, he argues that a "special motive" is necessary if the "world known in common and taken for granted" is to be brought in question.[25] Only when sociologists can estrange themselves from the "atti-tudes of everyday life," as Schutz puts it, can they discover the expectancies that give commonplace scenes their familiar, life-as-usual character. As we will see later, the "special motive" is exemplified in Garfinkel's experiments, in which he attempts to "make trouble" or "violate the scene," as the profes-sor did in the example at the beginning of this section.

It should be clear by now that ethnomethodology does not aim to "explain" human behavior or to show, for example, why places and genera-tions vary in their suicide and divorce rates or why religion "really" exists. The emphasis in this perspective is on description, and the subject matter—people's methods of making sense of their social world—poses different questions from those asked by traditional sociology.

---

[23]See Alfred Schutz, "The Stranger: An Essay in Social Psychology," in Open University, *School and Society: A Sociological Reader* (London: Routledge and Kegan Paul in association with Open University Press, 1971), p. 32. See also Simmel's essay on the stranger in Kurt Wolff, trans. and ed., *The Sociology of Georg Simmel* (Glencoe, Ill.: The Free Press, 1950), p. 402.

[24]Ibid., p. 34.

[25]Garfinkel, *Studies in Ethnomethodology*, p. 37.

Dorothy Smith's work is an example of this "nontraditional" approach to sociology. Her call for a woman-centered sociology could, in itself, be described as a "violation of the scene" for more traditional sociologists. The following description of her approach reveals her debt to Garfinkel:

> It proposes an insider's sociology, that is, a systematically developed consciousness of society from within. . . . Beginning from where subject is actually located returns us to a social world arising in and known in and through the ongoing actual activities of actual people.[26]

Ethnomethodologists are interested in the interpretations people use to make sense of social settings. Hugh Mehan provides us with a graphic illustration of the incorrect assessments made about students by teachers who interpret test results without examining the children's own perceptions and understandings of the testing materials. As Mehan describes:

> The California Reading Test consists of a number of words, sentences and paragraphs along the left side of the page contained in an arrow which points to a series of three pictures arrayed along the right side of the page. The child is told to "mark the picture that goes best with the words in the arrow."
>
> One question has the word "fly" in the arrow pointing to pictures of an elephant, a bird, and a dog. The correct answer to this (obviously) is "the bird." The answer sheets of many of the first grade children showed that they had chosen the elephant alone or along with the bird as a response to that question. When Mehan asked them why they chose that answer, they replied: "That's Dumbo." Dumbo, of course, is Walt Disney's flying elephant, well known as an animal that flies, to children who watch television and read children's books.[27]

Mehan concludes that when children apply the word *fly* to an elephant, this may be "evidence to the tester that the child cannot abstract the similar features of objects and has 'impoverished' conceptual abilities. But this conclusion denies the actual complexity and richness of the child's day to day lived life." According to the way the tester views and interprets the test, the child has shown an inability to use some of the background skills of conceptual thought. But the children, who do not yet necessarily know the "right way" to answer the test, may have made sense of it—differently, yes, but on the basis of conceptual skills nonetheless. Incorrect answers, therefore, can result from a discrepancy between adult and student views of the world. Rather than take the question and the responses on the test sheet at

---

[26]Dorothy Smith, "Sociological Theory: Methods of Writing Patriarchy," pp. 34–64, in Wallace, ed., *Feminism and Sociological Theory* (Newbury Park: Sage, 1989).

[27]Hugh Mehan, "Ethnomethodology and Education," in D. O'Shea, ed., *Sociology of the School and Schooling* (Washington, D.C.: National Institute of Education, 1974), p. 20. See also Hugh Mehan, "Structuring School Structure," *Harvard Educational Review*, 48 (1978), 50–51.

their "face value," as the teachers did, Mehan probed for the way the student interpreted the question and the answer. The child's response told Mehan what meaning that particular student got out of the situation; in a real sense, the student was "accounting for" a previous action by showing how she or he had made sense of the task. This notion of "accounting" is one to which Garfinkel has devoted considerable attention.

ACCOUNTING

Accounting is people's ability to announce to themselves and others the meaning they are getting out of a situation. Accounting involves both language and meaning; people are constantly giving linguistic or verbal accounts as they explain their actions. Garfinkel urges ethnomethodologists to call attention to reflexive practices: "by his accounting practices the member makes familiar, commonplace activities of everyday life recognizable *as* familiar commonplace activities; . . . on each occasion that an account of human activities is used . . . they [should] be recognized for 'another first time' . . ."[28]

For instance, when a child is asked to "tell about" his or her own creative production and then proceeds to interpret the figures, shapes, and colors in the drawing to another person, the child is giving an "account." If an art teacher is truly interested in the student's own interpretation of a drawing, that teacher will carefully phrase the request as something like, "Tell me about it," so as to invite an interpretation from the student's own world of meaning; from the "account" will emerge the student's meaning.[29]

Much of the accounting that people "make" to each other about their behavior is done in an abbreviated form, because commonplace conversation assumes a "common understanding" of many things that are "left out" of the conversation. Terms that require mutual understanding and that are not explicated verbally Garfinkel calls "indexical expressions." One of the assignments Garfinkel gives to his students is to "report common conversations by writing on the left side of a sheet what the parties actually said and on the right side what they and their partners (in the conversation) understand that they were talking about.[30] The result is that much more is written on the right-hand side than the left-hand side. What is "left out" on the left-hand side is related, as Garfinkel puts it, to "the previous course of the conversation, or the particular relationship of actual or potential interac-

[28]Garfinkel, *Studies in Ethnomethodology*, p. 9. See also John Heritage's excellent chapter entitled "Accounts and Accounting," in his *Garfinkel and Ethnomethodology*.

[29]See Marvin B. Scott and Stanford M. Lyman's much cited article, "Accounts," *American Sociological Review*, 33 (February 1968), 46–62.

[30]Garfinkel, *Studies in Ethnomethodology*, p. 38.

tion that exists between user and auditor."[31] Garfinkel refers to this practice of "filling in" the meanings to talk as the "et cetera" principle; it is a "shorthand" way of talking.

Accounts and meanings in any situation are largely dependent on the nature of the situation. Garfinkel points out that the meanings two people attach to any interaction are linked to its location and time, the persons present, the purpose or intention of the actors, their knowledge of each other's intentions—all of which are aspects of indexicality. Garfinkel is saying that social interaction is explicable only in context, and contextual relevance is at the heart of ethnomethodology's concerns.

Garfinkel mentions a related issue, the "sanctioned properties of common discourse."[32] This refers to people's expectation that there will be no interference with the conduct of everyday affairs in the form of questions about what is "really said." In other words it is expected and required that people *will* understand plain, everyday talk so that common conversational affairs can be conducted without interference. To illustrate the "sanctioned character" of these properties, Garfinkel presents the following experiment: "Students were instructed to engage an acquaintance or a friend in an ordinary conversation and, without indicating that what the experimenter was asking was in any way unusual, to insist that the person clarify the sense of his commonplace remarks."[33]

Below is one student's account of this experiment:

> The subject was telling the experimenter, a member of the subject's car pool, about having had a flat tire while going to work the previous day.
> (S) I had a flat tire.
> (E) What do you mean, you had a flat tire?
> She appeared momentarily stunned. Then she answered in a hostile way. "What do you mean, 'What do you mean?' A flat tire is a flat tire. That is what I meant. Nothing special. What a crazy question."[34]

This account is a good illustration of "sanctioned character" because the subject actually became hostile. Also, she attempted to "make sense" of the situation by treating it as a "crazy question." Obviously, there are many occasions when the question "What do you mean?" is perfectly acceptable and, in fact, is expected for purposes of clarification. But there are other occasions, like the one just described, when the question becomes a "violation of the scene" for the subject. The student actually "made trouble" by questioning indexical expressions based on mutual understanding, and the question introduced a sense of distrust into the situation. The subject at-

[31]Ibid., p. 40.
[32]Ibid., p. 41.
[33]Ibid., p. 42.
[34]Ibid.

tempted to make order of a disorderly scene. Her announcement that it was a "crazy question" was her way of assembling an orderly scene.

It is important to study how people build "accounts" of social action while doing that action, because making sense of a situation is involved in giving linguistic accounts of social interaction. (As Garfinkel puts it, "To do interaction is to tell interaction.") It is not surprising, therefore, that many ethnomethodologists are engaged in conversational analysis, for these endeavors are at the heart of ethnomethodology's concerns.

For instance, Fishman analyzed conversational activities of couples in their homes from the perspective of the socially structured power relationships between men and women. She found several general patterns. For instance, both men and women regarded topics introduced by women as tentative, and many of these were quickly dropped. By contrast, topics introduced by men were treated as topics to be pursued, and they were seldom rejected.[35]

Roy Turner has made the point that exchanges of utterances can be regarded as "doing things with words." As examples he cites the "I do" of a wedding ceremony, the "I apologize" after stepping on someone's toe, and the "I'll bet you five dollars that Chris Evert will win." Turner argues that these utterances are clearly activities.[36] Because accounts are in the form of "talk," descriptive sentences of actual conversations and respondents' own interpretation of conversations, word-for-word, are important data for ethnomethodologists. This is illustrated by the methods used by sociologists who are "doing ethnomethodology," to which we now turn.

DOING ETHNOMETHODOLOGY

The various methods that have been used by ethnomethodologists to gather data for analysis include open-ended, or depth, interviews; participant observation; videotaping; the documentary method of interpretation; and ethnomethodological "experiments," often called "breaching experiments." The meaning that the individual imparts to everyday life situations is of prime importance to ethnomethodologists. Therefore, we can expect to see them conducting open-ended depth interviews with people, because this is an excellent way of gathering data that convey subjective meaning. Two projects employing this methodology were Garfinkel's jury deliberation study and Mehan's school testing study. Garfinkel had taped sessions of the actual jury deliberations, but the personal interviews with the jurors revealed the sources of the knowledge that they drew on in order to do the

[35]Pamela M. Fishman, "Interaction: The Work Women Do," *Social Problems*, 25 (1978), 397–406.

[36]Roy Turner, in Jack D. Douglas, ed., *Understanding Everyday Life* (Chicago: Aldine, 1970), p. 170.

work of jurors. Thus, Garfinkel's interviews with jurors revealed the follow-ing about how the jurors knew what they were doing in doing the work of jurors:

> Jurors learned the official line from various places: from the juror's hand-book; from the instructions they received from the court; from the procedure of the *voir dire* when jurors were invited by the court to disqualify themselves if they could find for themselves reasons why they could not act in this fash-ion. They learned it from court personnel; they learned it from what jurors told each other, from TV, and from the movies. Several jurors got a quick tutoring by their high school children who had taken courses in civics.[37]

In like manner, Mehan used personal interviews with students who had been tested to get at their own interpretations of the test questions as well as their own meaning of their responses to the test questions. Another example is the case study of a transsexual reported by Garfinkel in "Passing and the Managed Achievement of Sex Status in an Intersexed Person."[38] Most of the data presented there were gleaned from thirty-five hours of tape-recorded conversations with Agnes, a nineteen-year-old girl raised as a boy, who was constantly experiencing the risks and uncertainties involved in learning to act and feel like a woman. Agnes learned from her fiancé's direct admonitions to her and from his critiques of other women that she should not insist on having things her way and that she should not offer her opinions or claim equality with men. From her roommates and other women friends Agnes learned "the value of passive acceptance as a desir-able female trait."[39]

Depth interviewing combined with participant observation can high-light the problematic areas of an individual's everyday life, areas that might otherwise have never been brought to light. For instance, in his study *Passing On*, David Sudnow says that his ethnomethodological perspective enabled him to spot the ambiguity of the bereaved status and thus to highlight the "essentially troublesome character of the normative elements in grief."[40] Sudnow notes:

> Bereaved persons apparently have considerable difficulty in their manage-ment of the properties of their own situation. They frequently don't know at what point they should undertake activities typically engaged in prior to death, and a large part of their difficulty derives from the sheer fact of their known status as a bereaved, which leaves them open to being treated sorrow-

---

[37]Garfinkel, *Studies in Ethnomethodology*, p. 110.

[38]Ibid., pp. 116–85.

[39]Ibid., p. 147.

[40]David Sudnow, *Passing On: The Social Organization of Dying* (Englewood Cliffs, N.J.: Prentice-Hall, Inc., 1967), p. 140.

fully no matter how they might conduct themselves. It is felt that only with time do they lose their status as bereaved in the eyes of others and cease to encounter treatments as a grievous person, and that time can often come long after they have ceased regarding themselves in that fashion.[41]

Functionalists like Parsons, for instance, maintain that grief is functional for the release and reduction of tension, and they assume that the roles of the bereaved and those around the bereaved are societally clear-cut. Ethnomethodologists like Sudnow may be revealing to us the limits of the culturally created role. There are wide gaps in the cultural prescription, and individuals experience the gaps very sharply. For example, Sudnow's research shows that the bereaved person may be anxiously asking, "How am I supposed to act here?"

Another method used by sociologists who are "doing ethnomethodology" is called the "documentary method of interpretation." Garfinkel credits Mannheim with the label and quotes his definition, as the search for "an identical homologous pattern underlying a vast variety of totally different realizations of meaning." Garfinkel says:

> The method consists of treating an actual appearance as "the document of," as "pointing to," as "standing on behalf of" a presupposed underlying pattern. Not only is the underlying pattern derived from its individual documentary evidences, but the individual documentary evidences, in their turn, are interpreted on the basis of "what is known" about the underlying pattern.[42]

To Garfinkel, the documentary method is something people are constantly using as they continually interpret and reinterpret each others' behavior and look for underlying patterns. One use of the documentary method by an ethnomethodologist is found in a study of the convict code by D. Lawrence Wieder.[43] As a participant observer at a halfway house, Wieder—after several months and many conversations with residents—detected a code that was operative. The code included prohibitions against snitching, copping out, taking advantage of other residents, messing with other residents, and trusting staff, as well as positive injunctions to share what you had to help and show loyalty to other residents. "Telling the code" did not simply describe, analyze, and explain a situation in that environment. It was also the way residents actually guided conduct. For instance, when a resident terminated a conversation by saying, "You know I won't snitch," he was not only negatively sanctioning the prior conduct of the person with whom he was interacting and thereby terminating the conversa-

---

[41]Ibid., p. 137.
[42]Garfinkel, *Studies in Ethnomethodology*, p. 78.
[43]See Turner, *Ethnomethodology: Selected Readings*, pp. 144–72.

tion; he was also pointing out potential consequences if his associate persisted. Thus, "telling the code" was extremely persuasive.

Wieder describes an instance of the use of the documentary method:

> An example of the use of this method is provided by the interpretation of a remark I overheard during my first week at halfway house. I passed a resident who was wandering through the halls after the committee meetings on Wednesday night. He said to the staff and all others within hearing, "Where can I find that meeting where I can get an overnight pass?" On the basis of what I had already learned, I understood him to be saying, "I'm not going to that meeting because I'm interested in participating in the program of halfway house. I'm going to that meeting just because I would like to collect the reward of an overnight pass and for no other reason. I'm not a kiss-ass. Everyone who is in hearing distance should understand that I'm not kissing up to staff. My behavior really is in conformity with the code, though without hearing this (reference to an overnight pass), you might think otherwise."[44]

Wieder continues,

> I thereby collected another "piece" of talk which, when put together with utterances I had heard up to that point (which permitted me to see the "sense" of this remark) and used with utterances I had yet to collect, was employed by me to formulate the general maxim, "Show your loyalty to the residents."[45]

Wieder explains that to be able to see an utterance like that as an expression of an underlying moral order, he had to know some of the particulars of that underlying order to begin with, so his participant observation and interviews with residents were crucial. An example of the everyday use of the documentary method is presented by Jeffrey Alexander. "Reporters," he says, "employ the documentary method in their own perceptions of events, and the products of their investigations document the events for their readers."[46]

A final method, or way of "doing ethnomethodology," is to engage in an ethnomethodological "experiment" or "breaching experiment," in which researchers disrupt ordinary activity, or, as Garfinkel puts it, "violate the scene." When they do this, the researchers are interested in what the subjects do and what they look to in order to give the situation an appearance of

[44]Ibid., p. 160.

[45]Ibid.

[46]Jeffrey C. Alexander, "The Mass News Media in Systemic, Historical and Comparative Perspective," in Elihu Katz and T. Szecsko, eds., *Mass Media and Social Change* (London: Sage, 1981), pp. 17–51.

order, or to "make sense" of the situation.[47] The professor's experiment with her class, which we mentioned at the beginning of this section, is an example of such an experiment.

However, although some ethnomethodologists find ways to "make trouble" themselves so that they can study how people attempt to bring order out of chaos—and many of Garfinkel's own student assignments are this type of endeavor—we would like to enter a note of caution. We suggest that a rather acute sensitivity is required for researchers who decide to "violate the scene" and thus "create" ethnomethodological data. For example, when one of the authors gave Garfinkel's "boarder" assignment to her students, there were some disturbing results. To summarize briefly, in this assignment the students were to spend "from fifteen minutes to an hour in their homes imagining that they were boarders and acting out this assumption. They were instructed to conduct themselves in a circumspect and polite fashion. They were to avoid getting personal, to use formal address, to speak only when spoken to."[48]

A distressing result we found with our own students is related to the question of sensitivity and trust. One of the students who attempted to complete the boarder assignment was a recently divorced woman with two young children. The children were so threatened by the shattering of their world at home when the mother began to act out the boarder role that the mother ended the experiment immediately. However, it took her at least a month to reassure the children that their world was not shattered; she went to great lengths to prove herself with them after that incident, until they finally came to the point where they felt they could trust her again. In retrospect she felt that it was too soon after their father's departure from the home. When the mother became a boarder, she was, in a sense, leaving the children also.

Garfinkel's concept of trust explains how people comply with a certain order of events and is, as we have seen, close to Parsons' idea of shared normative expectations. How do people perceive and interpret their daily lives and how do objects and events and facts come to be seen as normal, as making sense? Garfinkel's answer is "trust." That is, rules are ambiguous, and they are perceived and interpreted differently; but the actor "trusts" the environment in the face of this uncertainty.[49]

The notion of trust is an important element in the incident with the divorced mother and her children. Their reaction to her taking on the role

---

[47]We have found, incidentally, that students tend to get a better grasp of what ethnomethodology is all about by completing some of the experiments and/or assignments mentioned by Garfinkel. (See especially the experiments on pp. 38, 42, 47, 79, and 85 in *Studies in Ethnomethodology*.)

[48]Garfinkel, *Studies in Ethnomethodology*, p. 47.

[49]Aaron V. Cicourel, *Method and Measurement in Sociology* (New York: The Free Press, 1964), p. 206.

of boarder should underscore the complexities involved in the decision to "violate the scene." Our position is that certain ethical questions should be addressed in advance, well before the ethnomethodologists go out into the field to "make trouble."

The ways ethnomethodologists "do ethnomethodology" underscore the differences between what they do, how they go about doing it, and the way other sociologists do their work. The differences between ethnomethodology and symbolic interactionism are particularly interesting, since both are inductive social-psychological perspectives limited primarily to the microsociological level, and both use qualitative data.

METHODOLOGICAL COMPARISONS

Like symbolic interactionism, ethnomethodology is a social-psychological approach concerned with individuals rather than roles and social structures. However, its questions are different from those of symbolic interactionism. Cicourel points out that notions like Cooley's "looking-glass self" and Thomas's "definition of the situation" presuppose that meanings can be accepted as self-evident. What ethnomethodology is interested in, according to Cicourel, is the properties of meanings, or the structure of the "rules of the game." The ethnomethodological question is, "How do the rules of conduct (or the rules of the game) inform the actors about the nature of their environment?" Or, as Cicourel puts it, "How does the actor go about making sense of his environment in socially acceptable ways?"[50]

Though the methods used by symbolic interactionism and ethnomethodology are essentially the same, they are used in a different way because ethnomethodology asks different questions. Ethnomethodologists, for instance, are constantly seeking situations where they can analyze subjects who are "making sense" of a situation—situations in which meaning is "problematic." What are obvious places for such phenomena? Many data would be available to any researcher who could follow immigrants around during their first few weeks in a new country. The same could be said for the first few weeks in a college student's campus life. Places where new or unexpected situations occur frequently (like the wards frequented by David Sudnow, where announcements of deaths were made) are also rich in ethnomethodological data.

Let us recall the example of the baseball player and Mead's "generalized other," which we discussed in Chapter V. Mead's analysis dealt with the ability of the player to have the mind-set of all the other players on the team. Thus the player on first base would automatically know the meaning of the situation regardless of whether a fly, a strike, or a walk occurred at

[50]Ibid., p. 198.

home plate. Ethnomethodologists view the meaning of such a situation as problematic. Someone working from an ethnomethodological perspective would be more interested in the ways players "make sense of" the situation, as evidenced by their reactions when the umpire or another player acts unexpectedly, than in what was going on in the minds of the players. Ethnomethodology asks, What methods would the player use in constructing and maintaining a sense of order?

Sudnow explicitly points to this problematic stance as an important difference between symbolic interactionism and ethnomethodology. He contrasts his own study of death and dying with that of Glaser and Strauss (*Awareness of Dying*), which we discussed in Chapter V, and states:

> Their analysis is not treated as a problematic phenomenon. Their central interest, of considerable social-psychological importance, is the management of information in interaction. . . . I have found it necessary, being less concerned with interaction between staff and patient and more concerned with the organization of ward activities to regard the very phenomenon of dying as troublesome, an understanding of its sense requiring location of those practices which its use warrants.[51]

Sudnow adds that he feels that, from an organizational perspective, awareness of dying is irrelevant for a considerable number of people. If one is interested, as ethnomethodologists are, in studies of "naturally organized activities of an everyday nature," then the degree of the patient's awareness of dying is, for ethnomethodologists, not important. What *is* important to Sudnow is how people in the ward "make sense" of a dying situation—that is, the ways all the people involved present to the world an orderly social scene on the ward.

The differences in approach are again apparent if we recall the experiment in which students were instructed to bargain with a sales clerk for merchandise that had a standardized price.[52] This is another of the experiments Garfinkel uses, although when we discussed it in Chapter V, we did not identify it with him. What was Garfinkel's focus in this experiment? Quoting Parsons, Garfinkel argues that because of the "internalization" of the standardized expectancy of the "institutionalized one price rule," that is, because of "background expectancies," student-customers would be fearful and shamed, and sales clerks would be anxious and angry. (An important piece of contextual information is the location of this experiment. It took place in the United States rather than in Mexico, for instance, where the standardized expectation is bargaining.) Though many of Garfinkel's students *were* fearful, many of those who completed six bargaining episodes learned that they could bargain successfully and planned to do so in the

---

[51]David Sudnow, *Passing On*, pp. 62–63, fn. 2.
[52]Garfinkel, *Studies in Ethnomethodology*, pp. 68–70.

future, thus illustrating that the "internalization of the one price rule" was, in fact, problematic. In this respect they were constructing a new social reality for themselves and for the merchants.

As we stated in Chapter V, the symbolic interactionist perspective would concentrate instead on the self-interaction of the sales clerk and on what the sales clerk was "saying to herself" as she confronted this surprising situation. The sales clerk's definition of the situation and its meaning for her would be the focus for symbolic interactionism; all Garfinkel says about the clerk is, "A few showed anxiety; occasionally one got angry."[53] Ethnomethodology would want to know what methods or "accounting practices" the sales clerks look to in order to give this situation a semblance of order. Do they ask the student-customer questions; impugn motives; consult an oracle, a god, or an astrology calendar; ask for a repeat of the request; label the student-customer crazy; or simply ignore the incident? The taken-for-granted, or the contextual, features of the situation would certainly be a central part of the ethnomethodological interpretation of the action. Since Garfinkel emphasizes the fact that meanings are situationally dependent— that is, that interaction is characterized by indexicality—such contextual features as the location and time of the interaction between the sales clerk and customer, the persons present during the incident, and the sales clerk's knowledge of the intentions of the customer would have to be "fleshed out" to get to the meaning of the situation.

Basically, both perspectives deal with qualitative data, but neither would argue that quantitative data has no value. Some, like Cicourel, are known for their sophisticated use of quantitative data. In his article "The School as a Mechanism of Social Differentiation," Cicourel employs such "hard" data as SCAT scores and grade-point averages in his analysis of school counselors' ratings and student achievement types, and he shows that the student's progress is contingent upon the interpretations, judgments, and action of school personnel.[54] However, Cicourel attacks the overconfident stance of the survey researcher when he says: "The nature of the inferred role of the other is a problem seldom addressed by sociologists. (For example, how does the subject decide the meaning of questionnaire items?)"[55]

Questions like this are important for those who deal only with "hard" data. You may recall that we discuss the problem of misinterpretation of test items in the study of school children by Mehan.

---

[53] Ibid., p. 69.

[54] Aaron V. Cicourel and John I. Kitsuse, "The School as a Mechanism of Social Differentiation," in Jerome Karabel and A. H. Halsey, eds., *Power and Ideology in Education* (New York: Oxford University Press, 1977), pp. 282–92, from Aaron V. Cicourel and John I. Kitsuse, *The Educational Decision-Makers* (New York: Bobbs-Merrill, 1963).

[55] Cicourel, *Method and Measurement in Sociology*, p. 212.

Like Blumer,[56] Cicourel raises serious questions about measurement systems in use in sociology. He says that even the written word is "subject to the differential perception and interpretation of actors variously distributed in the social structures."[57] Moreover, quantitative analysis leaves out what Cicourel calls the "inner horizon" of subjective social action as outlined by Weber; instead it concentrates on the "outer horizon," or distributions like occupational prestige scales or social class rankings. The "inner horizon," which both symbolic interactionism and ethnomethodology highlight, includes "idiomatic expressions, course of action motives, institutional and innovational language"—all of which are unclarified in the "outer horizon" of distributions.[58] Cicourel says that without the inner horizon, social research is a "closed enterprise rather than an open search for knowledge relative to a given era."[59]

A good example of the value of the inner horizon is given by Sudnow in *Passing On* when he discusses the counting of deaths. He mentions the value the hospital administrators place on a general demographic inventory of deaths, but he notes that the ward personnel do not add up the daily death counts in any systematic way. However, rather special varieties of death are not only counted but remembered in some detail; these include suicides, death from barium enema exams, deaths of very young children, mothers who die in childbirth, and patients who die during the course of a doctor's routine morning round. What Sudnow brings to our attention are noteworthy deaths, "those which take place in settings where death is uncommon, those which result from accidents or diagnostic and treatment errors, and those which result in the very young patient."[60] In other words, these are the deaths that don't "make sense" and that are correspondingly ripe for ethnomethodological analysis, since they offer the possibility of learning how people manage the discrepancies between what is expected or appropriate and their own unsettling experiences.

As will be apparent from its stress on participation and the "inner horizon," ethnomethodology also resembles symbolic interactionism in that it must deal with researchers' possible bias as they interpret the subjective data they have collected. To his credit, Sudnow admits that his descriptions are made by a middle-class observer; he concludes that ethnography is "continually plagued by the import of such descriptive biases."[61] The problem of bias, of course, must be dealt with by all researchers, no matter what perspective they espouse. However, the bias is probably more "out front"

[56]See Chapter V.
[57]Cicourel, *Method and Measurement in Sociology*, p. 221.
[58]Ibid., p. 223.
[59]Ibid., p. 224.
[60]Sudnow, *Passing On*, pp. 40–41.
[61]Ibid., p. 176.

with ethnomethodologists, because they tend to become practitioners in a deeper sense than the other perspectives, so the danger may be more acute.

Finally, both ethnomethodologists and symbolic interactionists use participant observation, case studies, depth interviews, and biographies as methodological techniques. However, in discussing participant observations, Garfinkel stresses the role of the researcher as "practitioner" and emphasizes the participant over the observer's role. He says that researchers must be part of the world they are studying and must know it well.[62] Another way of putting it is to say that ethnomethodology is involved in "studies of activities, not theories about activities."[63] As Psathas describes it, it is like learning how to swim. Though a person can learn a lot from reading books about swimming, the only way to become a swimmer is to do it, to get in the water and swim. We sense that what ethnomethodologists are really saying is that to know what ethnomethodology is you must "do" ethnomethodology.

PART TWO
Peter Berger: The Social Construction of Reality

BACKGROUND

Another branch of phenomenological sociology is represented by the work of Peter Berger. Born in 1929 in Vienna, Austria, Berger earned his B.A. at Wagner College in 1949 and his M.A. and Ph.D. in 1950 and 1954 at the New School for Social Research, where he studied under Alfred Schutz. Subsequently, he taught at the Hartford Seminary Foundation, the New School for Social Research, Rutgers, and Boston College. Currently he is University Professor at Boston University.

The theoretical underpinnings for Berger's work appear in *The Social Construction of Reality* (1966) which he coauthored with Thomas Luckmann. Much of Berger's writing has focused on the sociology of religion, and here his most important work is *The Sacred Canopy* (1969). Berger's interest in religion is not accidental; he studied for a time at Lutheran Theological Seminary in Philadelphia and at Yale Divinity School. A past president of the Society for the Scientific Study of Religion, Berger has published numerous articles and a half dozen books on religious topics.[64] He has also

[62]Personal Interview, September 1975.

[63]See George Psathas, "Misinterpreting Ethnomethodology." Paper presented at American Sociological Association annual meeting, New York, 1976, p. 5.

[64]For example, *The Noise of Solemn Assemblies*, *The Sacred Canopy*, *Rumor of Angels*, and *The Heretical Imperative*.

developed an interest in the area of social change, as is evidenced in his books *The Homeless Mind* (1973) and *Pyramids of Sacrifice* (1975). His most recent work, coauthored with his wife, Brigitte Berger, is *The War over the Family* (1983). We will look first at the key concepts of Berger's theory and then at some applications of his phenomenological position.

KEY CONCEPTS

In *The Social Construction of Reality*, Berger and Luckmann take a sociology of knowledge approach. They focus on the "processes by which *any* body of 'knowledge' comes to be socially accepted *as* 'reality.' "[65] By "reality construction" they mean the process whereby people continuously create, through their actions and interactions, a shared reality that is experienced as objectively factual and subjectively meaningful. They assume that everyday reality is a socially constructed system in which people bestow a certain order on everyday phenomena, a reality which has both subjective and objective elements. By subjective they mean that the reality is personally meaningful to the individual. By objective they are referring to the social order, or the institutional world, which they view as a human product.[66]

An excerpt from Berger's book *The Sacred Canopy* may help clarify their position:

> Worlds are socially constructed and socially maintained. Their continuing reality, both objective (as common, taken-for-granted facticity) and subjective (as facticity imposing itself on individual consciousness), depends upon specific social processes, namely those processes that ongoingly reconstruct and maintain the particular worlds in question. Conversely, the interruption of these social processes threatens the (objective and subjective) reality of the worlds in question. Thus each world requires a social "base" for its continuing existence as a world that is real to actual human beings.[67]

According to Berger and Luckmann, alienation is a loss of meaning: there has been a disintegration of the socially constructed knowledge system. Developing nations, for instance, where modernization is eroding traditional worlds, are experiencing this kind of alienation.[68] Only by recon-

---

[65]Peter L. Berger and Thomas Luckmann, *The Social Construction of Reality* (New York: Doubleday, 1966), p. 3.

[66]The subjective element is borrowed from Weber's *verstehende*, and the objective from Durkheim's social facts. See pp. 238 and 21.

[67]Berger, *The Sacred Canopy* (New York: Doubleday, 1969), p. 45.

[68]See Peter Berger, Brigitte Berger, and Hansfried Kellner, *The Homeless Mind* (New York: Random House, 1973). This concept of alienation is very different from the Marxist concept discussed in Chapter III and closer to Durkheim's notion of anomie.

structing a knowledge system so that it brings with it a rediscovery of meaning can these nations' alienation be alleviated.

The heart of this theory deals with the question of how everyday reality is socially constructed. As Berger and Luckmann put it, "How is it possible that subjective meanings *become* objective facticities?"[69]

Berger and Luckmann's phenomenological analysis is focused on the subjective experience of the reality of everyday life, the "here and now." This reality also includes past and future. As they explain it, "My attention to this world (of everyday life) is mainly determined by what I am doing, have done or plan to do in it." But their focus is not on a self-contained world, for the reality of everyday life is described as an "intersubjective world, a world that I share with others."[70] Berger and Luckmann are, like Goffman, convinced that face-to-face interaction is where the *real* action is. In fact, they state that face-to-face interaction is the prototype of social interaction and that all other cases of social interaction derive from it.[71] In contrast to Goffman, whose actors appear to be reading scripts which were written by others, Berger and Luckmann's actors improvise and create their own scripts.

The fact that Berger and Luckmann include objective reality as well as subjective reality in their framework makes it more than a purely microsociological approach. Instead their theory can be viewed as an attempt to bridge the micro- and macrosociological levels of analysis, an attempt made by only a few social theorists.[72] The key concepts of Berger and Luckmann's theory, which they describe as "moments" of a dialectical process, are *externalization, objectivation,* and *internalization.*

Externalization

Berger and Luckmann label the first "moment" in the continuing dialectical process of the social construction of reality externalization, wherein individuals, by their own human activity, create their social worlds. They view the social order as an ongoing human production. The social order is both the "result of past human activity," and it "exists only and insofar as human activity continues to produce it."[73] Thus, externalization has two dimensions. On the one hand, it means that human beings can create a new social reality, like forming a new friendship or starting a new business. On the other hand, it means that human beings can re-create social institutions by their ongoing externalization of them, like maintaining and renewing old friendships or like paying income taxes.

[69]Berger and Luckmann, *The Social Construction of Reality*, p. 18.
[70]Ibid., pp. 22 and 23.
[71]Ibid., p. 28.
[72]See, for instance, Randall Collins, p. 159, and Peter Blau, p. 212.
[73]Berger and Luckmann, *The Social Construction of Reality*, p. 52.

In order to understand externalization better, let us look at the creation of a new friendship. Two people who find their interaction mutually rewarding become friends. This friendship is a new social reality; their newly forged "we-ness" is a social reality which did not previously exist. The friends themselves actively and willingly produced this new social entity. Friendship is an ongoing human production in the sense that every time the friends interact, they re-create the friendship. Thus, friendship is an institution which is both external to and produced by human beings. Other examples of externalization are creating and maintaining a marriage, a new business, or a new occupation.

The "moment" of externalization, then, is the moment of production in the dialectical process. It is in the externalization phase of reality construction that Berger and Luckmann see individuals as creative beings, capable of acting on their own environment. This concept is akin to the "I" phase of the social self, an idea borrowed from George Herbert Mead.[74] In short, externalization means that individuals create society.

Objectivation

Objectivation is the process whereby individuals apprehend everyday life as an ordered, prearranged reality that imposes itself upon but is seemingly independent of human beings. For the individual, as Berger and Luckmann put it, "the reality of everyday life appears already objectified, that is, constituted by an order of objects that have been designated *as* objects before my appearance on the scene."[75]

Language is the means by which objects are so designated. Berger and Luckmann explain, "The common objectivations of everyday life are maintained primarily by linguistic signification. Everyday life is, above all, life with and by means of the language I share with my fellowmen (sic). An understanding of language is thus essential for any understanding of the reality of everyday life."[76] To return to the example of friendship again, objectivation means that the friendship between two people which resulted from their interactions confronts the two friends as a social reality. When the friends refer to this reality as "we," they are using language to designate the friendship as an objective social reality. Other people, hearing that the two are friends, understand what the relationship means.

In his field work at a nursing home, Gubrium used the concept of objectivation to analyze the status of senility among the patients. He argued that knowledge about senility and incipient senility emerged in the process of the everyday work done by health care personnel to categorize behavior as senile or nonsenile. When senility is realized in this way people seem to

---

[74]See Chapter V, p. 244.
[75]Berger and Luckmann, *The Social Construction of Reality*, p. 22.
[76]Ibid., p. 37.

accept the natural objective status of senility.[77] Once designated as such, the status of senility acts back on those who have been so labeled. For instance, Gubrium found that patients tend to believe senility is contagious. He quotes two patients: (1) "You spend too much time around 'em, you get to be nuts before your time." (2) "That crazy stuff is catchy, you know. They'll set you as goofy as they are."[78] To illustrate the social construction of reality in the case of senility, Gubrium makes the point that it is taken for granted that confused, disoriented, or agitated behavior is considered senile when the individual engaging in such behavior is aged. However, the manifestation of the very same symptoms in a younger individual is believed to be "obviously" something else.[79] Thus, senility is an objective reality which has consequences for the people so labeled.

In short, objectivation means that society is an objective reality which has consequences for the individual, because it "acts back on" its creator. And this brings us to our next concept.

Internalization

The third "moment" of the dialectical process is internalization, a kind of socialization by which the legitimation of the institutional order is assured. For Berger, successful socialization means that there is a high degree of symmetry between both objective and subjective reality and objective and subjective identity. Internalization for Berger is what socialization is for Parsons in that individuals internalize (make their own) the objectivated social reality, with the result that "everyone pretty much *is* what he is supposed to be." There is no problem of identity, for "everybody knows who everybody is and who he is himself."[80]

A study of the reentry of Vietnam veterans illustrates some of the problems caused by a lack of symmetry between objective and subjective identity. As the researchers put it, "There is a change of identity as one moves from the war world. The civilian turned soldier has an acute sense of the war as having made him different through and through, not merely identifiably different." And though the veteran wants to be reincorporated into the taken-for-granted social reality of home, he finds that his war world cannot be mutually shared in his home world. He must "get his head out of Nam," as one veteran put it.[81] In short, he is *not* what he is "supposed to be," and the identity problem is acute.

---

[77]Jaber F. Gubrium, "Notes on the Social Organization of Senility," *Urban Life*, 7, no. 1 (April 1978), 27.

[78]Ibid., p. 38.

[79]Ibid., p. 26.

[80]Berger and Luckmann, *The Social Construction of Reality*, p. 164.

[81]Robert R. Faulkner and Douglas B. McGaw, "Uneasy Homecoming: Stages in the Reentry Transition of Vietnam Veterans," *Urban Life*, 6, no. 3 (October 1977), 308 and 315.

As we mentioned above, Berger's definition of socialization is very similar to Parsons', that is, the internalization of social norms and values. Berger, however, distinguishes between primary and secondary socialization. Primary socialization refers to what individuals undergo in childhood when they encounter the significant others with whom they identify emotionally. "The child takes on the significant others' roles and attitudes, that is, internalizes them and makes his own."[82] Secondary socialization is "any subsequent process that inducts an already socialized individual into new sectors of the objective world of his society."[83] Basically secondary socialization is a later phase in the acquisition of knowledge, and it concerns more specific roles. It takes place under the auspices of specialized agencies, like modern educational institutions.

The social construction of reality theory argues that whenever individuals engage in internalization, they are conforming to the expectations of existing social institutions, and they are *also re-creating that social institution.* The creation of a new institution occurs in the moment of externalization; once externalized, it is objectified and once objectified, it acts back on the individual as an internalized entity. As Berger and Luckmann sum it up: "Society is a human product" (externalization); "society is an objective reality" (objectivation); "man is a social product" (internalization).[84]

Returning once again to our example of friendship, let us consider its institutionalization. When two individuals create a friendship in the moment of externalization, it becomes an object (objectivation), which then acts back on them as something they have internalized. Thus, forming a friendship can have various consequences for the friends in question, such as the use of a friend's time, energy, and other resources. Consider for a moment the whole gamut of behaviors expected of a friend: visiting a friend in the hospital or caring for a friend when she or he is sick, giving advice to a friend, lending money, giving gifts, writing letters, and even spending whole days with a friend. In short, an institution which I helped create is acting back on me whenever a friend demands my time (objectivation); and when I choose to meet those demands (internalization), I am re-creating (externalizing) that institution again. As an individual I can act and react; I can create new institutions and re-create (and thus maintain) old ones, but in either case reality is grounded in the ongoing process of interaction and negotiation.

As we mentioned above, Berger and Luckmann see the central question for sociological theory as: "How is it possible that subjective meanings

---

[82]Berger and Luckmann, *The Social Construction of Reality*, pp. 131–32.
[83]Ibid., p. 130.
[84]Ibid., p. 61.

become objective facticities?"[85] Their primary interest is in the factors that make a given world more or less "real" and fully internalized.

An issue related to internalization is what Berger and Luckmann call *reification*, "the apprehension of the products of human activity *as if* they were something else than human products—such as facts of nature, results of cosmic laws, or manifestations of divine will. Reification implies that man is capable of forgetting his own authorship of the human world, and further that the dialectic between man, the producer, and his products is lost to consciousness. The reified world is, by definition, a dehumanized world."[86]

In *The Sacred Canopy*, Berger pictures the individual who reifies his social world as one who is living an alienated and meaningless life. As Berger puts it, "The actor becomes *only* that which is acted upon."[87] The dialectic is lost, and the individual is no longer free but is a prisoner of his or her destiny. Berger discusses the role of religion in this reification process:

> One of the essential qualities of the sacred, as encountered in 'religious experience' is otherness, its manifestation as something *totaliter aliter* [totally other] as compared to ordinary, profane human life. . . . The fundamental 'recipe' of religious legitimation is the transformation of human products into supra-or non-human facticities. The humanly made world is explained in terms that deny its human production.[88]

Thus, to the degree that religious beliefs convince individuals that they are *not* masters of their own fates, or that patriotism or anticommunism are sacred beliefs, or that blind obedience is a moral duty—to that degree religion, according to Berger, is aiding and abetting the reification process.

Finally, the theory of the social construction of reality argues that roles as well as institutions can be reified. For instance, when an individual says, "I must act in this way because of my position. I have no choice," that individual is demonstrating a reified lock-step mentality. Such a mentality minimizes the choices available to people, and it exemplifies the situation wherein individuals have, indeed, forgotten their authorship of the human world.

This does not mean that responsible behavior and firm commitments imply reification. Berger's theory takes account of individuals who reaffirm their responsibilities and choices, while being mindful of other alternatives available to them. A friend who willingly gives scarce time or money in the name of friendship and a parent who says, "I must do this because of my responsibility to my child," are consciously re-creating social reality rather than reifying their positions.

[85] Ibid., p. 18.
[86] Ibid., p. 89.
[87] Berger, *The Sacred Canopy*, p. 86.
[88] Ibid., pp. 87 and 89.

CONCLUSION

As we have seen, phenomenology is not only a new perspective; it is also far from being conventional or traditional sociology. It is both unfamiliar to and distrusted by many mainstream sociologists. Since sociology journals tend to favor quantitative studies, it is not surprising that phenomenologists typically find it difficult to get their work published, a dilemma they share with symbolic interactionists. The emergence of journals like *Journal of Contemporary Ethnography* (formerly called *Urban Life and Culture*) was extremely important because it created a channel for the publication of ethnographic studies. Now, however, even a mainstream journal like *American Sociological Review* has symbolic interactionists and phenomenologists serving as editors and associate editors. In addition, there are an increasing number of publications devoted exclusively to theory, for example, *Sociological Theory, Current Perspectives in Sociological Theory, Theory and Society,* and *Theory, Culture and Society*.

Other characteristics shared by symbolic interactionism and phenomenology include the view of the individual as an active, knowledgeable (and even sometimes emotional) subject, and a disdain for any research methodology in which the individual is passive. To use C. Wright Mills' terms, both perspectives have a negative view of "grand theory" and "abstracted empiricism."

One of the things ethnomethodology shares with functionalism is that it has been the subject of an attack by a president of the American Sociological Association in a presidential address. We will recall that George C. Homans used his presidential address as an occasion to attack Parsons, Smelser, and the functionalists. In like manner, Lewis Coser chose in his presidential address to attack path analysis and ethnomethodology. His chief criticism was that the ethnomethodological perspective ignores "institutional factors in general, and the centrality of power in social interaction in particular."[89]

Why does Garfinkel, for instance, "make trouble" or "violate the scene"? He does not aim to change the social system but simply to see what people do to bring back a semblance of order when their social world is disrupted. Garfinkel doesn't "make trouble" to illustrate that the social system is exploitative or to point up imbalances in power and resources. Rather, in functionalist terms, he is introducing strain into a situation, and he is interested in how people bring this particular situation back to equilibrium.

Berger's theory of the social construction of reality is like functionalism in defining socialization as the internalization of societal values and norms. Berger's position, however, differs from Parsons' in that the former views the individual as capable of taking a critical stance toward the

[89]Coser, "Presidential Address: Two Methods in Search of a Substance," p. 696.

social order. However, although Berger reminds us that the social order is a human product, he never addresses the question of whether some people are in a better position than others to create social reality. Berger's theory lacks the tools necessary for the analysis of power relationships, a shortcoming shared with ethnomethodology and symbolic interactionism.

Hence, phenomenology's concerns would not appeal to macrosociologists whose main interest is in distinguishing among the origins of different social institutions and studying social change. Neither would it appeal to social scientists like George Homans, who give priority to establishing general explanatory propositions.

What is the future of phenomenology? One of the indicators that its early demise is unlikely is the current increase in publications and the continued interest in sessions devoted specifically to this perspective at annual sociological meetings, both regional and national. Phenomenology and symbolic interactionism have different and complementary contributions to make at the level of microsociological analysis.

VII

ALTERNATIVE
PERSPECTIVES

This chapter discusses some theoretical developments which fall outside the dominant sociological traditions. Each nonetheless exerts considerable influence on both empirical sociology and the work of other theorists.

Overall, these perspectives also reflect a renewed interest in general laws about social behavior and in defining their potential and limits. In Chapter I we noted that one of the great divides in sociological theory has always been over the possibility of developing deductive theorems. Throughout the history of the discipline, there has been a very active debate about whether the scientific model is appropriate to the study of society. Human behavior is purposive, and if you tell people that something is going to happen because social laws predict it, they may, unlike fruit flies or crystals, set out to prove you wrong. Nonetheless, the physical sciences offer an impressive model to copy, explaining whole groups of phenomena with a few powerful laws. The continuing development of statistical techniques and the use of computers to examine huge bodies of data have encouraged sociologists to look for comparable patterns. So, too, has recent work in related disciplines, notably psychology, linguistics, and biology.

The one unifying feature of structuralist developments is just such a concern with general principles of social structure. American structuralism concentrates on developing abstract theorems to explain such social phenomena as integration and relies heavily on quantitative computer-based techniques. French structuralism, by contrast, attempts to identify common conceptual schemes. The structuration theory of Anthony Giddens also deals with the nature of social explanation and with the relevance of the scientific model. While Giddens' theory reaches quite different conclusions from structuralism and argues that general deductive theorems cannot be derived in sociology, it too develops some very general and inclusive explanatory concepts. Finally, sociobiology has created enormous arguments among sociologists by attempting to identify recurring features of human society that derive from our biological capacities and limitations.

PART ONE
Structuralism

Structure is one of those words which we use easily until we try to define it. Then whole books appear trying to describe what it means. However, in all definitions there exists the notion that, if you describe the structure of something, you are describing how the important bits of it fit together. The interesting part is, of course, identifying what is important, and why. For example, a building has a structure—a skeletal underpinning to which we can add different things but which also limits what we can do. In remodeling a house, it is important to be clear about its structure. If you pull down a structural wall, the whole house will be at risk and may even come crashing down.

When sociologists make structure the main concern of their work, it is because they believe in the possibility of establishing *general* statements about society—or, more specifically, about how the world as we experience it is formed by some underlying structure.[1] A paleontologist trying to work out what a dinosaur actually looked like works from the bones out, but can only do so because scientists have worked from the flesh in with other animals to establish the principles relating a skeleton to the whole. All structuralists attempt the same sort of thing—but there the resemblances between them end. Of the two major groupings into which contemporary theorists can be divided, the French are concerned almost exclusively with human thought and language. The active strain in Anglo-Saxon work, by contrast, looks to the relationships between people—outside, and not inside, the individual.

FRENCH STRUCTURALISM

To the foreign reader the most striking thing about French structuralist writing is that it is "all about words." Whereas American and British social scientists, brought up in an empiricist tradition, tend to concentrate on people's actual behavior in trying to understand society, French intellectuals are far more inclined to look at what people say and how they think. This is almost certainly related to the place of intellectuals in French society, where they write for a general literary public rather than within a particular academic discipline. The two French structuralists best known outside France—Claude Lévi-Strauss and Michel Foucault—have worked in different disciplines but shared a readership.

Sociology does not, in general, put forth concepts and language as the *cause* of things rather than the result. It is thus worth pointing out how fundamentally some recent ideas and words *about* ideas and words have affected the way we understand ourselves. For example, the linguist Noam Chomsky has argued for the existence of a "depth grammar" shared by all human languages.[2] What this means is that all languages—and therefore the way all human beings understand and communicate about the world—have fundamental features in common. If we can comprehend this underlying structure and its "transformational rules" we will have learned something very important about the sort of creatures we are. The fact that in all

[1]See the discussion of structure in Chapters II and V.

[2]Noam Chomsky, *Cartesian Linguistics, A Chapter in the History of Rationalist Thought* (New York: Harper and Row, 1966), and *Aspects of the Theory of Syntax* (Cambridge, Mass.: M.I.T. Press, 1965).

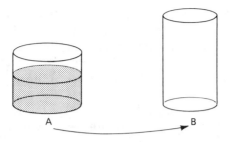

FIGURE 7-1   Conservation of Quantities

human languages sentences must have subjects and predicates "structures" our experience.

The Swiss psychologist Jean Piaget has transformed the way in which we think about child development and, in consequence, our own nature by his work on children's modes of reasoning. Piaget, like Chomsky, is concerned with how we, as humans, "know" the world—how we interpret it and how our understanding is tied up with our underlying nature and genetic inheritance. The most famous of his experiments showing how adult reasoning develops only gradually in a child involve the "conservation of quantities."[3] This is shown most dramatically if you pour a given quantity of liquid from glass A to glass B (see Figure 7-1). Once the liquid is in B, young children will generally be convinced that there is now a larger quantity present than there was before. Similarly, it is not at all obvious to young children that if you count a group of objects first in one order and then in another, the answer "must" be the same. A "conservationist" view of quantities (and the world) develops only slowly.

The common element in Chomsky's and Piaget's work is the search for the structure of thought and perception. Because the way we see and understand the world affects the way we act, understanding social behavior must involve understanding the laws of language and the intellect.[4] It is a search for just this understanding that marks French structuralism.

Claude Lévi-Strauss: Claude Lévi-Strauss was born in 1908, the son of an artist and grandson of a rabbi. His first regular academic post was as a professor of sociology at the University of São Paulo in Brazil, from where he led an anthropological expedition to central Brazil. After serving in the

[3]See especially Jean Piaget, *The Language and Thought of the Child* (London: Routledge and Kegan Paul, 1959), and *The Child's Construction of Reality* (London: Routledge and Kegan Paul, 1958). A good summary of Piaget's thought is to be found in Margaret Donaldson, *Children's Minds* (London: Fontana, 1971).

[4]Piaget, in his discussion of structuralism, defines it as the search for a whole, "self-regulating" system of laws. "[T]he elements of a structure are subordinated to laws, and it is in terms of these laws that the structure . . . is defined." Jean Piaget, *Structuralism*, trans. and ed. Chaninah Maschler (London: Routledge and Kegan Paul, 1971), p. 7.

French army in 1939–40, he made his way to New York and taught at the New School. In 1949, after his return to France, his *Elementary Structures of Kinship* first brought him wide recognition.[5] In 1950, he became Director of Studies at the University of Paris (École Pratique des Hautes Études), and in 1959 he was appointed to the Chair of Social Anthropology at the Collège de France.

Although Lévi-Strauss first became famous for the analysis of kinship structures, he is today most associated with the analysis of myth—specifically, with the attempt to identify constants underlying the apparently endless variety of stories and subject matter. He believes that there are patterns common to all human thought, and that these can be found in the myths and classification structures of any tribe or culture. To borrow an analogy from his own work, the myths and structures of different societies resemble a theme in music. Every note may be changed, but it is still the same tune.

For Lévi-Strauss thought processes are what *make* us human. Rather than the thoughts of people deriving from the societies in which they live, it is the societies which are different concrete "workings-out" of the same thought processes. He says, at one point, that "all social life, however elementary, presupposes an intellectual activity in man of which the formal properties cannot, accordingly, be a reflection of the concrete organization of society."[6] In other words, we must "think" in some sense before we can have any social life—therefore, the conceptual scheme underlying social life is fundamental. The bulk of Lévi-Strauss' work is an attempt to extract conceptual universals and develop a method for analyzing myth in these terms.

For all its apparently abstruse nature, this is also a theoretical perspective with important political implications. Because it sets very strict limits to the malleability of human beings and of human societies, it also denies the possibility of a "new man," made by a perfect society. On the contrary—future man will share the same "deep" mental structures as his predecessors, and therefore his society will be similar as well. As Edmund Leach, the foremost British expositor of Lévi-Strauss, points out, to a structuralist history offers images of past societies which were "structural transformations" of those we know now—no better and no worse. Intellectual Paris was not slow to recognize the "anti-Marxism" of Lévi-Strauss' ideas, and structuralism was attacked and supported in precisely these terms.[7]

Rather than try to summarize all of Lévi-Strauss' ideas, we will illustrate them with a particular example—his analysis of how all societies cook

---

[5]Claude Lévi-Strauss, *The Elementary Structures of Kinship*. See Chapter IV, p. 180.

[6]Claude Lévi-Strauss, *Totemism* (Boston: Beacon Press, 1963), p. 96.

[7]The Marxist sociologist Tom Bottomore notes that "a Marxist thinker cannot be a "pure" structuralist . . . for the Marxist theory has as its starting point the idea of historically distinct social structures." Tom Bottomore, "Structure and History," in Peter M. Blau, ed., *Approaches to the Study of Social Structure* (New York: The Free Press, 1975), p. 169.

food, "define" food as belonging to different categories, and have categories which are similar.[8]

The argument is not that there is some innate structure which leads us directly to classify food as "food." Instead, Lévi-Strauss looks for some underlying principle of organizing our thought which, when it meets the real world, produces certain ways of categorizing food. He believes that we introduce order into experience by dividing the continuum of space and time into discontinuous segments—different things, different events. Specifically, we see things in terms of binary opposites. Thus, red, at a traffic light, is seen as the "opposite" of green—although actually they are both parts of a continuous color spectrum. Having identified opposites, we then define something as intermediate—in the case of the traffic light, amber.[9]

In the case of food we have two opposites. Food can be raw (in its original state) or changed. In addition, it can be changed by nature—bacteria—so that it is rotten, or it can be changed by human beings—that is, cooked. The intersection of these two opposites—"normal-changed" and "natural-cultural" gives us a typical Lévi-Straussian schema (see Figure 7-2). What Lévi-Strauss is arguing here is that, *because* the natural world is this way and *because* we divide things into separate, opposing categories, all peoples end up with a set of "cooking" categories. Indeed, the similarities between their categories can be referred back to this triangle. We all, he claims, have a "boiling" category because it reduces food to something comparable to its rotten state; a "roasting" category in which there is only partial cooking (changing); and so on. In myth, too, we can find a logical order beneath the apparently inconsequential collections of character and incident. This encompasses the main experiences and dilemmas of people's existence and is also expressed in terms of "binary oppositions."[10]

Many social scientists' reaction to Lévi-Strauss' work has been one of skepticism. There is, they argue, frequently a feeling of sleight of hand. Awkward facts seem to be ignored—where, for instance do frying and grilling, which are far from universal, fit into the "raw-cooked" triangle? Nonetheless, there is almost always something in the analyses which makes sense. We *do* all divide up food into surprisingly similar categories—food for banquets, food suitable for children—even though what is in one category in one place may be in another somewhere else. Equally, we now acknowledge and study the common elements and underlying structure in

[8]This discussion owes much to Edmund Leach's exposition of Lévi-Strauss' ideas, especially in Edmund Leach, *Lévi-Strauss* (London: Collins, 1970) and Edmund Leach, ed., *The Structural Study of Myth and Totemism: A.S.A. Monograph 5* (London: Tavistock Publications, 1967).

[9]This example is used by Leach to illustrate Lévi-Strauss' argument.

[10]Leach, *The Structural Study of Myth and Totemism*, provides a collection of essays by anthropologists on Lévi-Strauss' exposition of a Tsimshian Indian myth from Alaska, and it is an excellent introduction to his approach.

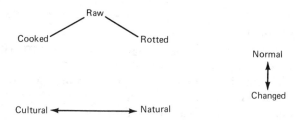

FIGURE 7-2   A Simplified Version of Lévi-Strauss' "Cooking schema." (Adapted from "Le Triangle Culinaire," *L'Arc* [Aix-en Provence] 26 [1965], 19–29.)[11]

the myths of different societies. The current move away from extreme "culturalism"—or the rejection of all cross-cultural generalizations—and towards a search for universals owes much to Lévi-Strauss' influence.[12]

Michel Foucault (1929–1984)   Although Lévi-Strauss became something of a cult figure in Britain and America during the late 1960s, the work of Michel Foucault has only recently become well known. This may be partly because it does not obviously "belong" to any one discipline. The chair at the prestigious Collège de France which he held at the time of his sudden death was in history and systems of thought. His degrees, however, were in philosophy, psychology, and psychopathology. His books combine vivid contemporary descriptions of torture, madness, and prisons with abstruse discussions of the structure of knowledge; straight historical narrative with predictions of the end of our society; and philosophy with psychology.

What gives Foucault's work unity is that it is, as we noted earlier, "all about words." Take, for example, *Madness and Civilization,*[13] probably the best known of Foucault's works published in English. Foucault explores the way people have thought and written about madness, and he examines the changes that have taken place between the Middle Ages and modern times. He shows how considerable these changes have been and relates them to the general outlook of the time. His sources are books, laws, treatises, and legends, plus the art of the period, such as pictures of the "ships of fools" bearing madmen whom sailors had been paid to transport away.

To Foucault, the prison and the asylum exemplify the modern world. In premodern times, torture and public floggings and executions were the state's main tools for securing order.[14] Then came a major transition, to the

[11]Figure 7-2 is discussed in Leach, *Lévi-Strauss.*

[12]See p. 348 for the anthropologist Robin Fox's description of how his impatience with anthropology's compartmentalization of cultures led him to sociobiology.

[13]Michel Foucault, *Madness and Civilization: A History of Insanity in the Age of Reason* (New York: Random House, 1965).

[14]Michel Foucault, *Discipline and Punish: The Birth of the Prison* (London: Allen Lane, 1977), and *Madness and Civilization.*

use of confinement—for convicted criminals, but also (and often, at first, in the same place) for the insane and the indigent. An "entire population . . . almost overnight found itself shut up, excluded more severely than the lepers"[15] of the Middle Ages. "In a hundred and fifty years, confinement had become the abusive amalgam of heterogeneous elements."[16]

We commonly see the advent of the modern mental hospital and the decline of the death penalty as signs of progress. Foucault, however, sees them as epitomizing a shift in the way power is exercised in a society. They embody discipline and deprive those involved of liberty. In this, they are more extreme than, but nevertheless similar to, the other major institutions of modern life—for example, the factory or the modern school.

Foucault's work is distinguished as much by its method as by its conclusions. He concentrates on textual analysis because he seeks structures of knowledge. The particular way in which we see and comprehend the world is, in his view, what defines an age, and this governs the ways in which power is exercised. Doctors, prison governors, lawyers, and politicians are not seen by Foucault as individuals who consciously develop institutions which will secure their positions. Rather, the viewpoint of an age—in our case, the "scientific" view—means that people naturally see things in a certain way. The actions follow. Thus, in the early nineteenth century, suddenly "everywhere we find the same outrage, the same virtuous censure"[17] of the way the insane and criminals are imprisoned together. Similarly, throughout Europe and the United States, in the space of a few decades, "modern" codes of law were drawn up and "the entire economy of punishment was redistributed. . . . At the beginning of the nineteenth century . . . the great spectacle of physical punishment disappeared; the tortured body was avoided."[18] Both were incompatible with the whole emerging "scientifico-legal complex."[19]

It is this approach which makes Foucault's work a part of structuralism—although in later years he rejected the label.[20] In The Order of Things[21] (the book which made him famous) and in The Archaeology of Knowledge,[22] he puts forward the notion of an "episteme" which defines an age. The modern episteme was formed at the end of the eighteenth century and bound up with

[15]Foucault, Madness and Civilization, p. 45.

[16]Ibid.

[17]Ibid., p. 227.

[18]Foucault, Discipline and Punish, pp. 7 and 14.

[19]Ibid., p. 23.

[20]See Edith Kurzweil, The Age of Structuralism: Lévi-Strauss to Foucault (New York: Columbia University Press, 1980).

[21]Michel Foucault, The Order of Things: An Archaeology of the Human Sciences (London: Tavistock Publications, 1970).

[22]Michel Foucault The Archaeology of Knowledge, trans. A. M. Sheridan Smith (London: Tavistock Publications, 1972).

the shift of language toward objectivity; but is no more universally valid or permanent than its predecessors.

Having read Foucault once, one cannot look at modern society in quite the same way again. This is not to say, however, that his approach is not open to criticism—for the attempt to go beyond narrow, empiricist disciplinary study does not make irrelevant the latter's emphasis on testing one's ideas against the evidence. Piaget himself has been one of Foucault's harshest critics, stating that "beneath the cleverness there are only bare affirmations and omissions."[23] There is no real method behind his selection and elaboration of an episteme's characteristics. Rather "he relies on intuition and substitutes speculative improvisation for methodical procedures."[24] And is it reasonable to imply that institutional change derives almost entirely from some underlying and apparently autonomous "world view," and that people's conscious motives and decisions are hardly relevant?

A more general criticism can be applied to French structuralism as a whole: namely, that it is dangerous to rely so heavily on the written and spoken word. Those who write and tell tales, and whose words survive, are only a fraction of a society. They are unquestionably its products in the sense of being the people they are because of when and where they live. However, especially in the written word, there is much that is individual to the writer and much more that is specific to the outlook of the "writing" classes alone. It is dangerous to believe that one can somehow deduce social institutions directly from ideas, just as it is dangerous to see ideas as simply a "superstructure" mirroring the economic institutions below.

It is worth returning here to the work of Piaget himself—or rather to the testimony of a practicing psychologist. Smedslund, after years of work in the Piagetian tradition, concluded eventually that its emphasis on cognition was one-sided.[25] Children's behavior could not, he found, be described adequately in terms of the presence or absence of certain structures of thought. Too often, following Piaget's approach meant presenting children with tasks which were new to them, atypical, more like the mathematics and science of a Western classroom than anything else. Smedslund came to see other features of their lives and nature—rejection at home, feelings of jealousy—as far more important than their stage of intellectual development, and he noted that the relative sophistication of their behavior outside the class was often strikingly unrelated to their "Piagetian" stage of development. He concluded not that Piaget was wrong but that structures of thought are just one influence, one factor, to be considered alongside others.

[23]Piaget, *Structuralism*, p. 130.

[24]Ibid., p. 133.

[25]J. Smedslund, "Piaget's Psychology in Practice," *British Journal of Educational Psychology*, 47 (1977), 1–6. See also P. C. Wason and P. N. Johnson-Laird, *The Psychology of Reasoning: Structure and Content* (London: Batsford, 1972).

AMERICAN STRUCTURALISM: PETER BLAU

Most American sociologists have not been greatly attracted to French structuralism. However, this does not mean that they have abandoned all interest in finding general principles which shape apparently different organizations and communities. Indeed, interest in such general, structural principles has been given a new lease on life by the mathematicians' colonization of the social sciences and the increasing availability of computer programs with which one can search for regularities in huge bodies of data.[26]

The most ambitious recent attempt to advance structuralist theory is that of Peter Blau in his *Inequality and Heterogeneity: A Primitive Theory of Social Structure*.[27] Compared to, say, Foucault's approach, Blau's work is very much in the standard scientific tradition of sociology. He is interested in "theorems" which can be tested (and falsified) empirically. Moreover, whereas French structuralists emphasize concepts[28] and intellectual processes, Blau's subject matter is distinctively "social." The division of labor, intermarriage, patterns of friendship, and social mobility figure greatly in his studies.

Primitive Social Structure

In *Inequality and Heterogeneity*, Blau sets out a theory of social structure through a set of axioms (or assumptions) and derived theorems and corollaries. His main concern is in fact more narrow than the label implies and is the same as that of Durkheim and Parsons—what integrates a society? His major assumption, which is central to the answer he gives, is that "some kind of social association is necessary for integration. . . . [T]he integration of various groups and strata in society cannot rest solely on their functional interdependence: it requires some actual social interaction among their members."[29] Consequently, his theorems deal with the structural factors which tend to affect interaction and, thereby, social integration.

Blau starts with the point that a "social structure is delineated by its parameters"[30]—that is, by the characteristics which distinguish people from each other and thereby affect their social relationships. In our society,

[26]See, for example, the recent publication sponsored jointly by the *American Journal of Sociology* and the *Journal of Political Economy:* Christopher Winship and Sherwin Rosen, eds., *Organizations and Institutions: Sociological and Economic Approaches to the Analysis of Social Structure,* Supplement to the *American Journal of Sociology,* 94 (1988).

[27]Peter M. Blau, *Inequality and Heterogeneity: A Primitive Theory of Social Structure* (New York: The Free Press, 1977).

[28]Although Parsons resembles them in noting: "I am a cultural determinist, rather than a social determinist," in Talcott Parsons, *Societies: Evolutionary and Comparative Perspectives* (Englewood Cliffs, N.J.: Prentice-Hall, Inc., 1966), p. 113.

[29]Ibid., p. 5.

[30]Ibid., p. 6.

gender and occupation are "parameters"—eye color is not. Blau is not interested in whether such characteristics are acquired or ascribed, but rather in whether they are nominal or graduated.[31] "A nominal parameter divides the population into subgroups with distinct boundaries. There is no inherent rank-order among these groups. . . . Sex, religion, race, and occupation are nominal parameters. A graduated parameter differentiates people in terms of a status rank-order. . . . Income, wealth, education and power are graduated parameters."[32] The resulting "differentiation" among people can, in turn, be classified according to whether it involves heterogeneity or inequality. "Heterogeneity or horizontal differentiation refers to the distribution of a population among groups in terms of a nominal parameter. Inequality or vertical differentiation refers to the status distribution in terms of a graduated parameter."[33]

Both inequality and heterogeneity create "barriers to social intercourse" and, therefore, to social integration.[34] However, the way and degree to which they do so are a function of structural factors: notably group size and social mobility. Indeed, Blau argues, a whole set of social phenomena derive from the fact that, for any two groups, other things being equal, *"the rate of intergroup associations of the smaller group must exceed that of the larger."*[35]

There is nothing mysterious about this. It is not that members of small groups are more inclined to look for friends outside their group because it is restricting. Nor is it because they feel insecure and want to "integrate" themselves. It is simply that, as a general rule, the situation cannot be avoided. Figure 7-3 shows why.

Let us suppose that the As and the Xs are members of two groups who work in the same corporation—and also play tennis on office courts after work. In any given week, it is very likely that any given A will work closely with an X, but that will still mean that most of the Xs do not work with an A. Even if every A, in that same week, plays a tennis match with at least one X, many of the latter will still have no contacts with an A. If you draw a line from each of the As to a second X, many Xs will be left unlinked.

This seems obvious enough, but, in fact, people do not necessarily recognize it. As Blau points out, many liberal Americans wonder (or indeed worry) about having few or no black friends. But as long as there are far fewer blacks than whites in the United States this is bound to happen. Similarly, people sometimes comment that, for example, Jews, or Mormons, or Christian Scientists are "cliquish"—that they have no friends from these

---

[31]Compare with Parsons' theory of social structure expressed in terms of pattern variables.

[32]Blau, *Inequality and Heterogeneity*, p. 7.

[33]Ibid., p. 9.

[34]Ibid., p. 10.

[35]Ibid., p. 21.

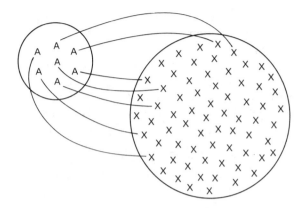

FIGURE 7-3   Intergroup Associations for Groups of Different Sizes

groups. But just as if every black in America had one or two good friends who were white, most whites still would have no black friends, so the same is true for Jews, Mormons, Christian Scientists, or any other minority group.

Thus, Blau points out, from this one theorem one can produce a good "probabilistic"[36] answer to such questions as "Is racial intermarriage more prevalent among blacks or among whites?" or "Are Jews, or are Christians, more likely to engage in premarital sexual intercourse with members of the other religious group?" Although cultural factors, such as strength of religious convictions or levels of sexual inhibition in a group, may have some effects on individuals' behavior, there is no need to look for a "cultural" hypothesis. A structural one, about group size, will do well.[37]

Scott Smith and his colleagues decided to test Blau's hypotheses by looking at the experiences of female employees in a large federal bureaucracy.[38] We can see what Blau would expect—that the fewer females there are, the more their social associations will be with male colleagues, and vice versa. But is it what one would normally predict? Would you expect a woman's magazine, for example, to argue that things will be easier for a woman who goes to work in a predominantly male environment, or to warn that, in that case, a woman will have to be especially tough and determined? Rosabeth Moss Kanter, for example, in *Men and Women of the Corporation*,[39]

[36]That is, one that will usually turn out to be correct when tested.

[37]However, group size is unlikely, very often, to be a complete explanation. Intermarriage between the brown and red-haired is likely to exceed that between whites and blacks because hair color is not a "salient parameter"—people do not think about it in their social relationships.

[38]Scott J. Smith, Charles M. Bonjean, William T. Markham, and Judy Corder, "Social Structure and Intergroup Interaction: Men and Women of the Federal Bureaucracy." *American Sociological Review*, 47 (October 1982), 587–99.

[39]Rosabeth Moss Kanter, *Men and Women of the Corporation* (New York: Basic Books, 1967).

put forward a quite different argument from Blau's: namely, that when there are a few "token" women, men will *heighten* cultural boundaries and freeze the women out.

Smith and his colleagues relied on questionnaire data and could not, unfortunately, look at whether the women were ever perceived as "token" in the sense that they had been appointed *because* they were women. However, with this one proviso, Blau's predictions were borne out. Male-female contacts were more frequent the lower the percentage of the group that was female, and such higher frequencies actually tended to increase the amount of social support which females received from male co-workers. Group structure generates association, but association seems, in turn, to generate liking—at which point we are back to psychology.[40]

Blau also provides a number of interesting comments on the implications for social interaction of the classical "pyramidal" social structure formed by "graduated parameters" such as wealth, education, or social status. Quite inevitably, "most people are insulated from social contacts with the élite." However many hands a senator or Member of Parliament shakes, most citizens will never meet their elected representatives. And while quite a few nineteenth-century dukes married actresses, only a few of the many thousand actresses had the fortune to marry dukes. It is not surprising that "class lines may appear to be less rigid to persons in upper than those in lower strata."[41]

Some even more general conclusions follow. Although heterogeneity creates barriers to social intercourse, "much heterogeneity weakens these barriers."[42] The more heterogeneity, the smaller the groups and hence the greater the possibility of intergroup association. Conversely, any factors which tend to increase the relative size of the lower groups in a society—for instance, higher fertility or large-scale immigration of poor people—will tend to reduce association (and integration).[43]

Terry Blum used data on interethnic and interreligious social contacts at the individual level to examine Blau's theory and found that ethnic and religious heterogeneity did indeed encourage such relations.[44] In addition, Blau and Schwartz have tested a number of Blau's key theorems. They used 1970 census data to see whether the theorems predict rates of

[40]And, indeed, exchange theory. See p. 195. A comparable pattern emerges even within marriages. There is a direct relationship between the quality of a marriage and the simple *quantity of time* people spend together, with the latter proving far more important than, e.g., similarity of life-style. Paul W. Kingston and Steven L. Noch, "Time Together Among Dual Earner Couples," *American Sociological Review*, 52, no. 3 (June 1987), 391–400.

[41]Blau, *Inequality and Heterogeneity*, p. 50.

[42]Ibid., p. 257.

[43]And, by definition, increase inequality.

[44]Terry C. Blum, "Structural Constraints on Interpersonal Relations: A Test of Blau's Macrosociological Theory," *American Journal of Sociology*, 91, no. 3 (November 1985), 511–21.

intermarriage in metropolitan areas correctly.[45] Using categories such as occupation, mother tongue, birth region, and race, they looked at the effects of heterogeneity and of group size. Blau's theorems that "small group size promotes intergroup relations" and that "heterogeneity promotes intergroup relations" were indeed confirmed. For example, the more an area's population was scattered across groups with different mother tongues and the more diverse the birthplaces of its inhabitants, the higher its rate of intermarriage.[46]

Blau and Schwartz's study also looked at the effects of *intersection* and its obverse, *consolidation*, on intermarriage rates. Intersection and consolidation are mirror image terms, describing the degree to which "various dimensions of differentiation are related."[47] They introduce a rather different idea from heterogeneity, although they will often be associated. Imagine an apparently fairly heterogeneous community in which there are five racial groups, five main occupational categories, and five religious groupings. It would be quite conceivable for each racial group to have its own religion *and* to be overwhelmingly concentrated in one occupational category. In that case, you would have very little intersection, but a great deal of consolidation.

Blau's original theory was simply that "intersection promotes and consolidation impedes intergroup relations." However, the data showed that what is really crucial is that there should be *multiple* intersection of different groups.[48] If, for example, you look simply at whether those with a given mother tongue tend to belong to different occupational groups, you won't be able to predict which areas have the highest intermarriage rates between people from different groups. If, however, you look at how far local people with the same mother tongue tend to differ in terms of occupation, race, and religious affiliation, you will. Multiple cross-overs are closely related to high intermarriage rates.

As Blau and Schwartz explain, the hypotheses here derive directly from Simmel's insights into the "web" of group affiliations, work that also inspired Coser's work on conflict.[49] They argue, "If social differences along various lines are closely related, they consolidate group boundaries and class distinctions and strengthen the barriers between insiders and outsiders."[50] Conversely, "crosscutting social differences put individuals at the intersection of a web of group affiliations that exert diverse and often counteracting

[45]Peter M. Blau and Joseph E. Schwartz, *Crosscutting Social Circles: Testing a Macrostructural Theory of Intergroup Relations* (Orlando, Fla.: Academic Press, 1984).

[46]Heterogeneity was operationally defined as the chance expectation that two random persons belong to different groups.

[47]Blau and Schwartz, *Crosscutting Social Circles*, p. 85.

[48]Ibid., pp. 88–98. The theorem now reads, "The multiple intersection of independent dimensions of social differentiation promotes intergroup relations" (p. 90).

[49]See above pp. 150–55.

[50]Blau and Schwartz, *Crosscutting Social Circles*, p. 11.

pressures, weakening the hold any one group has on its members, widening the options of individuals and increasing their freedom."[51]

Durkheim Revisited

As we mentioned earlier, Blau's major interest is very much that of Durkheim and the functionalists. Thus, one of the most important parts of *Inequality and Heterogeneity* is a direct reworking of Durkheim's theory of social integration. Durkheim believed that, whereas primitive societies were held together by "mechanical solidarity" (shared beliefs), modern societies are held together by the interdependence that comes with the division of labor—"organic solidarity."[52] Essentially, Durkheim's argument is that the "division of labor," that is, increasing specialization, comes about through population growth and more frequent social interaction. The greater the division of labor, the more we depend on each other and the less self-sufficient we are. As the unions in a number of Western European countries have discovered, a group of workers in, for example, the water or electricity industry can hold a country or government for ransom. Fifty-five million Britons and two hundred fifty million Americans could not become self-sufficient hunters and gatherers even if they wanted.

However, Blau argues, although division of labor may make for functional interdependence, it does *not*, in and of itself, create integration. That depends, ultimately, on actual association between different members of a society, and it is perfectly possible to have high levels of interdependence without many of the workers involved actually meeting each other.

What really matters, Blau reiterates, is the degree of social association between people in a society. Thus, it is quite true that, "*the advancing division of labor increases the probability of social associations among different occupations,*"[53] but not equally and automatically in all circumstances. That will depend on the form it takes. The division of labor in South Africa clearly is highly advanced. The country is also, and equally clearly, not a well-integrated society.

To the extent that the division of labor produces greater *heterogeneity*—more groups than there used to be, and each one smaller—it will tend to promote integration. This will be more true, the more expert and specialized the groups are, for specialists are more likely to associate than are workers in routine jobs. Production-line workers at Ford Motor Company have no particular reason to meet mailmen or poster hangers in the course

---

[51]Ibid., pp. 83–84. Dahrendorf makes a related point when he argues that "superimposed" positions, where managers are also owners (and relatively rich), lead to greater tensions and more intense conflict. Blau and Schwartz show that the rate of violent crime in a metropolitan area is related to the "consolidation" of race and occupation, in other words, to how closely race is linked to poverty.

[52]See Chapter II, pp. 20–21 and 48.

[53]This is known as "Theorem 28." Blau, *Inequality and Heterogeneity*, p. 201.

of their work. Conversely, the more advances in the division of labor are associated with *inequality* of occupational status or income—with a few specialists and many workers in routine jobs, for example—the less they will promote integration.

Social integration will also be greater the more increases in the division of labor involve "outmobility" from groups—for example, peasants moving into the towns.[54] It will be lower, the more "salient parameters" are "consolidated," or, in ordinary English, the more particular jobs are reserved for or preempted by people from particular well-defined groups, with few or no social bonds to other groups. South Africa is probably the clearest case of such a society in the world today.

The original underlying insight here remains very much Durkheim's. The great advantage of Blau's reformulation is that, instead of one theory for preindustrial and another for industrial societies, the basic argument is the same for all. What vary are the factors which promote integration. It is also true that social association is something which many people feel instinctively to be important, even if it does not occur to them to turn it into a formal sociological theorem! In the United Kingdom, for example, most health care is provided through the National Health Service, funded by taxes, so that patients do not pay directly for anything. An increasing number of people take out additional insurance which allows one to get specialist consultations and operations privately. The health care, and indeed the doctors, are basically the same, but private care enables a patient to be treated sooner. Private health insurance of this kind arouses very strong emotions. Many politicians on the left attack it for creating "two nations," and people who use it are often loath to admit that they are doing so. The National Health Service is valued not only for its instrumental uses in providing health care, but also, and quite explicitly, because it brings people from all sectors of society together.

Against this, it must be noted that Blau does not actually do much to prove his theory. He *defines* social integration in terms of social association, then shows what promotes association. However, while societies with low intergroup association may not be very integrated in that sense of the term, it is only one possible sense. India, with its extremely strict caste divisions and taboos, even on the handling of Brahmins' food by the lower castes, has been one of the most stable societies in human history. Fragmented societies do not necessarily fall apart, and Blau's "theory" is thus more valuable for its clarification of the factors affecting social association than as a grand theory of social structure.

Networks and Structure Blau's structuralism is exceptionally axiomatic, but he is far from alone in attempting to formalize and quantify the "web of

---

[54]And keeping in touch with family and friends who remain behind.

group affiliations."[55] For example, a number of sociologists use the concept of *networks* in their structural analyses. Their aim is to describe the underlying shapes of people's contacts and specify how these shapes affect the behavior of those involved. The major difference between most "network analysts" and Blau is that the former are interested in explaining the behavior of individual people. The abstract concepts of institutional analysis are used insofar as they impinge directly on people through personal links.[56]

Network analysis is rather like a traffic engineer using nighttime photography to estimate traffic flows. If you take a long-exposure aerial photograph of a city's traffic at night, you get a pretty but seemingly shapeless pattern of thicker and thinner lines of light (from headlights) interspersed with dark. The pattern is not shapeless, however. If you take a series of photographs and superimpose them, the differences between thick and thin lines will become increasingly clear, reflecting differences in the volume of traffic.

Network analysts do something like this with social relationships, building up a pattern rather like a drawing based on aerial photographs. They also, and most importantly, try to specify "how this ramification influences the behaviour of the people involved in the network."[57] To stretch our own metaphor a little further, drivers react to what they know about traffic patterns (e.g., by trying to avoid busy roads) and are affected by them (e.g., being held up especially often at places where traffic flows tend to produce accidents). Social networks are things to which we react and which affect us. Just as there are particular types of road junctions which may be *generally* associated with high or low accident rates, so there may be *general* characteristics of social networks which[58] produce recurrent, patterned events and behavior.[59]

Clyde Mitchell suggests that network analysis is potentially most helpful in explaining what is going on in large-scale social situations.[60] In a

[55]Georg Simmel, "The Web of Group Affiliations," trans. Reinhard Bendix, in Kurt H. Wolff, Reinhard Bendix et al., *Simmel: Translation of Chapters from "Soziologie"* (New York: The Free Press, 1964).

[56]Barry Wellman equates network and structural analysis in "Network Analysis: Some Basic Principles," in Randall Collins, ed., *Sociological Theory 1983* (San Francisco: Jossey-Bass, 1983), pp. 155–200. Blau, conversely, argues that there is a fundamental difference between "structural" analysis and analyses conducted at the level of face-to-face relationships. See Chapter IV, Conclusion. See also B. Wellman and S.D. Berkowitz, eds., *Social Structures: A Network Approach* (Cambridge: Cambridge University Press 1988).

[57]J. Clyde Mitchell, "Social Networks," *Annual Review of Anthropology*, 3 (1974), 279–99.

[58]*Ceteris paribus.*

[59]Sociometry, or the study of patterns of friendship and liking, encouraged the development of statistical techniques for network analysis. Early sociometric studies generally asked people to name others they liked most and then mapped out the results, gradually revealing the structure of friendship in a group.

[60]Mitchell, "Social Networks," p. 280.

small-scale tightly organized society, it is possible to account satisfactorily for behavior in terms of, for example, kin relationships or the requirements for adolescents to be initiated into adulthood. In larger, more fluid societies, the "occupational structure" or the "economic system" is just not adequate to explain what is going on at the individual level. It may set boundaries—but people do not live within hermetically sealed occupational or economic groups, and one needs to look beyond, to how and where their lives crosscut them. Individual ties outside their main groups may be of prime importance for them, as the poet Dylan Thomas pointed out: "If you want to be a proper newspaperman," I said, "You got to be well known in the right circles. You got to be *persona grata* in the mortuary, see."[61]

Just as Blau reexamined Durkheim's theory of social integration, so Claude Fischer and his associates used network analysis to examine critically one of the most durable views of modern life: In the process of moving from agricultural village to urban industrial life we have been cut off from any "authentic" community and have become a "nation of strangers."[62] It should follow, Fischer argues, that it is from local social relations that people get initmate friendship and support and that people who have moved recently are more likely to be isolated and suffer psychologically.

In fact, however, data from Detroit did not indicate that men whose friends came from a local neighborhood group were a distinct or especially fortunate minority.[63] Modern communications enabled people to maintain friendships over distances and gain real support from them—in part, no doubt, because friendships which are established and maintained in modern societies are truly chosen by both parties, rather than wished upon them by propinquity.

Granovetter's notion of the "strength of weak ties" is concerned with the effects of network density: that is, with the number of links among the various members of someone's acquaintance.[64] He argues that people with very dense networks in which friends all know each other will, for that reason, tend to be relatively cut off from information and from contact with the wider population. Loosely knit networks and weak ties are very important not only in spreading information and fostering cohesion in a large

[61]Dylan Thomas, *Return Journey to Swansea*, a spoken recording (London: Caedmon, 1972).

[62]Claude S. Fischer, with Robert M. Jackson, C. Ann Stueve, Kathleen Gerson, Lynne McCallister Jones, and M. Baldassare, *Networks and Places: Social Relations in the Urban Setting* (New York: The Free Press, 1977). The phrase "a nation of strangers," cited by Fischer, is from Vance Packard, *A Nation of Strangers* (New York: McKay, 1972). See p. 31 for a discussion of the related ideas of Gemeinschaft and Gesellschaft.

[63]Fischer, *Networks and Places*, p. 165.

[64]Mark Granovetter, "The Strength of Weak Ties," *American Journal of Sociology*, 78 (6) (1973) 1360–68, and "The Strength of Weak Ties. A Network Theory Revisited," in Collins, ed., *Sociological Theory* (1983), pp. 201–32.

society, but also in furthering individuals' goals.[65] For example, "mere acquaintances" are more likely to give you a lead to a job opening than are your close friends, since by definition they move in different circles and have access to different information than you. "Weak" ties are also one important reason why middle-class communities generally do better at protecting themselves from undesired development than working-class ones. Somebody in a middle-class neighborhood usually knows somebody who can "drop a word" in the right place, or who is great at presenting evidence at a tribunal, or who can get coverage in the local press.[66]

A number of attempts, notably by Karen Cook and her associates,[67] have been made to link analyses of network structure with exchange theory. They involve specifying the nature of the links between network members—for example, whether they involve equal or unequal exchange. So far, however, the networks examined have tended to be quite small. This underscores a basic problem with this type of structuralist analysis, as practiced by Blau as well as others. Only computers make it possible, and even then it is hugely labor-intensive in terms of data collection, coding, and analysis. To date, the theories which have emerged have not added enough, compared to other methods, to encourage most sociologists to adopt this approach.[68]

PART TWO
Structuration Theory: Anthony Giddens

Anthony Giddens, a prolific British theorist, is currently Professor of Sociology at the University of Cambridge. He has commented extensively on the writings of the "classical" theorists, such as Durkheim, Weber, and, most notably, Marx. He has also written widely on the nature of sociological theory, and his views draw heavily and explicitly on such contemporary writers as Erving Goffman.

The fullest exposition of Giddens' ideas appears in his *Constitution of Society*,[69] in which he sets forth his *theory of structuration*. This theory contains a good deal about what such terms as "society" and "structure" might mean.

[65]See pp. 333–34 for Blau's similar argument. Another classic proposition of network theory is that "multistranded" relationships are more likely to be intense than single-stranded ones. In other words, the more numerous the links that join people, the more likely it is that they will honor obligations and be able to demand help successfully.

[66]Mitchell, "Social Networks," p. 283.

[67]See Chapter IV.

[68]There is also a notable surfeit of methodological work over actual empirical research. A useful review is provided by Ron Burt, "Models of Network Structure," *Annual Review of Sociology*, 6 (1980), 79–141.

[69]Anthony Giddens, *The Constitution of Society: Outline of the Theory of Structuration* (Cambridge: Polity Press, 1984).

It is not—very consciously not—a variant of the sort of structuralism expounded by Peter Blau. On the contrary, in proposing a synthesis of much that has been advanced as "macro" or "micro" theory, Giddens rejects Blau's stated position.

Giddens argues that most theorists have tended to be imperialists, claiming all the ground for their own favored concepts—whether these be "structure" and its constraining qualities (in the case of structuralism and functionalism) or action and meaning (as with symbolic interactionism and phenomonology).

> One of my principal ambitions in the formulation of structuration theory is to put an end to each of these empire-building endeavours. The basic domain of study of the social sciences, according to the theory of structuration, is neither the experience of the individual actor, nor the existence of any form of societal totality, but social practices ordered across space and time.[70]

This, in turn, involves recognizing that social theory must reconceptualize its subject matter "as a duality—the duality of structure."[71] It is as misleading to concentrate only on the activities of a "free agent" as it is to look only at structural constraints which set limits to free activity.[72] Both are necessary.

Giddens' key point is that human actors re-create, through their actions, the very social practices (and institutions) *which in turn constrain that action*. They may also modify and change them. Thus, human social life is formed and reformed in the course of the most normal, routine activities. Giddens expresses this by describing human action as essentially *transformational* and argues that "the structural properties of social systems exist only in so far as forms of social conduct are reproduced chronically across time and space."[73] This emphasis on social practices' continuation from day to day, or year to year—"time"—and in different places—"space"—runs through all Giddens' writings.

So, too, does Giddens' insistence that this is not a mechanistic repetitive process in which we simply reproduce exactly what came before. Because social practices are modified as well as reproduced, we must reject "the presumption that it is possible to formulate theorems of structural causation which will explain the determination of social action in general."[74] The creative aspects of human action—the individual side of the

---

[70]Ibid., p. 2.

[71]Ibid., p. xxi. Giddens defines structure as "rules and resources, recursively implicated in the reproduction of social systems." *Central Problems in Social Theory: Action, Structure and Contradiction in Social Analysis* (London: The Macmillan Press, 1979), p. 64. This definition is discussed further below.

[72]Giddens, *Constitution of Society*, p. 139. Giddens' view of the individual as a "knowledgable actor" resembles that of George Herbert Mead. See Chapter V.

[73]Ibid., pp. xxi and xxiii.

[74]Ibid., p. 227.

duality—makes this impossible.[75] Giddens' insistence on this point separates his "structuration" theory definitively from the "structuralism" of
theorists such as Blau.[76]

Diego Gambetta's empirical research, praised by Giddens for its concern with the "duality of structure," clarifies what this approach involves. In
Were They Pushed or Did They Jump? Gambetta studied Italian survey data in
order to understand people's different educational experiences.[77] He asked
why some individuals stay on at school, while others leave, and why some
choose vocational-track schools—a choice in Italy which makes it impossible
to go on to university—while others go to the academic high schools.

In Italy, as in other countries, there are big class differences in staying-
on rates. However, Gambetta argues, "since there are no overt forces of
coercion, educational destinations have somehow to be reached through
individual preferences and decisions."[78] Most writers about education tend
to see people as either being "pushed" by the "forces of social reproduction"—a typically macro view—or as "jumping" on the basis of rational choice
between alternatives.[79] Gambetta's aim was to see how far "educational behaviour [can] be represented as a product of intentional choice"[80] and how
far external processes in practice minimize individuals' degree of choice.

Gambetta looked carefully at the social factors bringing pressure to
bear on people, and at people's own choice between alternatives. "So, *were
they pushed or did they jump?*" he asks. "If anything they jumped. They
jumped as much as they could and as much as they perceived it was worth
jumping."[81] In other words, the better people's grades, the more likely they
(and you) are to stay on at school. The longer they stay on—and hence the
greater their investment—the likelier it is that they will plan to stay on
longer still. And the higher the economic returns to education in the region
where they live, the less likely they are to leave early. In every case, individual decisions are the crucial mechanism producing aggregated "institutional" results.

However, Gambetta also demonstrated that "not all children can jump
to the same extent and the number of pushes they receive in several direc-

---

[75]It follows that all social research must include important parts which are particular to
that situation and not to be deduced from general laws; it has a "necessarily cultural, ethnographic or 'anthropological' aspect to it." Giddens, *Constitution of Society*, p. 237.

[76]Or of Marxists such as Althusser. Giddens, *Central Problems in Social Theory*, Chapter 4.

[77]Diego Gambetta, *Were They Pushed or Did They Jump? Individual Decision Mechanisms in
Education* (Cambridge: Cambridge University Press, Studies in Rationality and Social Change,
1987).

[78]Ibid., p. 2.

[79]Bourdieu (see pp. 93–101) and Boudon (see pp. 203–6) exemplify the two approaches.

[80]Gambetta, *Were They Pushed?* p. 7.

[81]Ibid., p. 186.

tions varies tremendously in society." In the case of children from poorer homes, the sheer cost to their families of their staying on at school is of great importance; indeed, it is the major reason for differences between them and their middle-class counterparts. In addition, academically weak middle-class pupils "who are pushed upwards risk failures later on and are often in no position to make good use of the education they receive other than for satisfying tenacious family pride."[82]

Social Reproduction   Giddens identifies a number of factors which play a key role in the reproduction of social practices. Among these are mutual knowledge, autonomy and trust, and routinization. Here, Giddens' inspirations are largely writers associated with "micro" analysis, notably Goffman but also Schutz.[83]

Thus, in his analysis of everyday action, Giddens draws attention to the "vast bulk of the 'stocks of knowledge', in Schutz's phrase, or what I prefer to call the *mutual knowledge* incorporated in encounters."[84] This knowledge is essentially outside what Giddens calls "discursive consciousness," by which he means that people are not normally self-conscious about it or conscious of knowing it. Indeed, the knowledge about which they are self-conscious and about which they can hold forth is only a very small part of that with which they operate. An enormous amount of other mutual knowledge is used quite automatically.

Giddens himself gives an excellent example of what he means in the following transcript from a courtroom:

Public defender (PD): Your honour, we request immediate sentencing and waive the probation report.

Judge: What's his record?

PD: He has a prior drunk and a GTA (grand theft, auto). Nothing serious. This is just a shoplifting case. He did enter the K-Mart with intent to steal. But really all we have here is a petty theft.

Judge: What do the people have?

District Attorney (DA): Nothing either way.

Judge: Any objections to immediate sentencing?

DA: No.

Judge: How long has he been in?

PD: Eighty-three days.

Judge: I make this a misdemeanour by PC article 17 and sentence you to ninety days in County Jail with credit for time served.[85]

[82] Ibid., p. 187.
[83] See Chapters V and VI.
[84] Giddens, *Constitution of Society*, p. 4.
[85] Ibid., p. 330.

Each speaker here, as Giddens points out, assumes that the other participants know a vast amount about what a legal system is and how this particular one operates, as well as about "drunkenness" and "K-Marts." (You, as a twentieth-century reader, also can understand the passage without too much difficulty. Imagine the reaction of a ninth-century Viking to this passage.) What Giddens also underlines is that "by invoking the institutional order in this way—and *there is no other way* for participants in interaction to render what they do intelligible and coherent to one another—they thereby contribute to reproducing it."[86] Such exchanges are a necessary precondition of a legal system's continued existence.

Much of what Giddens says is to be found—as he makes clear—in the writings of microsociologists, such as the phenomenologists. His own concern is to relate this microanalysis to macro structures: to show how, far from being distinct concerns, the latter are created—and "reproduced"— on a continual basis by the former. Encapsulated in his analysis of courtroom dialogue, this is his distinctive contribution.

For the same reasons, Giddens lays great emphasis on the idea of *routinization.* Following Schutz again, he points out how we use formulae, or "typified schemes," in the course of our social life in order to get through routine, recurrent situations. People know general "rules" for doing particular types of social activity, and into these the particulars of a certain situation can be slotted. Moreover, "those types of rule which are of most significance for social theory are locked into the reproduction of institutionalised practices."[87] That is why studying day-to-day life is an integral part of any analysis of how institutional practices—macro topics—are maintained or reproduced. They are the prime expression of the "duality of structure" which is Giddens' main concern.

Giddens also stresses the way in which routinization is crucial to the individual for reasons that go beyond those of rational convenience. He argues that routine, *"psychologically linked to the minimizing of unconscious sources of anxiety,* is the predominant form of day-to-day social activity. . . . In the enactment of routines agents sustain a sense of ontological security."[88] In other words, they maintain a sense that their world is truly "real." Routine is important for ensuring the continuity of our own personalities, not just the continuity of institutions. We therefore have a "generalized motivational commitment"[89] to sustaining the routine and "tactfulness" of ordinary social intercourse.[90]

[86]Ibid., p. 331.

[87]Ibid., p. 22.

[88]Ibid., p. 282. Italics ours.

[89]Ibid., p. 64.

[90]Compare, for example, the reactions of people involved in Garfinkel's experiments in "violating" routine and trust, discussed in Chapter VI. Garfinkel's experiments demonstrate vividly "how important another's reaction to one's own action [is] in confirming the validity of

Giddens demonstrates the importance to us of routine, and the trust it engenders, by describing the effects of its absence. In particular,[91] he draws on Bruno Bettelheim's famous account of his experiences as a prisoner in Dachau and Buchenwald, two Nazi concentration camps.[92] The camps were a place where the ordinary routines of life were systematically and deliberately destroyed. Violence against an individual was an ever-present threat and might descend without warning. All toilet activities were carried out in public, under the control of the guards, as a deliberate way of denying people control and privacy. Prisoners—torn from their family and familiar environments, frequently without warning—were in many cases tortured and set to senseless tasks, without any ability to plan for the future. In these circumstances, Bettelheim records, "I . . . saw fast changes taking place, and not only in behaviour but personality also." Those who managed to maintain some small control in their daily lives were able to survive—albeit with regression to childlike attitudes and with marked and volatile mood swings; but with time, prisoners' personalities were "reconstructed" so that they actually came to identify with their oppressors, the camp guards.

Giddens sees the camps as an extreme example of "critical situations" in which normal routine is radically disturbed, and he draws parallels with the behavior of, for example, revolutionary mobs. Here, too, people become more suggestible; their behavior regresses to that associated with childhood; and they fall under the influence of a leader or demagogue. "The radical disruption of routine produces a sort of corrosive effect upon the customary behaviour of the actor, associated with the impact of anxiety or fear. . . . [A]n impressive feature of protracted critical situations is that changes occur in the personalities of those exposed to them, in spite of their conscious resolution to resist. . . . But a critical situation of a protracted type is precisely one that is radically removed from the habitual contexts of social reproduction."[93]

Study of critical situations and their effects leads us to a deeper understanding of the role of routine. We can see that socialization is not something that occurs once and for all during childhood. Instead, it is by creating and re-creating the familiar, through routine social relations, that our (acquired) personalities are sustained and anxiety contained. "*Continuity of*

---

the prior experience on which that action was based. . . . [W]ithout such confirmation the social world becomes unintelligible and seemingly unknowable." David Good, "Individuals, Interpersonal Relations and Trust," in Diego Gambetta, ed., *Trust: Making and Breaking Cooperative Relations* (New York: Basil Blackwell, 1988).

[91]Giddens, *Central Problems in Social Theory.*

[92]See Bruno Bettelheim, *The Informed Heart* (Glencoe, Ill.: The Free Press, 1960). Bettelheim later founded a famous school for disturbed children in Chicago.

[93]Giddens, *Central Problems in Social Theory,* pp. 126–27 passim.

social reproduction involves the continual 'regrooving' of established attitudes and cognitive outlooks."[94]

Giddens relates his arguments about the links between routinization, trust, and personality to the work of Goffman, whom he greatly admires. He feels that Goffman's work is too often seen as anecdotal, and nongeneralizable, when in fact he has described many of the crucial ways in which personality, individual behavior and "social structure" are intertwined. Control over one's body and the importance of keeping "face" in social interaction are two of Goffman's major concerns. So, too, is the difference between "front" and "back" regions. Giddens emphasizes that these are important general—and indeed necessary—parts of human society. The Nazi concentration camps depersonalized the inmates by destroying the differentiation between front and back regions, stripping away control from them, and making anything like a "normal" society impossible.

Social Structure   Giddens' concern with the "dynamics" of institutional survival is similarly evident in his definition of social structure: "Structure refers, in social analysis, to the structuring properties . . . which make it possible for discernibly similar social practices to exist across varying spans of *time* and *space* and which lend them 'systemic' form."[95] Structure consists of the "rules and resources recursively implicated in the reproduction of social systems,"[96] that is, the rules which are articulated in social interaction and tell people how to "do" social life, and the resources on which people can call to achieve their objectives.[97]

One distinctive aspect of Giddens' discussion is the emphasis he places on the physical dimensions of human action and social "structure." He is aware that we are biological creatures and that our bodies are very important to us and central to the whole process of "transformational" or social human action. His high opinion of Goffman's work is in considerable measure linked to Goffman's analyses of body management, for example, as seen in the discussion of front and back regions mentioned earlier.[98]

Giddens argues that the way in which daily life is routinized is closely linked to features of the human body, including the common paths followed by people through a life cycle. Among these features is the "limited capability of human beings to participate in more than one task at once"; hence, turn-

---

[94]Ibid., p. 128. Italics original.

[95]Giddens, *Constitution of Society,* p. 17 (italics ours). Similarly, "social systems . . . are organized as regularized social practices, sustained in encounters dispersed across time-space": their existence encompasses different days, weeks, years, and decades, as well as different places. Ibid., p. 83.

[96]Giddens, *Central Problems in Social Theory,* p. 64.

[97]"Resources" refer to a very wide range of phenomena, similar to those itemized by Collins. See Chapter III of this text. Giddens also emphasizes the importance of unevenly distributed resources.

[98]See also Chapter V.

taking is fundamental to activity. Another feature is the indivisibility of the body. You cannot have your arms playing tennis while your legs are doing the shopping! The whole awareness of self[99] and the way one behaves to "others" entail a "ramified control of the body."[100] Again, as the concentration camp discussion will have implied, trust and "ontological security [are] founded on an autonomy of bodily control within predictable routines and encounters."[101] The context of encounters, which Giddens sees as a key point of study for "structuration theory," includes the co-presence of actors, their body gestures, and expressions; "all social interaction is expressed at some point in and through the contextualities of bodily presence."[102]

This emphasis on the flesh and blood of interaction removes Giddens from the mathematical structuralism of Blau as much as from the focus on words of Foucault. However, Giddens does not seem to believe that there are important regularities which derive directly from the biological as such—he is no sociobiologist in the making. It is rather that his formulation of the "problem of order" as how "it comes about that social systems 'bind' time and space, incorporating and integrating presence and absence,"[103] directs him to the physical context of interaction.

The same perspective informs Giddens' rather distinctive classification of social types.[104] Giddens does not focus simply on economic forms of ownership, but also on a way in which societies today are quite different from any before. In the past, although some societies were (partially) literate and developed books and even a rudimentary postal system, *communication was essentially and overwhelmingly face-to-face*. Politicians' "whistle-stop tours" by railroad were a way of meeting potential voters. Conversely, emigrants to the New World knew that farewells were, literally, forever.

In the developed societies of our world, none of this is true. Presidential candidates communicate by television commercials, not by hour-long speeches to large crowds (and Romeo and Juliet could use the telephone today). President Gorbachev, in his bid to carry the Soviet population with him in his reforms, similarly has made constant use of television. In Giddens' terms, the "contemporary world system is, for the first time in human history, one in which absence in space no longer hinders system co-ordination."[105]

---

[99] In discussing the "I," Giddens draws on G. H. Mead. See above Chapter V and Giddens, *Constitution of Society*, p. 43.

[100] Giddens, *Constitution of Society*, p. 43.

[101] Ibid., p. 64.

[102] Ibid., p. 297.

[103] Ibid., p. 181.

[104] See especially Anthony Giddens, *A Contemporary Critique of Historical Materialism*. Vol. I: *Power, Property and the State* (London: Macmillan, 1981): see also Giddens, *Constitution of Society*, Chapter 4.

[105] Giddens, *Constitution of Society*, p. 185. See also Chapter III, pp. 105–6, of this text for discussion of Giddens' view of the "world system."

Giddens sees the past as dominated first by tribal and then by "class-divided" societies.[106] In tribal, and particularly *oral* (pre-literate) societies, the "dominant structural principle" involves tradition and kinship, depending on large amounts of direct interaction between people. In class-divided societies, tradition and kinship remain very important, but there is some "disentangling" of the two from the institutional spheres of politics—with its standing armies, government officials, and formal legal codes—and economics—with markets, currency, and formal property rights.[107]

Giddens' habitual concern with the "binding together" of social life over time and over space leads him here to focus on the role of writing and of the city. Thus, he argues, "Life is not experienced as 'structures' but as the *durée* of day-to-day existence. . . . In tribal and class-divided societies, the routinisation of daily life is governed above all by tradition. . . . [T]he significance of tradition in purely oral cultures is different from those in which some form of writing exists. . . . [It expands] the level of time-space distanciation."[108]

Viewed from this same perspective,

> the city cannot be regarded as purely incidental to social theory but belongs at its very core. . . . [T]he city is . . . a *storage container* that permits time-space distanciation well beyond that characteristic of tribal societies. . . . The city is the generator of the authoritative resources out of which state power is created and sustained. . . . [Cities] are the basis of whatever administrative-political integration is achieved in that society as a whole. . . . In class-divided societies cities are crucibles of power.[109]

It follows, then, that modern capitalism was not just another, more "developed"[110] form of class-divided society, but rather the "first genuinely global type of societal organization in history."[111] In it, state and economic institutions are fully "disembedded" from the family and from orally transmitted traditions. The administrative concerns and reach of the state expand enormously, while the economic system has built into it a continuing tendency to produce technological innovation and greater wealth. State socialist societies embody a different approach to generating wealth in a self-sustaining fashion. There, too, economy and polity are differentiated

---

[106]Here his analysis is in many respects similar to that of Habermas. See above Chapter III, pp. 123–26.

[107]Giddens emphasizes the differentiation of city from countryside in such societies.

[108]Giddens, *A Contemporary Critique of Historical Materialism,* Vol. I, p. 150.

[109]Ibid., pp. 140, 144, 145 passim.

[110]Giddens objects to accounts which portray history in strongly evolutionary form, pointing out that the "dissolution of states is no less common an occurrence than their initial formation" (*Constitution of Society,* p. 248). However, his own account does not differ much in its essentials from those of less self-conscious writers.

[111]Giddens, *Constitution of Society,* p. 183.

from the "old" world of kin and tradition, but "the economy has been made subordinate to the directive control of the political administration."[112] Today, therefore, we inhabit a "world economy" in which the "super-power blocs" of capitalism and state socialism actually coexist with class-divided and even a few tribal societies.

Giddens' style is often extraordinarily discursive, and his habit of repeating and elaborating upon his ideas in slightly different ways can make it hard to identify the central argument. Moreover, given how self-conscious he is about the process of theorizing, his own concepts and definitions are sometimes surprisingly imprecise. However, Giddens' efforts to integrate micro and macro concepts represent an important trend in current sociological theory. His elaboration of Goffman's work and his discussion of routine and trust are especially successful in showing how individual behavior and psychology inhere in institutional structures.

PART THREE
Sociobiology

Sociobiology is the study of the biological bases of human behavior, and consequently it attacks the predominant mode of sociological theory and analysis. Although contemporary theoretical perspectives vary considerably in their subject matter, view of mankind, and methods of analysis, they do share an emphasis on symbol and meaning. This is one of the things that has made them "sociological."

In recent years, however, many have attacked sociology (and anthropology) for implying that society is essentially symbolic, rather than a world of flesh-and-blood animals whose biology also affects their behavior. The critics argue that we should study the biological basis of people's social behavior—what Parsons labels the level of the "organism"—which they consider to be far more important than has commonly been admitted. This approach is usually called *sociobiology*, although the term is not universal. It is the one zoologist Edward Wilson used in his massive synthesis of work on "the systematic study of the biological basis of all social behavior."[113] In fact, Wilson's work deals almost wholly with animal societies and such features as their "dominance systems" (or pecking orders), rules of territoriality, and parental care. Nonetheless, it is his work which has made the public fully

---

[112]Anthony Giddens, *The Class Structure of the Advanced Societies* (London: Hutchinson, 1973), p. 252.

[113]Edward O. Wilson, *Sociobiology: The New Synthesis* (Cambridge, Mass: The Belknap Press of Harvard University Press, 1975), p. 4.

aware of the existence of sociobiology as a controversial approach to human behavior.

Sociobiologists argue that the human race is a product of evolution and that vast quantities of information are passed on by our genes. It follows that genes as well as environment play a role in society and that behavior has a biological base. The balance may be different for humans, just as animals and insects differ from one another, but the basic framework of analysis is the same.

> Sociobiology applies natural selection theory to behavior. It asserts that the behavior of an animal, like its anatomy, is the product of a process of biological evolution through natural selection. Any behavioral phenotype is the result of the interaction between genotype and environmental conditions. . . . [F]or man, culture is indeed a whole new evolutionary ball game. . . . However, human culture does not stand apart from biological evolution; it grew out of it and remains inextricably intertwined with it.[114]

Sociobiologists are not simplistic genetic determinists who claim that human behavior is directly controlled by genes. Rather, they believe that biological factors and genetic influences set limits to the range of possible behaviors. These limits and behavioral tendencies, they argue, result from evolution, just as does the behavior of other species, and they must be understood in the context of natural selection.

One of the best descriptions of this general approach has been given by the anthropologist Robin Fox. He describes how, as a young student,

> I had the litany chanted at me: "biological universals cannot explain cultural differentials. . . ." And of course at one level they cannot. Muslims, I was told, take off their shoes to go into church while Christians take off their hats. Now find a biological explanation for *that!* I was never sure I wanted to find any kind of explanation for it. It seemed to me an arbitrary thing. . . . [Nonetheless] I was plagued by the question: If we do not really know what biological universals there are, then how can we study the cultural differentials in the first place? How to study the variables without the constants?[115]

Fox argues that although there is a great deal of difference in the "symbolic disguises" worn by different societies and in the details of their culture and behavior, beneath these differences is a remarkable uniformity of social structure and social institutions. He predicts that if you could bring up children in isolation from any known culture, within a very few generations they would produce a society with a long list of concrete properties:

---

[114]Pierre L. van den Berghe, "Sociobiology, Dogma, and Ethics," *The Wilson Quarterly* (Summer 1977), 121.

[115]Robin Fox, "The Cultural Animal." *Encounter*, XXXV, no. 1 (July 1970), 33.

"laws about property, rules about incest . . . a system of social status and methods of indicating it . . . courtship practices . . . associations set aside for men . . . gambling . . . homicide, suicide, homosexuality, schizophrenia, psychosis, and neurosis, and various practitioners to take advantage of, or cure, these, depending on how they are viewed."[116] They would do this, he claims, because it is "in the beast."

In other words, Fox argues, we are not different in kind from other animals because we are "cultural" and they are "biological." Rather, we are a special kind of primate: a primate that produces cultures and that has endured as a "cultural animal." As the human being evolved, a biped dependent on his brains for survival, the capacity for cultural behavior was at a premium. Natural selection favored those who could develop cultural traditions and thus adapt rapidly to changing circumstances—for although cultural traditions may change slowly, they do so very rapidly compared to instinctive behavior and genetic material. The use of brain-dependent cultural activities and the growth of the human brain went hand in hand. Thus, "culture does not represent a triumph over nature," Fox argues. Rather, "in behaving culturally we are behaving naturally."[117]

THE "NEW BIOLOGY": SELFISH GENES
AND ALTRUISTIC CREATURES

The importance of biological factors in explaining human behavior is an issue which arouses extremely strong feelings among social scientists. This is hardly surprising, since at issue are what it means to be human and how far we can affect what we are and the sorts of societies we live in. At the same time, it is extraordinarily difficult to examine the role of biological factors directly and find out just how important they are. No one, after all, is denying that environment and culture both matter. But how are we to separate out the inextricably entwined?

One possibility is to look at some of the major theoretical advances which have been taking place in biology and ethology, and ask how far they really do illuminate human behavior. (If the answer is "very little," this does not, of course, prove that future developments might not do better—but it will, at least, counsel caution in using biology to help explain social behavior.) For this purpose, recent work on "altruism" is especially interesting, because it brings into play a number of quite distinct theories. Darwin's theory of evolution states that things survive if they are able to compete for resources in a successful—and stable—fashion. We now know that, among

[116]Ibid.

[117]Ibid., 40. In similar vein, Groves and Sabater Pi analyze similarities between human and apes in the use of a "fix-point" or home base for sleeping. Colin P. Groves and J. Sabater Pi, "From Ape's Nest to Human Fix-Point," *Man*, (n.s.), 20 (1985), 22–47.

living things, the basic unit of survival is the gene, because it is genes that replicate themselves. If an organism contains a gene which tends to promote its survival, then that gene will spread gradually.[118] Those descendants of the first organism which inherit the gene will tend to survive and reproduce relatively more successfully, and the gene will be replicated. The cockroach, which has remained unchanged for millennia, is produced by a particularly effective and stable set of genes. Man's probable ancestor, *Australopithecus*, no longer exists in that form, but we all carry genes which come in a direct line of descent from ancestors more or less akin to *Australopithecus*. Those inherited genes, of different origins but now traveling together, are, by definition, the results of selection (so far, at least). The behavior they govern has enabled organisms to survive and reproduce.

This basic theory of natural selection—in which the mechanism for Darwin's theory is provided by Mendelian genetics—is essentially one of what has been called "gene selfishness."[119] This is not to say that genes are *consciously* selfish. Rather the whole theory of natural selection implies it, for it states that the race goes, by definition, to the self-interested. If a gene promotes the survival of an organism, it will be reproduced. If it does not, it will not.[120]

One of the most obvious challenges to evolutionary theory has always been the existence of altruistic behavior—that is, behavior which apparently *does not* promote the survival of the creature exhibiting it.[121] Humans are quite often "altruistic," but so, apparently, are other animals, and not only where their children are concerned. Worker bees, for example, use their stings as a very effective defense of the nest—and die in doing so. Many small birds use an alarm call to warn of the approach of hawks or other predators—and in doing so draw attention to themselves.

One very common explanation which has been offered is that creatures behave in this way "for the good of the species." The individuals concerned may not benefit directly, but the way they act will help other members of the species to survive, reproduce, and replicate altruistic behavior. Robert Ardrey suggested that the world became populated with groups of self-sacrificing individuals because, as a species, they did better than

---

[118]*Ceteris paribus.*

[119]Richard Dawkins, *The Selfish Gene* (Oxford: Oxford University Press, 1976, and London: Granada, 1978), p. 7. Page references are to the Granada edition.

[120]Clearly this is not an instantaneous, either-or situation. Rather, over time, organisms with the (more successful) gene A will tend to do better than those with the (less successful) gene B. Over enough time, those with gene B may do badly enough that gene B becomes extinct. The persistence of sickle-cell anemia in parts of Africa shows how complex this process can be. Although sickle-cell anemia is often fatal, the responsible genes also provide protection against malaria and to this degree promote survival (and themselves survive).

[121]It is the consequences of the behavior which are important—so-called "altruistic behavior" has nothing to do with the supposed intentions of the creatures involved. Cf. Penelope J. Green, Charles J. Morgan, and David P. Barash, "Sociobiology" in Scott McNall, ed., *Theoretical Perspectives in Sociology* (New York: St. Martins Press, 1979), pp. 414–30.

selfish, noncooperating ones.[122] The idea has also appealed to sociologists and social psychologists. J. Philippe Rushton, for example, in discussing the way in which altruistic behavior develops in society, suggests that the need for mutual defense created "group loyalty and ultimately the altruistic willingness to sacrifice the self for the group."[123]

It is an appealing scenario, but unfortunately it never would have occurred. One reason is that it implies an ability to recognize and identify with one's "own" species, a characteristic which animals do not display. The second flaw in the "group-selection" theory is also very simple. It leaves the field wide open to the mutant gangster, who won't play by the rules. He is happy to let others sacrifice themselves for him, but sees no reason to do the same. He will simply take the pickings and do far better than the altruists at breeding. (Moreover, his offspring will very likely be gangsters, too.) This does not mean that *only* gangsters will survive: to continue the analogy, aggressive individuals of this sort fortunately attack each other as much as, or more than, their more timid co-citizens. This may help keep their numbers down and leave space for the rest to go on breeding, too. However, we cannot use "the good of the species" as a satisfactory explanation for alarm calls, bee stings, and the like, where the behavior is a *general* characteristic of the species.[124] A gene for such self-sacrificing behavior would not last long, let alone give rise to stable and universal traits.[125]

In explaining apparently altruistic behavior, modern biologists use a variety of explanations, depending on the situation in question. The most powerful single explanation, however—in the sense that it accounts for so many apparent puzzles—is that of *kin selection*. The argument is that apparently altruistic behavior may be highly "adaptive," even when it does not promote the survival and future reproduction of a given individual, so long as it does benefit *related* individuals.[126] This is much clearer once we realize that, in the long term, we are talking about whether particular *genes* survive and are passed on to more or less remote individuals. Suppose, for exam-

---

[122]Robert Ardrey, *The Social Contract* (London: Collins, 1970). Cf. the work of V. C. Wynne-Edwards.

[123]J. Philippe Rushton, *Altruism, Socialization and Society* (Englewood Cliffs, N.J.: Prentice-Hall, Inc., 1980), p. 29.

[124]See the work of J. Maynard Smith for a full discussion of how different categories (e.g., "hawk" and "dove") can coexist within a species in stable proportions. E.g., J. Maynard Smith and G. R. Price, "The Logic of Animal Conflicts," *Nature*, 24b (1973), 15–18. See also Dawkins, *The Selfish Gene*.

[125]Economists, who have recently been discussing very similar problems in the context of how large organizations, which depend on reciprocity, operate, refer to "free riders" or "opportunists." See, especially, Mancur Olson, *The Logic of Collective Action* (Cambridge: Harvard University Press, 1965); and Douglass C. North, *Structure and Change in Economic History* (New York: W. W. Norton & Co., Inc., 1981).

[126]In its present form, the theory owes most to the work of W. D. Hamilton; see especially "The Genetical Evolution of Social Behavior" (I & II), *Journal of Theoretical Biology*, 7 (1964), 1–16 and 17–52.

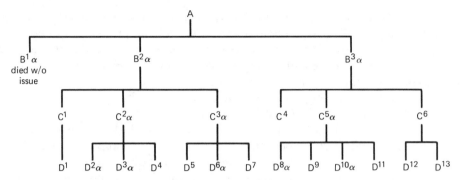

FIGURE 7-4   A Model of the Spread of an "Altruistic" Gene

ple, that individual A gives birth to three children (see Figure 7-4), all of whom share with A an "altruistic" gene α. They help each other in a number of situations, and eventually poor B^1 perishes, leaving no offspring. However, B^2 and B^3 are luckier; and the results of the cooperative behavior can be seen in the fact that they, between them, raise 6 children, 3 of whom possess α. By the fourth generation (D^1, D^2 etc.), there are 5 copies of α around instead of 3; whereas the noncooperating siblings (C^1, C^4, C^6) have only managed 3 adult offspring among them. In other words, the "sacrifice" of B^1 had a positive payoff in terms of natural selection. It promoted the spread of the relevant gene and was in that sense quite consistent with the "selfishness" of evolution.

If we go back to those kamikaze worker bees, we can see how the same logic applies. Because such behavior promotes the welfare of their genes, they care for and defend each other and the nest, generation after generation. They are sterile themselves; therefore, from the point of view of natural selection, it is the protection and care of the current and future queens (and their mates) which is selected for.[127] Worker bees who look after themselves will not promote the survival of their genes.

What kin selection points out is that something we take for granted—looking after one's children—is really only a special case of something more general. Any genetically based behavior which tends to help one's genes to survive will, by definition, tend itself to survive.

Altruistic behavior between unrelated individuals would seem, by contrast, to be an open invitation to "cheating," something bound to benefit the recipient at the donor's expense. However, Robert Trivers points out that there are certain situations in which cheating will not be worth-

---

[127]The particular social organization developed by ants, bees, and wasps is related to their very distinctive system of sexual reproduction, in which, for example, "sister" worker bees share more genes with each other than with their mother. See R. L. Trivers and H. Hare, "Haplodiploidy and the Evolution of the Social Insects," *Science*, 191 (1976), 249–63.

while.[128] Long-lived creatures which are likely to come into contact frequently and which have a high degree of mutual dependence are especially likely to meet with many opportunities for reciprocal altruism and, therefore, to benefit from practicing it. These are factors which also encourage kin selection, making it difficult to distinguish the two within a species. However, Trivers' theory provides a clear explanation for such remarkable behavior as that of "cleaner" fish, which enter other fish and clean the gills and mouths of predators without themselves (usually) being eaten.

The arguments of the "new biology" are extremely interesting in themselves. However, the question remains, Just how much do they contribute to explaining human society? When a functionalist talks about shared norms and values, for example, is this really just a misdescription of behavior which has evolved over the millennia because, when we lived in small kin-based groups, altruism and reciprocity promoted our reproductive success?

Some sociobiologists have tried to apply ideas such as kin selection directly to the particular social patterns of different societies. Suppose we take the practice of polyandry, in which several men share a wife. Sociobiologists may "explain" it by pointing out that, when it exists, it usually involves several *brothers* sharing a wife. Each man is therefore furthering the reproduction of his genes somewhat for every child born.[129] Equally, they point out that if the wife lives with the husband's family, the latter can attempt to make sure that her offspring really are his, whereas her family knows anyway that the children really are their descendants. Thus, "we humans seem, in general, to be doing a very good job of adhering to biology . . . 80% of all human societies have patrilocality as the dominant form of residence."[130]

"Strategies" for securing your (or your genes') reproduction, which include, for example, partrilocality, do indeed occur among animals. This is what gives the sociobiologists' analogies such vividness. However, many biologists are wary of regarding most of them as anything more than analogies. Among animals, one is talking about stable, instinct-based behavior. A creature does not practice polyandry one minute, polygyny the next. Squirrels in one wood are not patrilocal when those in the next are matrilocal. Dawkins, the author of *The Selfish Gene,* describes an occasion when he listened to anthropologists discussing kinship behavior in kin selection terms.[131] Did they really mean, he asked, that different tribes had been isolated so long that they had evolved distinctive mating patterns? Good

[128]Robert Trivers, "The Evolution of Reciprocal Altruism," *Quarterly Review of Biology,* 46 (1971), 35–57.

[129]David P. Barash, *Sociobiology: The Whisperings Within* (New York: Harper and Row, 1979, and London: Fontana, 1981). Subsequent page references are for the Fontana edition.

[130]Ibid., p. 144.

[131]R. Dawkins, *The Extended Phenotype: The Gene as the Unit of Selection* (Oxford and San Francisco: W. H. Freeman and Co., 1982).

gracious, no, they replied, they weren't talking about *genes*. But the point about ethologists is that they are talking about genes. Kin selection is a theory about gene-based evolution.

Similar dangers lurk in waiting for the sociobiologist who ventures into the field of "reciprocal altruism"—behavior between unrelated individuals which can be adaptive provided that the giver really will be the getter at some future date. Reciprocity as a norm has cropped up in a number of places in this book.[132] The suggestion that it may be biologically based is obviously a big claim for biology rather than sociology as a major explanatory force. Once again, however, what we are dealing with in humans is not, at root, instinctive—or no more than partly so. Barash, for example, gives as an example of an "important aspect of the biology of altruism" the behavior of the Chukchee people of Siberia, where the men traveled with the reindeer herds and shared their wives with each other. "As with the proverbial seaman who had a woman in every port, adult Chukchee males could count on finding one at every encampment. . . . The men making these arrangements . . . were not really altruistic at all. They profited from their generosity by the guarantee that they would receive equivalent benefits."[133]

The trouble is that formal wife sharing is not a common, let alone universal, characteristic of human societies. Consequently, we can explain Chukchee customs not only as well, but *better*, as a solution to a particular, concrete problem, without bringing in genes at all.[134] Reciprocity, trust, and cooperation among human beings are in general better explained by several factors than by just positing genetic inheritance. On the one hand, it is true that we do things for family members that we would not do for others[135] and that cooperating creatures often do better than non-cooperators. (Certainly, humans and ants are currently worldwide winners.) However, altruistic and other mutually rewarding behavior can also be arrived at rationally. Studies of people playing games show that collaboration leads to a gradual growth of trust and enduring cooperation.

---

[132]See especially Chapter IV.

[133]Barash, *Sociobiology*, p. 155.

[134]The temptation to substitute a telling analogy for argument is one to which even Edward Wilson succumbs on occasion. He notes that "Mother Theresa is an extraordinary person but it should not be forgotten that she is secure in the service of Christ and the knowledge of her Church's immortality." (*On Human Nature*, Harvard University Press, 1978, p. 165). But Mother Theresa is only a daughter of the Catholic Church in a spiritual sense, and to suggest that her behavior is like that of a kamikaze worker bee or alarm-sounding ground squirrel is nonsense. See Vernon Reynolds, *The Biology of Human Action*, 2nd ed. (Oxford: W. H. Freeman & Co. Ltd., 1980), for a general critique of sociobiology.

[135]Conversely, child abuse by step-parents is statistically far more likely than abuse by genetic parents, as traditional fairy stories recognize. See, e.g., Laura Betzig, Monique Morgerhoff Mulder, and Paul Turke, eds., *Human Reproductive Behaviour: A Darwinian Perspective* (Cambridge: Cambridge University Press, 1988), p. 12.

They also show how rarely, over the long term, it "pays" to be seen as untrustworthy.[136]

Does this mean that sociobiology really has nothing to offer the student of society? Certainly, its most hostile opponents have argued that the human being is essentially a creature of cultural norms, in whom biological universals extend no further than such basic activities as eating, excreting, and sleeping. They argue that Wilson, for example, is a product of an alienated culture and his own class prejudices and "joins the long parade of biological determinists whose work has served to buttress the institutions of their society by exonerating them from responsibility for social problems."[137] Many other social scientists, however, have been stimulated by sociobiology—not to see it as a replacement for their own disciplines but as a valuable reminder to take note of the physical aspects of social life. Talcott Parsons was especially intrigued by the possibility of elaborating on his first "system level," that of the biological organism. Psychologists and sociologists have been encouraged to treat human survival and reproduction as important influences on the survival of cultural and social practices as well as physical characteristics.

More generally, anthropologists have come to focus on reproductive success (measured by numbers of surviving children) in their analyses of social structure.[138] While emphasizing that cultural responses to environmental pressures vary widely, they also identify links between recurrent practices (and supposed "adaptation") and individuals' success (or "enhanced fitness"). They point out that female adultery is more common in societies where men care for their sisters' sons rather then their own. Female adultery is generally more common the more inheritance is matrilineal (i.e., from mother to child, rather than father to child).[139] Similarly, in tribal societies where men can count on plenty of support from their own kin, clan, neighbors, or age group, those who are wealthy tend to opt for "quantity" and acquire lots of wives, rather than "quality" in the form of particularly expensive marriages.[140] Conversely, in societies where marriage ties with other families are very important to a man's

[136]Patrick Bateson "The Biological Evolution of Co-operation and Trust," and David Good, "Individuals, Interpersonal Relations and Trust," in Diego Gambetta, ed., *Trust: Making and Breaking Co-operative Relations.* See also Chapter IV, pp. 209–11.

[137]Letter to the *New York Review of Books,* November 13, 1975, from the Cambridge, Massachusetts-based "Sociobiology Study Group."

[138]See, e.g., Betzig, Borgerhoff Mulder, and Turke, eds., *Human Reproductive Behaviour;* and N. A. Chagnon and W. Irons eds., *Evolutionary Biology and Human Social Behavior: An Anthropological Perspective* (North Scituate, Mass.: Duxbury Press, 1979).

[139]In these cases, there is less riding on whether a child's paternity is correctly identified.

[140]These patterns can be identified because, in tribal societies, there is a "bride price," which on marriage, the husband pays to the wife's family.

success, wealthy men will opt for quality rather than simply numbers of wives.[141]

BIOLOGY AND CULTURE

Social scientists who are interested in integrating sociobiology into their own disciplines can be divided roughly into those who are trying to use neo-Darwinian concepts to examine culture—those concerned with "cultural evolution"—and those who are interested in the ways in which "proximate" biological and environmental factors shape and set limits to our social lives. Two recent addresses—one by the psychologist and statistician Donald Campbell and one by sociologist Alice Rossi—illustrate these two approaches. Both, interestingly, were presidential addresses (to the American Psychological Association and American Sociological Association) intended by their authors to convince their fellow professionals of the importance of pursuing evolutionary and biological hypotheses.[142]

Campbell suggests that it may make sense to see human culture as the product of selective evolution, just as it does physical and psychological attributes. The fact that culture is not gene-based in the way that, say, the working of our kidneys is, does not mean that societies select their cultures almost at random. On the contrary, over time, it makes sense to see the "cumulated culture and social system"[143] as the product of adaptive evolution. This is clear enough for, say, tools; less so for rules of social organization. However, Campbell speculates,

> Since time immemorial, human populations have continually been reorganized under different organizational systems with different beliefs and customs. In this flux, there may well have been a selective retention of organizational principles and ideologies, independent of the fate of individuals, if these organizational forms and belief systems contributed to the social system functionality, as expressed in the conquest and conversion of other peoples . . . a complex division-of-labor, urban, apartment-house, stored-food society . . . has independently occurred for human beings a half-dozen times.[144]

---

[141]Marriage payments in tribal societies will commonly be related to the bride's age and/or to her family's position. Monique Borgerhoff Mulder, "Adaptation and Evolutionary Approaches to Anthropology," *Man* (N.S.), 22 (1987), 25–41; Betzig, Borgerhoff Mulder, and Turke, eds., *Human Reproductive Behaviour.*

[142]Donald T. Campbell, "On the Conflict Between Biological and Social Evolution and Between Psychology and Moral Tradition," *The American Psychologist* (1975), 1103–26; and Alice S. Rossi, "Gender and Parenthood," *American Sociological Review*, 49, no. 1 (1984), 1–19.

[143]Campbell, "On the Conflict Between Biological and Social Evolution," p. 1104.

[144]Ibid., p. 1106.

Such a view of human society as the product of biological *and* cultural evolution is known as "dual inheritance theory"[145] and bears some striking resemblances to functionalism. However, there are some important differences, too. Campbell notes that "the wisdom produced by any evolutionary system is always wisdom about past worlds"[146] and may be quite *harmful* in current circumstances. Moreover, he doubts whether the process is still continuing.

> Adaptive evolution is a negative feedback steering device, and therefore works best when the evolving social organization is a small part of the total environment, so that variations in the social organization do not substantially change the selective system, that is, the overall environment. . . . [O]ne might well doubt that any adaptive social evolution is going on at the level of nations today . . . [because] major nations are so few in number, and so much the dominant part of each other's environment.[147]

More specifically, Campbell and "dual inheritance" theorists differ from previous sociologists in seeing the interaction between biological and social factors as worth particular and special attention.[148] In discussing altruism earlier, we rejected the idea that creatures behave for "the good of the species" and argued that "kin selection" and "reciprocal altruism" also do not get us very far in explaining human behavior. Campbell agrees, emphasizing that "*social evolution has had to counter individual selfish tendencies which biological evolution has continued to select as a result of the genetic competition among the cooperators.*"[149]

Campbell argues that religion and morality have to be seen in terms of their "evolutionary adaptive value" as a way of counteracting necessarily selfish human nature and that we can and should look for links between culturally evolved systems and biologically evolved traits. One possibility is that of children's eager conformity, our "suggestibility to majorities and prestige figures," and obedience to authority. Indeed our "universal tendency for conformity to the opinions of others may be essential to an adaptive social custom cumulation."[150] In other words, we may possess

[145]For a formal elaboration of the basic postulates, see Peter J. Richerson and Robert Boyd, "A Dual Inheritance Model of the Human Evolutionary Process: Basic Postulates and a Simple Model," *Journal of Social and Biological Structures*, 1, no. 2 (1978), 127–54.

[146]Campbell, p. 1106.

[147]Ibid.

[148]See especially articles by William H. Durham and others, in *Human Ecology*, 10, No. 3 (Sept. 1982), an issue on "Biology and Culture." Also Thomas Dietz, "The 'New Environmental Paradigm,' Human Ecology and Environmental Sociology," *Environmental Sociology* (1978), 12–15.

[149]Campbell, p. 1115. Italics original.

[150]Ibid., p. 1107. This argument is developed further in Robert Boyd and Peter J. Richerson, "Cultural Transmission and the Evolution of Co-operative Behavior," *Human Ecology*, 10, no. 3 (1982), 325–51.

traits that not only help in our socialization but make us want to be socialized.

Charles Lumsden and Edward Wilson have taken such arguments the furthest. They argue that as we evolved from creatures with a far higher percentage of instinctive behavior, it is extremely unlikely that we would have shed all genetically based traits. Instead, they hypothesize that how we see and understand things—the processes of cognition which underlie social and cultural artifacts—are directed by "epigenetic rules," "genetically determined procedures that direct the assembly of the mind."[151] Lumsden and Wilson note that their ideas are basically consistent with the approach of "structuralists"—such as Chomsky or Piaget, who also postulate innate constraints—and argue that creatures whose cultural behavior is based on adaptive procedures of this type will, in the long term, fare better[152] than creatures whose choice of culture is unconstrained and ultimately random.

The problem with such hypotheses is that they are almost impossible to test. Skeptics argue that one does not, in fact, *have* to posit biological underpinnings to the transmission of cultures. One could also explain them as rational responses to immediate problems. If a pattern recurs, that may be simply because the problem does, too. Although some criticism of this type comes from commentators who are hostile to sociobiology, it is also advanced by authors who are themselves extremely interested in the relationship between biology and social organization.[153] Rather than looking to neo-Darwinian theory, however, they want social scientists to take adequate account of the direct and immediate effects on society of environmental pressures. For example, it is easy for middle-class Westerners to forget that, for much of the world, getting enough to eat is a daily struggle. Western social science, in turn, often pays little attention to the importance of life's most basic requirements.

To date, as noted earlier, it has been the anthropologists who have given most attention to the link between human survival and reproduction on the one hand and cultural and social practices on the other. One very clear-cut example is the use of maize in agricultural communities. Without special preparation (involving an alkali in the cooking), maize is of very little nutritional value. Whether wood ash or lime is used is not something that is obviously important to an anthropologist studying the agricultural peoples of the New World—yet, in fact, there is a very close relationship

---

[151]Charles J. Lumsden and Edward O. Wilson, *Genes, Mind and Culture: The Coevolutionary Process* (Cambridge, Mass.: Harvard University Press, 1981), p. 7. See also Charles J. Lumsden, "Cultural Evolution and the Devolution of Tabula Rasa," *Journal of Social and Biological Structures*, 6, no. 2, (1983), 101–14.

[152]In natural selection terms.

[153]See especially, Vernon Reynolds, *The Biology of Human Action* (Reading, England: W. H. Freeman & Co., Ltd., 1976), and Mark V. Flinn and Richard D. Alexander, "Culture Theory: The Developing Synthesis from Biology" in *Human Ecology*, 10, no. 3, (1982), 383–400.

between alkali use and cultivation or dependence on maize.[154] Societies which did not develop this process presumably died out or developed some alternative food source.

In a similar spirit Alice Rossi, in her 1983 address to the American Sociological Association, argued that "none of the theories prevalent in family sociology . . . are adequate to an understanding and explanation of human parenting because they do not seek an integration of biological and social constructs."[155] When discussing human reproduction and child rearing, the appropriate response to the fact that socialization may exaggerate biological differences is not, she argues, to pretend they do not exist. Rossi is interested in the evidence on directly sex-linked biological differences, but she is also interested in the changing and complex relationships between sexual identity and reproduction, and social behavior and experience. Thus, she points out that the increasing age at marriage of men, rising divorce rates, and increasing numbers of women choosing to bear children out of marriage mean an *increasing* differential in the percentage of each sex with family responsibilities. Sociologists need no reminder, she goes on,

> that the . . . subpopulation group [of young men] predominates in sexual violence, alcohol and drug abuse, crime and social deviance. Unattached males roam the interstices between socially cohesive groups, kill and are themselves killed and maimed, but the machine cultures of the West have shown no inventiveness in developing new social institutions capable of providing individual loyalty and social integration to replace the bonds of family. Our only answers have been armies and prisons.[156]

Too often, Rossi argues, sociologists treat behavior differences between the sexes as simply culturally determined. Thus, hormones which bring on puberty are treated as though they were simply signals that certain "appropriate" behavior can and should follow. In fact, among *young* men, there are high correlations between testosterone levels and aggression.[157] Although older men may have greater control, "older men are not all 'mature'. . . . [L]ife pressures can often escalate to the point that our thin veneer of socialized self-control is lost, with the results we see in our prisons, hospitals, shelters for battered wives or homeless men, and treatment centers for child victims of incest. . . . Feelings and thoughts are

---

[154]S. H. Katz, M. C. Hediger, and L. A. Valleroy, "Traditional Maize Processing Techniques in the New World," *Science*, 184 (1974), 765–73.

[155]Rossi, "Gender and Parenthood," p. 1. See also Alice Rossi, "A Biosocial Perspective on Parenting," *Daedalus*, 106, no. 2 (1977), 1–31.

[156]Rossi, "Gender and Parenthood," p. 5.

[157]Even after allowing for all other factors. Rossi's reference is to J. R. Udry, J. O. G. Billy, N. M. Morris, T. R. Groff, and M. H. Raj, "Serum Androgenic Hormones Motivate Sexual Behavior in Adolescent Boys," *Fertility and Sterility* 43, no. 1 (1985), 90–94.

molecular events in the brain that have chemical consequences"[158] and physical ones.

The Biology of Religion[159] by Vernon Reynolds and R. E. S. Tanner is the most comprehensive analysis to date of the interaction between aspects of culture and the organizing concepts of natural selection theory—individual survival and reproductive success. We referred to Reynolds earlier in this section as one of the most effective critics of sociobiologists who posit a direct link between biological traits and social behavior. In particular, he sees no reason to invoke genetic factors in explaining behavior which can be interpreted as a recurring response to enduring problems. At the same time, as an anthropologist and ethologist,[160] he is particularly interested in the way creatures deal with the fundamental and original "problem" of how to survive and reproduce in an uncertain physical environment.

As one might expect, Reynolds and Tanner emphasize the diversity of what is religiously ordained and sanctioned. At the same time, they are concerned with "whether and how religions can be seen as developments arising out of human efforts to deal with long-term survival prospects,"[161] which embody different (culturally developed) approaches to the same (biological and physical) problems. Specifically, they suggest that there are two distinct reproductive strategies—which a sociologist would describe as "ideal types"—in a world of uncertainty. One aims for high levels of reproduction, so that some offspring will be likely to survive whatever happens, and will involve, as a result, giving less attention to the care and preservation of any one child. The other involves the curbing of reproduction, but more concentrated care of the offspring who are produced, so that all or most who are born may survive.

Religions are—among many other things—clearly concerned with laying down rules about reproduction. If, in doing so, they are responding "adaptively" to the physical environment, one might expect each to embody, in more or less extreme fashion, either the "anti" or the "pro" birth strategy (see Table 7-1). Moreover, the way in which they develop should be related to how unpredictable the environment is. The more unpredictable and crisis-ridden, the more likely it is that "pro-natalist" rules, encouraging enough children for some to survive, will be incorporated into the corpus of religious rules.

The implications for reproduction of many religious rules are often extremely clear. For example, traditional Islam sets no lower age limit for

[158]Alice S. Rossi, "Growing Up and Older in Sociology," in Matilda White Riley, ed., *Sociological Lives*, p. 62. See also Alice S. Rossi, "Sex and Gender in an Aging Society," *Daedalus*, 115, no. 1 (1986), 141–169.

[159]V. Reynolds and R. E. S. Tanner, *The Biology of Religion* (London and New York: Longman, 1983).

[160]Reynolds is an expert on primate behavior.

[161]Reynolds and Tanner, *The Biology of Religion*, p. 3.

TABLE 7-1   Alternative Sets of Religious Rules Governing Reproduction

LIFE CYCLE	"ANTI-NATALIST RULES"	"PRO-NATALIST" RULES
Conception	Few better	Many better
Infanticide and abortion	Approved of	Disapproved of
Birth and childhood	Few births, more care	Many births, less care
Adolescence	Reproduction delayed	Early reproduction
Marriage	Late	Early
Celibacy	Approved of	Disapproved of
Divorce and widowhood	Remarriage disapproved of	Remarriage preferred
Middle and old age	Refrain from reproduction	Reproduction continued
Death	Shock, denial	Accepted as routine
Concepts of disease	More hygiene conscious	Less hygiene conscious
Treatment of disease	Intervention and cure	Resignation, passivity

Source: Adapted from Table 1.2, p. 14, in Reynolds and Tanner, *The Biology of Religion* (London: Longman, 1983). Reprinted by permission of the publisher.

marriage, and traditional Hinduism considers it appropriate for girls as young as eight to be married. Neither religion believes that there is any virtue in celibacy, whereas Christian countries have consistently been characterized by far higher percentages remaining unmarried and higher average age at first marriage.[162] However, while some religions fall clearly at one end or other of the anti- or pro-natalist spectrum, others—notably Buddhism and Judaism—have survived for millennia with rules, some of which suggest one strategy, and some, another.[163]

If a religion does indeed reflect the environment faced by its devotees, pro-natalist rules should be most common in conditions of greater uncertainty. It is there that the consequences of the environment—droughts, famines, diseases, etc.—are most likely to encourage the retention and codification of customs encouraging high birthrates. Using energy consumption and income[164] as their indicators, Reynolds and Tanner find that there is, indeed, a significant correlation. In countries with low incomes and energy consumption, life is consequently highly insecure, and religion is likely to encourage reproduction and vice versa.

The problem with this "test" of the thesis is that it is quite possible that low national incomes are as much the result as the cause of the inhabitants' approach to reproduction. Max Weber, in one of sociology's most famous analyses, suggested such a link between the "Protestant ethic" and economic success.[165] A second problem is that Buddhism and Hinduism both

[162]Peter Laslett, *The World We Have Lost* (London: Methuen, 1971).

[163]This will presumably mean an "in-between" birthrate. It is thus not in itself an unreasonable strategy; but it does call into question how far there really is feedback from the environment which tends to reinforce rules of one or other type.

[164]Strictly, GNP per capita (1975, US dollars).

[165]Max Weber, *The Protestant Ethic and the Spirit of Capitalism* (New York: Scribner's 1958).

originated in the same country, India, although the former (which is overall rather anti-natalist) is no longer important there. Judaism and Islam, also with very different attitudes, are both originally religions of desert nomads. It might also be objected that Christianity developed at a time of far greater uncertainty for its adherents than most face today. On the other hand, economic historians increasingly are bringing together evidence that non-European countries have, throughout history, experienced more natural disasters and higher rates of disease than did the countries where Christianity first took root (and Judaism survived).[166] Thus, Reynolds and Tanner, by using modern data for a single year, may have omitted much of the evidence most favorable to their thesis.

Biology and Sociology   It seems unlikely that many of the recent theoretical advances of the "new biology" will have much direct relevance to sociology. Models deriving optimum ratios of worker bees to drones will hardly be used to explain changes in human family size, nor will middle managers' behavior be best understood in terms of a baboon troop's. What *does* seem likely, is that sociobiology's development will encourage social scientists to treat reproduction, scarcity, and environmental uncertainty as factors which are quite as important in explaining human as animal behavior—even if the way we respond is very different. For example, it is an awareness of individual selfishness as a motivating force in the survival of any living organism that lies behind one sociologist's comments on Marxist analysis:

> A reductionist model of class conflict and solidarity in terms of individuals maximizing self-interest is . . . perfectly adequate to understand "collective behavior." [However, as class distinctions and class conflict disappear] selfish interests are even more likely to emerge. . . . This is why Marxism has been so relatively successful in accounting for class conflicts . . . and such an abysmal failure in predicting, much less changing, behavior in the utopian societies it attempted to create. Socialism has always foundered on the rock of individual selfishness.[167]

Other writers echo Rossi's plea not to see human beings as infinitely "plastic." Sociologists tend to take it for granted that society revolves around group membership, even though they are often more interested in social classes than in kinship. They are less happy with the fact that groups

[166]See, for example, E. L. Jones, *The European Miracle* (New York: Cambridge University Press, 1981). Insights which sociobiology provides into individual psychology and interpersonal relationships may also be highly relevant to sociological analysis. For example, when symbolic interactionists look at how people interpret meaning, bodily characteristics such as fatness or extreme shortness can be important for all those involved in interaction.

[167]Pierre L. van den Berghe, *The Ethnic Phenomenon* (New York: Elsevier, 1981), pp. 241–42.

require boundaries and the exclusion of people as well as their inclusion.[168] But creatures that have lived in groups through millions of years of evolution are very likely to have characteristics that strongly encourage identification with one's own group—and therefore, rejection of others.

In consequence, "sociobiology expects *every* racial group to be xenophobic. . . . [I]t expects, if anything, that every group feels itself superior to others."[169] This is because

> when it occurs in natural settings, xenophobia is a functional and adaptive trait in that it maintains the integrity of the social group. It ensures that group members will be socially familiar. . . . Xenophobia has apparently arisen in the course of natural selection and social evolution in those species and populations where discrete social groups are adaptively favoured.[170]

What it *may* also leave us with is "a residual and irreducible element of interracial hostility after all other historical, political, economic, social and psychological factors have been removed."[171] The implication is the same as Rossi's: not that we should excuse or accept, but that we should recognize the biology of human beings along with their culture and the constraints which this implies.

Similarly, although we have argued that it is inappropriate to use kin selection arguments to explain particular sorts of human kinship patterns, it is probably entirely appropriate to link our evolutionary past to the fact that human societies organize much of their behavior around kin.

> The Carnegie Medal for bravery is a peacetime equivalent of the Congressional Medal of Honor, and its bestowers unconsciously recognize the sociobiology of altruism by not giving the medal for bravery in saving the life of a relative. Helping a relative in distress is apparently expected. What is unexpected, and therefore worthy of a medal, is encountering danger to help a non-relative.[172]

Such a recognition does, indeed, imply a serious criticism of many of the perspectives discussed above. If you look back at the chapter on conflict theory, you will find a number of theorists with different ideas about how groups form in society, what sort of interests will be pursued, and the lines

[168]See the section on Lewis Coser, Chapter III.

[169]Vernon Reynolds, "Sociobiology and Race Relations," in Vernon Reynolds, Vincent Folger, and Ian Vine, eds., *The Sociobiology of Ethnocentrism. Evolutionary Dimensions of Xenophobia, Discrimination, Racism and Nationalism.* (London: Croom Helm 1987), p. 212.

[170]Johan M. G. van der Denneu, "Ethnocentrism and In-group/Out-group Differentiation," in Reynolds, Folger, and Vine, *Sociobiology of Ethnocentrism*, p. 22. See also Austin L. Hughes, *Evolution and Human Kinship* (New York: Oxford University Press, 1988).

[171]Reynolds, "Sociobiology and Race Relations," p. 211.

[172]Barash, *Sociobiology*, p. 135.

along which conflict will occur. In the whole chapter, however, there is extraordinarily little mention of family groups and ties.[173] Yet, if you think of your own family, you will probably find that its members cut across occupations, classes—and, especially through marriage—religious and even racial groups. If, as sociobiology suggests, there really is a basic "family feeling" among humans, just as there is among other creatures, then there is a built-in basis of group formation in all societies that sociologists must not ignore. Sociobiology does not only suggest the importance of biology to the sociology of the family, as Alice Rossi argues. It also implies that our relative neglect of this area in recent years is overdue for reappraisal.

[173]Collins is the main exception.

VIII

CONCLUSION

PART ONE
Social Theory and Understanding: The Value of Multiple Perspectives

Contemporary sociological theory ranges from the antideterminist inductive and descriptive approach typified by ethnomethodology to the predictive, deductive approach advocated by exchange theory. It encompasses the most detailed microsociological analysis in addition to functionalism's and conflict theory's efforts to analyze the determinants of large-scale social structure and social evolution. However, these differences do not mean that the major theoretical perspectives are totally incompatible with each other. On the contrary, they can offer complementary insights. Throughout this text, we have tried to show how each perspective helps us to understand concrete social phenomena and problems. We can illustrate the complementarity of their approaches if we return to the themes which have run throughout each chapter: formal education and the role of women in contemporary society.

EXPLORING FORMAL EDUCATION: FIVE VIEWS OF THE SCHOOL

In Chapter I, we raised two major questions about education in modern society. The first of these, which can hardly fail to strike any observer, is, What accounts for the enormous size of a modern education system? The second must equally well occur to anyone who has been through formal schooling and thinks back to his or her fellow students. It is, Why do some individuals do well when others fail and drop out? As we can now see, the first question is essentially "macrosociological," since it poses a question about social structure; consequently, functionalism and conflict theory offer the most by way of answers. The second question, by contrast, asks why our day-by-day experiences of school add up to academic success in some cases and to dropping out as soon as possible in others. Here the "micro" approaches of symbolic interactionism and phenomenology along with theories of rational choice prove most enlightening.

One common explanation for our enormous educational establishment refers to the general nature of industrial society. It is meritocratic and impersonal. Technical skills are necessary for many jobs, and, for most people, work and home are miles apart. Such a society, it is argued, demands our sort of school. Children have to undergo an extensive and prolonged education outside the home so that they will learn to see individual performance, not family ties, as the proper criterion for job placement and success. At the same time, they can learn complicated technical skills, and employers can discover, from school certification, who is capable of performing different jobs.

Functionalism analyzes education in just such terms. In Chapter II, we described Talcott Parsons' classic account of the American school system,[1] in which he discusses how the elementary school teaches children the impersonal and achievement-oriented values of an industrial society, accustoms them to a world in which there is none of the unconditional affection and support provided by the family, and thus develops "the commitments and capacities for successful performance of their adult roles."[2] At the same time, it performs the equally important function of manpower allocation, identifying children as potentially fitted, or unfitted, for college and for particular jobs—a task that cannot be left to family ascription because special abilities and skills are so important in modern occupations. Other functionalists have extended the analysis, interpreting the continuing growth of the education system as a function of the increasing technical skills required of the labor force.[3] Others discuss the functions of different types of higher education, as when Burton Clark examines the way junior colleges accustom and resign people to limited career ambitions.[4]

Much of this analysis has become part of the way that not just sociologists but almost all those involved with education look at modern schooling, even when they are very critical of its role. It is, for example, exactly the view put forward by politicians throughout the developed and underdeveloped world when they spend massive sums on education so they can fit their societies for the "white-hot technological revolution."[5] Parents similarly try to impress on their children the need to study and acquire a skill if they are to do well in the modern economy.

However, there is also an alternative way of explaining the nature and growth of modern education. According to this explanation, the educational system is essentially a way of securing power and privilege in a technological age. One could argue that instead of directly passing on money or land, successful families today secure the position of their children by giving them education. Either because society considers a long, expensive education to be a superior qualification for holding certain positions or

---

[1]Talcott Parsons, "The School Class as a Social System: Some of Its Functions in American Society," in A. H. Halsey, Jean Floud, and C. Arnold Anderson, eds., *Education, Economy and Society* (New York: The Free Press, 1961). See also Chapter II.

[2]Ibid., p. 434.

[3]This case is argued explicitly by, among others, Burton Clark in *Educating the Expert Society* (San Francisco: Chandler, 1962).

[4]Burton Clark, "The Cooling-Out Function in Higher Education," *American Journal of Sociology*, 65 (1960). See Chapter II.

[5]The phrase is Harold Wilson's, former prime minister of the United Kingdom.

because middle- and upper-class families can provide far greater scholastic help to their children than can other families, a long formal education allows parents to pass on and secure position and status for their children. These same children might fare far less well in a world of self-made entrepreneurs and on-the-job training.

At the same time, one could view extended compulsory schooling as "indoctrinating" children into believing in the current form of society and teaching them the basic skills needed by "factory fodder." In this view, schooling is a useful way to maintain the status quo to the benefit of those in charge. Finally, there is the related argument that people who have a lot of education, however acquired, have a stake in increasing the importance of education in the job market. Their efforts to do so encourage the upward spiral of educational requirements and the educational system's continued growth.

The conflict theorists discussed in Chapter III analyze education in this way, as a factor in the competitive struggle for resources rather than a contribution to a society's functioning. Norman Birnbaum and Pierre Bourdieu, for example, both question the degree to which schooling identifies skills objectively. They argue instead that families with the wherewithal to secure good education for their children use the system to ensure for them a superior social position.[6] Cultural traits that mark "top people" out, so that those without the right habits of speech and manners can be discriminated against by educated insiders are, such theorists argue, at least as important a product of education as any technical skills.

Finally, these theorists emphasize the dynamics of conflict, rather than technological change, when they analyze the continuing expansion of education. Collins, for example, argues that people with an education, like any other group with particular resources, want to secure for themselves the maximum potential benefits. They attempt to make high educational requirements a prerequisite for job entry and to exclude those without formal certificates. The attempt by large numbers of people to obtain the required certificates and the continuing attempt by educated groups to protect their privileged position lead, Collins argues, to an educational spiral, in which the formal educational requirements for job entry are being raised continually.[7] Raymond Boudon, from a rational choice perspective, complements Collins' argument by showing how individuals' choices will, almost always, tend to result in longer courses being taken rather than shorter ones. People calculate that if they take short courses,

---

[6]Norman Birnbaum, *The Crisis of Industrial Society* (New York: Oxford University Press, 1969); Pierre Bourdieu and Jean-Claude Passeron, *The Inheritors*, trans. R. Nice (Chicago: University of Chicago Press, 1979).

[7]Randall Collins, "Functional and Conflict Theories of Educational Stratification," *American Sociological Review*, 36 (1971), 1002–19, and *The Credential Society: An Historical Sociology of Education and Stratification* (New York: Academic Press, 1979).

they risk being pushed aside in the job market by other people who have taken longer ones. Multiply these individual choices, and, obviously, one is left with a continuing expansion of the average size of higher education and its average length.[8]

Which set of explanations is correct? Probably both and neither. A modern society does demand very real and complex skills, and its schools help accustom children to an impersonal environment. At the same time, educational qualifications are undoubtedly a resource in people's continual struggle to secure a good life for themselves; and a heavy emphasis on formal education suits those with such qualifications and the ability to help their children get them. What is important for our purposes here is that these two accounts, each embodying very different insights, also derive from two of the major perspectives discussed in this book: functionalism and conflict theory.

In similar fashion, rational choice theory, symbolic interactionism, and phenomenology offer different but complementary answers to our second question: Why does one particular student fail while another succeeds? One possible explanation is that a student's decisions and behavior depend, basically, on the costs and benefits which that student perceives. Students who find that hard work and good behavior bring them rewards that they value, including parental approval or respect and status from their peers, will behave in one way. Students who find that they get praise and good grades even when they do little work will respond accordingly. Students whose peer group admires and rewards rebels, who do not see academic rewards as something they can attain, or who believe their school to be so bad that what it offers is not worth acquiring, will respond rationally to these very different signals.

The rational choice theories discussed in Chapter IV are the most closely associated with this emphasis on the costs and benefits of different actions. They underline the importance of looking at the choices offered by a school not simply in terms of whether pupils come from families able to send them to "top" schools, but in terms of the day-to-day options that face the children themselves. When George Richmond looked in this way at his own ungovernable classroom, he was able to alter affairs dramatically by changing the pattern of rewards.[9] Before, continual war with the teacher at least offered students fun and peer-group status. Once there were tangible benefits to be gained from study, however, the balance swung the other way. Richmond's "micro-economy game," by paying students and introducing a competitive game they enjoyed, resulted in a classroom where students worked hard and willingly.

[8]Raymond Boudon, *The Unintended Consequences of Social Action* (London: Macmillan, 1982).

[9]George Richmond, *The Micro-Society School: A Real World in Miniature* (New York: Harper & Row, 1973).

It is also possible, while retaining an emphasis on students' daily experiences, to focus not on rational choice but on the interaction between teachers and students. Teachers may misinterpret such things as students' accents or styles of speech, responding, for example, with a "Don't talk to me like that" when they hear what seems to them cheeky or insubordinate. They may react to behavior that is symbolic to them of a student unlikely to do well in school. Conversely, students may interpret teachers' behavior as evidence that they do or do not take their job seriously, or do or don't care about whether any particular student learns or succeeds. If both sides behave to each other on this basis, both their general relationship and the students' school careers will be influenced accordingly.

Symbolic interactionists address students' success or failure in this way. Their perspective enabled Colin Lacey to explain why some children succeeded and others failed in an English "grammar school" (academically selective high school). He showed how the interaction between students and teachers created and reinforced both the images each held of the other and the way they behaved. For example, boys whom teachers saw as buffoons or potential dropouts came increasingly to see themselves in this way and to behave accordingly.[10]

Finally, there is yet another way of explaining a particular student's failure or success. One can go beyond looking at how people generally interpret aspects of each other's behavior to look at the minute details of speech and conversation—at how students understand particular questions and problems. Here, the emphasis is on the fact that teachers' statements or items on a test do not have a single, shared, and self-evident meaning, even though we all tend to assume that they do. A child's apparent "failure" on a test may not be a result of ignorance or stupidity. Instead, the child may understand a question in a perfectly coherent but "wrong" way. Similarly, to grasp fully why another child is a "success," we must see how the teacher "understands" the questions and the way the child's answers fit with the teacher's assumptions and preconceptions.

Phenomenology's contribution to understanding scholastic success and failure is to be found in such analysis of the speech patterns, concepts, and assumptions involved in conversations between teacher and child and whether the child's answers or conduct are seen as "right" or "wrong." In his description of how small children's tests were interpreted and graded, for example, Hugh Mehan applied ethnomethodology's concern with underlying assumptions of shared meaning to understanding how teachers

---

[10]Colin Lacey, *Hightown Grammar: The School as a Social System* (Manchester: Manchester University Press, 1970). A good discussion of the scope of educational sociology of this "interpretive" type can be found in Jerome Karabel and A. H. Halsey, eds., *Power and Ideology in Education* (New York: Oxford University Press, 1977), Ch. I. See also Carl Werthman, "Delinquents in Schools," in *School and Society: A Sociological Reader,* prepared by the Open University School and Society Course Team, (London: Routledge with Open University Press, 1971).

assess an answer as correct. He demonstrated how a child's perfectly coherent and accurate reasoning may, because of the way he or she interprets the materials, produce answers different from those the teacher and test compiler consider "obviously" right. Similarly, Aaron Cicourel and John Kitsuse showed how guidance counselors' interpretations and assumptions result in records being assessed as "good" or "poor" and in students being labeled and treated accordingly.[11]

EXPLORING THE ROLE OF WOMEN IN CONTEMPORARY SOCIETY

The second theme which has run through this text is that of gender, in particular the role of women in contemporary society. Here, too, we started with two apparently puzzling questions. The first was why female college graduates in full-time employment in the United States have lower average annual earnings than full-time male workers who are only high school graduates. The second was why men and boys, at home, school, and work, tend consistently to be more aggressive and dominant, and girls and women more caring and "supportive." How can the multiple perspectives of sociology build up answers to each of these questions?

One possible explanation for gender-linked income differentials is that they follow from, or contribute to, the complex and interdependent roles undertaken by people in modern industrial societies. As we said in Chapter II, functionalism does indeed provide such an explanation. Parsons sees sex role differentiation as one important way in which families—and societies—respond to the need of systems to carry out different tasks. In pattern variable terms, there is a need for expressive leadership but also for instrumental leadership. In AGIL terms, there is a need for adaptation—securing enough resources—but also for latent pattern maintenance and the transmission of societal values. Role differentiation, Parsons would argue, is a more effective way of fulfilling system needs than if everyone tried to do everything.

Thus, according to functionalist analysis, primary responsibility for breadwinning and instrumental leadership is allocated to men, and primary responsibility for the family and expressive leadership to women. This gender-based societal response to the need for both kinds of role is, according to this argument, reflected in the labor market. Higher average earnings for men reflect a combination of giving higher pay to people who have the "main" occupational responsibilities; men doing more overtime (for the same reasons); and women's choice of less well-paid but

[11]Hugh Mehan, "Ethnomethodology and Education," in D. O'Shea, ed., *Sociology of the School and Schooling* (Washington, D.C.: National Institute of Education, 1974); Aaron Cicourel and John Kitsuse, *The Educational Decision-Makers* (New York: Bobbs-Merrill, 1963).

"caring" occupations which are consistent with their general expressive role.[12]

There is, however, another very different explanation of income inequalities, generally and in this specific, gender-linked case. This explanation is phrased in terms of self-interest and the activities of organized interest groups, and it is presented by the conflict theorists discussed in Chapter III. Marxist feminists, for example, argue that gender has to be used alongside class in analyzing inequalities and see societies as patriarchies in which power relations favor men at the expense of women. Thus, for Zillah Eisenstein the sexual division of labor is a basic mechanism of control, of preserving men's superior (and better paid) position. Classifying a job as a "woman's" job is a way to justify paying less and treating the occupation concerned as somehow inferior.

Conflict theorists in the "analytic" tradition are less likely to provide explanations which invoke cohesive "patriarchal" organization by men to oppress women. Instead, they see gender as one dimension among others in terms of which people organize and act self-interestedly. Collins and Chafetz, for example, both point out that women are almost universally inferior to men in their access to wealth, power, and other valued resources. They note, however, that there are big variations between societies and that one needs to look at factors specific to a situation as well as to universal differences.[13]

In explaining women's lower average earnings in the contemporary United States, analytic conflict theorists give considerable weight to universal biological differences. All societies, they note, have found it more efficient for those who bear the children also to do the caretaking. It can be arranged otherwise, but this will be more troublesome and less "obvious" a solution. Thus, women's child-care responsibilities affect their choice of occupation and the time they devote to it in a way that is not true for men. Not only do women more often work part-time, they also choose jobs which—like teaching—fit in relatively well with child care (and other family responsibilities). The fact that women are interested in these jobs for reasons other than the material rewards means, in turn, that employers can offer wages which are lower than they would have to pay in an "open" market. Women are caught in a double bind, one made worse by such factors as the long distances that, in modern society, often separate home and work place; the attitudes which encourage them to aim for "women's" jobs; and the fact that established occupational groups have a strong interest in continuing to structure jobs so that they are difficult for women to do.

---

[12]Miriam Johnson provides a feminist critique, within the general functionalist model, of this analysis. She sees the process of "inclusion" as gradually promoting equal pay and opportunity for women albeit to the accompaniment of tension and strain. See Chapter II, p. 52.

[13]See Chapter III, pp. 96 and 163–65.

Rational choice theory provides a perspective on women's earnings which is quite similar to that of analytic conflict theorists such as Janet Chafetz. It looks at the logic of men's and women's choices and shows how they make them freely and rationally *within a set of social constraints and values*. Thus, when Gerson studied women's career paths, she found that many women made a conscious choice not to pursue their careers actively because they valued personal relationships more. Others became very successful at work, but often after, and because, relationships had failed. Again, Luker found that women in the pro-life movement were very often full-time mothers and housewives to whom raising a family and "nurturing" were the most important things a woman could do.[14]

The individual choices and decisions of women like these will, on a large scale, help to produce and perpetuate average national earnings which are lower for women than for men. Rational choice theory does not posit "patriarchy" as an explanation, but it does refer to values and decisions which are gender-linked, or specific to women—values and decisions which simply do not affect men in the same way.

It is exactly these sorts of values which inform theorists' answers to the second of our questions about women in contemporary society. At issue here was why men and boys tend to dominate a situation and show aggression, while girls and women tend to assume supporting roles and provide nurture and support. It is predominantly the micro perspectives which address this question; and their explanations are not conflicting so much as concerned with different levels of analysis.

Deferring to men and nurturing can be viewed as quintessentially non-self-interested and therefore not amenable to explanation in rational choice terms. However, rational choice theory does set out to explain such behavior, alongside the altruism of political activists, blood donors, etc. The women studied by Luker, activists for *and* against abortion, behaved in this way in order to affirm and confirm the values they held and their own self-image. What is interesting about the pro-life group, in particular, is their belief that there are things which it is particularly women's role to provide—that women *should* be the nurturers, the homemakers, the peacemakers.

Similar values are invoked in rational choice theorists' analyses of the dynamics of power within a family. While decision making is to a large extent a function of who earns most, it is also obvious that women defer to men—and to their children—in ways which can only be explained by values. Thus, in families where women are the main earners, they are generally careful not to exploit their greater potential power to the full.

Rational choice theory delineates a set of values which many women hold and which certainly can help explain the pattern of women's behavior. The theory does not, however, explain how women come to hold these

[14]See Chapter IV, pp. 230–31.

values in the first place. Symbolic interactionists, by comparison, are particularly interested in detailed analysis of the process by which people take on particular identities—such as that of a "traditional" wife and mother. Nancy Chodorow, notably, argues that female children strongly and consciously identify with their mothers, so they develop, generation by generation, a "high relational capacity." All sorts of signals from society as a whole reinforce them in their belief that this is a "suitable" thing to do.[15] Thus, Raphaela Best points out how girls at school are able to express emotions openly, whereas boys get laughed at as cry-babies when they do. Erving Goffman shows how the way men and women are depicted in something as apparently unimportant as advertisements again reinforces people's ideas of what is "appropriate" male and female behavior. Janet Lever shows how the games children play reinforce and perpetuate traditional gender-based roles and the separation of the sexes.[16]

Phenomenology, as usual, goes even further into the microstructure of human interaction and the way in which our identities, themselves bound up with our values, are created. In the work of writers such as Pamela Fishman, we can see how women's "tentativeness" in conversation is reinforced. Similarly, Garfinkel, in his story of Agnes,[17] who undergoes a sex-change, describes how she was able to learn, from direct and indirect signals, what the appropriate behavior was for someone who wanted to be a woman. Among the important things Agnes learned were that she should not offer her opinions and that "passive acceptance" is a desirable female trait.[18]

In sum, each of the major perspectives of contemporary sociological theory succeeds, in its different way, in helping us understand one of the major determinants of our daily lives and experiences. In doing so, moreover, it complements rather than contradicts the insights provided by others. A similar pattern could be found and traced in many other spheres—for example, voting patterns or the workings of a government bureaucracy or standing army. This is the reason, ultimately, that each perspective is

---

[15]Although there is no overt disagreement among microtheorists in their analysis of women's relative lack of aggression, we should note that a number of macrotheorists (male and female) reject Chodorow's theories as inadequate and unable to account for change.

[16]See Chapter V, pp. 286, 287, 280 and 248.

[17]Harold Garfinkel, *Studies in Ethnomethodology* (Englewood Cliffs, N.J.: Prentice-Hall, Inc., 1967). See also Chapter VI.

[18]A full discussion of male/female differences in behavior carries one into the vexed and uncertain area of biological influences. While these cannot be treated fully within a sociological text book, sociobiologists such as Alice Rossi warn against the danger for sociology of ignoring physical and biological factors. On the particular question of male aggression, the evidence is conflicting. Thus, in K. B. Hoyenga and K. Hoyenga, *The Question of Sex Differences* (Boston: Little, Brown, 1979), research is reported which shows that changes in testosterone levels in human males do not consistently predict changes in aggressive behavior. However, while pure biological determinism finds little support, there is also a body of research linking testosterone and testosterone exposure in the womb to relative aggression later. See e.g. J. R. Udry et al., "Serum Androgenic Hormones"; Alice S. Rossi, "Sex and Gender"; and the work of D. Olwens.

recognized as an important part of modern theory and why so many practicing sociologists are eclectic in their approach, drawing on the insights of different perspectives in accordance with their interests and concerns.

PART TWO
Historical Trends

In discussing the major theoretical perspectives of contemporary sociology we have concentrated on their intellectual content and contributions to sociological understanding. However, they are also part of the social scene themselves, and their popularity does not depend on their internal qualities alone. At different times during the last thirty years, different approaches have been more or less popular and influential. Theory is as dynamic a body of ideas today as it has ever been.

In American sociology, particularly, three distinct phases are apparent. In the 1950s, functionalism was the most influential perspective, and theorists' concerns were predominantly macrosociological. In the 1960s and 1970s, neo-Marxist and analytic conflict theory were increasingly important, and there often seemed to be more people interested in finding things wrong with functionalism than there were sociologists using its approach. At the same time, especially in the United States, interest in the details of person-to-person encounters increased sharply. Symbolic interactionism and, increasingly, phenomenology influenced even those sociologists whose main interest was in macrosociology. The result, in the 1980s, was a third phase of increasing concern with the links between macroanalysis and microanalysis and with ways of integrating the two when analyzing concrete phenomena.

We cannot pretend to offer a full and original analysis of these changes, but a number of social developments were probably influential. First is the different social experience of different generations of sociologists. One does not have to believe that ideas are straightforwardly determined by people's social positions to agree that the questions sociologists ask, and the perspectives they adopt in trying to answer them, will be shaped by their own lives. So will the degree to which a reader finds the question sensible and interesting or the answer convincing. Many of the sociologists who were active in the 1950s had fathers in the ministry and backgrounds where gradual social reform was advocated as a means of aiding disadvantaged groups and integrating them into society. They were working in a period when there was a general political consensus, and many intellectuals believed in an "end of ideology." Functionalism's emphasis on common norms thus seemed an appropriate way to examine society. Younger sociologists' interests were formed during the era of the Vietnam War, a period of renewed political and ideological strife. Whatever their own political preferences, they had their attention turned to the origins of conflict and importance of ideology. Meanwhile, the New Left produced a group of young left-wing sociologists with a great interest in the Frankfurt School.[19]

In addition, during the 1960s old cultural conventions broke down, and "alternative life-styles" flourished, especially in the United States. There was increasing interest in the way people's relationships with each other are created and affected by their mode of communication. "Humanists" also attacked science for ignoring the emotional and artistic sides of human experience. Alongside the demonstrations and controversies splitting the United States, many turned away from involvement in any organizations. It seems likely that these currents made younger sociologists more interested in the details of interaction, more aware of how one's world, or one's "reality," could be created in an immediate way by oneself and the people around one. By contrast, during the 1950s people were aware of a different sort of social change. The importance in the economy of small businesses and farms was fast shrinking, and increasing numbers of people were being employed by large organizations. This focused the attention of many of the most able sociologists on organizations and the industrial firm—on "structural" questions rather than microsociological analysis.[20]

A third factor affecting the direction taken by sociological theory was probably the similar shift in interest taking place in the intellectual world at large. Since 1945, phenomenology has become increasingly well known outside Germany. Its criticisms of mainline social science and its concern with the subjective aspects of reality have influenced many more sociologists than just the self-declared phenomenologists. English and American philosophers have also been increasingly interested in the active, or "intentional," aspects of perception and in the way our thoughts and experiences rest on shared assumptions and irreducible concepts.[21] Stephen Toulmin

---

[19]It is important to remember that the period did not simply produce left-wing critiques. It refueled political and ideological debate across the spectrum, producing not only a new generation of radicals but also a "new conservatism" concerned about the growth in state power and intervention, the use of the courts to make social policy, etc. This side of the renewed ideological character of intellectual debate is less apparent in sociology than in the intellectual scene as a whole, where, for example, the discovery of Marcuse by some is balanced by the discovery of his contemporary, Hayek, by others.

[20]See, for example, Peter M. Blau and W. R. Scott, *Formal Organizations* (San Francisco: Chandler, 1962), or Amitai Etzioni, *A Comparative Analysis of Complex Organizations* (New York: The Free Press, 1961).

[21]The work of P. F. Strawson (e.g., *Individuals: An Essay in Descriptive Metaphysics* [London: Methuen and Co., Ltd., 1959]) is especially important in this area. Noam Chomsky's work on "depth grammar," in which he has argued for the existence of a grammar shared by all human languages (and rooted in the genes of the individual) also became very well known during this period. See Noam Chomsky, *Aspects of the Theory of Syntax* (Cambridge, Mass.: M.I.T. Press, 1965).

has noted a change among philosophers of science (and social science) with similar implications. He has argued that during the 1960s they became increasingly concerned with how perceptions and theories were rooted in the "historical temporal world" and in the general conceptual framework of an age.[22]

Curiously enough, the relative decline in sociology's status during the late 1970s and early 1980s probably stimulated the integration of such theories into mainline sociology. With the decline of 1960s-style "counterculture," America and Western Europe alike found students moving to subjects with more immediate relevance in the job market. The discipline ceased to be highly fashionable and linked with political activism, developing instead into one social science discipline among others. A weakened link with political activism in turn meant that American sociologists, in particular, became more interested in academic developments elsewhere. Especially in the area of theory, they looked more to other disciplines and to other countries—moves which are in any case mutually reinforcing, since in Europe the barriers between different social science disciplines are far less defined. A growing interest in such theorists as Habermas, Giddens, and Foucault meant growing influence for theorists who themselves are interested in the "micro" roots of macrosociology and well acquainted with phenomenological analysis. Similarly, the growing influence of rational choice theory, reentering sociology via political science and economics, also meant a renewed focus on the micro-macro interface.[23]

This focus does not mean that we have, or are likely to have in the near future, a single integrated theory or the breakout of peace among warring theorists. It is not even clear that this would be a good idea. As Steven Lukes observes, those who have made significant contributions in the social sciences "have all been, in their several ways, one-sided, one-eyed, exaggerating, unreasonable and unjudicious, focusing obsessively on certain relationships or aspects of social life and blind to others. Indeed, their very one-sidedness and obsessiveness is a precondition for whatever insight they attain."[24] What recent trends do confirm is that major theoretical perspectives are not totally incompatible with each other. When it comes to analyzing a particular area of social life, like formal education, or answering a puzzling question, such as why women are paid less than comparably qualified men, different perspectives offer *different and often complementary* insights.

[22]Stephen Toulmin, "From Form to Function: Philosophy and History of Science in the 1950s and Now," *Daedalus* 106.3 (Summer 1977), 159.

[23]Although sociobiology's influence remains relatively small, it is concerned with the society-wide implications of individual behavior and of gene-based individual characteristics.

[24]Steven Lukes, "Subject to Survey," *Times Literary Supplement* (October 1985), 1163, cited in Gambetta, *Were They Pushed or Did They Jump? Individual Decisions in Education* (Cambridge: Cambridge University Press, Studies in Rationality and Social Change, 1987), p. 167.

SELECTED BIBLIOGRAPHY

ABRAHAMSON, MARK, *Functionalism*. Englewood Cliffs, N.J.: Prentice-Hall, Inc., 1978.

ADORNO, THEODOR, ET AL., *The Authoritarian Personality*. New York: Harper & Row, 1950.

ALEXANDER, JEFFREY C., ed., *Durkheimian Sociology: Cultural Studies*. New York: Cambridge University Press, 1988.

————, ed., *Neofunctionalism*. Beverly Hills, Calif.: Sage, 1985.

————, *Theoretical Logic in Sociology* (4 vols.). Berkeley: University of California Press, 1982.

————, *Twenty Lectures: Sociological Theory Since World War II*. New York: Columbia University Press, 1987.

AVINERI, SHLOMO, *The Social and Political Thought of Karl Marx*. Cambridge: Cambridge University Press, 1968.

BELLAH, ROBERT N., "Civil Religion in America," *Daedalus*, 96 (1967), 1–21.

————, "DURKHEIM AND HISTORY," *American Sociological Review*, 24 (1959), 447–61.

BERGER, PETER L., *The Noise of Solemn Assemblies: Christian Commitment and the Religious Establishment in America*. Garden City, N.Y.: Doubleday, 1961.

————, *A Rumor of Angels: Modern Society and the Rediscovery of the Supernatural*. Garden City, New York: Doubleday, 1970.

————, *The Sacred Canopy: Elements of a Sociological Theory of Religion*. New York: Doubleday, 1969.

————, BRIGITTE BERGER, AND HANSFRIED KELLNER, *The Homeless Mind*. New York: Random House, 1973.

————, AND THOMAS LUCKMANN, *The Social Construction of Reality*. New York: Doubleday, 1966.

BLAU, PETER M., ed., *Approaches to the Study of Social Structure*. New York: The Free Press, 1975.

————, *The Dynamics of Bureaucracy: A Study of Interpersonal Relationships in Two Government Agencies*. Chicago: University of Chicago Press, 1955.

————, *Exchange and Power in Social Life*. New York: John Wiley, 1964.

————, *Inequality and Heterogeneity: A Primitive Theory of Social Structure*. New York: The Free Press, 1977.

————, AND JOSEPH E. SCHWARTZ, *Cross-cutting Social Circles: Testing a Macrostructural Theory of Intergroup Relations*. Orlando, Fla.: Academic Press, 1984.

————, AND W. RICHARD SCOTT, *Formal Organizations*. San Francisco: Harper & Row, 1962.

BLUMER, HERBERT, "Comments on 'Parsons as a Symbolic Interactionist'," *Sociological Inquiry*, 45 (1975), 59–62, 68.

————, "Going Astray with a Logical Scheme," *Symbolic Interaction*, 6 (1983), 127–137.

————, "Sociological Theory in Industrial Relations," *American Sociological Review*, 12 (1947), 271–78.

————, *Symbolic Interactionism: Perspective and Method*. Englewood Cliffs, N.J.: Prentice-Hall, Inc., 1969.

————, "The World of Youthful Drug Use" (manuscript). Berkeley, California: University of California, School of Criminology, 1967.

BOCK, KENNETH, "Evolution, Function, and Change," *American Sociological Review*, 28 (1963), 229–37.

BOTT, ELIZABETH, *Family and Social Network*. London: Tavistock Publications, 1957 and 1971.

BOUDON, RAYMOND, *The Unintended Consequences of Social Action*. London: Macmillan, 1982.

BOURDIEU, PIERRE, *Outline of a Theory of Practice*, trans. R. Nice. Cambridge: Cambridge University Press, 1977.

———, AND JEAN-CLAUDE PASSERON, *The Inheritors*, trans. R. Nice. Chicago: University of Chicago Press, 1979.

BURAWOY, MICHAEL, *Manufacturing Consent*. Chicago: University of Chicago Press, 1979.

BURAWOY, MICHAEL, AND THEDA SKOCPOL, eds., *Marxist Inquiries: Studies of Labor, Class and States*. Chicago: University of Chicago Press, 1982.

CAMPBELL, DONALD T., "On the Conflict between Biological and Social Evolution and between Psychology and Moral Tradition," *The American Psychologist* (1975), 1103–26.

CHAFETZ, JANET SALTZMAN, *Feminist Sociology: An Overview of Contemporary Theories*. Itasca, Ill: Peacock, 1988.

———, *Sex and Advantage: A Comparative, Macro-Structural Theory of Sex Stratification*. Totowa, N.J.: Rowman and Allanheld, 1984.

———, AND ANTHONY GARY DWORKIN, *Female Revolt: Women's Movements in World and Historical Perspective*. Totowa, N.J.: Rowman and Allanheld, 1986.

CHODOROW, NANCY, *The Reproduction of Mothering*. Berkeley: University of California Press, 1978.

———, *Feminism and Psychoanalysis*. New Haven: Yale University Press, 1989.

CHOMSKY, NOAM, *Aspects of the Theory of Syntax*. Cambridge, Mass.: The M.I.T. Press, 1965.

CICOUREL, AARON V., AND JOHN I. KITSUSE, *The Educational Decision-Makers*. Indianapolis: Bobbs-Merrill, 1963.

———, *Method and Measurement in Sociology*. New York: The Free Press, 1964.

COLEMAN, JAMES S., "Foundations for a Theory of Collective Decisions," *American Journal of Sociology*, LXXI (1966), 615–27.

———, *Individual Interests and Collective Action*. New York: Cambridge University Press, 1986.

———, *The Mathematics of Collective Action*. Chicago: Aldine, 1973.

COLLINS, RANDALL, *Conflict Sociology: Toward an Explanatory Science*. New York: Academic Press, 1975.

———, *The Credential Society: An Historical Sociology of Education and Stratification*. New York: Academic Press, 1979.

———, "Functional and Conflict Theories of Educational Stratification," *American Sociological Review*, 36 (1971), 1002–19.

———, *Sociology Since Midcentury*. New York: Academic Press, 1981.

COMTE, AUGUSTE, *The Positive Philosophy*, trans. Harriet Martineau. New York: Calvin Blanchard, 1958.

COOK, KAREN, ed., *Social Exchange Theory*. Newbury Park, Calif.: Sage, 1987.

COOLEY, CHARLES HORTON, *Human Nature and the Social Order*. New York: Scribner's, 1922.

COSER, LEWIS A., *Continuities in the Study of Social Conflict*. New York: The Free Press, 1967.

———, *The Functions of Social Conflict*. Glencoe, Ill.: The Free Press, 1956.

———, *Greedy Institutions: Patterns of Undivided Commitments*. New York: The Free Press, 1974.

———, ed., *The Idea of Social Structure: Papers in Honor of Robert K. Merton*. New York: Harcourt Brace Jovanovich, Inc., 1975.

———, *Masters of Sociological Thought*. New York: Harcourt Brace Jovanovich, Inc., 1977.

———, "Presidential Address: Two Methods in Search of a Substance," *American Sociological Review*, 40, no. 6 (December 1975), 691–700.

DAHRENDORF, RALF, *Class and Class Conflict in Industrial Society*. Stanford, California: Stanford University Press, 1959.

——, *Essays in the Theory of Society*. Stanford, Calif.: Stanford University Press, 1968.

——, *The New Liberty*. London: Routledge and Kegan Paul, 1975.

DAVIS, KINGSLEY, "The Myth of Functional Analysis as a Special Method in Sociology and Anthropology," *American Sociological Review*, 24 (1959), 757–72.

DAWKINS, RICHARD, *The Extended Phenotype: The Gene as the Unit of Selection*. Oxford and San Francisco: W. H. Freeman and Company Publishers, 1982.

——, *The Selfish Gene*. Oxford: Oxford University Press, 1976.

DEEGAN, MARY JO. *Jane Addams and the Men of the Chicago School: 1890–1918*. New Brunswick, N.J.: Transaction, 1986.

——, AND MICHAEL HILL, eds., *Women and Symbolic Interaction*. Boston: Allen and Unwin, 1987.

DENZIN, NORMAN, *On Understanding Emotion*. San Francisco: Jossey-Bass, 1984.

DJILAS, MILOVAN, *The New Class: An Analysis of the Communist System*. New York: Holt, Rinehart and Winston, 1957.

DOUGLAS, JACK D., ed., *Understanding Everyday Life*. Chicago: Aldine, 1970.

DURKHEIM, EMILE, *The Division of Labor in Society*. Glencoe, Ill.: The Free Press, 1964.

——, *The Elementary Forms of the Religious Life*. New York: Collier Books, 1961.

——, *Moral Education*. New York: The Free Press, 1973.

——, *The Rules of Sociological Method*. Edited with an introduction by Steven Lukes. Translated by W. D. Halls. New York: The Free Press, 1982.

——, *Suicide*. Glencoe, Ill.: The Free Press, 1951.

EISENSTEIN, ZILLAH R., *Capitalist Patriarchy and the Case for Socialist Feminism*. New York: Monthly Review Press, 1979.

EMERSON, R. M., "Exchange Theory, Part I: A Psychological Basis for Social Exchange"; and "Exchange Theory, Part II: Exchange Relations and Networks," in J. Berger, M. Zelditch, and B. Anderson, eds., *Sociological Theories in Progress*, Boston: Houghton-Mifflin, 1972.

——, "Power-dependence Relations," *American Sociological Review*, 27 (1962), 31–41.

ENGELS, FRIEDRICH, *The Origin of the Family, Private Property and the State*, trans. Alick West. New York: Penguin, 1972.

FARIS, R. E. L., *Chicago Sociology 1920–1932*. Chicago: University of Chicago Press, 1970.

FERGUSON, KATHY E., *Self, Society and Womankind*. Westport, Conn.: Greenwood Press, 1980.

FESTINGER, LEON, *A Theory of Cognitive Dissonance*. Evanston, Ill.: Row, Peterson, 1957.

FOUCAULT, MICHEL, *Discipline and Punish: The Birth of the Prison*. Trans. Alan Sheridan. London: Allen Lane, 1977.

——, *Madness and Civilization. A History of Insanity in the Age of Reason*. Trans. Richard Howard. New York: Random House, 1965.

——, *The Order of Things: An Archaeology of the Human Sciences*. New York: Vintage Books, 1973.

FOX, ROBIN, *Kinship and Marriage*. Harmondsworth, Middlesex: Penguin, 1967.

FROMM, ERICH, *The Sane Society*. New York: Holt, Rinehart and Winston, 1956.

GARFINKEL, HAROLD, *Studies in Ethnomethodology*. Englewood Cliffs, N.J.: Prentice-Hall, Inc., 1967.

GERTH, HANS, AND C. WRIGHT MILLS, *Character and Social Structure*. New York: Harcourt Brace Jovanovich, Inc., 1953.

GIDDENS, ANTHONY, *Central Problems in Social Theory.* Berkeley: University of California Press, 1979.

———, *The Constitution of Society.* Cambridge, England: Polity, 1984.

———, *Profiles and Critiques in Social Theory.* Berkeley: University of California Press, 1982.

———, "Review Essay: Habermas' Social and Political Theory." *American Journal of Sociology,* 83, no. 1 (1977), 198–212.

GLASER, BARNEY G., AND ANSELM L. STRAUSS, *The Discovery of Grounded Theory: Strategies for Qualitative Research.* Chicago: Aldine, 1967.

GOFFMAN, ERVING, "The Arrangement Between the Sexes," *Theory and Society,* 4 (1977), 301–332.

———, *Asylums; Essays on the Social Situation of Mental Patients and Other Inmates.* New York: Doubleday, 1961.

———, *Encounters: Two Studies in the Sociology of Interaction.* Indianapolis: Bobbs-Merrill, 1961.

———, *Gender Advertisements.* New York: Harper Colophon, 1976.

———, "The Interaction Order," *American Sociological Review,* 48, no. 1 (February 1983), 1–17.

———, *Interaction Ritual: Essays on Face-to-Face Behavior.* Garden City, New York: Doubleday Anchor, 1967.

———, *The Presentation of Self in Everyday Life.* Garden City, New York: Doubleday Anchor, 1959.

———, *Stigma: Notes on the Management of Spoiled Identity.* Englewood Cliffs, N.J.: Prentice-Hall, Inc., 1963.

———, *Strategic Interaction.* Philadelphia: University of Pennsylvania Press, 1969.

GRANOVETTER, MARK, "The Strength of Weak Ties," *American Journal of Sociology,* 78 (1973), 1360–80.

GRATHOFF, RICHARD, ed., *The Theory of Social Action: The Correspondence of Alfred Schutz and Talcott Parsons.* Bloomington, Indiana: Indiana University Press, 1978.

HABERMAS, JÜRGEN, *Communication and the Evolution of Society,* trans. Thomas McCarthy. London: Heinemann Education Books, 1979.

———, *Legitimation Crisis,* trans. Thomas McCarthy. Boston: Beacon Press, 1975.

———, *The Philosophical Discourse of Modernity: Twelve Lectures,* trans. Frederick Lawrence. Cambridge, England: Polity, 1987.

———, "Talcott Parsons: Problems of Theory Construction," *Sociological Inquiry,* 51 (1981), 173–196.

———, *Theory and Practice,* trans. John Viertel. Boston: Beacon Press, 1973.

———, *The Theory of Communicative Action,* Vol. I, *Reason and the Rationalization of Society,* 1984; and Vol. II, *Lifeworld and System: A Critique of Functionalist Reason,* 1988. Cambridge, England: Polity.

HANDEL, WARREN, *Ethnomethodology: How People Make Sense.* Englewood Cliffs, N.J.: Prentice-Hall, Inc., 1982.

HAYEK, FRIEDRICH, See Von Hayek.

HEATH, ANTHONY, *Rational Choice and Social Exchange.* Cambridge: Cambridge University Press, 1976.

HERITAGE, JOHN, *Garfinkel and Ethnomethodology.* Cambridge, England: Polity, 1984.

HOCHSCHILD, ARLIE RUSSELL, *The Managed Heart: Commercialization of Human Feeling.* Berkeley: University of California Press, 1983.

HOMANS, GEORGE C., "Bringing Men Back In," *American Sociological Review,* 29, no. 5 (December 1964), 809–18.

———, *The Human Group.* New York: Harcourt Brace Jovanovich Inc., 1950.

———, "A Life of Synthesis," in *Sociological Self-Images: A Collective Portrait*, ed. Irving L. Horowitz. Beverly Hills, California: Sage Publications, Inc., 1969.

———, *The Nature of Social Science*. New York: Harcourt Brace Jovanovich, Inc., 1967.

———, "Social Behavior as Exchange," *American Journal of Sociology*, LXII (1958), 597–606.

———, *Social Behavior: Its Elementary Forms*. Revised edition. New York: Harcourt Brace Jovanovich, Inc., 1974.

———, "A Sociologist's Reaction," *The American Sociologist*, 12, no. 2 (May 1977), 69.

HORKHEIMER, MAX, *Critical Theory*, trans. Matthew J. O'Connell et al., New York: Continuum Books, 1972.

JOHNSON, BENTON, *Functionalism in Modern Sociology: Understanding Talcott Parsons*. Morristown, N.J.: General Learning Press, 1975.

JONES, E. L., *The European Miracle: Environments, Economics and Geo-politics in the History of Europe and Asia*. Cambridge: Cambridge University Press, 1981.

KEMPER, THEODORE, *A Social Interactional Theory of the Emotions*. New York: John Wiley, 1978.

KOLAKOWSKI, LESZEK, *Main Currents of Marxism*. Oxford: Clarendon Press, 1978.

KONRAD, GEORGE, AND IVAN SZELENYI, *The Intellectuals on the Road to Class Power*. New York: Harcourt Brace Jovanovich, Inc., 1979.

KORNHAUSER, WILLIAM, " 'Power Elite' or 'Veto Groups'?" in *Class, Status and Power*, eds. Reinhard Bendix and Seymour Martin Lipset. New York: The Free Press, 1966.

KUHN, THOMAS, *The Structure of Scientific Revolutions*. Chicago: University of Chicago Press, 1970.

LEACH, EDMUND, ed., *The Structural Study of Myth and Totemism*. London: Tavistock Publications, 1967.

LEMERT, CHARLES C., ed., *French Sociology: Rupture and Renewal since 1968*. New York: Columbia University Press, 1981.

LENIN, VLADIMIR I., *Imperialism: The Highest Stage of Capitalism*. New York: International Publishers, 1939.

LENSKI, GERHARD E., *Power and Privilege: A Theory of Social Stratification*. New York: McGraw-Hill, 1966.

LÉVI-STRAUSS, CLAUDE, *The Elementary Structures of Kinship*, rev. ed., London: Eyre and Spottiswoode, 1969.

———, *Totemism*. Boston: Beacon Press, 1963.

———, "Le Triangle Culinaire," *L'Arc*, 26 (1965), 19–29.

LEVINE, D., E. CARTER, AND E. MILLER, "Simmel's Influence on American Sociology II," *American Journal of Sociology*, 81 (1976), 1112–32.

LOUBSER, JAN J., RAINER C. BAUM, ANDREW EFFRAT, AND VICTOR LIDZ, eds., *Explorations on General Theory in Social Science: Essays in Honor of Talcott Parsons*. New York: The Free Press, 1976.

LUHMANN, NIKLAS, *The Differentiation of Society*. New York: Columbia University Press, 1982.

———, "Society, Meaning, Religion—Based on Self-Reference," *Sociological Analysis*, 46 (1985), 5–20.

———, "Tautology and Paradox in the Self-Descriptions of Modern Society," *Sociological Theory*, 6 (1988), 26–37.

LUKES, STEVEN, *Emile Durkheim: His Life and Work*. New York: Harper & Row, 1972.

LUMSDEN, CHARLES J., AND EDWARD O. WILSON, *Genes, Mind and Culture: The Coevolutionary Process*. Cambridge: Harvard University Press, 1981.

MALINOWSKI, BRONISLAW, *Crime and Custom in Savage Society*. London: Routledge and Kegan Paul, 1926.

MANIS, JEROME G., AND BERNARD N. MELTZER, eds., *Symbolic Interaction: A Reader in Social Psychology*. Boston: Allyn & Bacon, 1972.

MARCUSE, HERBERT, *Eros and Civilization*. New York: Vintage Books, 1955.

———, *One-Dimensional Man*. Boston: Beacon Press, 1964.

MARX, KARL, *Capital*, Vol. I, trans. Samuel Moore and Edward Aveling, ed. F. Engels. London: Lawrence and Wishart, 1961.

———, *The Eighteenth Brumaire of Louis Bonaparte*. New York: International Publishers, 1935.

———, *The Poverty of Philosophy*. Moscow: Foreign Languages Publishing House, n.d.

———, AND FREDERICK ENGELS, *The Communist Manifesto*. Harmondsworth, Middlesex: Penguin, 1967.

———AND FREDERICK ENGELS, ed., *Selected Works*, Vol. I. London: Lawrence and Wishart, 1962.

MAUSS, MARCEL, *The Gift*. Glencoe, Ill.: The Free Press, 1954.

McCALL, GEORGE J., AND J. L. SIMMONS, *Identities and Interactions*. New York: The Free Press, 1966.

McLEAN, IAIN, *Public Choice: An Introduction*. Oxford: Basil Blackwell, 1987.

MEAD, GEORGE HERBERT, *Mind, Self and Society*. Chicago: University of Chicago Press, 1934.

MERTON, ROBERT K., *Social Theory and Social Structure*. Enlarged Edition. New York: The Free Press, 1968.

MICHELS, ROBERT, *Political Parties: A Sociological Study of Oligarchical Tendencies of Modern Democracy*, trans. Eden and Cedar Paul. Glencoe, Ill.: The Free Press, 1958.

MILLS, C. WRIGHT, *Listen Yankee: The Revolution in Cuba*. New York: Ballantine, 1960.

———, *The New Men of Power*. New York: Harcourt Brace Jovanovich, Inc., 1948.

———, *The Power Elite*. New York: Oxford University Press, 1956.

———, "The Power Elite: Military, Economic and Political," in *Problems of Power in American Society*, ed. Arthur Kornhauser. Detroit: Wayne State University Press, 1957.

———, *The Sociological Imagination*. New York: Oxford University Press, 1959.

———, *White Collar: The American Middle Classes*. New York: Oxford University Press, 1951.

MOORE, BARRINGTON, JR., *Social Origins of Dictatorship and Democracy: Lord and Peasant in the Making of the Modern World*. Boston: Beacon Press, 1966.

MOSCA, GAETANO, *The Ruling Class*. New York: McGraw-Hill, 1960.

MULLINS, NICHOLAS C., *Theories and Theory Groups in Contemporary American Sociology*. New York: Harper & Row, 1973.

MÜNCH, RICHARD, "Talcott Parsons and the Theory of Action, I and II," *American Journal of Sociology*, 86 (1981), 709–39 and 87 (1982), 771–826.

NAGEL, ERNEST, *The Structure of Science*. New York: Harcourt Brace Jovanovich, Inc., 1961.

NISBET, ROBERT A., *The Sociological Tradition*. New York: Basic Books, 1966.

NORTH, DOUGLASS, *Structure and Change in Economic History*. New York: W. W. Norton & Co., Inc., 1981.

OLSON, MANCUR, *The Logic of Collective Action: Public Goods and the Theory of Groups*. Cambridge: Harvard University Press, 1965.

PARETO, VILFREDO, *The Treatise on General Sociology*. New York: Dover, 1963.

PARK, ROBERT E., AND ERNEST W. BURGESS, *Introduction to the Science of Society.* Chicago: University of Chicago Press, 1921.

PARSONS, TALCOTT, *Action Theory and the Human Condition.* New York: The Free Press, 1978.

———, *Essays in Sociological Theory.* New York: The Free Press, 1954.

———, "Evolutionary Universals in Society," *American Sociological Review,* 29 (1964), 339–57.

———, "On Building Social System Theory: A Personal History," *Daedalus* (1970), 826–81.

———, "Pattern Variables Revisited," *American Sociological Review,* 25 (1960), 467–83.

———, "The School Class as a Social System: Some of Its Functions in American Society," in *Education, Economy and Society,* eds., A. H. Halsey, Jean Floud, and C. Arnold Anderson. New York: The Free Press, 1961.

———, *The Social System.* New York: The Free Press, 1951.

———, *Societies: Evolutionary and Comparative Perspectives.* Englewood Cliffs, N.J.: Prentice-Hall, Inc., 1966.

———, ed., *Sociological Theory and Modern Society.* New York: The Free Press, 1967.

———, *The System of Modern Societies.* Englewood Cliffs, N.J.: Prentice-Hall, Inc., 1971.

———, AND GERALD M. PLATT, *The American University.* Cambridge: Harvard University Press, 1973.

———, AND EDWARD A. SHILS, eds., *Toward a General Theory of Action.* Cambridge: Harvard University Press, 1951.

———, ROBERT F. BALES AND EDWARD A. SHILS, *Working Papers in the Theory of Action.* Glencoe, Ill.: The Free Press, 1953.

PIAGET, JEAN, *The Child's Construction of Reality.* London: Routledge and Kegan Paul, 1958.

———, *Structuralism,* trans. and ed. Chaninah Maschler, London: Routledge and Kegan Paul, 1971.

POPPER, KARL, *The Logic of Scientific Discovery.* London: Hutchinson, 1959.

REYNOLDS, VERNON, *The Biology of Human Action.* 2nd edition. Reading, England: W. H. Freeman & Company, Publishers, 1980.

———, AND R. E. S. TANNER, *The Biology of Religion.* London and New York: Longman, 1983.

ROSSI, ALICE, "A Biosocial Perspective on Parenting," *Daedalus,* 106, no. 2 (1977), 1–31.

———, "Gender and Parenthood," *American Sociological Review,* 49, no. 1, (1984), 1–19.

SAHLINS, MARSHALL, D., AND ELMAN R. SERVICE, eds., *Evolution and Culture.* Ann Arbor: University of Michigan Press, 1960.

SCHUMPETER, JOSEPH, *Capitalism, Socialism and Democracy.* London: Unwin University Books, 1943.

———, *Imperialism and Social Classes.* Cleveland: Meridian Books, 1955.

———, *Ten Great Economists: from Marx to Keynes.* London: Allen and Unwin, Ltd., 1952.

SCHUTZ, ALFRED, *Collected Papers I: The Problem of Social Reality.* The Hague: Martinus Nijhoff, 1962.

———, "The Stranger: An Essay in Social Psychology," in *School and Society: A Sociological Reader.* Open University. London: Routledge and Kegan Paul, 1971.

SCOTT, MARVIN, AND STANFORD M. LYMAN, "Accounts," *American Sociological Review* 33 (1968), 46–62.

SHIBUTANI, TAMOTSU, ed., *Human Nature and Collective Behavior: Papers in Honor of Herbert Blumer.* Englewood Cliffs, N.J.: Prentice-Hall, Inc., 1970.

SIMMEL, GEORG, *Conflict,* trans. Kurt H. Wolff. Glencoe, Ill.: The Free Press, 1955.

————, *The Sociology of Georg Simmel,* trans. Kurt H. Wolff. Glencoe, Ill.: The Free Press, 1950.

SMELSER, NEIL, "Mechanics of Change and Adjustment to Change," in *Industrialization and Society,* pp. 32–48, eds. Berthhold F. Hoselitz and Wilbert E. Moore. Paris: Unesco-Mouton, 1963.

————, *Social Change in the Industrial Revolution.* Chicago: University of Chicago Press, 1959.

————, AND R. STEPHEN WARNER, *Sociological Theory: Historical and Formal.* Morristown, N.J.: General Learning Press, 1976.

————, *The Sociology of Economic Life.* Englewood Cliffs, N.J.: Prentice-Hall, Inc., 1963.

SMITH, DOROTHY, *The Everyday World as Problematic: A Feminist Sociology.* Boston: Northeastern University Press, 1987.

SPENCER, HERBERT, *The Principles of Sociology.* New York: Appleton, 1896.

STACEY, JUDITH, AND BARRIE THORNE, "The Missing Feminist Revolution in Sociology," *Social Problems,* 32 (1985), 301–316.

SZELENYI, IVAN, "The Intelligentsia in the Class Structure of State-Socialist Societies," in *Marxist Inquiries: Studies of Labor, Class and States,* eds., Michael Burawoy and Theda Skocpol. Chicago: University of Chicago Press, 1982.

————, WITH ROBERT MANCHIN, PÁL JUHASZ, BALINT MAGYAR, AND BILL MARTIN, *Socialist Entrepreneurs: Embourgeoisement in Rural Hungary.* Cambridge, England: Polity, 1988.

THIBAUT, JOHN W., AND HAROLD H. KELLEY, *The Social Psychology of Groups.* New York: John Wiley, 1959.

THOMAS, WILLIAM I., *The Unadjusted Girl.* Boston: Little, Brown, 1923.

————, WITH DOROTHY SWAINE THOMAS, *The Child in America.* New York: Alfred A. Knopf, 1928.

THOMPSON, JOHN B., AND DAVID HELD, eds., *Habermas: Critical Debates.* London: Macmillan, 1982.

TOURAINE, ALAIN, *The Self-Production of Society.* Chicago: University of Chicago Press, 1977.

TRIVERS, ROBERT, "The Evolution of Reciprocal Altruism," *Quarterly Review of Biology,* 46 (1971), 35–57.

TUCKER, ROBERT C., *Philosophy and Myth in Karl Marx.* Cambridge: Cambridge University Press, 1961.

TURNER, ROY, ed., *Ethnomethodology: Selected Readings.* Baltimore: Penguin, 1974.

VAN DEN BERG, AXEL, "Critical Theory: Is There Still Hope?" *American Journal of Sociology,* 86, no. 3 (1980), 449–78.

VEBLEN, THORSTEIN, *The Theory of the Leisure Class.* New York: Modern Library, 1934.

VON HAYEK, FRIEDRICH, *The Constitution of Liberty.* Chicago: Henry Regnery Company, 1972.

WALLACE, RUTH A., ed., *Feminism and Sociological Theory.* Newbury Park, Calif.: Sage, 1989.

WALLERSTEIN, IMMANUEL, *The Modern World System I: Capitalist Agriculture and the Origins of the European World-Economy in the Sixteenth Century.* New York: Academic Press, 1974.

————, *The Modern World System II: Mercantilism and the Consolidation of the European World-Economy, 1600–1750.* New York: Academic Press, 1980.

——, *The Modern World System III: The Second Era of Great Expansion of the Capitalist Economy, 1730–1840s.* New York: Academic Press, 1988.

WEBER, MAX, *The Protestant Ethic and the Spirit of Capitalism,* trans. Talcott Parsons. New York: Scribner's, 1958.

——, *The Religion of China: Confucianism and Taoism,* trans. and ed. Hans H. Gerth. Glencoe, Ill.: The Free Press, 1951.

——, *The Theory of Social and Economic Organization,* trans. A. M. Henderson and Talcott Parsons. New York: The Free Press, 1964.

WELLMAN, BARRY, "Network Analysis: Some Basic Principles," in Randall Collins, ed., *Sociological Theory 1983.* San Francisco: Jossey-Bass, 1983.

WHITE, HARRISON C., SCOTT A. BOORMAN, AND RONALD L. BREIGER, "Social Structure from Multiple Networks: I. Blockmodels of Roles and Positions," *American Journal of Sociology,* 81 (1976), 730–80.

WILLIAMS, ROBIN M., JR., "Change and Stability in Values and Value Systems," in *Stability and Social Change,* eds. Bernard Barber and Alex Inkeles. Boston: Little, Brown, 1971.

WILSON, EDWARD O., *On Human Nature.* Cambridge: Harvard University Press, 1978.

——, *Sociobiology: The New Synthesis.* Cambridge, Mass.: The Belknap Press of Harvard University Press, 1975.

WINCH, PETER, *The Idea of a Social Science and Its Relation to Philosophy.* London: Routledge and Kegan Paul, 1958.

WRIGHT, ERIK OLIN, *Class, Crisis, and the State.* London: New Left Books, 1979.

——, *Class Structure and Income Determination.* New York: Academic Press, 1979.

——, AND JOACHIM SINGELMANN, "Proletarianization in the Changing American Class Structure," in *Marxist-Inquiries: Studies of Labor, Class and States,* eds. Michael Burawoy and Theda Skocpol, supplement to vol. 88 of the *American Journal of Sociology,* 1982.

ZEITLIN, IRVING M., *Capitalism and Imperialism: An Introduction to Neo-Marxian Concepts.* Chicago: Markham Publishing Co., 1972.

INDEX